D0984747

THE RE-ENCHANTMENT OF THE WORLD

The Re-Enchantment of the World

Secular Magic in a Rational Age

EDITED BY
JOSHUA LANDY AND MICHAEL SALER

STANFORD UNIVERSITY PRESS

STANFORD, CALIFORNIA 2009

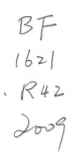
Stanford University Press
Stanford, California

This book has been published with the assistance of the Research Unit of the Division of Literatures, Cultures, and Languages at Stanford University.

Library of Congress Cataloging-in-Publication Data
   The re-enchantment of the world : secular magic in a rational age / edited by Joshua Landy and Michael Saler.
      p. cm.
   Includes bibliographical references and index.
   ISBN 978-0-8047-5299-2 (cloth : alk. paper)
   1. Magic—Social aspects. 2. Marvelous, The—Social aspects. 3. Rationalism. 4. Secularism. 5. Thought and thinking. 6. Civilization, Modern. I. Landy, Joshua. II. Saler, Michael T.
   BF1621.R42 2009
   909.8—dc22

                                                                     2008022442

Typeset by Thompson Type in 10/12.5 Palatino

O

Acknowledgments

This book is partially funded by a grant from the Research Unit of the Division of Literatures, Cultures, and Languages at Stanford University; the editors would like to thank Gregory Freidin and Roland Greene for their warm and magnanimous support. They are also grateful to Joanna Fiduccia for her invaluable, extensive, and expert assistance, to Trina Marmarelli for her sterling translation work, and to Norris Pope for his sage editorial advice.

"Jimmy's Garden" is reprinted from Margaret Morton, *Transitory Gardens, Uprooted Lives* (Yale University Press, 1993), by the courtesy of the author. Mallarmé's "Sonnet allégorique de lui-même" is reprinted from Carl-Paul Barbier, ed., *Documents Stéphane Mallarmé*, vol. IV (Paris: Nizet, 1973) with the permission of Nizet. Kauffmann's cover illustration of Ponson du Terrail's *Les Drames de Paris: Rocambole* (Paris: Jules Rouff, 1883–1886) is reprinted courtesy of the Bibliothèque des Littératures Policières, Paris. André Gill's "Portrait authentique de Rocambole" (*La Lune*, 11 November 1867) is reprinted courtesy of Special Collections, University of Michigan Library. Raphael's "Transfiguration" and Michelangelo's "Libyan Sibyl" are reprinted courtesy of Art Resource, New York.

Contents

Figures

Contributors

R. Lanier Anderson is an Associate Professor in the Department of Philosophy at Stanford University and co-director of Stanford's Literature and Philosophy Initiative. He has published numerous articles on Kant, Nietzsche, neo-Kantianism, and nineteenth-century philosophy.

Dan Edelstein is an Assistant Professor of French at Stanford University. His first book, *The Terror of Natural Right*, which has been accepted for publication by the University of Chicago Press, concerns republicanism and natural right theory in eighteenth-century France. He is currently working on a project concerning the "Super-Enlightenment."

Hans Ulrich Gumbrecht is the Albert Guérard Professor in Literature in the Departments of French and Italian and Comparative Literature at Stanford University. He is a fellow of the American Academy of Arts and Sciences. He is the author of over a thousand articles and several books, including *In 1926: Living at the Edge of Time* (Harvard, 1997), *In Praise of Athletic Beauty* (Harvard, 2006), *Production of Presence: What Meaning Cannot Convey* (Stanford, 2004), and *The Powers of Philology: Dynamics of Textual Scholarship* (University of Illinois, 2003).

Robert Harrison is the Rosina Pierotti Professor in Italian Literature in the Department of French and Italian at Stanford University. He is a fellow of the American Academy of Arts and Sciences. He is the author of *The Dominion of the Dead* (Chicago, 2003), *Forests: The Shadow of Civilization* (Chicago, 1992), *The Body of Beatrice* (Johns Hopkins, 1988), and *Gardens: An Essay on the Human Condition* (Chicago, 2008).

Joshua Landy is Associate Professor in the Department of French and Italian at Stanford University, and co-director of Stanford's Initiative in Philosophy and Literature. He is the author of *Philosophy as Fiction: Self, Deception, and Knowledge in Proust* (Oxford, 2004) and the editor, with Claude Bremond and Thomas Pavel, of *Thematics: New Approaches* (SUNY, 1995). He is currently working on a second book, *Formative Fictions: Literary Structure and the Life Well Lived.*

Andrea Nightingale is a Professor in the Departments of Classics and Comparative Literature at Stanford University. She is the author of *Genres in Dialogue: Plato and the Construct of Philosophy* (Cambridge, 1996) and *Spectacles of Truth in Classical Greek Philosophy: Theoria in its Cultural Context* (Cambridge, 2004). She is currently researching the philosophy and literature of ecology in the modern and postmodern periods.

Nicholas Paige is an Associate Professor of French at the University of California, Berkeley. Author of *Being Interior: Autobiography and the Contradictions of Modernity in Seventeenth-Century France* (Penn, 2001), he is currently completing *Fiction before Fiction,* a study of modes of fictional reference in the French novel from seventeenth-century romance to nineteenth-century realism.

Michael Saler is a Professor in the Department of History at the University of California, Davis. His research interests include modern European intellectual and cultural history and modern British history. He is the author of *The Avant-Garde in Interwar England: "Medieval Modernism" and the London Underground* (Oxford, 1999), and is currently working on a history of the rational enchantments of Imaginary Worlds during the late nineteenth and twentieth centuries.

Michel Serres is a member of the Académie Française, and a Professor of French in the Department of French and Italian at Stanford University. He is the author of numerous books, including most recently *Le mal propre: Polluer pour s'approprier* (Paris: Pommier, 2008); *Carpaccio: Les esclaves libérés* (Paris: Pommier, 2007); *L'art des ponts: homo pontifex* (Paris: Pommier, 2006).

Linda Simon is a Professor of English at Skidmore College. Her books include *Genuine Reality: A Life of William James* (Harcourt, 1997), *Dark*

Light: Electricity and Anxiety from the Telegraph to the X-Ray (Harcourt, 2004), and *The Critical Reception of Henry James: Creating a Master* (Camden House, 2007). She is General Editor of *William James Studies* and a past president of the William James Society.

Daniel Jiro Tanaka has taught at Vassar College and Clark University. He received his Ph.D. in German from Princeton, with a dissertation titled *Forms of Disenchantment: Kant and Neo-Kantianism in the Early Work of Walter Benjamin*. He is currently working on a book-length study of disenchantment in modern German thought.

Maiken Umbach is a Senior Lecturer in Modern European History at the University of Manchester. She is the joint editor of *German History*, the journal of the German History Society, and co-director of the Centre for Research on the Cultural Forms of Modern European Politics. She is the author of *Federalism and Enlightenment in Germany, 1740–1806* (Hambledon, 2000); she is the editor of *German Federalism: Past, Present, Future* (Macmillan/Palgrave, 2002) and co-editor, with Bernd Hüppauf, of *Vernacular Modernism: Heimat, Globalization and the Built Environment* (Stanford, 2005). She is currently working on her second book, *German Cities and the Genesis of Modernism, 1890–1930*.

Robin Walz is an Associate Professor of History and Chair of the Department of Social Science at the University of Alaska Southeast. His research focuses on French popular culture and fiction and French and European intellectual history. He is the author of *Pulp Surrealism: Insolent Popular Culture in Twentieth-Century France* (U. California, 2000). He is currently working on his second book, *Detectives, Avengers, and Elegant Criminals: Popular Characters and French Identity, 1815–1950*.

THE RE-ENCHANTMENT OF THE WORLD

Introduction: The Varieties of
Modern Enchantment

JOSHUA LANDY AND MICHAEL SALER

1

"The fate of our times," Max Weber famously wrote in 1917, "is characterized by rationalization and intellectualization and, above all, by
the 'disenchantment of the world.'"[1] Weber was in excellent company—Friedrich Nietzsche had preceded him in the 1880s, preceded in
turn by the German Romantics[2]—and he had powerful reasons to perceive Western modernity in the way he did. For while religious faith
continued to exert its hold over the vast majority of industrialized
souls, its claims had become considerably more modest. It now allowed secular law courts to adjudicate matters of morality; it permitted scientists to explain away the miracles of nature; it dismissed as
frauds those whom it had formerly persecuted as heretics; and most of
the time at least, it delegated cases of possession to psychologists and
psychiatrists. Stone by stone, the more baroque buttresses on the cathedral of traditional belief were being carted away to the museum of cultural history.

Weber's account was, however, incomplete. What he neglected to
mention is that each time religion reluctantly withdrew from a particular area of experience, a new, thoroughly secular strategy for re-
enchantment cheerfully emerged to fill the void. The astonishing
profusion and variety of such strategies is itself enchanting. Between
them, philosophers, artists, architects, poets, stage magicians, and ordinary citizens made it possible to enjoy many of the benefits previously

offered by faith, without having to subscribe to a creed; the progressive disenchantment of the world was thus accompanied, from the start and continually, by its progressive re-enchantment.

Let us insist right away on the words *secular* and *strategy*. When we speak here of re-enchantment, we do not have in mind the periodic resurgence of traditional ideas and practices (for example, the survival in some quarters of exorcism rites), or again the sporadic generation of new creeds, such as spiritualism, that have sought to replace the old. As Camus would say, to embrace such a creed is not to solve the problem of disenchantment but rather to change its terms on the sly.[3] Still less do we have in mind what one might call *insidious* re-enchantment, of the kind discussed at length by Theodor Adorno and others—the purported exploitation, that is, of a helpless population's unwitting tendency to invest media and markets with a mystical aura, in order to keep the capitalist system in place.[4] Instead, what this volume seeks to show is that there are, in the modern age, *fully secular and deliberate* strategies for re-enchantment, of which (to put the point another way) no one, however hard-bitten he or she may be, need feel ashamed.

The thesis of this volume, then, is that there is a variety of secular and conscious strategies for re-enchantment, held together by their common aim of filling a God-shaped void. Amid this unity, diversity is a positive requirement, since as Nietzsche understood so well, the God to be replaced served multiple functions simultaneously. If the world is to be re-enchanted, it must accordingly be reimbued not only with *mystery* and *wonder* but also with *order*, perhaps even with *purpose*; there must be a hierarchy of *significance* attaching to objects and events encountered;[5] individual lives, and moments within those lives, must be susceptible again to *redemption*; there must be a new, intelligible locus for the *infinite*; there must be a way of carving out, within the fully profane world, a set of spaces which somehow possess the allure of the *sacred*; there must be everyday *miracles*, exceptional events which go against (and perhaps even alter) the accepted order of things; and there must be secular *epiphanies*, moments of being in which, for a brief instant, the center appears to hold, and the promise is held out of a quasi-mystical union with something larger than oneself. Piece by piece, in a largely unwitting collaboration, modern intellectuals and creators have put together a panoply of responses to the Weberian condition, offering fully secularized subjects an affirmation of existence that does not come at the cost of naïveté, irrationalism, or hypocrisy.

2

To recognize the existence of such widespread, far-reaching, and wholesale efforts is at the same time to reach a new, and more nuanced, understanding of the nature of modernity.[6] It is to reject, first of all, the notion that any lingering enchantment within Western culture must of necessity be a relic, a throwback, a corner of unenlightened atavism yet to be swept clean (we will call this the *binary* approach); it is to reject, second, the notion that modernity is itself enchanted, unbeknown to its subjects, in a deceptive and dangerous way (we will call this attitude the *dialectical*); it is to accept, instead, the fact that modernity embraces seeming contraries, such as rationality and wonder, secularism and faith (we will term this final position *antinomial*). Of course, no one would deny the stunning longevity of atavistic yearnings within industrialized cultures, any more than contest the frequent employment within them of irrational beguilements as temptations to follow a party, subscribe to a cause, or consume a product. The point, however, is that these are not the only two options. There remains a third type of enchantment, unjustly overlooked, which is the modern enchantment *par excellence*: one which simultaneously enchants and disenchants, which delights but does not delude.

Of the three approaches listed above, the binary has been by far the most prevalent. Ever since the seventeenth century, elites have tended to define enchantment as the residual, subordinate "other" to modernity's rational, secular, and progressive side, as a form of duplicity associated with the "superstitions" of organized religion and the dogmatic authority of monarchical rule.[7] Reason, it was claimed, would free individuals from the thrall of such enchantments; science would affirm that what had been taken for centuries as "wonders" and "marvels," when examined empirically and without reliance on revelation, would be explicable in terms of uniform natural laws. Enchantments did not disappear entirely within the binary model, but were marginalized as residual phenomena both subordinate to and explicable by secular rationality. Wonders and marvels were relegated to the ghettoes of popular culture in the seventeenth and eighteenth centuries and mass culture in the nineteenth and twentieth.[8] In addition, enchantments became associated with the cognitive outlooks of groups traditionally cast as inferior within the discourse of Western elites: "primitives," children, women, the lower classes. Rational adults could partake of enchantments through the exercise of their imagination, but despite the protestations of Romantics, the imagination continued to be cast as inferior to reason, and as a potentially dangerous instigator of desire, throughout much of the nineteenth century.[9] (Indeed, nineteenth-century understandings of "culture" were formulated partly as a way to contain the transgressive desires of an unregulated imagination.)[10]

Those who sought alternatives to the prevalent discourse of modern disenchantment were often tagged by their critics as reactionary antimodernists engaged in a futile struggle to recapture "The World We Have Lost."[11] For example, the range of late nineteenth-century responses to the discourse of disenchantment has usually been treated as a regressive flight from the scientific and secular tendencies of modernity, a "revolt against positivism," in historian H. Stuart Hughes's well-known phrase.[12] The revolt was characterized by a fascination with spiritualism and the occult, a vogue for non-Western religions and art, and a turn to aestheticism, neo-paganism, and celebrations of the irrational will. Many participants in these movements seemed to accept the binary distinction between modernity and enchantment no less than their critics, as did their successors in the numerous counterculture movements of the twentieth century.[13] Similarly, Georges Bataille contrasted "primitive" cultures of enchanted energies and irrational expenditures with "modern cultures" distorted by a desiccated form of rationality. "The present world," he remarked in 1955, "tends to neglect the marvelous."[14]

Whereas the binary approach depicts contemporary turns to the irrational and spiritual as atavistic and marginal reactions to the secular rationality of the modern world, the *dialectical* approach posits modernity itself as inherently irrational, a mythic construct no less enchanted than the myths it sought to overcome. And whereas the binary approach concedes some merit to modernity,[15] the dialectical approach views modernity as uniformly oppressive and inhumane, a condition exacerbated by its hypocritical claims to reason, progress, and freedom. On the binary approach, then, modernity is disenchanted, both for good and for ill; on the dialectical approach, modernity is enchanted, deceptively and dangerously.

The dialectical approach is already implicit in the thought of Karl Marx, whose writings on modernity abound with metaphors and similes of enchantment—specters, ghosts, fetishes, and so forth—linking the modern world with the religious world it had supposedly sur-mounted,[16] and becomes explicit in the writings of Friedrich Nietzsche. For the latter, the Western commitment to reason and science is both ir-rational (it owes its origin to "the flame lit by a faith that is thousands of years old, that Christian faith which was also the faith of Plato, that God is the truth, that truth is divine") and destructive, in that the un-conditional will to truth, by exposing the value-neutral reality of the world, ultimately leads to nihilism.[17] Max Weber's thought could be interpreted as straddling the binary and dialectical approaches, as could that of Sigmund Freud, who warns in such later works as *Civilization and Its Discontents* (1930) that the repressive cultural forces of modernity, together with its advances in science and technology, might eventuate in the ultimate irrational act: humanity's self-destruction.[18]

It is thus not surprising that the most influential articulation of the dialectical approach was made by two philosophers who brought to-gether the various insights of Marx, Nietzsche, Weber, and Freud in a single, coruscating work. Max Horkheimer and Theodore Adorno, in the 1947 *Dialectic of Enlightenment*, indict Western modernity as a glob-alizing enchantment whose reliance on instrumental reason abolishes individuality, distorts human nature, and represses autonomy. Moder-nity becomes a self-legitimizing force that transcends its own proper-ties of self-criticism:

For the scientific temper, any deviation of thought from the business of manip-ulating the actual . . . is no less senseless and self-destructive than it would be for the magician to step outside the magic circle drawn for his incantation; and in both cases violation of the taboo caries a heavy price for the offender. The mastery of nature draws the circle in which the critique of pure reason holds thought spellbound.[19]

The dialectical approach of Horkheimer and Adorno defines nearly all forms of culture as complicit with the "totalitarian" logic of Enlight-enment, "high" as well as "low." The two gesture feebly towards a sav-ing remnant of "genuine" artistic expressions that remain inassimilable to reductive reason and its attendant logic of capitalist commodfica-tion, but on the whole the rational and secular tendencies of moder-nity stand condemned as the ultimate expressions of a beguiling form of enchantment: "The more completely the machinery of thought sub-jugates existence, the more blindly it is satisfied with reproducing it. Enlightenment thereby regresses to the mythology it has never been able to escape."[20]

Later exponents of the dialectical position include Michel Foucault, with his histories of madness and prisons,[21] and Terry Castle, whose stimulating collection of essays on eighteenth- and nineteenth-century Anglophone literature, *The Female Thermometer,* argues that enchantments were not eradicated successfully by the Enlightenment emphasis on reason but simply displaced from nature to the human psyche, resulting, ironically, in an even more powerful expression of the irrational. Echoing Horkheimer and Adorno, Castle observes that "the more we seek to free ourselves . . . from the coils of superstition, mystery, and magic, the more tightly, paradoxically, the uncanny holds us in its grip."[22] And in *The Secret Life of Puppets,* Victoria Nelson concurs that the supernatural, the religious, and the marvelous continue to be "operative in what we imagine to be the rational and scientific perspective we use to assess reality."[23]

The binary and dialectical approaches to the problem of modern enchantment continue to influence scholarship, but in recent years there has been a concerted attempt to rethink the discourse from a vantage point that rejects the "either/or" logic of both of these slants. Postcolonial scholars, for example, have argued that the binary approach was more ideological than real, a useful conceptual tool for Western colonial purposes that obscured the tensions and contradictions within the modern world; the seeming "universal" distinctions championed by the Western metropole between modernity and tradition, or secularism and superstition, often do not hold up, such scholars argue, when viewed from the "periphery" of non-Western cultures negotiating processes of modernization in complex ways.[24] And historians of science, religion, and mass culture have explored how multivalent and interdependent these phenomena have been, further complexifying the oppositions between science and religion, religion and rationality, rationality and mass culture.[25] These and related critiques have redirected the attention of historians from theoretical models to the competing conceptions of "modernity" propounded by historical subjects themselves, whose "alternative modernities" make legitimate claims upon our attention.[26]

Indeed, the binary and dialectical approaches are in the process of being replaced by the recognition that modernity is characterized by fruitful tensions between seemingly irreconcilable forces and ideas. Modernity is defined less by binaries arranged in an implicit hierarchy, or by the dialectical transformation of one term into its opposite, than by contradictions, oppositions, and antinomies: modernity is messy.[27] As a result of this reconceptualization, the long-accepted binary and dialectical approaches to modernity and enchantment are finally beginning to be called into question. There is a growing awareness, manifested in the work of James Cook, Simon During, and a handful of others,[28] that there are forms of enchantment entirely compatible with, and indeed at times *dependent* upon, those features of modernity usually seen as disenchanting the world.

Extending their work, which tends in each case to examine a single historical aspect or disciplinary perspective, the present volume seeks to lay the Weberian and Adornian ghosts, with their seemingly endless binary and dialectical plaints, to rest once and for all. Freed from the sinister spectres of *Kulturkritik*, antinomial theorists of modernity are at last able to put on display a set of enchantments that are *voluntary*, being chosen (*pace* Adorno) by autonomous agents rather than insidiously imposed by power structures, *respectable*, compatible as they are (*pace* Weber) with secular rationality, and *multiple*, being replacements, each one in its own way, for a polymorphous God.

3

When Western intellectuals speak of the disenchantment of the world, what they have in mind, as often as not, is a gradual decline in *mystery*. Little by little, physics has extended its reach into more and more areas previously occupied by metaphysics, as apparently inexplicable natural phenomena have found themselves susceptible, one by one, to strictly worldly explanations. Days of darkness mean nothing more than that the moon is in the way of the sun. Rainbows are neither visitations from Iris nor reminders of a covenant, but merely the result of prismatic refraction. And if a given mental illness can be cured by medication, then it is more likely to be an instance of chemical imbalance than one of diabolical possession. The shadow of God, as Nietzsche would have put it, has slowly retreated; it is now high noon.

Or is it? As Andrea Nightingale reveals, modern science is just as likely to *restore* mystery as to extirpate it from the natural world. Science—which once used, like philosophy, to grant wonder only instrumental value, as a step on the way to wonder-free knowledge and thoroughly unmysterious certainty—now becomes, paradoxically enough, the single most powerful generator of the marvelous. And not just because of the technological marvels it produces, but also and especially because of the limits it ends up setting to its own powers. "The highest that we can attain to is not Knowledge," Henry David Thoreau already realized, but "a sudden revelation of the insufficiency of all that we called Knowledge before." In other words, the quest for knowledge—rationality itself—can, and indeed should, lead to an admission of irremediable defeat; properly understood, the natural world can itself be a source of the wonder formerly found in contemplation of the divine.

Wonder, according to Linda Simon, is equally to be found within the human world. Charting William James's development as a philosopher, Simon maintains that his early disenchantment gave way to a form of faith compatible with secular modernity, one that willed a belief in possibility, supported by evidence from personal experience and sensations. In particular, James's turn to *language* became an important source of modern re-enchantment. Rather than rely on language as a conceptual tool, an approach which, he felt, led to reifications of experience, James emphasized the transitive, open-ended aspects of language. Re-enchantment, as James saw it, could be experienced in such simple—and magical—words as *or, but,* and (especially) *if.*

Surprising as it may sound, the enchanting possibilities latent in ordinary speech were also brought to the fore by none other than Ludwig Wittgenstein, the arch demystifier, problem dissolver, and foe of metaphysics. Wittgenstein's later philosophy provided an antidote to the disenchantment of his early philosophy, explains Michael Saler, by emphasizing the fecundity of interpretations that can be derived from everyday linguistic usage. For while such usage frequently testifies to widely shared grammatical confusions and seductions, it just as often indicates the specificity of individual perspectives, and thus a new *infinite,* understood as a potentially endless series of points of view. Strikingly, Wittgenstein—unlike his fellow cultural pessimists—was willing (indeed eager) to turn to mass culture as a resource for innovative perspectives, because it was unafraid of appearing "silly," and was thus free to advance unconventional hypotheses. Whereas other cultural pessimists often cited the commercialization of culture as contributing to the debasement of Western civilization, Wittgenstein indicated that it could generate forms of enchantment that were compatible with the secular rationality of his age.

So too for Michel Serres, whose lyrical essay concludes the volume, re-enchantment takes place through language, though in a strikingly different way. In place of a religious or mythical story of origins—a *Genesis*, a *Metamorphoses*—Serres offers us what he sees as a genuine, nonfanciful, potentially epistemology-generating access to the earliest period of human existence on earth. It is well known, he notes, that when we seek to make genuine contact with another individual we attend to the *style* of his or her utterances, not merely to the paraphrasable content. But the same thing, argues Serres, holds at a higher (or deeper) level. For just as the music of an individual conveys his or her essence, so too the music of a language conveys *its* essence. And if we listen carefully enough, paying attention so to speak only to the bass line and ignoring the melody, we may ultimately retrace our steps all the way back to the source of language in general, "the song of enchantment of the things themselves." Within the rational modern world, "music raises all the arts, codes all the sciences, breathes under languages, inspires all thoughts, better yet, gives rhythm to all numbers; under it, behind it, between it and the booming call of things and bodies, lies the mute mystery, coffer of all secrets. He who discovers it speaks, virtually, every language."

A second key way of understanding disenchantment is in terms of exile. For those still operating within the Judeo-Christian framework, humans find themselves placed on this planet for a reason (because, as Leibniz famously surmised, it is the best of all possible worlds); indeed, *individual* humans are placed at *specific* locations for reasons known to God. For Darwinians, by contrast, we are here simply because environmental factors favored the survival of organisms like us. There is no deeper explanation for our presence, still less for the presence of a particular organism at a particular place. How, under such circumstances, are we to feel at home on earth?

Robert Harrison suggests that we turn for an answer to the homeless, who surely have a more direct, literal, and pressing acquaintance with the modern predicament than anyone else. Their response, Harrison informs us, is to construct "gardens" amid desolate spaces, gardens made sometimes of flowers, or piles of leaves, but sometimes just of stuffed animals, milk cartons, or recycled refuse. The homeless garden, argues Harrison, provides a corner of order, a "still point of the turning world," and thus a point of contact between uprooted individuals and the world in which they live: a re-enchantment, in other words, of space. To understand this is not to aestheticize an appalling condition, or to diminish one's awareness of the reality of suffering; on

the contrary, it is to refuse the equal injustice, the equal projective reduction, of seeing *only* distress.

At a wider scale, Maiken Umbach contends, modern space may be
re-enchanted architecturally. This indeed, according to Umbach, was
the explicit goal of Josep Puig i Cadafalch, prominent Catalan politician and architect. Like his romantic predecessors, Puig turned to the
imagination in order to redress the rational and commercial excesses
of the modern world; unlike the Romantics, however, Puig was progressive, rather than nostalgic. Again like the Romantics (one thinks of
the vogue for medievalism in European literature and architecture during the nineteenth century), Puig recovered medieval motifs; in his
hands, however, these were consciously used to connote the forward-
looking and industrial traditions of the Catalan region. Puig thus deliberately mobilized an "imagination of place" against the "abstract
space" of modern architecture, melding tradition and modernity, imagination and reality, and showing, as Umbach demonstrates, that the romantic imagination could re-enchant the world without being either
escapist or reactionary.

Joshua Landy outlines a second main response to the world's
thoroughgoing arbitrariness, a response which he finds at work in the
poetry of Stéphane Mallarmé. Mallarmé, explains Landy, sets out to
remedy the predicament by creating an *alternative* world, one which
exists only in and through poetry, one where everything has to be exactly what and where it is. Not only does Mallarmé himself create just
such a perfect world, a world of absolute necessity, but he also provides his readers with a formal model and the skills required for the
creation of their own. In pointing to their own fictionality, the poems
accustom their readers in the divided attitude required to believe in
fictions they themselves have created. (Jean-Eugène Robert-Houdin's
magic performances work, says Landy, in exactly the same way.) Self-
reflexivity at large—a central feature of literary modernism—may have
emerged from this need to re-enchant the world.

More or less contemporaneously with Mallarmé, and operating
along similar lines, the "rocambolesque" made its appearance: evidence, according to Robin Walz, of the counterintuitive possibility for
mass production and consumption to yield specifically modern enchantments, both imaginative and self-aware. The creator of the popular antihero Rocambole, Ponson du Terrail, crafted highly sensational
serial fiction for newspapers, each installment ending on a cliffhanger

that brought readers back day after day. What distinguished Ponson from other *feuilleton* writers was the fact that his narratives relentlessly and flagrantly (rather than periodically and casually) defied all logic and probability; it was precisely these qualities that made them so attractive to a mass audience. Readers were being schooled in the conventions of genre fiction and welcomed Ponson's parodies that stimulated—and challenged—their rational and imaginative faculties. Whereas the early modern carnivalesque temporarily inverted established hierarchies before restoring them, the Rocambolesque that began with Ponson and continued through twentieth-century French culture promised endless subversions that accorded both with the commercial needs of the new publishing industry and with the imaginative needs of a new mass audience.

There is, however, a third type of response to contingency, involving neither literal nor metaphorical creation but instead a mental attitude, one which, according to Hans Ulrich Gumbrecht, is most often to be found in the semi-sacred space of the *stadium*. For spectator sports are, on Gumbrecht's account, the privileged site of today's "secular epiphanies," moments of being in which form suddenly emerges from chaos and in which we the audience, "lost in focused intensity," once again allow the world to be present to us, to touch us directly; in which, to put it another way, we allow ourselves once again to be, as we have in reality always been, part of the world. Such re-enchantment—a closing of the gap, a restoration of our sense of place within the cosmos, a revitalization of gratitude simply for what is—can, Gumbrecht promises, still be possible in an age obsessed with meaning at the expense of presence, ideas at the expense of sensations, minds at the expense of bodies. All we need to do is immerse ourselves in the epiphanies of form taking place before our eyes. And as forms continually emerge and re-emerge from chaos, spectator sports continually go philosophy one better by *embodying*, rather than merely asking, the age-old metaphysical question: why is there something as opposed to nothing?

There exist, then, fully secular strategies for rediscovering at-homeness in the world, order, necessity, intensity, wonder, and the infinite. What, however, of the supernatural? What of revelation, salvation, and redemption? Nicholas Paige sets out to answer the first question. As Paige sees it, new understandings of fiction permitted Enlightenment-era Europeans to find an acceptable outlet for their fascination with otherworldly phenomena in the protected space of literature. In the late seventeenth century, fairy tales and other stories began to treat discredited notions of the supernatural with ironic playfulness; readers were instructed to view the fantastic as an entertaining artifice that no longer laid claim to veracity. Then, in the mid-eighteenth century, "fantastic" and "realist" fiction were both understood as inhabiting an imaginative realm that was taken for "real" while readers inhabited it. Further, the imagination itself was seen as helping to constitute reality, a move that anticipated twentieth-century phenomenology and pragmatism. The new status accorded both to fiction and to the imagination has become widely accepted today, allowing for the re-enchantment of the world through all fictional genres; but it was the Enlightenment that originally gave birth to the possibility for experiencing fiction as the site of a disenchanted enchantment, one which is "real" only as long as the story lasts.

According to D. Jiro Tanaka, Walter Benjamin and Ernst Bloch—and indeed a large number of less self-reflective moderns—find a new locus, within the material world, for the mystical revelation. While emptying out the *content* of gnosticism, Tanaka writes, Benjamin and Bloch preserve its *structure,* which is that of an asymmetrical dualism. There are, in each case, two worlds, the imperfect (ours) and the perfect. The asymmetry lies in the fact that crossworld transit is in one direction only: no way to force our way into the mystery, but only a hope, if we make ourselves properly receptive, of catching periodic messages vouchsafed to us from the other side. When such esoteric wisdom arrives, however, it is transformative, perhaps even world saving. (Hence, as Tanaka puts it, Benjamin and Bloch end up not just in "profane illumination" but in a "secular soteriology.") The most perspicuous example is that of the self. If certain strains of psychology are right, the deepest parts of the mind are inaccessible to conscious scrutiny yet indirectly palpable and, when disclosed, redemptive. It is surely no accident that the Surrealists, Benjamin's darlings, were influenced by Freud: the unconscious served, for them, as a thoroughly immanent and secular site of re-enchantment.

Dan Edelstein points toward the possibility of a secular form of collective salvation—a secular messianism, in other words—in his essay on Georges Sorel. Edelstein's is a revisionary view of Sorel, for the latter's blend of myth and politics is often seen as leading inexorably to fascism (Mussolini was a great admirer of Sorel). Edelstein, however, recovers an important aspect of Sorel's ideas that Mussolini, among many others, missed: the attempt to reconcile mythic, "enchanted" thought with a rational and secular form of politics. Sorel believed that modern politics had become disenchanted by ideologies that enumerated the social goals to be achieved. Disagreeing with established conceptions of ideologies, he complained that they spoke to the head, not to the heart, and thus were ineffective; genuine political change would only occur if deliberative thought was complemented by emotional fervor. Sorel's concept of "myth" thus stressed the necessity of galvanizing people to act by appealing to their emotions and reason simultaneously. Political myths would provide individuals with the overarching meaning and purpose that Max Weber believed had been permanently lost in the modern, disenchanted world. Edelstein argues that Sorel's strategy remains relevant for contemporary political life: enchantment need not be reason's opposite, but can instead be its partner.

When it comes to individual redemption, one could be forgiven for thinking that there is simply no hope of its rational replacement. As R. Lanier Anderson shows, however, not only can the Christian concept be replaced, but the replacement actually turns out to be superior to the original. Anderson starts from Friedrich Nietzsche's "eternal recurrence" thought experiment, in which the reader is asked to imagine how she would react if informed that she will live her life over again, and indeed continue to do so an infinite number of times. To greet this news with ecstasy would be to indicate consonance between her life and her values, and hence a fully authentic and unified existence; to greet it with horror, by contrast, would be to indicate the need for redemption. Redemption, here, takes the form of an altered understanding of the events which we find it hard to will back. If we can see them as contributing to an overall life which we endorse—if, that is, we can change our life into one in which apparent setbacks turn out to have been indispensable conduits to success—then we will have redeemed it. Like Raphael, painter of *The Transfiguration,* I will have taken negative elements and made them positive, by virtue of their contribution to a powerful totality. And we will have surpassed the Christian offer of redemption: as Anderson points out, Christianity does nothing to affect the (negative) value of the negative events themselves, but only offers us a future compensation. In short, "what Christianity promises is not the redemption *of* my life, but a redemption *from* my life."

Nietzschean redemption is thus not only less fraught with metaphysical assumptions than its Christian counterpart, and not only just as workable, but also, it turns out, considerably more *effective*.

There is a genuine urgency, an existential pathos, about the essays in this volume. The world is, in every traditional sense, disenchanted; a life lived in rigorous confrontation with disenchantment is an impoverished life (even Camus, for all his emphasis on lucidity, had an ethics of intensity to offer by way of compensation); and it will not do, either, to revert to prior forms of wonder, order, and redemption. No, the world must be enchanted anew—human flourishing requires it—for those who wish to be consistent in their adoption of secular rationality. It must be enchanted with *dignity*, which is to say in concord with secular rationality, in full awareness of pluralism and contingency. And it must be *multiply* enchanted, so as to satisfy again all the pressing demands formerly satisfied by religion. Fortunately, it is.

CHAPTER 1

"Broken Knowledge"

ANDREA NIGHTINGALE

> We have heard of a Society for the Diffusion of Useful Knowledge.
> It is said that knowledge is power, and the like. Methinks there is
> equal need of a Society for the Diffusion of Useful Ignorance, what
> we will call Beautiful Knowledge . . . What we call knowledge is
> often our positive ignorance; ignorance our negative knowledge.
>
> —Thoreau, "Walking"

WHERE AND HOW DO WE dwell? Weber famously claimed that we live
in an age of disenchantment (*Entzauberung*), an age in which reason,
rejecting religion in favor of science, has destroyed traditional modes
of wonder and enchantment. As Heidegger observed, the rise of modern science was rooted in a particular epistemology: the valorization of
"certainty" and the demotion of wonder. Francis Bacon, one of the
early fathers of modern science, eloquently articulated this point: deni-
grating wonder as "broken knowledge" ("contemplation broken off, or
losing itself"), he claimed that scientists must repair this by the
achievement of scientific knowledge.[1] Modern science searched for a
mode of inquiry and of knowledge that would not break down or collapse into wonder. It developed a specific "economy of attention"—attention to nature—that aimed towards "certain" knowledge and
technological control.[2] This scientific economy of attention (which was
but one of many possible modes of attention) treated the natural world
as a complex machine that could be studied, known, and "mastered"
by humans.

In "economizing" our attention, we look at some things while blinding ourselves to others. Nietzsche has reminded us that there are blind
spots in all pursuits of knowledge.[3] In these intellectual pursuits, there
lurks a desire not to know certain things—a sort of passion for ignorance. The scientific approach to nature demoted all forms of understanding that did not seek to achieve certainty. One such mode of
understanding involves the attempt to apprehend nature (and our
place in nature) in bodily and experiential terms—to attain knowledge
that will always be partial, broken off. It is based on a completely different economy of attention, one that attends to nature in ecological
rather than scientific terms. An ecological approach to nature is
grounded in partial and perspectival modes of apprehension—"situated" knowledge. The philosophical ecologist attempts to understand
the kinship between humans and nonhumans through bodily forms of
engagement. This kinship, however, has its limits: human awareness
of time and death separates us from nonhuman nature. We are, then,
both situated and unsituated in the natural world, and our efforts to
achieve an ecological mode of dwelling must honor both sides of this
equation. The oscillation between bodily and intellectual explorations
of nature generates a mode of understanding that "breaks off" in wonder: wonder is the origin of ecological philosophy, but also its (ongoing) culmination.

In this essay, I examine the problem of being "at-home" and, at the
same time, "homeless" in the natural world. I conceive of "ecology" in
the original sense of the Greek words, that is, a discipline that offers an
"account" (*logos*) of the "household" (*oikos*) where we dwell. Western
thinkers have offered various *logoi* about the "household" in which we
humans live (or should live). Certainly the *logos* we use about the
earthly "household" is directly linked to the manner in which we
dwell, the values that we hold. I begin by looking at Augustine's discussion of time and the body, which illustrates the premodern Christian notion of being "homeless" on earth. In the *Confessions*, Augustine
develops a specific "economy of attention"—what he calls *attentio*—
which sets the stage for modern reconceptions of the natural world. I
then examine Descartes's *Discourse on Method*, which elevates scientific
knowledge and its "economy of attention" over all other modes of
understanding. This text articulates an ideology that legitimizes the
technological control of earth and promises a "home" created by science. The technology developed in modernity served to maximize our

distance from a home on earth, effectively creating a home away from home. I then turn to a text that sets forth a different conception of human dwelling: Thoreau's *Walden*. This book, which has become a sort of bible for ecologists, does not offer a simple account of going "home" to nature. Thoreau is well aware that humans have a complex relation to nonhuman nature: we are earthly beings whose consciousness pulls us away from earth. His meditation on dwelling offers a powerful response to the problem of the human experience of temporality and bodily finitude. Thoreau develops a radically different mode of "attention" to the natural world—one in which the fear of death and wonder at life grounds our capacity for enchantment. Nature kills, but it also enchants.

The fact that humans are conscious of temporal change and the vagaries of the body (which will ultimately die) raises the problem of human dwelling. Traditional, premodern religion had offered an "enchanting" solution to this problem, based on a specific economy of attention. Consider Augustine's approach to this issue in his discussion of temporality in the *Confessions*. As Augustine argues, human life is "distended" in time. In our mental and conscious life, we are simultaneously pulled into the past (*memoria*) and into the future (*expectatio*). We do not simply dwell in the present: indeed "no time is wholly present."[4] As Augustine puts it, "life is a distention (*distentio*) in several directions."[5] This "distention" of the mind has important existential ramifications. The experience of "distention" in time, Augustine claims, is both a fact of human life and a sign of original sin. We humans are self-conscious beings, aware of bodily transience; our minds continually drag us backwards and forwards, away from bodily presence. Obviously, the desires, pains, and agitations of the human body are directly linked to time—to our experience of what Ricoeur calls the "sorrows of time."[6] Augustine describes the human experience of distention as that of being "scattered" in time—scattered, because we are never stable, never in one temporal or bodily "place." We live, then, in a sort of existential diaspora: our minds—our consciousness of time—estrange us from nature, offering us no real home on earth. According to Augustine, our bodies, too, are not fully natural: the expulsion of Adam and Eve from the garden "infected" the human body, which was thereafter "diseased." This conception of a body denaturalized by original sin, together with the mind's "scatteredness" in time, resulted in a devaluation (if not rejection) of life on earth. The premodern Christian identified himself as homeless on earth, and sought for a home elsewhere.

Augustine eloquently articulates the Christian solution to this existential problem: the Christian god, who offers humans a "true" home in the afterlife, outside of time and nature. As Augustine puts it: "I am scattered in times whose order I do not understand. The storms of incoherent events tear to pieces my thoughts, the inmost entrails of my soul, until that day when, purified and molten by the fire of your love, I will flow together to merge into You."[7] Of course this "homecoming" occurs in a "future" which lies beyond time: "I can find no safe place to settle my soul in, but in you alone. There let my scattered pieces (*sparsa*) be gathered together, and from you let no part of me depart."[8] In uniting with God in the afterlife, the Christian departs from the homelessness caused by the sins and sorrows of time, and by his "unnatural" (postlapsarian) body.

In Augustine's narrative, the Christian, though homeless on earth, journeys towards a "place" outside of time and nature. What, then, can a person do while he or she is "scattered" in time? According to Augustine, *attentio*—attention—is the discipline that serves to organize the scattered pieces of one's temporal and bodily experiences. Let us look briefly at Augustine's "economy of attention" since it well illustrates premodern Christian "enchantment" and its focus on God at the expense of nature. In Augustine, *attentio* operates by focusing on an action, event, or discourse (short or long), for example a psalm, a single event, or a life narrative.[9] Past, present, and future can be held together by the act of attention—*attentio* can arrange the pieces of one's life into a cohesive narrative (i.e., a teleological Christian narrative, which is the only way to achieve a coherent life story). Note that this "attentive" narratological arrangement both generates and justifies a higher mode of attention: *attentio* to or contemplation of God. The act of focusing one's attention on God offers the Christian a temporary stilling of the vagaries of the mind. To be sure, this discipline of attention does not overcome time and the body—there is no escape from this in the fallen world. But it does keep the mind focused, and prevents it from wandering into sinful thoughts.

As in all economies of attention, there is blindess and insight: one chooses what to attend to and what to ignore. Augustine is rich in refusals—refusals to see and know the world. Curiosity, in particular, is roundly rejected as a sinful form of attention. In *Confessions* 10,

Augustine describes his avoidance of curiosity and his attempts to blind himself to nature:

there are many respects, in tiny and contemptible details, where our curiosity is provoked every day. . . . I now do not watch a dog chasing a rabbit when this is happening at the circus. But if by chance I am passing when there is hunting in the countryside, it distracts me from thinking out some weighty matter. The hunt turns me to an interest in the sport, not enough to lead me to alter the direction of the beast I am riding, but shifting the inclination of my heart. Unless You had proved to me my infirmity and quickly admonished me either to take the sight as the start for some reflection enabling me to rise up to You or wholly to scorn and pass the matter by, I would be watching life an empty-headed fool.[10]

Here, Augustine indicates that the proper view of nature is no view at all. The correct response to one's curiosity at the natural world is to avert one's attention from all bodily beings. To observe the bodily world results in distraction and, indeed, stupidity.

When I am sitting at home, a lizard catching flies or a spider entrapping them as they rush into its web often fascinates me. The problem is not made any different by the fact that the animals are small . . . When my heart becomes the receptacle of distractions of this nature and the container for a mass of empty thoughts, then too my prayers are often interrupted and distracted.[11]

In this economy of attention, the Christian disciplines himself to ignore the bodily world and focus on God. He rejects curiosity and embraces divine contemplation.

Augustine's "solution" to the sorrows of time tends to repel postmodern readers. Certainly his attacks on sexuality and the body dismay and, at times, revolt us (though it no doubt produced enchantment in many premodern readers). And his rejection of the natural world is hardly appealing, offering no viable mode of dwelling responsibly on earth. But, in this sexually liberated age, are we any more comfortable with our bodies, with our place in the natural world? Consider Stephen Hall's recent book *Merchants of Immortality*, which examines scientific attempts to prolong human life by developing cloning, stem cell research, and "longevity genes." Consider also the modern response to our estrangement from the natural world: the technological alteration of the earth and the human body.

We need not accept Augustine's Christian doctrines and his ontological theories to understand the experience of being "scattered in time," "homeless" in the natural world. The modern rejection of religion does not do away with our anxiety about time and death, and does not alter our ambivalent relationship to the earth and bodily life. Not surprisingly, secular modern science deals directly with the very same issues addressed by Augustine: with the problem of transience, bodily vicissitudes, and death. In place of religious solutions to our existential and physical problems, technology offers us the prolongation of life, the alteration ("enhancement") of our bodies, and the eventual goal of making death "optional." Modern science promises us a new mode of dwelling—a material home away from the earthly home.

Let us look, now, at Descartes's *Discourse on Method* and its meditation on dwelling. This text features a prominent and quite pertinent trope— the comparison of the development of a system of knowledge to the construction of a house. I take seriously Descartes's housebuilding metaphors because they illustrate his conception of how and where we should dwell. Let us focus in particular on Descartes's claim that he will destroy the "household" of social beliefs (i.e., traditional beliefs about the world), and rebuild a wholly new system guided by the technological "mastery" of the earth.

In the *Discourse on Method,* Descartes offers an autobiographical account of his construction of a new way of thinking. He begins with a reflection on building practices:

One of the first [ideas] that occurred to me was that there is less perfection in a work produced by several persons than in one produced by a single hand. Thus we notice that buildings conceived and completed by a single architect are usually more beautiful and better planned than those remodelled by several persons using ancient walls of various vintages along with new ones.[12]

Descartes goes on to observe that this same principle applies in science and philosophy: these fields have been developed by numerous laborers with manifold materials, and they have thus offered a hodgepodge of unreliable conclusions. Turning his back on this joint project, Descartes steps forth as a sort of rugged individualist who proposes to build a house all by himself, with brand new materials. At first, he insists that his project is simply a private endeavor: "It is true that we never tear down all the houses in a city just to rebuild them in a different way and to make the streets more beautiful; but we do see that individual owners often have theirs torn down and rebuilt."[13] Later, however, Descartes suggests that his new "dwelling" will surpass those on offer, and bring great benefits to humankind. Indeed he explicitly promises that his new project will not only provide epistemic certainty, but be eminently useful for practical life.[14]

Descartes claims that he aims not only at speculative philosophy but a good and moral life: "I firmly believed that by this means I would succeed in conducting my life much better than if I built only on the old foundations."[15] Throughout the early part of the treatise, Descartes emphasizes the moral thrust of his project. He explicitly poses the question of what sort of morality he will adhere to while he pursues his investigations. Where will he dwell when he demolishes his old system of living and thinking (his "old house") and labors to build something new? What sort of ethical beliefs and practices should he adopt in this interim period? Descartes decides that he will have to live in a temporary or "provisional" sort of house:

> In planning to rebuild one's house it is not enough to draw up the plans for the new dwelling and tear down the old one . . . We must see that we are provided with a comfortable place to stay while the work of rebuilding is going on. Similarly in my own case; while reason obliged me to be irresolute in my beliefs, there was no reason why I should be so in my actions. In order to live as happily as possible during the interval I prepared a provisional code of morality for myself.[16]

In this "provisional" dwelling place, Descartes will live according to traditional morality: during the time that he is constructing his new system, he will follow the laws and customs of his society.

In keeping with traditional values, Descartes adopts the ethic of self-mastery as one of the key principles of his provisional morality:

> My third maxim was always to seek to conquer myself rather than fortune, to change my desires rather than the established order, and generally to believe that nothing except our thoughts is wholly under our control . . . Thus, making a virtue out of necessity, we no more desire to be well when we are sick, or to be free when we are in prison, than we now desire bodies as incorruptible as diamonds.[17]

Descartes's ideal of self-mastery involves the rejection of the desire to control nature and other externals—"we no more desire to be well when we are sick." This is fundamentally at odds with Descartes's later claim that we must "master and possess nature." Of course the principle of self-mastery in this early passage is part of Descartes's "provisional" morality: he later abandons this principle and proclaims that science will make us "well when we are sick" and, indeed, will enable us to control the natural world.[18]

Descartes adopts a provisional morality as a place to stay while he conducts his private experiments. He then proceeds to tear down his old "house" in the act of rejecting everything he knows: doubting his senses, beliefs, and ideas, he comes to discover a firm foundation of knowledge within himself (in the famous "cogito" arguments, which I will not address here). Descartes's frequent use of the metaphors of building and dwelling in the early parts of the text invites us to anticipate the construction of a unique and exceptional new house later on, after he has made his philosophical discoveries. We also anticipate that there will be a major moving project at the end of the road. What will Descartes's new "household" consist of? What sort of morality and community will we find in this new domicile?

We may infer the answer to the question about community. Only "thinking things" can be members of Descartes's new household: the corporeal world, and all its distinct parts, is essentially a machine that has no life or agency. Let me briefly rehearse Descartes's "proof" of the ontological distinction between animals and humans, since this provides the foundation for his new conception of the human being and human dwelling. As Descartes says in section IV, the mind is a substance completely separate from the body: "I concluded that I was a thing or substance whose whole essence or nature was to think, and which, to exist, has no need of space nor of any material thing or body. Thus it follows that this ego, this mind, by which I am what I am, is entirely distinct from the body."[19] The human being, in short, has no dependence on the animal and bodily realm, which is made up of material mechanisms.[20] Needless to say, Descartes's declaration of independence has serious ethical and ecological ramifications.

Descartes's ontology is based on a specific economy of attention: we do not need to attend to animals or other nonhuman beings in ethical, behavioral, or emotional terms, since they are merely machines. In studying animals, Descartes blinds himself to most of their behavior and actions. He looks instead at one key thing: that animals do not possess human language, which "proves that they are not rational, and that nature makes them behave as they do according to the dispositions of their organs: just as a clock, composed only on wheels and springs can count and measure the time."[21] In short, the body of an animal is "a machine created by the hand of God."[22] Even when animals try to make themselves heard, Descartes hears bells and whistles instead of cries of pain. He does, of course, attend to the bodily world—the whole point is to master nature by science. But his attention to nature is that of a mechanical engineer. He encourages others to follow him in this discipline of attention in a memorable description of a dead animal: "Those who are not well versed in anatomy will find less difficulty in understanding what I am going to say if they will take the trouble, before reading this, to have the heart of some large animal cut open before them."[23] Here and elsewhere, Descartes encourages the reader to "see" the animal as a complex machine that can be fully known and understood by science. He attends to the natural world with the goal of achieving scientific certainty and technological control.

Descartes's economy of attention is tied up with a specific account of curiosity and wonder. *Contra* Augustine, Descartes considers wonder as useful for the pursuit and acquisition of knowledge. Useful, but only to a certain degree. As he says in *The Passions of the Soul*: wonder— the "attention to unusual and extraordinary objects"—is beneficial insofar as it leads to knowledge. One must avoid wondering too much, however, and thus "perverting the use of reason." We must "free ourselves" from wonder by achieving knowledge and certainty; otherwise, we will end in the state of "blind curiosity," which characterizes "men who seek out things that are rare solely to wonder at them and not for the purpose of knowing them."[24] Curiosity and wonder, if pursued for the wrong ends, can harm reason and prevent one from achieving knowledge. Wonder is useful initially as the origin of inquiry, but must be eliminated by the attainment of certainty. There is no room for "broken knowledge" in this philosophy.

We turn now to a crucial—and quite surprising—move in the text. In part IV, Descartes has gone deep into his own mind to discover the speculative truths about human nature and god. At this point, we may imagine that his ultimate goal is the theoretical contemplation of divine truth and essence (which many previous philosophers had proclaimed the highest and best activity for humans). But, in part V, Descartes turns abruptly to the physical world, focusing exclusively on his scientific endeavors and discoveries. For the rest of the treatise (and in the three treatises that follow the *Discourse*—the *Optics, Meteorology,* and *Geometry*), he devotes his attention to scientific knowledge and its application. Indeed, in part V, he explicitly privileges the practical application of scientific knowledge over "speculative" philosophy:

As soon as I had achieved some general notions about physics . . . I noticed how far they might lead and how they differed from the principles accepted up to this time . . . And they have satisfied me that it is possible to reach knowledge that will be of much utility in this life: and that instead of the speculative philosophy now taught in the schools we can find a practical one, by which, knowing the nature and behaviour of fire, water, air, stars, the heavens, and all the other bodies which surround us . . . we can employ these entities for all the purposes for which they are suited, and so make ourselves the masters and possessors of nature.[25]

As Robert Harrison suggests, Descartes's method "promises neither salvation nor wisdom but rather power . . . that is to say the appropriation of the power traditionally assigned to God."[26]

What are we to make of this abrupt move from the identification of the human as *res cogitans* in part IV to the treatment of man as *homo faber* in part V?[27] Where, we may ask, do humans actually dwell? At one moment we seem to be at home in our minds—since, as Descartes claims in part IV, the human being is a rational substance that is independent from the body.[28] But, in parts V and VI, he offers a very different answer to this question. For he now claims that humans are *dependent* on the earth—a point which slips out near the end of the treatise. After asserting that scientific knowledge can contribute to the "general good of mankind," Descartes claims that it will be particularly beneficial to human health. He follows this up with a surprising claim: "For the mind is so dependent on the humors and the condition of the organs of the body that if it is possible to find some way to make men wise and more clever than they have been so far, I believe that it is in medicine that it should be sought."[29]

Here, Descartes appears to reverse his earlier arguments. Now the mind is so dependent on the body that it can actually be altered and improved by changing the bodily state! If we take this passage seriously, it becomes clear that a profound sense of mortality and death haunts this seemingly optimistic text. Descartes's project, I suggest, is grounded in the fear of bodily death and disease, and in the aspiration for the transcendence of the body and the ravages of time. His earlier declaration of humans' ontological independence from *res extensa* evaporates in the face of bodily deterioration and death.

Ultimately, Descartes offers an incoherent answer to the question of human dwelling: if our bodies not only affect our dispositions but the very functioning of our minds, we can't dwell only in the mind; yet we also don't belong in nature. At the end of the text, Descartes points to an alternative solution, namely that we develop science to the point where we can destroy and remake the natural world to construct a space made especially for human beings. Note that, at the close of the text, Descartes does not return to the metaphor of house building that launches the *Discourse on Method*: in the course of the text, he switches from the metaphor of house building to that of the path (*methodos*). In the end, Descartes offers us a path rather than a place of dwelling: a path that aims, ultimately, at the complete technological reconstruction of the natural world. A path that leads us out of nature, to a home away from home. Even a partially reconstructed "house" on earth is an unsatisfactory place to dwell, and serves only as a resting spot on the path that will (in the long run) lead us to transcend our animality.

In the *Discourse on Method*, we witness the development of an ideology that relegates ethical wisdom to the status of the "merely provisional." Ethical wisdom is displaced by scientific knowledge. By the end of the treatise, practical wisdom is taking its dictates from science, rather than the other way around. In the ideology of modern science, technical reasoning sets itself up as the "master" of practical reasoning. Who or what, then, can control the direction of science? Who decides which "paths" to take? If we follow this ideology to its extreme, we will even transcend humanistic values—we humans will not even be answerable to ourselves.

Descartes's ideological constructions are very much with us in the present historical moment. For a number of his basic assumptions and inferences continue to be shared today. First, the belief in the essential superiority of human over nonhuman beings. Second, the claim that this superiority gives humans the right to dominate nature. Certainly the majority of people in the West do not believe that we have ethical responsibilities towards animals (let alone plants, rivers, etc.). And, while most people would deny that animals are machines (as Descartes claimed), we nonetheless treat our machines with more consideration than the animals that feed us. Correlatively, while many of us accept that humans are in fact animals rather than separate ontological substances, we still persist in believing that we are superior to all nonhuman beings and justified in using them for our own ends. Finally, we reflect Cartesian thinking in our aspiration to become independent from nature—in our quest to make death "optional." These beliefs and ideologies justify our hostile assaults on the earth, and our rejection of nature as the basis of human dwelling.

But science has yet to conquer the sorrows of time. In spite of the amenities offered by technology (many of which are cause for celebration) nature strikes back, and we are left scattered in a fragile and frightening world.

Henry David Thoreau develops a different epistemology and a radically new economy of attention in his "experiment" at Walden Pond. In *Walden*, Thoreau proposes a practical and a philosophical mode of living. In some ways, his project resembles that of Descartes: turning his back on society, he engages in a philosophy that combines theory and practice.[30] Like Descartes, Thoreau explicitly rejects traditional "households" and searches for a new mode of dwelling. But here the similarities end. For Thoreau creates a physical house to dwell in, and labors in the fields and forests of Concord. At the same time, he creates a house in words, not only in his descriptive account of his house and housekeeping at Walden Pond, but in his wide-ranging poetic and philosophic discourse. In *Walden*, Thoreau develops several different disciplines of attention. At times, he attends extensively to the natural world: this *attentio* involves both a direct bodily engagement with nature—especially through work—but also the activity of viewing and contemplating nonhuman beings. At other times, he pays careful attention to literature and culture, exploring the ways in which language and rationality separate humans from nature.

Thoreau sets out to "know" nature. A curious, observant, and passionate man, Thoreau had a lifelong love affair with the earthly world. His curiosity and his investigations of nature, however, do not aim at scientific certainty. Thoreau engages in physical and intellectual activities that lead to a mode of understanding rooted in wonder. Or, perhaps better, uprooted, since wonder carries us outside ourselves, takes us to a distant, unknown region. Again and again, Thoreau stumbles upon a broken form of knowledge: "At the same time that we are earnest to explore and learn all things, we require that all things be mysterious and unexplorable, that land and sea be infinitely wild, unsurveyed, unfathomed by us because unfathomable."[31] Thoreau does not romanticize nature; rather, he celebrates its mysteries and ultimate unknowability. "We know not where we are."[32] Can we know where we are in the natural world? What sort of knowledge would this be? At best, we would know it partially, perspectively. Consider Thoreau's description of this kind of understanding in "Walking": "the highest that we can attain to is not Knowledge, but Sympathy with Intelligence. I do not know that this higher knowledge amounts to anything more definite than a novel and a grand surprise on a sudden revelation of the insufficiency of all that we called Knowledge before."[33] The realization of the insufficiency of accepted knowledge results in the "breaking" of knowledge and the "surprise" of wonder. Thoreau calls this mode of wonder "beautiful knowledge."[34]

Thoreau's wonder pulls him into nature. It leads him to experiment with a mode of dwelling that includes ongoing physical contact with nature. Thoreau's construction of a house—so lovingly described—engages him directly with nonhuman beings: wood, rocks, clay, iron. This laborious, bodily endeavor brings Thoreau to know certain parts of nature with his own body. Thoreau's body is marked and scarred by his work, and the house itself no doubt contains the slough of the man's body (blood, sweat, hair). Thoreau constructed a house in the woods where he lived and labored for two years. His house was only a mile from Concord, located in a rural rather than a wild region. His experiment was deeply and quite deliberately *domestic*. He not only builds a house and grows vegetables, but does his own shopping, cooking, and house cleaning. In a moving chapter on "Solitude," Thoreau responds to the question—frequently put to him—whether he was lonely in the woods. His answer: "I was never alone." Here, Thoreau affirms the presence of nonhuman beings in his *oikos*—his household. As he puts it in a striking phrase: "I am no more lonely than . . . the first spider in a new house."

What is this first spider, this new house? Perhaps Thoreau is suggesting that *he* is the "first spider and the "new house" is the unique one that he himself has built. But this is too simple. Rather, Thoreau sets forth a paradox: there is no such thing as a first spider and, indeed, no such thing as a new house. There is no singular spider or singular house: if there were, then a living being might end up in profound loneliness. But spiders and houses exist in the community of nature. Consider Thoreau's own house. As he explains in some detail, he made his house with recycled materials: he buys and dismantles an old cabin in order to get the wood and nails; he retrieves and recycles the old to create something new. This same issue of recycling emerges in a lovely passage on housecleaning, where Thoreau takes all his wooden furniture out of doors in order to sweep his floor. He notices how strange the furniture looks outside, and then realizes that these items have themselves come from the trees which they now sit beneath.[35] How new, then, is his house and his furniture? In these passages, Thoreau reminds us that we borrow from the earth—and we give our bodies back when we die. We are recyclers and, indeed, recycled into the earthly habitat.

Thoreau's physical house is, itself, a work of art, a sort of temple that eventually became a site of pilgrimage. Thoreau took the wood, stones, and sands of his local region and created a structure that transformed our experience of—and "eye for"—Walden Pond and its woods. We must emphasize, however, that Thoreau did not want his readers to view his house as a final, fixed object—as an end to his dwelling project. In one highly metaphorical passage, Thoreau constructs in words a quite different house—a dream house that differs vastly from the one that he built:

I sometimes dream of a larger and more populous house, standing in a golden age, of enduring materials . . . which shall still consist of only one room, a vast, rude, substantial, primitive hall without ceiling or plastering, with bare rafters and purlins supporting a sort of lower heaven over one's head . . . a cavernous house, wherein you must reach up a torch upon a pole to see the roof; where some may live in the fire-place, some in the recess of a window, and some on settles, some at the end of the hall, some at another, and some aloft on rafters with the spiders, if they choose; a house which you have got into when you have opened the outside door, and the ceremony is over; where the weary traveller may wash, and eat, and converse, and sleep, without further journey; such a shelter as you would be glad to reach in a tempestuous night . . . where you can see all the treasures of the house at one view, and every thing hangs upon its peg that a man should use; at once kitchen, pantry, parlor, chamber, store-house, and garret; where you can see so necessary a thing as a barrel or a ladder, so convenient a thing as a cupboard, and hear the pot boil . . . A house whose inside is as open and manifest as a bird's nest. (pp. 290–91)

In this baroque passage, Thoreau invites us to "wander beyond" the physical house he built at Walden Pond. We must wander so that we do not get fixated on Thoreau's particular house or his philosophic project.

What, then, is Thoreau dreaming about? The dream passage seems, at first, to exhibit a nostalgic fantasy of a "primitive" life in the "golden age." Yet it has nothing in common with traditional golden-age scenarios. In Hesiod's famous account of the Golden Age, humans did not work, had no metal implements, and never encountered a rainstorm. Thoreau offers us here a very different conception of a "golden age"—an age where human culture somehow settles into nature. First, Thoreau suggests that his dream house is more or less identical to the natural world: a "nest" with the heavens as a roof—a vast habitat that includes numerous species of living beings. But Thoreau also portrays the house as a dwelling for human beings with their artifacts and technologies—one that offers people shelter from a tempestuous storm. An impossible house. An *unheimlich* house. Thoreau's excursus on his dream house—with its weird oscillation between nature and culture—calls our attention to the problematic but necessary association of humans and nonhumans. It reminds us that Thoreau's own house is a tenuous and provisional experiment that confronts the problem of human dwelling on earth.

In writing *Walden*, Thoreau recycled his housing project in the material of language. Thoreau, then, created two pieces of art, two works that "bring the earth into the open": [36] an architectural edifice and a literary text. Thoreau makes a simple house and a complex literary work—his discursive recycling is far more elaborate than his construction of a house in the woods. The house took months to build; the book took years and years to write. Thoreau uses the word "extra-vagant" to describe his own discourse. He inserts the hyphen to emphasize the Latin roots of the word: "wandering" (*vagare*) "beyond" (*extra*) traditional limits.[37] Thoreau develops an extra-vagant, wandering-beyond mode of discourse to capture the complexity of his art of living. Certainly his discourse goes well beyond the literal description of the house and neighborhood at Walden Pond.

Walden is extravagant, in part because it rejects a transcendental evasion of the bodily world. It wanders beyond the transcendentalism that gave Thoreau his first intellectual community. The Transcendentalists claimed that human beings will discover a divine, immaterial principle by engaging with nature in the right way. As Emerson suggests, a walk in the woods is an opportunity to discover God, and to develop one's spirituality. Transcendentalism conceives of nature as a "symbol" for God, and thus a mere pointer to a higher reality. It is a stepping-stone on the path towards transcendence. Ultimately, this philosophy endorses a dualistic scheme that privileges mind and God over nature. Emerson makes this clear in his famous essay "Nature." Consider an amazing passage at the end of the essay—a passage that offers us a house outside of physical nature:

The immobility or bruteness of nature is the absence of spirit; to pure spirit it is fluid, it is volatile, it is obedient. Every spirit builds itself a house, and beyond its house a world . . . Know then, that the world exists for you. For you is the phenomenon perfect . . . Build therefore your own world. As fast as you conform your life to the pure idea in your mind, that will unfold its great proportions . . . So fast will disagreeable appearances, swine, spiders, snakes, pests, mad-houses, prisons, enemies, vanish; they are temporary and shall no

more be seen. The kingdom of man over nature, which comes not with observation . . . he shall enter without more wonder than the blind man feels who is
gradually restored to perfect sight.[38]

In this disturbing passage, Emerson uses the metaphor of house building, but he invites us to dwell in a spiritual house—one that transcends
nature, with its "sordors and filth." The transcendental philosopher
ends up blinding himself to nature and, indeed, to human culture:
everything from spiders to madhouses "will no more be seen."

As his work matured, Thoreau rejected the dualistic philosophy of
the transcendentalists (and thus also to Platonic/Christian and Cartesian dualism). To counteract this pervasive mode of thinking, Thoreau
experiments with new and different discourses. He finds ways to blur
the boundaries between humans and nonhumans. For example,
Thoreau often identifies humans with animals, plants, and other earthly
entities—with the *humus* that grounds our humanity (*humanus*).

What is man but a mass of thawing clay? The ball of the human finger is but
a drop congealed. The fingers and toes flow to their extent from the thawing mass of the body . . . Is not the hand a spreading *palm* leaf with its lobes
and veins? The ear may be regarded, fancifully, as a lichen on the side of the
head . . . The nose is a manifest congealed drop or stalactite.[39]

In this rococo piece of writing, Thoreau invites us to consider our affinity to clay, leaves, lichen, and stalactites. We grow and flow from earth
like every other nonhuman being.

Next, we humans find kinship with insects. For example, after witnessing an elaborate battle between two colonies of ants, Thoreau exclaims: "I was myself excited somewhat even as if [the ants] had been
men. The more you think of it, the less the difference."[40] The humble
insect figures largely in the last chapter of the book. First, Thoreau introduces the notion of "the human insect."[41] He challenges his readers
to confront their own diminutive presence in the vast ecological community, and to acknowledge their relations to the humbler members of
the earthly household. In the famous closing passage of the text,
Thoreau compares the philosophic person to a "strong and beautiful
bug which came out of the dry leaf of an old table of applewood, which
had stood in a farmer's kitchen for sixty years . . . [hatched] from an
egg deposited in the living tree many years earlier still."[42] The book
ends with this profoundly anti-transcendental gesture—this image of
the "human insect" hatching out of the "dead, dry life of society."

Can we accept Thoreau's claim that human and nonhuman beings live in a common "household"? That there is a kinship between humans and nonhumans? As Thoreau says of his solitary life in the woods: "I was so distinctly made aware of the presence of something kindred to me, even in scenes which we are accustomed to call wild and dreary."[43] Humans are animals, but they are a distinct kind of animal. We humans are both inside and outside of nature: "I go and come with a strange liberty in Nature, a part of herself";[44] "We are not wholly involved in nature."[45] We are earthly terrestrial beings, but also "without earth" (*sans terre*).[46]

Thoreau developed both the intellectual and the physical aspects of human life. As a thinker immersed in literature and philosophy, he was fully engaged in the cultivation of discourse. At the same time, he sought to know the world with and through his body. Let's start with the body. With the contact of bodies. In his experiment at Walden Pond, Thoreau sets out to "know nature," both his own and that of nonhumans. In building a house, cultivating vegetables, and investigating his nonhuman "neighborhood," he develops a sort of carnal knowledge of the earth: "it was a singular experience, that long acquaintance which I cultivated with beans, what with planting, and hoeing, and harvesting, and threshing, and picking over, and selling them . . . [and] I might add eating them, for I did taste. I was determined to *know beans*."[47]

Here, we do not find a human subject standing over a natural object. Rather, Thoreau depicts an interaction of human and nonhuman beings: "What shall I learn of beans and beans of me?"[48] In seeking for bodily knowledge, Thoreau anticipates phenomenological conceptions of understanding. As Heidegger claims, "the closest kind of association [with the beings around us] is not mere perceptual cognition, but, rather, a handling, using, and taking care of things which has its own kind of knowledge."[49] Part of Thoreau's project focuses on his efforts to handle, use, and take care of things in this Heideggerian sense— efforts that involve manual labor and bodily activity, which offers "its own kind of knowledge." Nietzsche claimed (metaphorically) to do "philosophy with a hammer." Thoreau does philosophy with a physical hammer—and a kitchen broom, an axe, a hoe, and a fishing rod. Thoreau's body came to know bodily, material beings. In his view, our knowledge comes first from the senses and the body. As Thoreau puts it in "Walking," "unless our philosophy hears the cock crow in every barnyard within our horizon, it is belated."[50] The philosophy that focuses only on reason is belated: it comes after bodily knowledge, following in its wake.

Thoreau reexamines the boundaries between the mind and the body, between intellectual and bodily apprehension. In one provocative passage, he conceives of the mind as a special bodily organ suited for particular modes of knowledge:

The intellect is a cleaver; it discerns and rifts its way into the secret of things. I do not wish to be any more busy with my hands than is necessary. My head is hands and feet . . . My instinct tells me that my head is an organ for burrowing, as some creatures use their snout and fore-paws, and with it I would mine and burrow my way through these hills.[51]

In comparing the mind to "hands and feet," Thoreau blurs the distinction between the intellect and the body. In calling the human mind "the snout and forepaws" of a burrowing animal, he blurs the distinction between humans and animals.

Of course the mind, however material in its form, burrows with the paws (so to speak) of *logos*—paws that cannot "touch" the physical world. The very activity of human cognition and self-consciousness pulls us away from nature, and precludes us from being fully at home on earth. While our bodies ally us with nonhuman beings, our minds are (as Augustine suggested) "distended" in time: our mental awareness of bodily transience distances us from nature and unsettles us from earth. As Harrison beautifully observes,

We humans do not speak the language of nature's self-inclusion, but one of extraneous excess. Our *logos* is the outside of things—a boundary of finitude at which we are lost but which, in return, enables us to utter words at all. The words "tree" and "rock" are utterable because *logos*, in its longing, projects us beyond the containment of trees, rocks, wind and forests. In excess of the earth, we dwell in longing as in a house turned inside out.[52]

As self-conscious beings aware of time and bodily vicissitudes, we are longing (and unbelonging) beings. Our minds reach out beyond ourselves—beyond bodily and temporal presence. We are extravagant beings. This existential extravagance subjects humans to the sorrows and joys of time. In a distant echo of Augustine's notion of "distention," Thoreau suggests that we are pulled into the past as well as the future: "we loiter in winter when it is already spring."[53] Thoreau does not, however, see temporal "distention" as a sign of sin: rather, it is a basic fact of human life.

Thoreau speaks directly to the problems and possibilities of time: "In any weather, at any hour of the day or night, I have been anxious to improve the nick of time, and notch it on my stick too; to stand on the meeting of two eternities, the past and the future, which is precisely the present moment; to toe that line."[54] This passage does not celebrate "living in the present." First, Thoreau says that he is always anxious: anxiety pulls him towards the future, a future that is unknown. Second, Thoreau aims to "improve" the present time by (later) notching it on his stick. As Cavell suggests, this reference to notching the present on one's stick is a metaphorical image of the act of writing. In claiming to "notch" his present experience on his stick, Thoreau indicates that he will offer a written account of this event later in his life.[55] He can only "improve" his present experiences in the temporality—the extravagance—of language.[56] Thoreau, then, acknowledges that humans are both inside and outside of nature. He accepts human finitude and longing (as well as unbelonging), and responds by cultivating a peculiar form of enchantment. He offers not the (cold) comforts of transcendence but temporal pleasures and a profound sense of wonder at the natural world.

Thoreau develops specific disciplines of attention that lead to understanding, sympathy, and wonder. Part of his attention is directed towards intellectual and literary issues. Another part focuses on visual, aural, and tactile experiences—a bodily attention to the earthly realm. Thoreau very deliberately tacks back and forth between these economies of attention. For example, after the chapter titled "Reading" (which discusses classical literature and the art of reading), he turns immediately to a chapter called "Sounds." The opening of this chapter responds directly to the activity of reading, and offers a radically different discipline of attention:

But while we are confined to books, though the most select and classic, and read only particular written languages . . . we are in danger of forgetting the language which all things and events speak without metaphor, which alone is copious and standard. Much is published, but little printed. The rays which stream through the shutter will be no longer remembered when the shutter is wholly removed. No method nor discipline can supersede the necessity of being forever on the alert. What is a course of history, or philosophy, or poetry, no matter how well selected, or the best society, or the most admirable routine of life, compared with the discipline of looking always at what is to be seen?[57]

Unlike a fixed written text, nature is "published" in the continuing and transient events of the physical world. Here, Thoreau recommends the "discipline of looking always at what is to be seen." The activity of perceiving and attending to the physical world forms the basis of Thoreau's cultivation of reading and writing, and his engagement with discourse leads him to look again at nature: the two activities are intertwined in Thoreau's philosophy.

Nature kills: Thoreau knows that humans are creatures that die and become recycled in the natural world. "Man is a mass of thawing clay."[58] In a passage at the end of "Spring," Thoreau describes his encounters with dead animals:

> We are cheered when we observe the vulture feeding on the carrion which disgusts and disheartens us and deriving health and strength from the repast. There was a dead horse in the hollow by the path to my house, which compelled me sometimes to go out of my way, especially in the night when the air was heavy, but the assurance it gave me of the strong appetite and the inviolable health of Nature was my compensation for this.[59]

The sight of dead animals "disheartens us," no doubt because it reminds us of our own death. Here, Thoreau acknowledges the human fear of death. Yet he claims that the dead animals nonetheless "cheer" him because they remind him of the health of the ecosystem. For Thoreau, dead animals evoke both fear and wonder. They confront us with our own mortality, but also lead us to wonder at life, at the vitality of the earth.

Nature enchants: even while acknowledging that nature kills, Thoreau finds wonder and pleasure in nature. For this reason, Thoreau devotes endless curiosity and attention to the natural world. Consider the following passage from "Spring":

> Few phenomena gave me more delight than to observe the forms which thawing sand and clay assume in flowing down the sides of a deep cut on the railroad . . . When the frost comes out in the spring, and even in a thawing day in the winter, the sand begins to flow down the slopes like lava, sometimes bursting out through the snow and overflowing it where no sand was to be seen before. Unnumerable little streams overlap and interlace with one another, exhibiting a sort of hybrid product, which obeys half way the laws of currents, and half way that of vegetation. As it flows it takes the forms of sappy leaves or vines, making heaps of pulpy sprays a foot or more in depth, and resembling, as you look down on them, the laciniated lobed and imbricated thallusses of some lichens; or you are reminded of coral, of leopards' paws or birds' feet, of brains or lungs or bowels, and excrements of all kinds.[60]

This account of sand vegetation well illustrates Thoreau's particular mode of wonder. Here, Thoreau revels in the vision of entrails and excrement: this scene is "excrementitious in its character, and there is no end of the heaps of liver lights and bowels, as if the globe were turned inside out."[61] Thoreau is deliberately—and extravagantly—dwelling on the excrementitious aspects of nature. He finds beauty and wonder in the shit of the world. Here, Thoreau confronts the *humus* that is the basis of human life—and marvels at it. One could argue that the fear inspired by nature and death actually grounds the activity of wonder.

Consider, for a moment, Heidegger's conceptions of "astonishment" and "wonder." In Heidegger, "astonishment allows the unusual to grow, precisely as what is extraordinary, into what overgrows all usual powers and bears in itself a claim to a rank all its own. Astonishment is imbued with the awareness of being *excluded* from what exists in the awesome."[62] Wonder—which Heidegger elevates over astonishment—focuses on the ordinary:

in wonder, what is most usual of all and in all, i.e. everything, becomes the most unusual . . . Everything in what is most usual becomes in wonder the most unusual in this one respect: that it is what it is . . . while wonder must venture out into the most extreme unusualness of everything, it is at the same time cast back wholly on itself, knowing that it is incapable of penetrating the unusualness by way of explanation, since that would precisely be to destroy it.[63]

In Thoreau, we can find a unique synthesis of Heidegger's conceptions of "astonishment" and "wonder"—a synthesis that exhibits a radically different response to the natural world. First, Thoreau expresses "astonishment" in his experience of the extraordinariness of nature and his own sense of *exclusion* from it. At the same time, he experiences "wonder" in recognizing the unusualness of things that are usual, and in refusing to explain this strangeness (and thus destroy it). Thoreau goes further. He fears and marvels at the fundamental mystery of the bodily world: "I fear bodies, I tremble to meet them. What is this Titan that has possession of me? Talk of mysteries! Think of our life in nature—daily to be shown matter, to come into contact with it—rocks, trees, wind on our cheeks. The solid earth! The actual world! the *common sense*! Contact! Contact! *Who* are we? *Where* are we?"[64]

Ultimately, we should not articulate Thoreau's mode of wonder in Heideggerian terms (though this exercise is, I think, useful and illuminating). For Thoreau differs from Heidegger in fundamental ways. In particular, he confines his attentions exclusively to beings (not to Being). In addition, Thoreau has a different conception of the agency of nonhuman beings. In a deeply anthropocentric move, Heidegger separates "world-possessing" humans from animals and inanimate parts of nature—the former are "poor in world" (*weltarm*) and the latter "without world" (*weltlos*).[65] All nonhumans lack *Dasein*, and for that reason are "deprived" and inferior to humans (rather than simply different). Heidegger offers a lengthy analysis of animals, arguing that they are "poor in world" because they are captive to their environment and can only "move within instinctual drives."[66] Animals cannot, then, "attend to" beings—that is, attend to them "as something"— and are thus determined entirely by their instinctive impulses. In *Dependent Rational Animals*, Alasdair MacIntyre challenges this Heideggerian view. Citing recent scientific studies, he claims that many higher animals

do not merely respond to features of their environment, they actively explore it; they devote perceptual understanding to the objects that they encounter, they inspect them from different angles, they recognize the familiar, they identify and classify, they may on occasion treat one and the same object first as something to be played with and then as something to be eaten, and some of them recognize and even grieve for what is absent.[67]

Anticipating this nonanthropocentric view, Thoreau recognizes that animals have their own modes of intelligence. He also sees interdependence of the ecosystem and identifies human and nonhuman beings as members of a single, living world.[68] Nonhumans differ from humans in important ways, but are not inferior or "deprived" for this reason. In fact, Thoreau identifies nonhuman beings as kindred to humans and equal members of the earthly *oikos* (i.e., the earthly *community*). For Thoreau, the nonhuman beings in nature are (paradoxically) both akin and alien to us: they are kindred to us even as they signal our estrangement and unbelonging. Thoreau expresses this paradox in a passage on getting lost in the woods: in his lostness, Thoreau comes to "appreciate the vastness and strangeness of nature" even as he realizes "the infinite extent of our relations."[69] Nature is strange and alien, but it is also related to us in an infinite number of ways. This sense of belonging and unbelonging marks a unique mode of wonder: an enchantment at the earth that grounds our death.

We may ask what Thoreau's mode of enchantment has to offer us in the twenty-first century. Given the extensive ecological deterioration of the earth and the sickening facts of the wars going on at present, shouldn't we abandon wonder and just be shocked and outraged? Is wonder really appropriate at this horrifying moment? I would argue that it is not only appropriate but necessary. If we cannot develop the capacity to wonder at the nonhuman world, then we will have no real motivation to save it. Without Thoreau's mode of wonder, we will end up "solving" every ecological problem with technology rather than exercising restraint and setting limits to our desires. If we develop Thoreau's discipline of attention and his capacity for enchantment, as I believe, we will enter into an ethical and, indeed, an erotic relationship with the world. If we can begin to see the beauty, intricacy, and complex symbiosis of nonhuman beings in the natural world, then we will want to let these beings be. Careful attention to the natural world will, within a very short time, boggle the mind. Knowledge will break, and wonder will take the lead.

CHAPTER 2

Bewitched, Bothered, and Bewildered:
William James's Feeling of "If"

LINDA SIMON

WHEN WILLIAM JAMES titled his 1895 address to the Young Men's Christian Association "Is Life Worth Living?" he echoed a question that was on the minds of many of his contemporaries. Pessimism, melancholy, passivity: these feelings, characteristic of the age, seemed to James evidence of a "sick shudder of the frustrated religious demand," a frustration caused by the advent of science and the consequential denigration of faith. Faith in an attentive God, in an eternal moral order, perhaps even in the immortality of the soul, could alleviate despair. But educated men and women increasingly felt that belief in the supernatural amounted to superstition; that science alone would afford intimacy with nature; that the logical and rational must prevail over the intuitive and sentimental. The world could be known through methodical inquiry, science assured James's contemporaries, and that world consisted of matter.

Sharing the anxieties of the age, James came to believe that the essential question in the debate between science and religion centered on the meaning of knowing: What, James asked, could we know of the empirical and unseen world? How do we know what we know? Does faith emerge at the limits of knowing, or does faith imbue all belief— even in the empirical, even in ourselves? These questions resonate for us still, inflaming a cultural, and sometimes political, divide focused on the meaning of faith and of truth, the nature of inquiry and evidence: what David Hollinger calls "a distinctive cluster of hopes and aspirations about a culture based on science."[1]

For James, truth did not emerge solely from the empirical. He argued for a meaning of knowing that did not preclude uncertainty, individual perspective, and personal desire—and a conception of faith that offered an alternative both to church-centered worship and to abject commitment to the powers of science. In his vision, faith could take myriad expressions, and a search for the ineffable could satisfy what he called the "craving of the heart to believe that behind nature there is a spirit whose expression nature is."[2] James defined this spirit not as the God of Christianity (although he allowed for that conception), but rather as mysterious energies that could be apprehended intuitively and investigated scientifically.

James argued, furthermore, that intellectualizing—the "calculation" that Max Weber saw as the means to mastery of reality—was not the only way of knowing the world. Intuition mattered; personality mattered: in James's universe—a universe inherited, in part, from Romantic poets and artists—the self rose exalted, empowered to interpret, invent, and vitalize reality. With each individual, the world was reborn. Central to James's writings on philosophy, psychology, and spirituality is the idea of novelty. A world without the possibility of the new, a world that is consistent and predictable: such a world would be nothing less than catastrophic. For James, novelty is implicit in a "cosmological theory of *promise*," a theory that posits an unstable, inconstant universe containing not merely the tangible, but the miraculous and astonishing: what James called, admiringly and longingly, "wild facts."[3] The universe that James celebrated was discontinuous, prismatic, chaotic; a universe in which life was "always off its balance," a universe that heralded uniqueness and idiosyncrasy, in which each individual had authority to make meaning through self-reflection, empathy, prescience, and faith.[4] His was a universe, as Paul Croce has argued, in which metaphysical certainty did not depend on epistemological certainty. "The fallibility of scientific and religious knowledge was a chief lesson of his education," Croce writes; "finding a way, despite those limitations, to attain truth and its positive fruits was the challenge of his adulthood."[5]

This essay examines James's conception of that challenge: his resistance to a narrowing of perception and possibility dictated, as he saw it, by philosophical systems, by scientific and historical explanations of experience, by habit—and even by the conventions of language. "We ought to say a feeling of *and*, and a feeling of *if*, a feeling of *but*, and a feeling of *by*, quite as readily as we say a feeling of *blue* or a feeling of *cold*," James wrote. "Yet we do not: so inveterate has our habit become of recognizing the existence of the substantive parts alone, that language almost refuses to lend itself to any other use."[6] A feeling of "if" is the most crucial in this list. Besides provoking sensations of irritability, tension, anxiety, and restlessness that made him feel alive and even exhilarated, the notion of "if" portended for James the possibility that experience transcended the material and affirmed his investigation of—and faith in—the inexplicable, uncanny, and subliminal. The feeling of "if" characterizes the essence of James's psychology, focused as it is on the fluid encounters between self and external world, and the complicity of the individual in creating that world; and of his philosophy of pragmatism and pluralism, terms for a process of knowing a universe that can, and does, and inevitably must change—continually, unpredictably, wildly. The world, James wrote jubilantly, is a "delicious mess of insanities and realities, strivings and deadnesses, hopes and fears, agonies and exultations," especially the exultation of surprise.[7]

Psychologist and philosopher, intellectual and academic, James yearned for wildness in the same way that Thoreau felt "a strange thrill of savage delight" at glimpsing a woodchuck one evening, and, he confessed, feeling "strongly tempted to seize and devour him raw; not that I was hungry then, except for that wildness which he represented."[8] In 1854, when Thoreau retreated to Walden Pond, wildness seemed in danger of being tamed by prescribed social politeness, middlebrow churches, and an increasingly mechanized world; rebelliously, Thoreau wanted to ingest not only nature's raw power, but also an uninhibited, irrational, impetuousness—a whimsicality, even a selfishness, that was not expected behavior for mid-nineteenth-century gentlemen. The woods around Concord became, for Thoreau, a primal wilderness in which he could immerse himself, dazzled and bewildered.

Wildness lies at the heart of bewilderment. Etymologically, *wild* derives from roots meaning *willed* or *willful, uncontrolled* and, indeed, *uncontrollable*. If bewilderment means disorientation and confusion, it also means liberation from the merely rational and material. The bewildered give themselves permission to reject the notion that nothing exists except matter. "[M]aterialism's sun sets in a sea of disappointment," James wrote.[9]

For James, wildness was inherent in a multi-layered universe—a multi-verse, he called it—where surfaces and appearances offered only a partial representation of reality, including the reality of one's identity. If the external world was kaleidoscopic, the internal world offered wondrous complexities. Everyone, James believed, consisted of a multiplicity of selves; hidden, or subliminal, selves might be more authentic than the "social self" that one presented to various constituencies. These subliminal layers of self exerted force that shaped and influenced the social self; to discover and recognize these hidden selves led to an enriched understanding of one's true identity.

It was also possible, James suggested, that identity was shaped by forces outside of oneself, energies from what he called a "mother-sea" that filtered into one's consciousness. These energies comprised part of the hidden universe that might offer its secrets. Beyond the "accredited and orderly facts" that science had discovered, he said, "there ever floats a sort of dust-cloud of exceptional observations, of occurrences minute and irregular and seldom met with" that urged him not only to investigate, but even more importantly, to "renovate" the idea of what science is, what perception can encompass, and what, in fact, we mean when we say *we know.*[10]

Where the Wild Facts Are

James believed that systems, paradigms, and intellectualized orderliness—whether from philosophy, science, or religion—preclude our apprehending reality. Coloring within the lines, as it were, seemed to him to limit one's perceptions. "James detested any system of the universe that professed to enclose everything," his colleague George Santayana observed; "we must never set up boundaries that exclude romantic surprises."[11] In addition, systems inhibited creativity: hypotheses were more exciting than theories, which seemed to James an encumbrance. "In the presence of theories of any sort," Santayana remembered, "he was attentive, puzzled, suspicious, with a certain inner prompting to disregard them."[12] For James, the philosopher's project was to open doors to various and perhaps contradictory ways of making meaning and discovering truths; he called this perspective *pluralism,* and sometimes even *radical pluralism,* terms that generated considerable misunderstanding among readers who expected from him, as from any philosopher, some template that could be imposed on experiences to wrest order from apparent chaos, to find coherence in disparate occurrences. "Whether materialistically or spiritualistically minded," James wrote, "philosophers have always aimed at cleaning up the litter with which the world apparently is filled. They have substituted economical and orderly conceptions for the first sensible tangle; and whether these were morally elevated or only intellectually neat, they were at any rate always aesthetically pure and definite, and aimed at ascribing to the world something clean and intellectual in the way of inner structure." In contrast, pluralistic empiricism, he admitted, "offers but a sorry appearance. It is a turbid, muddled, gothic sort of affair, without a sweeping outline and with little pictorial nobility."[13] Its nobility, for James, was its welcome recognition of what he saw as a vast, mysterious, and complex reality that included the ineffable and was complicated by each person's idiosyncratic responses.

For James, science was an even worse offender than philosophy, focused as it was purely on probing and categorizing the material world, and denying one fact that seemed obvious to James and would become increasingly obvious to physicists in the next century: the scientist's role as perceiver and experimenter. Trained in chemistry at the Lawrence Scientific School, and teaching physiology and anatomy as his first professional position, James had emerged from the scientific community skeptical about its claims of objectivity and dispassion. He admitted, for example, that he once had manipulated an experiment in order to demonstrate a principle to his students.[14] But even more significant than such duplicity was science's underlying assumption that laws existed and, once discovered, could serve to explain the natural—that is, the perceivable—world. James preferred to believe in nature's capriciousness or, at least, in inaccessible secrets. Although scientists maintained that objectivity resulted from gathering and testing large amounts of empirical data, such researchers seemed to James nothing more than a sect of ardent devotees. Scientists, according to James, held "a certain fixed belief,—the belief that the hidden order of nature is mechanical exclusively, that non-mechanical categories are irrational ways of conceiving and explaining such things as human life."[15] Like members of any sect, scientists refused to acknowledge contradictory data, rejecting experiences or observations that James believed deserved investigation. Yet science proved alluring to many precisely because of the apparent verifiability of its theories. "There is included in human nature an ingrained naturalism and materialism of mind which can only admit facts that are actually tangible," James wrote. "Of this sort of mind the entity called 'science' is the idol. Fondness for the word 'scientist' is one of the notes by which you may know its votaries;

and its short way of killing any opinion that it disbelieves in is to call it 'unscientific.' "[16]

Philosophy and science each claimed authority to interpret reality, and each imposed concepts that threatened to limit experience. "With concepts," he insisted, "we go in quest of the absent, meet the remote, actively turn this way or that, bend our experience, and make it tell us whither it is bound." Instead of questioning and analyzing the vagaries of our experiences, he wrote, "We *harness* perceptual reality in concepts in order to drive it better to our ends."[17] This notion of harnessing experiences and perceptions seemed to James to "negate the inwardness of reality altogether": that is, concepts ignored personal responses and perceptions, and instead conflated individual experiences and forced generalizations.[18] Concepts, he said, were necessarily historical; the past, therefore, explained the present, and by doing so proscribed novelty. These two ideas—the historicity of concepts and their negation of humanity's variety—contradicted James's intuitions about knowing. James championed perception and urged his readers to become attentive to their experiences, to be open to the new and unexpected, to find new language to represent to themselves what they experienced, and especially to believe that their own identity, personality, needs, and desires shaped their knowledge of reality. "[T]o understand life by concepts," he wrote, "is to arrest its movement, cutting it up into bits as if with scissors, and immobilizing these in our logical herbarium where, comparing them as dried specimens, we can ascertain which of them statically includes or excludes which other."[19] James refused to live in a dead and dried world that could be examined and observed but not altered, a world whose surface could be explored, but not its depths, and a world that did not account for his *self* as a shaper of it.

Concepts, then, threatened to obscure awareness, forcing people to believe they knew what they saw or felt before an experience even had taken place. Concepts, James wrote, "guide us over the map of life . . . But this map, which surrounds the present, like all maps, is only a surface; its features are but abstract signs and symbols of things that in themselves are concrete bits of sensible experience."[20] If we distill experiences as abstractions, James feared, then such processes as activity and causation cannot fully be apprehended. Similarly, *"Personal identity is conceptually impossible"* because "ideas" and "states of mind" are discrete concepts, as is "soul" or "ego"; and *"Motion and change are impossible"* because events are "all separately conceived."[21] James's rejection of scientific and philosophical systems was motivated, in part, by his desire to account for the importance of the complexity of feelings, perceptions, and states of being that comprised the protean self. One path to self-knowledge, he believed, involved close attention to one's responses to the intricacy and contingency of experiences. "The deeper features of reality are found only in perceptual experience," he wrote. "Here alone do we acquaint ourselves with continuity, or the immersion of one thing in another, here alone with self, with substance, with qualities, with activity in its various modes, with time, with cause, with change, with novelty, with tendency, with freedom."[22]

Hidden Selves

Although James established a psychology laboratory at Harvard, much experimental research at the time focused on perception and nerve action rather than on exploring the essence of selfhood. Victorian psychology, eager to break from its origins in philosophy and borrowing its methods from physiology, devoted much attention to investigating neural pathways and quantifying responses, particularly responses to such stimuli as light and sound. Stop clocks were important laboratory equipment, but reaction-time experiments did not interest James, nor others of his colleagues who wanted not so much to understand brain and nerves as to understand will, self, and soul. For this project, introspection—observing one's own feelings and responses—was the primary means of investigation.[23] Discoveries resulting from introspection led to generalizations about the workings of all minds, about what James called "the absolute world-enigma" of consciousness.[24] As a psychologist writing the first comprehensive American psychology textbook, James found himself in the uncomfortable position of defending and explaining such generalizations, while at the same time aware of the limitations of both the introspective method and the language available to him to describe mental states. Still, his own introspection supported the basic tenets of a psychology that emphasized the self's integrity and autonomy. For James, each individual stood at the center of his or her world, shaping that world through responses to experiences, understanding that world through analysis of those experiences, and being shaped by the world through encounters, observations, and perceptions.

"Personal histories," James wrote, "are processes of change in time, and *the change itself is one of the things immediately experienced*."[25] Although his readers might assume that personal histories were summaries of events in one's life, for James the most significant parts of those histories were transitions among experiences; indeed, for James, transitions, "whether disjunctive or conjunctive in content, are themselves experiences, and must in general be accounted at least as real as the terms which they relate."[26] Or even more real. The coherence of experiences and their significance to each "mind" or "personal consciousness" depended on the idiosyncratic transitions that knit experiences, one to the next. Those transitions, James said, could be expressed as "grammatical particles. With, *near, next, like, from, towards, against, because, for, through, my*—these words designate types of conjunctive relation arranged in a roughly ascending order of intimacy and inclusiveness."[27] It is telling that in this list of prepositions, adjectives, and conjunctions, there is one possessive adjective, *my*, indicating the most intimate and inclusive conjunctive relation in a messy, whirling universe: the conjunctive relation that gathers together what James called floating and dangling experiences and claims them for a single ego. Transitions, he said, were experienced as a "halo of felt relations" or a "felt fringe of relations," a penumbra surrounding every thought and feeling that creates an aura suggesting "affinity" or "discord."[28]

James objected to schools of philosophy that "discredited" the importance of the "plain conjunctive experience . . . the empiricists leaving things permanently disjoined, and the rationalists remedying the looseness by their absolutes or substances, or whatever other fictitious agencies of union they may have employed."[29] For James, each person expressed his or her identity most forcefully and authentically through conjunctive relations: "Life," he insisted, "is in the transitions as much as in the term connected; often, indeed, it seems to be there more emphatically, as if our spurts and sallies forward were the real firing-line of the battle, were like the thin line of flame advancing across the dry autumnal field which the farmer proceeds to burn."[30] He believed this to be true of everyone because it seemed so incontrovertibly true for himself.

In the reality that James wanted to inhabit, the reality that he claimed he did inhabit, the self was ceaselessly in motion, buffeted and resisting, striving or retreating. In all of his discussion of mind, therefore, we can sense James's frustration with the nouns he felt forced to use to describe thinking, feeling, and awareness, since nouns slammed experiences against a wall, so to speak, and forced them to become stilled objects. Once experiences were expressed as nouns, James perceived them as dead, unchanging. His student Gertrude Stein took up the project of refreshing language through repetition and unexpected juxtaposition of words. James himself tried to create a new visual, sensual metaphor for subjective life as streaming thought "without breach, crack or division."[31] That streaming was characterized by sensations that seemed like "an alternation of flights and perchings," with the perchings representing the resting places—where thoughts and feelings were focused—and the flights representing the "transitive parts" of the stream.[32] Of course, transitions were the most elusive, since once one stopped to consider them, they became resting places and lost their pliant quality of tendency.

The act of perceiving was complicated, also, by a shimmering halo surrounding all experiences. When we are aware of hearing thunder, for example, James cautions us that "what we hear when the thunder crashes is not thunder *pure,* but thunder-breaking-upon-silence-and-contrasting-with-it . . . The thunder itself we believe to abolish and exclude the silence; but the *feeling* of the thunder is also a feeling of the silence as just gone." We never can perceive only the present moment, embedded as it is in the trembling aura of other moments. What we call the present stands as a beginning, a possibility for novelty, an idea that for James felt intoxicating. Finally, each moment of perception was impossible—happily—to duplicate by anyone else. "Our own bodily position, attitude, condition," James wrote, "is one of the things of which *some* awareness, however inattentive, invariably accompanies the knowledge of whatever else we know."[33] Our awareness of some attitudes or conditions flowing or floating somewhere beneath our conscious, perceiving self—this, for James, was the realm of the subliminal that fascinated him, as it did many of his contemporaries.

James rejected—"mistrusted" is how he put it—the term *unconscious,* which seemed threatening in its suggestion of passivity or abdication of will.[34] Although he conceded that such states as sleeping, fainting, coma, and epilepsy interrupted normal waking consciousness, still he believed that these interruptions did not sustain the notion that the unconscious existed "in an incessant and fine-grained form" somewhere in the mind.[35] Even a sleeping mother, he asserted, awoke upon hearing her baby cry, proof, therefore, of an enduring state of consciousness. Rather than subscribe to the idea of unconsciousness, James argued that one or another feeling of consciousness might dominate one's thoughts at any given time; consciousness might be layered into substrata.

James was more comfortable, then, with the concept of the subconscious, aware as he was of the controversy that the term generated. As late as 1910, James's Harvard colleague Hugo Munsterberg, recognizing "no consensus of opinion . . . as to the class of phenomena to which the term 'subconscious' shall be applied," published a symposium that aired the views of such noted researchers and scholars as Pierre Janet, Joseph Jastrow, Theodore Ribot, and Morton Prince.[36] Responses ranged from the empirical to the spiritual. The subconscious might be evidence only of "pure neural processes"; or it might consist of dissociated ideas that split off from the main consciousness. These dissociated states might produce aberrant feelings or behavior, or they might aggregate into "a large self-conscious personality, to which the term 'self' is given," a definition that described multiple personality or alternate consciousness. The possibility of an alternate self hidden in one's layered consciousness hinted at the notion that one could lead two—or perhaps more—lives: one as a socialized member of society, another as someone defiant, subversive, perhaps outrageous and even dangerous. Robert Louis Stevenson's *Dr. Jekyll and Mr. Hyde* was not alone among hugely popular, and titillating, tales of multiple personality.

More conservatively, some psychologists held that the subconscious should be a term ascribed to that part of consciousness "outside the focus of our attention" and perceived, as it were, "out in the corner of our mind's eye"; Morton Prince, for one, believed the term *co-conscious* was more accurate than subconscious. Janet believed that the subconscious always implied pathology; but others—notably British psychical researcher Frederic W. H. Myers—countered that the subconscious was not merely a repository of fragmented thoughts, but a richly varied site where "the main reservoir of consciousness and the personal consciousness becomes a subordinate stream flowing out of this great storage basis of 'subliminal' ideas." This subliminal consciousness might even be "part of a transcendental world."[37]

It should come as no surprise that James was captivated by Myers's imagination. Whether Myers's claims would be proved valid or not, James hailed him for acknowledging much more complexity in the human mind than other writers had, and for asserting that the workings of the subconscious were not pathological. Before Myers put forth his ideas, James said, the human mind had been considered "largely an abstraction. Its normal adult traits were recognised. A sort of sunlit terrace was exhibited on which it took its exercise. But where that terrace stopped, the mind stopped; and there was nothing farther left to tell of in this kind of philosophy but the brain and other physical facts of nature on the one hand, and the absolute metaphysical ground of the universe on the other."[38] In contrast to theorists who sought to prove the existence of "mind" as a unified entity, Myers suggested that consciousness "aggregates and dissipates."[39] The recognition of a complex subliminal self supported James's own idea, put forth in *The Principles of Psychology* and elsewhere, that any single person consisted of several selves: the material (or body), the social (consisting of multiple identities recognized by different constituencies), and the spiritual self, which James saw as the essence of one's identity.

By "spiritual self" James meant the sense each of us has of an active inner life: "of our ability to argue and discriminate, of our moral sensibility and conscience, of our indomitable will." Through introspection, anyone reflecting on interactions with the external world will discover "a spiritual something . . . which seems to *go out* to meet these qualities and contents, whilst they seem to *come in* to be received by it. It is what welcomes or rejects. . . . It is the home of interest."[40] Reflecting on one's spiritual self, James asserted, generated a feeling of ambiguity and possibility. "What we are," he said, "is always lined with the notion of what we *might* be, or *might have been*. We continue our past, but we seem to ourselves not always to be passively transmitting its push, but from time to time to re-direct it ourselves . . . Somewhere in the universe something must genuinely happen. Why not here, in the bosom of our several phenomenal lives?"[41] His description of his "palpitating inward life" is characterized by tension: "a constant play of furtherances and hindrances in my thinking, of checks and releases, tendencies which run with desire, and tendencies which run the other way."[42] For James, this tension felt challenging, energizing: "If this life be not a real fight, in which something is eternally gained for the universe by success, it is no better than a game of private theatricals from which one may withdraw at will. But it *feels* like a real fight," he insisted, "—as if there were something really wild in the universe which we, with all our idealities and faithfulnesses, are needed to redeem; and first of all to redeem our own hearts from atheisms and fears."[43]

This "wildness," however, was itself a source of enchantment for James. With all his hopes pinned on indeterminacy and instability, with his conviction that Nature was "a jungle, where all things are provisional, half-fitted to each other, and untidy," with his rejection of a "Sunday-school conception" of spirituality, James welcomed proof of a transcendental realm of vibrant energies.[44] For James, redemption from "atheisms and fears" was not an effort to find consolation in an omnipotent authority—although he recognized that desire in others—but precisely to inspire a release of will and energy in order to engage in the daily battle of living fully.[45] He claimed not to share in the intensity of beliefs that he documented in *The Varieties of Religious Experience*; he admitted, in a postscript to that book, his "inability to accept either popular Christianity or scholastic theism." Instead, he characterized himself as a "piecemeal" supernaturalist, one who believed in some larger power that "need not be infinite, it need not be solitary," only "friendly" to human needs and ideals. He decided to believe, too, in the chance of salvation. Chance in itself seemed to him as marvelous as the possibility of the soul's immortality. "No fact of human nature is more characteristic than its willingness to live on a chance," he wrote. "The existence of the chance makes the difference . . . between a life of which the keynote is resignation and a life of which the keynote is hope."[46] If he did not profess faith in a Christian God, he did, most forcefully, have faith in "a universe in which uncontrollable accidents and miracles (for such are new beginnings) can occur." The universe, therefore, is never completely knowable but always "incomplete and growing by addition of new parts. . . , its fate quivers, and . . . among the forces that decide its history are ourselves."[47]

James's faith in the vagaries of the universe fueled his participation in psychical research, which began in earnest in the early 1880s. As a member of the London Society for Psychical Research and a founding member of the American branch, James headed investigations of mediums, whose powers he included among wild, and, he hoped, probable, facts. As suspicious as he was of the materialism championed by scientific method, still he hoped that rigorous investigation and accumulation of data would lead to credible conclusions about trance states and the transmission of messages from the dead to the living. James's colleagues in these societies included scientists and philosophers frustrated by mainstream science's exclusion of phenomena too easily designated as "occult": telepathy, clairvoyance, hallucinations, evidence (such as ghosts) of human immortality. Psychical researchers also investigated hypnotism, dreams, automatic writing, and multiple personality; in fact, in the 1880s and 1890s, many articles on the mind that would later appear in journals of psychology could be found only in the *Proceedings of the Society for Psychical Research*. Among James's

British colleagues were Henry Sidgwick, lecturer in moral science at Cambridge University; Arthur Balfour, who later became England's prime minister; William Fletcher Barrett, a physicist and member of the Royal College of Science in Dublin; and physicist Sir Oliver Lodge. In America, members included Edward Pickering, head of the Harvard Astronomical Observatory; Charles Sedgwick Minor, professor of anthropology at Harvard; and Simon Newcomb, head of the astronomy department at Johns Hopkins, who became the organization's first president. Like James, these men hoped to distinguish occult phenomena from popular, and often duplicitous, spiritualism; and they hoped, too, as James wrote to his friend Thomas Davidson, to afford themselves a "glimpse into a world of new phenomenal possibilities enveloping those of the present life."[48]

James experimented in automatic writing and hypnotism, using his Harvard students as subjects, but he conducted much of his psychical research in dimly lit rooms in and around Boston. There, he would participate in sessions with mediums, witness the diaphanous appearance of apparitions, and feel tables turn beneath his fingers. After attending scores of séances, often with Harvard colleagues, James finally discovered a medium, Leonora Piper, whose abilities seemed incontrovertible. "If you wish to upset the law that all crows are black," James remarked, "you must not seek to show that no crows are; it is enough if you prove one single crow to be white. My own white crow is Mrs. Piper." Her powers touched James directly: she claimed to have messages from his young son, who had died shortly before James began to attend her sittings; and she divulged information about him and his family that he believed she could not know except through uncanny powers. Based on his experiences with Mrs. Piper, science, he exclaimed, "lies prostrate in the dust for me," and he hoped fervently that science could be "built up again in a form in which such things may have a positive place."[49] The new science for which James yearned allowed for "capricious, discontinuous, and not easily controlled" experiences. Most significantly, he envisioned a science that allowed for experiences generated by "peculiar persons": that is, a science in which "personal forces" served as "the starting-point for new effects." His science would be a discipline that refused the "systematic denial . . . of personality as a condition of events."[50] Psychical research, then, besides immersing James in wildness, underscored the essential participation of each individual to enhance, embolden—in fact, to create—the universe.

The Word "or"

Participation is the essence of pragmatism, the philosophical perspective for which James is renowned. Misunderstood by many of his colleagues, pragmatism often is confused with political expediency because James focused on the consequences of holding one idea rather than another. James, however, conceived of *consequences* as a term far more embracing than simply "what works." As David Hollinger explains, "Whatever else the pragmatist theory of truth entailed, it carried with it the sense that truth was a condition that happened to an idea through the course of events as experienced and analyzed by human beings." Purpose, need, and desire necessarily shape truth. Pragmatism celebrated inquiry, but, as Hollinger argues, "that inquiry could change the world . . . In contrast to the moralists who hailed or lamented the scientific enterprise as the exploration of a one-way street, down which orders for belief and conduct came from 'nature,' the pragmatic tradition carried a faith in inquiry's reconstructive capabilities in the most rigorous of the sciences and in everyday life."[51] Pragmatism's reconstructive capabilities, James discovered in his own life, applied to one's sense of identity and authority.

In June, 1877, James, thirty-five, wrote to his fiancée Alice Howe Gibbens, trying to explain what he considered to be his peculiar nature. "[T]he best way to define any man's true character," he said, "would be to seek out the particular mental or moral attitude, in which, when it came upon him, he felt himself most deeply and intensely active & alive. At such moments there is a voice inside which speaks & says '*this* is the real me!'" For James, such moments were characterized by "active tension, of holding my own as it were, & *trusting* outward things to perform their part so as to make it a full harmony, but without any *guarantee* that they will. Make it a guarantee," he added, "— and the attitude immediately becomes to my consciousness stagnant and stingless. Take away the guarantee, and I feel . . . a sort of deep enthusiastic bliss, of bitter willingness to do and suffer anything."[52] James had not always defined tension and struggle as exciting, energizing feelings. He remarked, late in his life, that "the word 'or' names a genuine reality,"[53] but this reality—of choices, chances, and the bliss of "active tension"—seemed inaccessible to him throughout his youth. Until the mid-1870s, in fact, he believed that in any struggle he would be defeated, and if he trusted anything, it was his inability to get what he wanted out of life.

When we read James's earlier letters to his friends and family, we see a man convinced that he had limited capacity to stand up against any forces at all. He felt doomed to recline. At the age of twenty-six, writing from Europe to his friend Oliver Wendell Holmes, he described himself as languid, tired, and thoroughly bored. "Much wd. I give for a constructive passion of some kind," he wrote. "In the past year if I have learned little else, I have at least learned a good deal that I previously did not suspect about the limits of my own mind. They are not exhilarating." He was filled, he said, with "a vague emptiness" where he knew he should have feelings. Even professionally, he saw little to interest, and surely not to excite, him. He could not do the laboratory work required for research (his back hurt when he stood for too long), and he feared that his predilection for empiricism rather than idealism or theology would stand in the way of a career as a philosopher. For several months, he confessed to Holmes, he had been "leading a most desultory life quite sick & weak a part of the time . . . and the rest of the time demoralized."[54] Two years later, he confessed to another friend that he felt dead intellectually.[55]

The sickness, weakness, listlessness, and hopelessness began around 1860, when James, at eighteen, considered the possibilities of his future. Throughout his peripatetic youth, accompanying his family to and from Europe, and being schooled inconsistently at home (literally, by his father) and in various academies abroad, James succumbed to his father's interpretation of the empirical world and of his own feelings. He often doubted his ability simply to know his own mind, much less to direct his future and make decisions; he became, to use the popular nineteenth-century medical term, *neurasthenic*: depressed, anxious, melancholy, and given to morbid thoughts. These feelings intensified as he grew into manhood. Circumscribed both by society's expectations for a suitable career and by his father's hopes that he would follow in his footsteps and become a self-taught, and preferably eccentric, philosopher, James, after bouts of indecision, insisted on following his own lights: he would become an artist, a decision that his father vehemently opposed. We can see in James's defense of his decision a portent of his later yearnings: art, he said, afforded him "spiritual impressions the intensest and purest I know."[56] Moreover, being an artist did not exclude—and in fact could enhance—his spiritual and religious life, which was his father's central concern. For James at the time, trying to wrest himself from his father's domination, becoming an artist seemed likely to give him some authority to interpret and translate what he perceived and, at the same time, become recognized publicly for his aesthetic contributions.

Soon, however, his lack of artistic passion and, as he saw it, lack of startling talent made him despondent about this choice for a career; earning a living as an artist seemed to portend serious compromises (he might end up merely painting portraits of the rich and famous), so he took a different path entirely, enrolling at the Lawrence Scientific School of Harvard University. Although his father had professed a desire to see James become a scientist, if not a philosopher, his definition of that role was far different from the kind of training that James would undergo at the Lawrence Scientific School.

For Henry James Sr., a true scientist was someone who would search after a unifying theory of nature; someone whose ultimate mission was to find what Emerson called an "occult relation" among all natural phenomena: in short, a theory that revealed God as the ultimate creative force, professed sympathy between humans and all other living entities, and enriched one's sense of humanity.[57] Fearful that his son would become merely a technician, Henry Sr. reluctantly gave in, allowing a decision that reflected as much James's rebellion against his father as it did his desire to explore a reality beneath the surface of everyday experience. James thus found himself free to embark on this path, yet for much of the next decade, all of his decisions—to continue studying science, to enroll in the Harvard Medical School, to accompany naturalist and anti-Darwinist Louis Agassiz on a research trip to Brazil, to travel to Europe—were fraught with indecisiveness; self-recrimination; suicidal thoughts; and ailments that included backaches, indigestion, headaches, eye strain, and depression. James was in a sorry state.

Around 1870, this sorry state began to change. One reason—the reason James himself gave for a sudden spark of optimism—came from his reading of French philosopher Charles Renouvier, who persuaded James that to believe in free will was, in fact, a choice. This idea—and James took it almost as a commandment—countered the pervasive pessimism that had characterized his life. Once he believed in his own free will, James decided emphatically, he could act on that belief. He could, then, make choices without feeling that they were dictated by overwhelming forces: his father, most prominently, and his community, as well. Along with James's reading of Renouvier came increased opportunities to choose and to act purely on his own behalf. The major change came when he was offered, and accepted, a replacement teaching position at Harvard. Besides earning a living for the first time in his life, James also earned the esteem of his students and joined a community of colleagues. He enjoyed teaching, not least because it gave him a feeling of power over others; in fact, he discovered, he enjoyed working. In addition, he was writing—for money, he told friends—but still his reviews were being published. From two sources, then, he received validation for his talents, and the recognition of a certain social self—competent, intellectually impressive—that he so deeply coveted. Besides his professional success, he experienced the validation of another social self: suitor, when, in 1876, he met Alice Gibbens.

Their courtship echoed the trajectory of indecision that had characterized all of James's life, but eventually—they married in 1878—he decided to cast his "vote" for a universe that included love, a wife, and the responsibility of providing for a family. And he felt that his anxiety over the decision was a positive experience: "Need and struggle are what excite and inspire us; our hour of triumph is what brings the void."[58] He decided to take a chance because chance, he said, was in fact "exactly the same thing as the idea of gift."[59] The man who had been afraid of risk became one who celebrated free will, who energetically confronted what he called the "either-or." "The world seems to us genuinely unfinished," he wrote, "and as if our beliefs and acts might be additions, originating *now*, and giving it a turn this way or that, according to their nature."[60] Restless, alert, easily agitated, James had become a man who breathed deeply of life, and if he settled now and again into the depressions that benighted his younger years, he also rose out of them with an enthusiasm, generosity of spirit, and openness that his friends and colleagues noted again and again. He felt, he said, "the squeeze of this world's life" in the possibilities of each moment. "Our sense of 'freedom,'" he wrote, "supposes that some things at least are decided here and now, that the passing moment may contain some novelty, be an original starting-point of events, and not merely transmit a push from elsewhere . . . , that the next turn in events can at any given moment genuinely be *ambiguous, i.e.,* possibly *this,* but also possibly *that.*"[61]

Novelty stands at the center of James's vision because the individual is at the center of the multi-verse. In each human life, James insisted, there is the possibility of new perceptions, new ideas, new transitions. Biography, he wrote, "yields a perfect effervescence of novelty all the time. New men and women, books, accidents, events, inventions, enterprises, burst unceasingly upon the world."[62] Being, which is itself mysterious, is not the universe's final word. To deny that there can be anything new, to assume, he said "that the universe has exhausted its spontaneity in one act, shocks our sense of life."[63]

James, from his nineteenth-century vantage point, helped to create the restless pluralism, prismatic vision, and dazzling sense of simultaneity that characterized the generations that succeeded him. He lived in a world of dawnings, surges of sensation, cascades of darkness, and crescendos of light. He protested against the feeling of "foreignness" and alienation that seemed to him inherent in a rationalist, monist, materialist universe, and championed a kind of pluralism that would put him into an intimate relationship to experiences and sensations.[64] His world allowed for faith, especially faith in the improbable. "For here possibilities, not finished facts, are the realities with which we have actively to deal" he wrote; "and to quote my friend [and brother-in-law] William Salter, of the Philadelphia Ethical Society, 'as the essence of courage is to stake one's life on a possibility, so the essence of faith is to believe that the possibility exists.'"[65]

CHAPTER 3

Waste Lands and Silly Valleys: Wittgenstein, Mass Culture, and Re-Enchantment

MICHAEL SALER

"Never stay up on the barren heights of cleverness, but come down into the green valleys of silliness."

—Ludwig Wittgenstein[1]

I. Disenchanted Enchantment

In the first half of the twentieth century, pulp fiction was read enthusiastically by mass audiences on both sides of the Atlantic, and just as enthusiastically disparaged by elites as evidence for the decline of Western culture. Ludwig Wittgenstein, ambivalent on many issues, belonged to both camps. He devoured any issues he could find of *Detective Story Magazine* published in America by Street and Smith, while nevertheless insisting that Oswald Spengler's *Decline of the West* was "completely in touch with what I have often thought myself."[2] When it came to his own vocation of philosophy, however, Wittgenstein shed any ambivalence, let alone nuance: philosophy was easily trumped by American mass culture, which provided more "mental vitamins & calories."[3] Writing to his friend Norman Malcolm in 1948 to thank him for his most recent shipment of *Detective Story Magazine* from the United States, Wittgenstein stated, "Your mags are wonderful. How people could read *Mind* if they could read Street & Smith beats me. If philosophy has anything to do with wisdom, there's certainly not a grain of truth in *Mind*, & quite often a grain in the detective stories."[4]

Of course, this and similar statements about the poverty of philosophy and the muse of mass culture could be taken as hyperbole, just another of Wittgenstein's eccentricities, on a par with his washing dishes in the bathtub or reaching for a poker while debating philosophic niceties with Karl Popper. Reading detective fiction might have no more significance for Wittgenstein than as escapism, akin to his description of movies as a "shower bath," washing away his tensions.[5] (Jean-Paul Sartre shared a love for mysteries with Wittgenstein, although in other respects their reading tastes seem not to have coincided; acknowledging his own addiction in his 1964 autobiography, Sartre added, "Even now, I read the "Serie Noire" more readily than I do Wittgenstein.")[6]

But we know that Wittgenstein perceived pulp fiction, and American mass culture in general, as more than a mere diversion. It wasn't just that he used pulp catchphrases in his conversations, claiming that faith was "as plain as a sock on the jaw," or that one of his aims in visiting Dublin was to "case the joint."[7] Nor was it that he seemed to read pulp fiction more than other forms of literature.[8] (A former student claimed that this scion of one of the most cultured families in Austria-Hungary was "in many ways a lowbrow.")[9] Wittgenstein found mass culture to be enlightening. He demonstrated its nutritive value by using examples drawn from the pulps during a 1936 lecture, arguing that confusions in language are more revealing when discussed "in a silly detective story" than when discussed "by a silly philosopher."[10] Further, in diary entries for the early 1930s he acknowledged the "extraordinarily beneficial effect" American films had on him—not just in terms of a "rest for the mind," but also in terms of productive stimulation: "And there I am truly gripped and moved by thoughts. That is, as long as it is not frightfully bad it always provides me material for thoughts and feelings."[11] The man who proclaimed, in *Philosophical Investigations* (1953), that his aim in philosophy was "To shew the fly out of the fly-bottle,"[12] found a similar liberation via *Detective Story Magazine*, as he told Malcolm in 1948: "when I opened one of your mags it was like getting out of a stuffy room into the fresh air."[13]

How might we reconcile this "lowbrow" Wittgenstein with the "highbrow" Wittgenstein also found in biographical portrayals: the Wittgenstein who read Augustine, Kierkegaard, Tolstoy, and William James, among others, who could whistle entire symphonic movements with breathtaking accuracy, and who once told Bertrand Russell that the boat race the two of them were witnessing was a waste of time, for "nothing is tolerable except producing great works or enjoying those of others"?[14] The Wittgenstein who agreed with many other contemporary cultural pessimists that Western Civilization was on the point of catastrophic collapse, and that modern culture was disenchanting, "alien and uncongenial" to him?[15]

Wittgenstein's apparently paradoxical embrace of modern mass culture while decrying the disenchantment of the world can best be addressed by examining his positions regarding the re-enchantment of the world. The shifts from his "early" philosophy, as represented by the *Tractatus Logico-Philosophicus* (1922) to his "late" philosophy, as represented by the *Philosophical Investigations*, mirrors a range of responses to the widespread view that modernity was "disenchanted"—that the rational, secular, and commercial tenets of the modern precluded the wonder and spontaneity that had characterized earlier periods in the West. In his earlier philosophy, Wittgenstein largely accepts the disenchantment thesis, whereas in his later philosophy he finds a philosophic approach that reconciles the rational and secular currents of modernity with the possibilities of spontaneity and wonder.

During the late nineteenth century, the widespread discourse of the disenchanted nature of a rational, secular modernity in the West provoked an opposite reaction, a turn to the nonrational, ineffable sources of spirituality and wonder. Symbolist poets and painters, vitalist philosophers, spiritualists and occultists: all represented a "revolt against positivism," which seemed a dominant tendency of the *fin-de-siècle*.[16] Wittgenstein's *Tractatus* reflects the stark oppositions within the culture between disenchanted reason and mystical enchantments. It famously distinguishes between the logical "facts" of the world that can be spoken—the disenchanted "picture theory"—and the realm of values, aesthetics, and spirituality that cannot be spoken. The enchantments of transcendent meanings are not to be found through rational philosophy, which can only clarify the logical relations among facts. Enchantment is not a "state of affairs" in the world; whereas for Aristotle and Descartes, philosophy begins in wonder, Wittgenstein argues in the *Tractatus* that philosophy reveals nothing of ultimate significance. Enchantment is ineffable, not philosophical.

During the interwar period, however, Wittgenstein modified his philosophic views. Rational philosophy could disenchant, by describing things as they were, but it could also re-enchant the state of affairs, by depicting alternative ways of viewing them that revealed their contingency and malleability: as he stated in 1948, "life's infinite variations are essential to our life."[17] He no longer believed in essential logical structures underlying propositions; instead, there existed a multiplicity of language games in which words derived their meanings. At times, however, he suggests that intimations of the infinite variations of life are not to be found in the "high" culture of modernity, which embodied many aspects he disliked: the emphasis on science, technology, progress, and instrumental rationality. Modern, bourgeois culture was one in which "taste" predominated, and Wittgenstein argued that taste "cannot create a new structure; it can only make adjustments to one that already exists . . . Giving birth is not its affair."[18] Instead, Wittgenstein valued "silliness," which could generate originality and suggest possibilities. He maintained that many of his own thoughts were "silly," but hoped they would bear original fruit, new sources of enchantment too often concealed by the modern, scientific approach to thought.

In many respects Wittgenstein remained until his death a cultural pessimist, but he did believe that modernity contained an important resource for the generation of originality through silliness: mass culture (especially in its American form). Whereas many interwar intellectuals saw American mass culture as part of the problem, for Wittgenstein it was part of the solution, a saving resource for the modern Waste Land. This was why Street and Smith's *Detective Fiction Weekly* was more valuable than *Mind* in his view: popular narratives, because they were dismissed by most elites, were not constrained to be tasteful and promulgate conventional views. They could afford to be "silly" and experiment, to be original within the unpoliced ghetto walls of their genre conventions. The French surrealists, for similar reasons, also turned to mass culture for the re-enchantment of modernity, and in this sense the otherwise rather rigid Wittgenstein might be likened to them, and to a few other interwar thinkers who found value in a form of culture disdained by most contemporary intellectuals.[19]

Thus Wittgenstein's philosophy, especially in its later manifestations, articulates both the disenchantments of modernity and the means by which it could be re-enchanted through its own rational, secular, and commercial tenets. Friedrich Nietzsche's observation in *The Gay Science* that "the world has become 'infinite' for us all over again, inasmuch as we cannot reject the possibility that it may include infinite interpretations"[20] serves as an enchanting counterpoint to Max Weber's disenchanting metaphor of modernity as an "iron cage"; it is an observation that Wittgenstein's later philosophy, with its emphasis on multiple perspectives ("seeing-as"), embraces. However, whereas Nietzsche despised mass culture, Wittgenstein embraced it.

The "silliness" of mass culture serves to generate infinite interpretations in the face of genteel culture's more staid, "tasteful" conventions.

II. The "Marvelous Spirit"

Wittgenstein was part of a generation that accepted the view, most famously expressed by Weber, that the modern world was "disenchanted." Otto Weininger and Oswald Spengler were among its proponents whom Wittgenstein admired, and he shared Weber's own concern that scientific naturalism was ensnaring humanity within an "iron cage of reason." As Peter C. John has argued, Wittgenstein always held that the capacity for wonder was valuable.[21] However, Wittgenstein believed that the positivistic spirit of contemporary science dampened humanity's sense of wonder at the inherent possibilities of existence, which Wittgenstein described in 1929 as his own "experience par excellence": "the best way of describing it is to say that when I have it I wonder at the existence of the world. And I am then inclined to use such phrases as 'how extraordinary that anything should exist' or 'how extraordinary that the world should exist.'"[22] Wittgenstein's own cultural pessimism was certainly darkened by his tendency toward depression and by his participation in both world wars, as a soldier on the front in the First and a volunteer at an English hospital in the Second. These sobering experiences, and his sense that the narrowly instrumental aims of modern science had become predominant in modern Western culture, led him to assume a nuclear holocaust was likely following World War Two.[23] Norman Malcolm recalled, "It was Wittgenstein's character to be deeply pessimistic . . . [he felt] that our lives are ugly and our minds in the dark."[24]

Wittgenstein also felt that it was his duty as a philosopher to disenchant, especially from the beguilements of professional philosophy: "Philosophy is a battle against the bewitchment of our intelligence by means of language."[25] He insisted that there were no occult qualities that needed to be unearthed by philosophers, and warned against "the mystifying use of our language": "We are most strongly tempted to think that there are things hidden . . . And yet nothing of the sort is the case."[26] But during the interwar period his efforts at disenchantment were not concerned merely with the vanquishing of pseudo-problems, leaving the world as it was; disenchantment was the preliminary step toward re-enchanting the world. Wittgenstein tellingly mixed the two when he described the virtues of his method in 1931, likening it to one of his favorite genres, the fairy tale: "The solution of philosophical problems can be compared with a gift in a fairy tale: in the magic castle it appears enchanted and if you look at it outside in daylight it is nothing but an ordinary bit of iron (or something of that sort)."[27]

The result of such a disenchanting practice was not to be used for erecting an iron cage of reason, but rather for dismantling it. Exorcising pseudo-problems enabled one to see the world in all its marvelous diversity and contingency, a stance Wittgenstein emphasized in his later philosophy that he began developing upon returning to Cambridge University in 1929. Echoing Hamlet's admonition to Horatio that there are more things in heaven and on earth than are dreamt by philosophy, he explained in a lecture how his linguistic analyses liberated individuals from the constraints built by scientists and maintained by philosophers:

What I give is the morphology of the use of an expression. I show that it has kinds of uses of which you had not dreamed. In philosophy one feels *forced* to look at a concept in a certain way. What I do is suggest, or even invent, other ways of looking at it . . . Thus your mental cramp is relieved, and you are free to look around the field of use of the expression and to describe the different kinds of uses of it.[28]

Wittgenstein's new method of locating the meaning of language in its everyday use was intended, in part, to re-awaken the sense of wonder that had been occluded by the positivistic insistence of his times that there was only one way of seeing things. In 1930, as he began to move away from his earlier emphasis on the logical structures inhering in language and the world adumbrated in the *Tractatus Logico-Philosophicus*, he read Sir James Frazier's *The Golden Bough*. He was appalled by Frazer's relegation of an enchanted attitude to existence to so-called "primitives." Frazer, he argued, was incapable of understanding "a different way of life from the English one of his time" and simply echoed the faith in progress of many in the West; his explanations "would be no explanations at all if they did not appeal to an inclination in ourselves."[29] Wonder at the world, Wittgenstein argued in his notebooks for that year, "has nothing to do with [a people] being primitive." Wonder was fundamentally an orientation to existence (what he would refer to in *Philosophical Investigations* as "seeing-as"),[30] rather than a primitive mindset that had been supplanted by a more "evolved" West. If wonder seemed absent from the modern West, that was largely the fault of its narrow scientific orientation. He believed that "Man has to awaken to wonder—and so perhaps do peoples. Science is a way of sending him to sleep again."[31] Philosophy as he conceived it would be like the kiss awakening the sleeping prince in fairy tales, for "Working in philosophy . . . is really more a working on oneself. On one's interpretation. On one's way of seeing things. (And what one expects of them.)"[32] That new way of seeing things would evoke wonder at the diversity and originality of life, as it often did for him: as he wrote in 1931, "The joy of my thoughts is the joy of my own strange life."[33]

This notion of wonder as emerging from a particular orientation to the world provided the answer to the question he asked about the definition of *enchantment,* a term recurrent in contemporary discussions of modernity that nevertheless remained frustratingly ambiguous. Wittgenstein was one of the few on either side of the debate about disenchantment to ask what "enchantment" actually meant, which was the necessary prelude to discovering if re-enchantment was even possible: "How do I know that someone is enchanted? How does one learn the linguistic expression of enchantment? What does it connect up with? With the expression of bodily sensations? Do we ask someone what he feels in his breast and facial muscles in order to find out whether he is feeling enjoyment?"[34]

He did not pursue this inquiry further, but in many other remarks does return to what might be regarded as an implicit answer, his notion that seeing the world from a vantage point, a "seeing-as," leaves it the same and changes it utterly: "We see, not change of aspect, but change of interpretation." This was a feat of prestidigitation that was real rather than a trick, a form of enchantment that did not deny the rational and secular tenets of modernity but coexisted with them. Just as he had stated in the *Tractatus* that "The world of the happy man is a different one from that of the unhappy one,"[35] so too might he have later said that the world of the enchanted man is different from that of the disenchanted one. Indeed, he came very close to saying this in 1931 in his reflections on miracles and the "marvelous," which are often associated with "enchantment": "It is a miracle only when *he* does it who does it in a marvelous spirit. Without this spirit it is only an extraordinarily strange fact . . . When I read in a fairy tale that the witch transforms a human being into a wild animal, it is also the spirit of this action, after all, that makes an impression on me."[36] In his later philosophy, Wittgenstein's highly original similes, questions, and thought experiments worked in this marvelous spirit, transforming hackneyed expressions and common conventions into evocatively strange "forms of life" reflecting the spontaneity and diversity of "language games."

His later philosophy was both disenchanting and re-enchanting, describing the world as it was, exorcising pseudo-problems created by the misuse of language, and revealing how that which remained was multifarious and even mysterious.

But this raises the question: how might one attain such a marvelous spirit or orientation in the face of all the pressures during the interwar period to conform to more conventional, "disenchanted" views? Or, rather, how did Wittgenstein attain it? How could he move from a severe emphasis on logical structures of language in his early philosophy to the more playful understanding of language as a provisional and open-ended game played by the malleable rules of grammar? In person he could be remarkably inflexible about conduct, manners, and beliefs; how could he nevertheless maintain, "The concept of a living being has the same indeterminacy as a language"? And how could a philosopher who focused on the detritus of everyday life—*Detective Fiction Weekly*, games, toothaches, and other "trivial" examples—overcome his powerful fear of being seen as ridiculous? "For there is nothing I am more afraid of," he wrote in 1931, as he was developing his new insights, "nothing I want to avoid so *unconditionally* as ridiculousness. And yet I know that this is a cowardice like any other, & that cowardice having been expelled everywhere else has its last unconquerable citadel there."[37]

These questions have complex answers, but one response involves the importance Wittgenstein came to place on the idea of "silliness." As we shall see, he associated mass culture, at least in its American variety, with silliness, and silliness with a fruitful way to attain the marvelous spirit and see the world anew: to re-enchant it. "Silly" mass culture proved a solvent to the rigidities of science and philosophy. It also served as a bracing tonic for Wittgenstein himself, full of "mental vitamins & calories," allaying his anxieties about the waning of traditional high culture in the modern world and the question of his own originality and genius. He was one of the few cultural pessimists of the interwar period, let alone philosophers, who saw mass culture as a potential source of insight and renewal.

III. Elite and Mass Cultures: The Solvent of Silliness

Wittgenstein disliked any form of cowardice—he had chosen to fight on the front lines during the First World War to overcome his fears—and he would certainly have wanted to free himself from the fear of appearing ridiculous. To many of his upbringing and profession, mass culture was often equated with the "ridiculous" if not the reprehensible. By the interwar period, however, Wittgenstein expressed his deep appreciation for aspects of mass culture alongside more traditional "high culture." The ridiculous and the silly, as well as their concrete manifestations in films and pulp fiction, became objects for reflections published posthumously in *Culture and Value*. In several of these reflections, we witness Wittgenstein grappling with the distinction between elite and mass cultures, just as he had tackled the apparent distinction between enchantment and disenchantment. In both instances, he demonstrated that simply binary oppositions between the terms were untenably reductive. Just as the modern, "disenchanted" world could be seen as enchanted from particular orientations, so too could "mass culture," by virtue of its "silliness," be shown to have redeeming features that cultural pessimists had missed. The elite faith that worthy cultural expressions could be identified partly by "taste" led them to ignore or misread elements of culture they deemed tasteless.

Prior to 1914, Wittgenstein himself believed in a clear hierarchy of tastes. He had told Bertrand Russell in 1912 that "good taste is genuine taste and therefore is fostered by whatever makes people think truthfully," including the study of mathematics.[38] As he matured, his frustrations with the stifling prejudices of his own upper-middle-class background, as well as those of English high society, fueled his contempt for bourgeois conventions, including the notion of "genuine taste." His developing philosophical views unmasked taste as merely a cultural product. In 1947 he remarked that taste is a reflection of conventions, and having it denotes neither originality nor the ability to appreciate originality: "Taste makes adjustments. Giving birth is not its affair. Taste makes things ACCEPTABLE. For this reason I believe that a great creator has no need of taste; his child is born into the world fully formed."[39]

Wittgenstein sensed that his own bourgeois fear of being seen as "ridiculous" (the opposite of "acceptable") posed a threat to his potential originality as a thinker. Freeing himself from such limiting prejudices so that he could give reign to his own unique insights, as well as live authentically, was critically important to him, inspiring the wider aim of his philosophy to relieve a "mental cramp," show "the fly out of the fly-bottle." His reflections on mass culture and "silliness" in *Culture and Value* document the gradual change in orientation he attained about the liberating—and thus re-enchanting—possibilities of silliness, particularly as they were expressed in modern mass culture. In a remark of 1930, for example, he presents a fairly conventional "cultural pessimist" view of mass culture as artificial, lacking in soul:

A modern film is to an old one as a present-day motor car is to one built 25 years ago. The impression that it makes is just as ridiculous and clumsy and the way film-making has improved is comparable to the sort of technical improvement we see in cars. It is not to be compared with the improvement—if it's right to call it that—of an artistic style. It is much the same with modern dance music too. A jazz dance, like film, must be something that can be improved. What distinguishes all these developments from the formation of a *style* is that spirit plays no part in them.[40]

By 1946, however, he appears to reject the cultural pessimists' dichotomy between an organic "culture" and a soulless "civilization" as merely a linguistic construction that provides a particular (and pernicious) orientation towards existence:

It is very *remarkable* that we should be inclined to think of civilization—houses, trees, cars, etc.—as separating man from his origins, from what is lofty and eternal, etc. Our civilized environment, along with its trees and plants, strikes us then as though it were cheaply wrapped in cellophane and isolated from everything great, from God, as it were. This is a remarkable picture that intrudes on us.[41]

Wittgenstein was not embracing the modern world wholeheartedly—in several respects he remained a cultural pessimist throughout his life—but he was searching for seeds of regeneration within it. That which appears as cheaply wrapped in cellophane may be critical for reorienting how we perceive and inhabit the world. As he stated in *Philosophical Investigations,* "The aspects of things that are most important to us are hidden because of their simplicity and familiarity . . . And this means: we fail to be struck by what, once seen, is most striking and powerful."[42]

Mass culture tended to be dismissed by many interwar intellectuals precisely because it was simple and familiar, but Wittgenstein paid attention to it; he said he learned from it and tried to convey what he had learned. He found American mass culture instructive not just because it represented the sort of everyday, "trivial" aspect of life that most took for granted, but because it was unselfconscious and didn't take itself seriously, like so-called "high culture." It wasn't afraid of being playful, of advancing unconventional ways of looking at the world. By being "silly," it was able to do what Wittgenstein himself aspired to do, providing he could get over his own fears of appearing "ridiculous." He wrote in 1947 that "A typical American film, naïve and silly, can—for all its silliness and even *by means of it*—be instructive. A fatuous, self-conscious English film can teach one nothing. I have often learnt a lesson from a silly American film."[43]

Silliness was key for Wittgenstein because he recognized his own tendency to be rigid and self-conscious; there were internal as well as external iron cages he had to dismantle. As we have seen, one of Wittgenstein's methods of re-enchanting a world disenchanted by a narrowly positivistic worldview was to dissolve reifications of language. He demonstrated the diversity of meanings words could have, depending on how they were used in a given language game. If "to imagine a language means to imagine a form of life,"[44] Wittgenstein's method of providing alternative—and often highly imaginative—readings of common expressions revivified the world by revealing its infinite potentials. But in order to present alternatives to conventional views, which included those of his own profession, Wittgenstein had to risk looking foolish. While he always had a fondness for "nonsense," enjoying Lewis Carroll and engaging in silly jokes with select friends, he also took himself, and life, very gravely.[45] He knew he had to unwind to be creative and reimagine the given, but never relinquished the conviction that "life is far more serious than what it looks like at the surface. Life is frightfully serious."[46]

Mass culture was silly, never "serious" for the puritanical Wittgenstein, partly because it was pleasurable to him. By this measure, however, philosophy itself could not be considered serious either. In 1932 he wrote that, "My philosophical work now seems to me like a diversion from the difficult, like a distraction, an enjoyment to which I do not devote myself with an entirely good conscience. As if I were going to the cinema instead of nursing a sick person." The same conjunction of pleasure, mass culture, and philosophy recurs in a conversation of 1947, in which he stated, "We are not 'interested' in things that are really important, e.g., in the death of our friend. We are interested in cinema and philosophy. Ideas never make any real change unless it hurts us to recognize them."[47]

But if mass culture could never be serious, there were nevertheless corresponding virtues to its intrinsic silliness. A silly orientation toward the world enabled one to express fruitful insights without self-censorship on the grounds of conventional taste. Detective fiction, films, and other "low cultural" expressions could contain genuine wisdom despite their crude formulations. Indeed, crude formulations might be indices of a fundamental honesty that is lost when burnished to the artificial standards of conventional taste. By flying under the radar of elite cultural norms, "mediocre" expressions could contain the living spirit of truth that "hovered over the ashes" of the modern Waste Land: "A mediocre writer must beware of too quickly replacing a crude, incorrect expression with a correct one. By doing so he kills his original idea, which was at least still a living seedling. Now it is withered and no longer worth *anything*. He may as well throw it on the rubbish heap. Whereas the wretched little seedling was still worth something."[48]

Wittgenstein wrote about cognate terms to silliness, emphasizing their similar value. Silliness was related to humor, for example, and humor itself was a productive perspective, akin to wonder: "Humor is not a mood but a way of looking at the world."[49] In *Culture and Value*, Wittgenstein also praised the stupid, the trivial, the cheap, and the humble. One of his most frequently cited aphorisms, "If people did not sometimes do silly things, nothing intelligent would ever get done,"[50] is surrounded by others in praise of folly: "Don't, *for heaven's sake*, be afraid of talking nonsense! But you must pay attention to your nonsense";[51] "Our greatest stupidities may be very wise";[52] "Every idea that costs a lot carries in its train a host of cheap ones; among these are even some that are useful."[53]

Even Wittgenstein's understanding of his own work is positioned somewhere within the silly-serious continuum: "What I am writing here may be feeble stuff; well, then I am just not capable of bringing the big, important things to light. But hidden in these feeble remarks are great prospects."[54] Frequently troubled by his pride and arrogance, he sought the humility enjoined by the Christian gospels, and this was a factor in his self-identification with an "abased" form of culture associated with the people rather than the elites. In interwar Europe, "cosmopolitan" mass culture, especially Hollywood films, could also be linked pejoratively with the Jews. It is striking that Wittgenstein at times feared that he might not be a "genius" (associated with traditional high culture) but rather merely a "talented" Jew (associated with mass culture and its reproductive nature). In a 1931 remark, he wrote: "Amongst Jews 'genius' is found only in the holy man. Even the greatest of Jewish thinkers is no more than talented. (Myself for instance.) I think there is some truth in my idea that I really only think reproductively."[55] By

1940 he has found a way to maintain that "genius" need not be defined in such a restrictive way. By having the courage to be true to his insights—by conquering his cowardly fear of appearing ridiculous—he might, for all his "Jewish," "reproductive" talents, lay claim to that title: "One might say: 'Genius is *talent* exercised with courage.'"[56] Analogously, mass culture might also share in that distinction, and be worthy of consideration.

Wittgenstein at times appraised his own work in terms of its overt imperfections and its honest insights, the same traits he found in American mass culture. He may not have been a Brahms, but perhaps closer to the composers of his beloved musical comedies featuring Carmen Miranda and Betty Hutton: "My style is like bad musical composition."[57] He may not have been a Goethe, let alone a Chandler or a Hammett: "A writer far more talented than I would still have only a minor talent"; "You have to face the faults in your own style. Almost like blemishes on your face."[58] He may not have been a Rembrandt, but was perhaps closer to the painters of the covers of *Detective Story Magazine*: "And after all a painter is basically what I am, often a very bad painter too."[59] Of course, Wittgenstein also could hold higher opinions of his work, but it is notable how often he identified with the world of imperfect and unpretentious artists, the world of silly films and pulp magazines rather than of *Mind*.

IV. "April is the Cruelest Month" / "April Fools!"

Wittgenstein clearly found affinities between his own work and that of mass culture, especially in their collective efforts to ring silly changes on conventional outlooks, thereby revealing the contingent, malleable, and provisional aspects of language. But we've had to draw out inferences from disparate remarks in order to make this case, as Wittgenstein himself was usually not very explicit about the specifics of mass culture, about how a "silly American film" or "silly detective story" might clarify our understanding and re-enchant the world. His biographer Ray Monk advances some persuasive connections between Wittgenstein's intellectual and personal styles and some of the themes often found in the contemporary pulps and films he enjoyed. Hard-boiled private eyes, for example, tended to be laconic and oriented toward action—they preferred to "show" rather than "say," in one of Wittgenstein's fundamental distinctions, mocking the pretensions of deductive problem solvers like Sherlock Holmes. And, like the heroes of the westerns that he also loved, they were individualists who valued freedom over conformity.[60] These qualities characterized Norbert Davis's mystery *The Mouse in the Mountain* (1943), which Wittgenstein particularly enjoyed.[61] He said he re-read it with "great pleasure," and he commended it to others; he even tried to find Davis's address so that he could send a fan letter.[62] Monk believes that Wittgenstein especially appreciated the novel's humor, and it is a book that relishes silly situations and zany exchanges.[63]

But these exchanges are not just enjoyably silly: they provide what Wittgenstein would call a "perspicuous representation" of how language is used in different language games. In *Philosophical Investigations*, Wittgenstein argued that we risk misunderstanding how a word is being used when we lack a view of the entire context in which it is situated, and consequently interpret terms from a perspective that is not connected to the language-game being played.[64] He warned against the dangers of uncritically assuming that words have essential meanings divorced from how they are used: "We remain unconscious of the prodigious diversity of all the every-day language-games because the clothing of our language makes everything alike."[65]

Davis's *The Mouse in the Mountain* provides several instances of perspicuous representations, demonstrating the different interpretations of language that ensue when two cultures clash because each assumes the other is playing the same language game. The novel, like *Philosophical Investigations*, shows in a descriptive fashion how linguistic meaning depends on grammar and use rather than any mystical "essence" that inheres in words; this "silly" novel is entertaining, but also instructive. While it is risky to infer how Wittgenstein might have read it, one could imagine him deriving some pleasure from seeing a number of his hard-won insights being played out on the pages of a popular novel, when more "serious" philosophers were repeating the mistakes refuted by this "ridiculous" work.

Davis delights in the linguistic confusion that ensues when a group of Americans are involved in a criminal investigation conducted by the local officials in Mexico. One exchange between Doan, the American detective, and Obrian, a Mexican sergeant, highlights the arbitrary uses of place names; it also reminds the reader (as Wittgenstein did in *Philosophical Investigations*) of the mistakes that can result when one argues from analogy, as if all terms adhered to a single rule:

"What army is this, anyway?" Doan inquired.

"The Mexican army, dumbness," said Sergeant Obrian. "I can speak your lingo on account I used to be a waiter in double New York."

"Where?" Doan said.

"New York, New York. It ain't New York City—didn't you know that? It's New York. Just like Mexico City is Mexico."[66]

Davis also plays with the tendency speakers have to impute invariant qualities to a term, a fallacy Wittgenstein exposed through the numerous "intermediate cases" he constructed in the *Philosophical Investigations.*[67] When the American Janet Martin admits to the Mexican investigator Captain Perona that she has read a mysterious diary of his ancestors, the Captain responds,

"It is incredible . . . No one in our family ever read it. It was so very difficult. Only professors can read such old-fashioned script."

"I'm a professor."

"Oh, no. You are a woman."

"I'm—a—professor!"

"How strange."[68]

And in a later exchange between the two, Perona discusses his brother, who knows about the United States because he was educated "At a place called Harvard. It was very unfortunate, but we could do nothing about it." Janet, puzzled, asks him why he thought this was "unfortunate." He responds, "He is the third son, you see, and we could not afford to give him a good education [in Mexico]."[69]

Many of the exchanges in the novel are like this; Captain Perona himself ponders if "this fantastic nonsense has the faintest relation to truth."[70] While it is impossible to say with certainty how Wittgenstein would have responded, it seems reasonable that he would have felt the novel was truthful precisely because of its fantastic nonsense. Norbert Davis's form of silliness was instructive and liberating, providing the overview of linguistic usages that Wittgenstein focused on in his own work: "A main source of our failure to understand is that we do not *command a clear view* of the use of our words.—Our grammar is lacking in this sort of perspicuity. A perspicuous representation produces just that understanding which consists in 'seeing connexions.'"[71]

In T. S. Eliot's "The Waste Land" (1922), we witness a different attempt to see connections, to bring together the fragments of the modern, disenchanted world into a larger, organic totality that had allegedly characterized the premodern, enchanted world. The narrator tries to do this aesthetically, by uniting disparate histories, cultures, and styles within a single work: "These fragments I have shored against my ruins."[72] Wittgenstein's own emphasis on the perspicuous representations that reveal underlying connections is a related way of re-enchanting an atomistic world, even as it disenchants in other respects. Did he perceive a similar shoring of fragments against our ruin within examples of "silly" mass culture, such as *The Mouse in the Mountain*?

What we can say with certainty is that for Wittgenstein, wonder was attainable in the modern no less than the premodern world; it did not require a renunciation of the rational, secular, and even commercial tenets of modernity for enchantments to flourish. All it required was the right orientation to the world. That orientation could take different forms, and silliness was one of them—an orientation he associated with mass culture. "The green valleys of silliness" could re-enchant "the barren heights of cleverness." For all of his cultural pessimism, he never defined modernity solely as a "Waste Land," and for all his critical asperity, he never lost sight of marvels. He reconciled reason and wonder through a disenchanted enchantment.

Wittgenstein's last words were not about silliness, but rather enchantment: "Tell them I've had a wonderful life."[73] Yet silliness, so closely interwoven with wonder, was never far from his thoughts. Indeed, he once said that a "good philosophical work could be written that would consist entirely of *jokes*."[74] He never wrote such a work. Perhaps he felt Carmen Miranda and Norbert Davis had gotten there first.

CHAPTER 4

Homeless Gardens

ROBERT HARRISON

HISTORY HAS NO MEMORY of the great majority of the gardens that have graced the earth over the centuries—gardens being by nature impermanent creations that only rarely leave behind any evidence of their enchantments—nor should it. Gardens are not memorials. They may be places of memory, or places that inspire recollection, but, apart from a few lofty exceptions, they are not created to immortalize their makers or defy the ravages of time. Just why we create them at all is a question to which there are probably more answers than one suspects or can give. Common sense assumes that gardens first came into being as a by-product of agriculture, or as a kind of primitive agriculture, yet we might do better to credit the intuition of poets in this matter, if only because their vocation, which is as old as the world itself, gives them a certain "feel" for origins. The poet W. S. Merwin, for example, is not convinced that agriculture was the source of gardening; he believes that gardens had spiritual or aesthetic beginnings, and that, if anything, agriculture arose as a consequence of gardening, not the other way around. He can muster no more hard evidence for his conviction than those who claim the contrary, yet if gardens are to agriculture what poetry is to prose, then there are at least analogical reasons to believe that gardens came first.

We are on less speculative grounds when we declare, in general sympathy with Merwin, that gardens are bound up with a set of distinctly human, as opposed to merely animal or economic, needs. The difference between a human and animal need is that the former can go unmet, unacknowledged, and unheeded without threatening a person's physical survival, yet that does not make its demands on us any less radical and essential. Humans do not have a need for gardens per se, but gardens, it seems, answer an array of human needs. This is evidenced by the fact that even in the most disenchanted of habitats, where the premium is on survival, they have a way of cropping up where you would least expect them. In 1993 Diana Balmori and Margaret Morton published a book of photographs with commentary titled *Transitory Gardens, Uprooted Lives*, which they dedicated "to the uprooted individuals who have tilled the streets of New York City in search of a home and, in the process, have laid bare the meaning of *garden.*" The book offers a visual and written record of the makeshift gardens that homeless individuals, with painstaking effort and care,

FIG. 4.1. Jimmy's Garden, from Margaret Morton, *Transitory Gardens, Uprooted Lives* (Yale University Press, 1993). Photograph © Margaret Morton 1991.

created for themselves in some of the most degraded urban areas of New York City. They are made of diverse, largely random materials: toys, stuffed animals, flags, found objects, milk cartons, recycled trash, piles of leaves, at times a simple row of flowers: "anything of possible value is taken up, and many things that do not seem useful are made so."[1] These are not the sort of municipal or private gardens of the ruling class that traditional studies of garden art are most familiar with. They are "*compositions* made in open spaces, compositions that have been constructed from a variety of elements and that, through their detachment from the usual conditions in which gardens are made, liberate the word *garden* from its cultural straitjacket."[2]

Balmori and Morton remark, and their photographs confirm, that each of these transitory gardens (which may last a day, a week, or a month) has a unique personal signature, yet all of them arise from a common source in the individuals who, lacking the bare necessities of life, made them. The authors do not presume to offer facile sociological or psychological explanations for the genesis of the compositions, except to say that they offer evidence of an irreducible will to creative expression in their makers. This is no doubt true: the urge to create, express, fashion, even beautify, is undeniably human. There is something universally childlike about it. But why gardens, and why gardens as unlikely as these? Looking at their images, it strikes one that, for all their diversity of styles, the gardens in question speak of various other fundamental urges, beyond that of creative expression.

The first has to do with creating a pocket of repose in the midst of turbulence, a "still point of the turning world," to borrow a phrase from T. S. Eliot. A sanctuary of repose, of self-gatheredness, is as basic a need as shelter, so much so that where the latter is lacking the former becomes all the more urgent. The gardens of the homeless, which are in effect homeless gardens, introduce form where it was not discernible, and in so doing they give composure to a segment of the inarticulate milieus in which they take their stand (almost defiantly). Composure here means precisely that: the self-gathered boundedness of form, within whose limits a precinct is opened up. It is evident from the photographs how the precinct in question emanates from but also encircles the garden's compositional material, creating an open enclosure that provides the amorphous environment with a measure of human orientation, which is the first step in making oneself at home (repose is a kind of orientation). These gardens visibly gather around themselves the spiritual, mental, and physical energies that their surroundings would otherwise dissipate, disperse, and dissolve. Their compositional formality, however loose or improvised it may be, puts in place a temporary matrix of containment, or delimitation, where before there was only an indifferent urban extension. By liberating the self-gathering and sheltering powers of form, they secure the differentiated limits necessary to human repose.

The second need which these gardens appear to respond to, or to arise from, is so innate that we are barely ever conscious of its abiding claims on us. I mean our biophilia, or better, our chlorophilia. Deprived of green, of plants, of trees, we succumb to a demoralization of spirit whose causes we often misidentify in favor of some existential, psychological, or neurochemical etiology, until one day we find ourselves in a garden or park or countryside and feel the oppression vanish, like magic. I don't deny that there are chlorophobes in our midst—we will encounter a few later in this study—but for most of us a habitat without chlorophyll is a form of spiritual death. And yet we create such habitats for ourselves day in and day out, all around the world. Why? How can the dechlorification of our life worlds, both inside and outside, meet with such little resistance, indeed with so much cooperation, from us? Maybe it has to do simply with the lack of conscious awareness of how deeply this need runs in our veins, of how "the force that through the green fuse drives the flower/drives my green age; that blasts the roots of trees/is my destroyer."[3] Or maybe—indeed, most probably—the reasons are more perverse.

In most of the transitory gardens of New York City the actual cultivation of plants is unfeasible, yet even so (or perhaps even *more* so) the compositions, to judge from their images, represent attempts to conjure up the spirit of plant and animal life, if only symbolically, through the clumplike arrangement of materials, the introduction of colors, the small pools of water, and the frequent presence of petals or leaves, as well as stuffed animals. On display here are various fantasy elements whose reference, at some basic level, seems to be the natural world. It is this implicit or explicit reference that fully justifies the use of the word "garden," albeit in a "liberated" sense," to describe these synthetic constructions.

Certainly there is no mistaking the chlorophiliac urge on display in the various "community gardens" that have sprung up not only in New York but in inner cities all across America. These are most often vacant urban lots that have been transformed—by homeless people, squatters, tenement dwellers, and others—into sanctuaries of dense vegetation. Here the premium is on green leafy things, on vegetables, on the verdant in its exuberant sprouting forms (grass lawns in fact are rare). Community gardens tend not to have the compositional character of the transitory gardens; they seem rather like uninhibited, almost anarchic celebrations of chlorophilia. One of the most ordinary phenomena of our terrestrial continents, namely the profusion of plant life, here takes on the character of an improbable miracle. These recreated fragments of Eden in postlapsarian landscapes of our own making show, by contrast, just how insane our late modern unworlding of the world—our desecrating war on the earth—really is.

Entire neighborhoods have been transformed by the presence of such gardens, many of which, as if by their power of enchantment, have created communities where none existed before. The following anecdote may serve as a real-life parable. A few years ago Karl Paige and Annette Smith happened to meet on the median of Quesada Avenue, near Newhall Street, in the Bayview District of San Francisco. Paige, a retired man who grew up on a farm in Mississippi, had come to the median with his saw to cut down a dying bush. Smith, a one time farmer's daughter born in Alabama, had come to dig up worms as fishing bait for her brother. Engaging in conversation, they decided it would be worthwhile to try to plant a garden there on the median. After obtaining permission from the city, they began to clear the grounds of the beer cans, engine oil, old batteries, spark plugs, refrigerators, brake pads, mattresses, and fast-food flotsam that had come there to die. They then ploughed and fertilized the soil, sowed a generous variety of seeds, and, cordoning the area off with yellow tape, they carefully nourished the marigolds, geraniums, snapdragons, cacti, basil, kale, and peanuts that soon enough began to sprout. The wonder of such a garden in their midst brought out the surrounding residents, many of whom met each other for first time around the flowers, herbs, and vegetables.

Several other gardens have since cropped up in the neighborhood, and now, where drug pushers, addicts, and vagrants once urinated, trashed, and engaged in turf wars, there are different kinds of congregations. "I feel absolutely blessed to live on this block," declared one resident to a local reporter. "I'll come home, and people will be in the gardens. Instead of just running in the house, I talk to the neighbors." Another resident: "More and more over the last few months, people have been leaving their houses to gather in the center of the garden. Some people have met one another for the first time near the collard greens."[4]

Demotic comments such as these confirm in a literal way what many classics of Western literature and philosophy suggest in traditionally figurative terms, namely the connection between gardens and forms of conviviality. In ancient, medieval, and modern texts I have in mind, the garden all too frequently appears as a place of conversation, dialogue, friendship, storytelling, in short, communilization. In the same way the compositional gardens represent a gathering of form, the community gardens of Bayview—and presumably all the others across America—bring about a gathering of people. This gathering-power of the garden helps explain why gardens are not only topics and sites of conversation, but in many instances are associated, in the text in question, with the very ideal of conversation.

Although no interlocutor seems to be present in them, the transitory gardens of New York also partake in this spirit of social intercourse. Insofar as they involve an affirmation, declare their human authorship, invite recognition, and call for a response, they represent speech acts, as it were, not in the banal sense of making "social statements" but in the sense of militating against and triumphing over imposed conditions of speechlessness. They represent "raids upon the inarticulate," to borrow once again from T. S. Eliot's *Four Quartets*. While there is certainly an irrepressible urge for creative expression at work in them, one senses that alongside or perhaps even beneath this urge lurks an even more urgent need to break through the barriers of aphasia and become loquacious, the way poems, for example, are loquacious. In effect these gardens amount to the beginning of a dialogue, and the interlocutor is whoever takes the time to notice and wonder at them. That is why the transitory gardens evoke even more starkly and more poignantly than do community gardens the distinctly human need that went into their making, namely the need to hold converse with one's fellow human beings.

Intimately related to this need for converse is the striving for eloquence, for when it comes to intercourse with one's fellow human beings in the public realm (and community gardens already *are* the public realm), securing the means of expression is not enough. Only through eloquence does one do justice to the medium in and through which one partakes of the blessings of conversation. Indeed, there is no rigid distinction here between the medium and the blessing, for the medium *is* the blessing, and asks to be enhanced. The striving for eloquence takes the form of an active and sustained *cultivation* of the means of expression—verbal or otherwise—one that aims not just at mastery but at a fulfillment of the potential of fluency, which in the case of human beings always requires effort. If the "flowers of rhetoric" was a conventional figure of speech in the classical and medieval traditions, it is because eloquence calls for a kind of tending or gardening.

Both the compositional gardens and community gardens under consideration here testify to the formidable adversities that some of our essential dispositional needs must frequently confront and overcome in our exasperated era in order to be affirmed, acknowledged, or fulfilled. Many if not most of these adversities are of our own making: the disfiguration of our lived worlds, the desertification of habitat, the degradation of community, the deprivation of voice, or the desocialization of human relations. This raises the question once again of whether there is not at bottom a perversity in our drive to prosper which actively conspires against the basic conditions under which human beings realize their fragile, mortal happiness. At times it seems that nothing makes us as anxious as the prospect of making ourselves happy—almost as if we believed, subconsciously or otherwise, that happiness necessarily comes at the expense of history, and that the history of the uprooting of human beings from the earth must go forward at all costs, as if this were a destiny rather than the sum of choices we make day by day in both the private and public spheres. It is at best only a half truth, what philosophy has traditionally claimed about happiness being the goal of all human action and aspiration. If humans are the strangest of the many strange things on Earth, as the poets tell us, it is because we have a way of conspiring against our natures, of working against our most basic dispositions, of putting ourselves under the compulsion to remain ill at ease in the world. History thrives on our discontent, or so we believe, and we seem to feel better about ourselves when we do history's bidding, even when it makes us wretched.

It's a strange and beautiful planet we live on—a mortal Eden that places heavy demands on our care—and maybe one day we will learn how to live on it less fitfully. Meanwhile we remain a nervous, unsettled species, more so now than at any other time in history. It is tempting to say that we have reached a point where we must now wrest our happiness from the historical forces that trample upon its prospects, that we must take those prospects into our own hands, over against the environments and institutions that have been imposed on us, both with and without our consent. That is easier said than done, however, for it would require of us to know what our most essential human needs and desires are. And nothing seems more out of reach at present than self-knowledge.

When we say, along with Voltaire, *"il faut cultiver notre jardin,"* we usually mean that we must cultivate our garden in the face of, or in spite of, history. The dictum implies that our personal efforts can only reach so far, and that history itself is beyond our capacity for cultivation. To a certain extent that is true, but where does history start and our garden stop? Is the cultivation of one's garden not always and already an activity that takes place within the realm of history? Gardens are havens, to be sure, yet while it offers sanctuary from the bustle of Paris, the Jardin de Luxembourg opens its precinct at the very heart of the city. Eden may lie outside of history, but human gardens take their stand in the disenchantment of history, and in so doing they make history. After all, Voltaire does not say: *il faut cultiver son jardin,* but *notre jardin.* *Notre jardin* refers to the world of human plurality: the shared public realm where human speech and deeds, as Hannah Arendt says, determine the course of history. To cultivate our garden is to cultivate history. Every garden, however personal or private, is *our* garden. There is no such thing—politically speaking—as a garden in the singular. In its challenge to history, a transitory garden in New York City that lasts a day *is* history. And history is never just yours or mine. It is always ours.

That history has no memory of most of the gardens of history does not mean that those gardens did not make history, even if only by turning away from it. In the final analysis—although we are in a realm where there is no finality—history is not the sum total of what is remembered. It is the terrifying, ongoing, and unending conflict between the forces of destruction and cultivation, both of which probably arise from the same source in us, namely care. It takes a creature of care to be as careless as human beings can be. Heidegger puts it well when he declares: "Only where there is care is there neglect."[5] To which one must add: only where there care is there recklessness. There is so much about us that remains opaque, mysterious, and unfathomable, but nothing more so than the subterranean connection between our capacity for destruction—even self-destruction—and our capacity for devotion. This is the legacy of care, which obliges us to strive time and again to become what we already are, that is, human. The burden of that legacy is that we can either succeed or fail in the endeavor to become human, and that we can never succeed once and for all. Indeed, the mark of our strangeness is that we can be abundantly human and starkly inhuman at one and the same time.

Such ambivalence cannot, or should not, obscure the simple fact that, as human beings, we come into our own, some innate potential in us gets activated, some life-affirming principle liberates its powers of redemption, when we take it upon ourselves to care for things, especially living things. This is perhaps the most fundamental of those dispositional needs which the transitory and communal gardens of inner cities reveal beneath the platforms on which we carry on our business and negotiate our relations: the need to care, and to cultivate. Yet in the same way that we create habitats that starve our chlorophilia, we create what Heidegger calls "unworlds" that fail to foster this human need to foster, help, enable, bring to fruition, in short to hand one's care over to something that is not oneself. Unlike the law of self-interest, which operates in us without any need of cultivation, the lesson of taking care of things is one that we must learn from others. Others must first cultivate its potential in us, and we in turn must cultivate it in others. Can one teach children anything more life enhancing than how to take care of things? Those who care for us the most are not those who spare us the burdens of care but those who liberate its vocation in us. These are the gardeners of the soul, as it were, and re-enchanters of the world.

CHAPTER 5

The Modernist Imagination of Place and the Politics of Regionalism: Puig i Cadafalch and Early Twentieth-Century Barcelona

MAIKEN UMBACH

1

In 1933, Martin Heidegger contrasted the alienation of life in the modern city with the authenticity of his rural abode. In a radio broadcast titled "Creative Landscape: Why do we stay in the provinces?" he claimed that his philosophical work had "an inner relationship [. . .] to the Black Forest and its people [which] comes from a centuries-long and irreplaceable rootedness in the Alemannian-Swabian soil."[1] Like the European Romantics and fin-de-siècle cultural pessimists before him,[2] Heidegger saw an opposition between place—as concrete, immutable, and authentic—and space—as abstract and utopian. In this view, the problem of modernity is that it is predicated on space, evident in the visual abstractions of modern architectural functionalism, and in the political abstractions of ideal-typical spaces such as Habermas's public sphere.[3] The self-appointed high priests of antimodernism have not, of course, been able to halt the progress of modernization. Yet place remains a powerful point of orientation in the modern world. Indeed, place-based politics witnessed a remarkable revival in the final decades of the twentieth century. The collapse of the Soviet Union brought ethnically and nationally based identities back to the fore. Even in Western Europe, the birthplace of the "high modernist ideologies,"[4] recent decades have seen multiple revivals of the particular, the local, and the regional.[5] How do we account for this longevity of place as a mental category?

Perhaps, as Bruno Latour suggested, we have never arrived in modernity.[6] Alternatively, the endurance of place can be conceptualized as modernity's omnipresent "other": every Enlightenment *utopia* producing its dialectical opposite, in this case a *topos*.[7] Others have defined the modern instead as "a matter of movement, of flux, of change, of unpredictability,"[8] and thus classified the endurance of place as yet another instance of modernity's inherent heterogeneity.[9] This essay takes a different line, by suggesting that modernism had much more room for the sentiment of "place" than is commonly acknowledged. The decisive decades around 1900 involved not so much a destruction of place as a creative re-imagination of place within a modern environment. This argument builds on a recent historiography that highlights the modern character of notions of *Heimat* and domesticity, so long vilified as purely reactionary.[10] Such revisions should not lead us to underestimate the intellectual dangers of real antimodernism, and its essentializing rhetoric of place-based authenticity. This differed from what I want to call the modernist imagination of place in that only the latter was self-conscious, and involved a process of fictionalization.[11] In this way, place's emotional significance could be recaptured without denying the heterogeneous and multiple identities that characterize life in a (post)modern world of high geographical and social mobility. Of course, the term *fictionalization*, and its close corollary, *re-enchantment*, are themselves problematic. They might conjure up the image of a Disneyesque dreamworld that signals a retreat from politics. Yet, like the dichotomy between space and place, the dichotomy between reality and fantasy is misleading. For Heidegger, the mountains of the Black Forest "spoke," as long as the listener was silent. For the modernist champions of place, by contrast, the voice of a landscape emerged only in the mind of the beholder, between the lines of the concrete and the abstract, the inner and outer worlds, the spiritual and the political parameters of the self. Place, for these modernists, was located *between* reality and the imagination. It therefore offered no retreat from modern life, and was no antidote to the city. Instead, the modernist imagination of place became a vehicle for an alternative form of political practice, engaging with the institutions and discourses of the modern world, but challenging the claim of the nation-state to be their only legitimate forum.

To demonstrate this, I shall focus on a case study that casts light on the connection between cultural representations of place and "real" place-based politics. The setting is Catalonia around 1900. In the early modern period, the region had lost its political autonomy, and gradually had been reduced to a Spanish province. In the mid-nineteenth century, Catalonia rose to new prominence, as Barcelona became Spain's first industrial city. Culture assumed a vital role in the revival of particularist and ultimately separatist sentiments in Catalonia. A central figure in this process was Josep Puig i Cadafalch. As a politician, he played a leading role in promoting the political re-assertion of Catalonia's autonomy from the Spanish state. In 1902, he became president of the newly founded Catalan *Lliga Regionalista,* and between 1917 and 1923, he served as the second president of the *Mancomunitat de Catalunya,* an administration that prefigured the autonomous government of the region which would finally be realized in the post-Franco era. Puig was very much a man of the "real world," a shrewd politician. Yet he was also an eminent cultural figure. A champion of what we might call the Catalan discourse of *Heimat,* he advocated a notion of heritage that was firmly centered on the medieval.[12] Puig played a pioneering role in the rediscovery and restoration of early medieval ecclesiastical architecture. As a result, the Catalan Romanesque came to be regarded as the spiritual *locus* of the region's historical identity. And finally, Puig was also one of the leading architects of his time.[13] As a pioneer of the Catalan *modernisme* movement, he helped transform the *Eixample,* Barcelona's dramatic late nineteenth-century urban extension, from a universalist urban planning dream into a three-dimensional advertisement for Catalan identity politics. Puig's architecture came to define the essence of modern Catalanism, and helped to bridge the gap between the country's medieval legacy and the modern industrial city. It is thus a prime example of an imagination of place which, while highly aware of its premodern roots, was thoroughly modernist in orientation.

2

The principality of Catalonia, with Barcelona at its heart, experienced its political heyday during the Middle Ages. In the early modern period, its independence was gradually eroded. In the nineteenth century the region became significant once again, yet this time the reasons were economic. With a vibrant textile industry, Catalonia was the first part of Spain to industrialize. The 1888 World Fair in Barcelona became a showcase of the city's new industrial wealth.[14] The elite of textile manufacturers who had benefited from this trend were champions of technological innovation and scientific progress. Like most liberals, they were afraid of worker unrest and anarchism.[15] More unusually for liberals, they supported economic protectionism.[16] Both in the domestic and the Spanish colonial markets, Barcelona's textile manufacturers stood to lose out to cheaper English imports, while the Spaniards had as yet no sizeable domestic industry to protect.[17] Such policy differences underpinned the debate over legal codification. The law was central to the emerging ideology of Catalanism. At the beginning of the eighteenth century, Catalan political bodies were dissolved, official use of the Catalan language prohibited, and Catalan public law abolished. Civil or "foral" law came to be celebrated as the only remaining institutional manifestation of Catalan autonomy.[18] National codification in the mid-nineteenth century threatened this. Catalan law was predicated on the concept of a stem family with testamentary liberty. By contrast, the draft Spanish code was centered on the nuclear family, with an emphasis on a community property system and partible inheritance.[19] Catalans cited two reasons for their law's superiority. Testamentary liberty created a sense of continuity between generations, and protected the status of the father as the head of the Catalan household, in the *casa pairal* just as much as in the world of industry.[20] This led to the second, more modern argument. Testamentary liberty resembled the English legal system, and was seen as conducive to industrialization. Joaquim Cadafalch suggested that one only needed to compare the English Industrial Revolution to the lethargy of French (and Spanish) economic development to see which system was superior.[21] Jacobson identified this fusion of historical and pro-industrial arguments as the Roman Catholic equivalent of [Weber's] Protestant ethic.[22] Such arguments gained particular currency in the later nineteenth century, at a time when the Spanish state experienced a fiscal crisis that was precipitated by the disintegration of the Spanish empire.[23] The "crisis" of Spain gave Catalans the opportunity to revive old claims to a separate identity, which found their first institutional manifestation in the *Unió Catalanista* in 1891.[24] This group drew up the manifesto for what became the first Catalanist political party, the *Lliga Regionalista*, of which Puig i Cadafalch was a founding member and the first president. While some historians have challenged the economic determinism that reduced the *Lliga's* Catalanism to a mere fig leaf of business interests,[25] it is certainly true that its support came, first and foremost, from Barcelona textile manufacturers, and that its agenda was wedded to the further-ing of Catalonia's industrial development.[26]

Parallel with these political trends, a heightened sense of cultural Catalanism had emerged in Barcelona from the middle of the nine-teenth century, which came to be associated, in turn, with the move-ments of *Renaixença, modernisme,* and *noucentisme.* The first, the so-called *Renaixença*—literally, the revival—involved a folkloristic re-discovery of Catalan traditions. The year 1859 saw the foundation of the *Jocs Florals,* festivals of Catalan poetry readings that were modeled on medieval bardic competitions.[27] Gradually, Catalan was trans-formed from a spoken idiom, that had survived principally in the countryside, to a literary language, championed by poets such as Jacint Verdaguer. These activities culminated in the 1906 First International Congress of the Catalan Language, the 1907 foundation of the *Institut d'Estudis Catalans,* and the publication in 1913 of Pompeu Fabra's *Normes ortogràfiques.*[28] And from the late 1880s, such achievements were also inscribed into Barcelona's urban fabric through monuments to the cultural heroes of Catalan culture, which adorned the boulevards *(passeigs)* and intersections of the *Eixample* district.[29] The political clas-sification of this movement has proved tricky. Few would dispute that economic modernization contributed to Catalonia's cultural dynamic during the second half of the nineteenth and early twentieth centuries. Nevertheless, in view of the fact that what was Catalan was defined, above all, in terms of history, Catalanism is still widely seen as anti-modern, and as such contrasted with the more liberal nationalism of Spain.[30] Such a classification is misguided, in that it confuses an advo-cacy of "place" with a rejection of things modern. History was not re-vived here as an end in itself. *Renaixença* and *modernisme* were driven not by a generic appreciation of the pre-industrial past, but rather, by a search for precedents which could be invoked to challenge the hege-mony of the Spanish state. The Middle Ages preceded early modern absolutist state building, and in the Catalan case, coincided with com-plete political independence. To associate the Middle Ages with partic-ular cultural productivity, therefore, was a highly topical contention in nineteenth-century Spain. Moreover, this medieval legacy was cre-atively re-imagined. This was not unique to the Catalan case. In many European countries, the gothic revival challenged the aesthetic and po-litical universalism of the classical idiom.[31] National and municipal authorities opted for the gothic to represent their unique identity. The rebuilding of the British Houses of Parliament in this style is a case in point, the construction of countless neomedieval town halls another.[32] Towards the end of the nineteenth century, this medievalism required a more populist edge. The Middle Ages were romanticized and represented in increasingly fanciful and fantastic images.[33] This new medievalism served as a window onto a magical and fundamentally "other" realm to the ordered cosmos of post-Renaissance Europe, akin to Orientalism.[34] Yet it was by no means antimodernist. Even aside from Ganim's world fairs,[35] examples of the fusion of "spectacular" consumer culture and the gothic idiom abound, from department stores to Bruno Taut's visionary glass house.[36] This gothicism provided an enchanted looking glass onto the miracles of the modern metropolis and industrial culture more generally. Yet as the gothic became commercialized, it also became universalized—and hence less useful for those who saw medievalism as a launchpad for projects of regional autonomy. Puig belonged to a generation of intellectuals who turned their attention to more geographically specific and even earlier precedents in their quest to re-invent place and defy territorial homogenization. The new precedent was the Romanesque, or what Puig himself later labeled the *premier art roman*.[37]

3

By international standards, the tiny rural Romanesque churches in the Catalan Pyrenees that attracted the attentions of Puig and his followers seem primitive. The Lombard Romanesque in Northern Italy was much more refined; indeed, where finer marble capitals feature in the Catalan Romanesque, they had usually been executed by Lombard craftsmen. Yet the simplicity of the Catalan architectural heritage was not a problem for its new champions. It served as an antidote to the alleged over-refinement and decadence of Spanish high culture. As Puig explained in his three-volume *L'architectura romànica a Catalunya*, the roughness of the Catalan Romanesque was emblematic of the honest character of the Catalan people.[38] The restorations that were undertaken under Puig's direction, and which he documented in scholarly publications, often exacerbated this primitivism, to the point of historical falsification.[39] Crucially, the frescoes that covered many of the walls and all apses in the churches concerned were transferred to Barcelona in 1921, and put on public display in a museum environment.[40] Ostensibly, this was done for conservationist reasons,[41] but the real trigger was provided by the threat of the frescoes' removal from Catalonia, into a private collection in Boston.[42] The conflict over ownership of the frescoes, entailed, among other things, a duel between Lluís Plandidura, a private collector who sold frescoes from the Romanesque church of Mur to the Museum of Fine Arts in Boston, where they remain today, and Folch i Torres, director of Barcelona's Board of Museums, a protégé and former student of Puig, who has been described as a "militant Catalanist."[43] This conflict provoked the direct involvement, politically and financially, of the *Mancomunitat de Catalunya*, in the question of how to keep the frescoes in Catalonia. In 1919, it was decided to purchase all frescoes for the Museus d'Art i Arqueologica, the predecessor of the National Museum of Catalan Art (MNAC).[44]

As well as protecting the region's heritage, moving the frescoes to Barcelona had other, ideologically desirable side-effects. In the museum, they formed a new connection between the city and the surrounding country: Barcelona became the showcase for what was Catalan. In engineering this transfer, the sense of authenticity itself became mobile, the world of the remote Pyrenean villages was transformed into a culture that could be exhibited, and was thus creatively reconstituted. Puig's architecture, as we shall see later, developed this theme further. At the same time, removing the frescoes transformed the churches in question. Exposing the bare stone, Puig made the churches even more archaic. Moreover, the loss of frescoes removed much of the original iconography, and with it, these churches' association with political power. This point requires elaboration.

For early Christian communities, who often met in barns, the sacred character of a church space was constituted only during the gathering of the faithful.[45] Only later did ecclesiastical space become sanctified, and hierarchical. The simple square room of the early hall churches was transformed into the basilica, with a hierarchy of three naves.[46] Frescoes now adorned the walls, and the central fresco in the apse would depict God, later Jesus (or more rarely the Virgin and the child), seated on a throne, as king of the earth and Heaven, in much the same pose as a worldly ruler. In most Romanesque churches in the Catalan Pyrenees, the old hall church shape had survived. This affinity with early Christian meeting places suited Puig's intentions. He was one of the first, but by no means the only, modernist to idealize the seemingly egalitarian character of early Christian architecture.[47] The removal of the frescoes further diminished any sense of hierarchy, in eliminating the religiously motivated contrast between interior and exterior. This

manipulation further enhanced the view of these churches as spontaneous communal gathering places. It appealed to a modern religious
sensibility, which was marked less by hierarchy, order, and obedience,
and more by sentiment, community, and introspection. In this way, the
restoration of Catalonia's rural churches conjured up an imagined community of Catalans, with roots that were spiritual and thus pre-, or
more accurately, extra-political—and thus fundamentally different to
the institutions of the Spanish church and state.[48]

Puig's particular achievement lay in making this imagined community compatible with modern, industrial Catalonia. As a scholar of the
Romanesque, Puig developed a theory of progress that safeguarded
what was ideologically valuable about Catalan "primitivism," but
made this compatible with technological innovation. To this end, Puig
overturned conventional classifications of architectural history. Andrea Mesecke argued that Puig's method "proceeds in a historical-
genetic manner, in contrast to the approaches of intellectual history,
philosophy and aesthetics practiced by German art historians. Together
with [. . .] the American Arthur Kingsley-Porter, who alongside Puig i
Cadafalch rediscovered the Romanesque architecture of Lombardy,
he [Puig] was the founding father of a new sub-discipline of art geography."[49] This comparison is not particularly helpful. It is true that
Kingsley-Porter agreed with some of Puig's findings, yet he himself
wrote that their methods were "fundamentally different."[50] The only
real similarity between the two men was that both rejected state-
centered approaches. At the time, most architectural historians propa-
gated an unapologetic nationalism, culminating in declarations such
as those that "the German Volk was the true hero" of art history.[51] This
was not a specifically German trend: almost identical formulations can
be found, for example, in the work of French art historian Raymond
Rey.[52] Against this tide, Kingsley-Porter and Puig i Cadafalch examined supranational artistic milieus and trajectories of influence. Yet
they did so for very different reasons. Kingsley-Porter rejected national
paradigms because "he was interested in the essence of art, to which
he attributed an extra-temporal, not historically conditioned power. [. . .]
Art history [. . .] contributed to prolonging and intensifying the aesthetic enjoyment of the work of art [. . .] enabling the spectator to experience a state of excitement comparable to that of the artistic creator."[53]
Kingsley-Porter was uninterested in the economic and technological
factors that influenced architecture, and defined "positivism" in art

history as his principal enemy.[54] Yet positivism and an interest in technological determinants of progress were precisely what characterized Puig i Cadafalch's approach.

Puig, too, saw Lombardy and Catalonia as closely connected regions.[55] His broader aim was to demonstrate that Catalonia had been at the heart of a regional network of particularly dynamic cultures, which defined the very meaning of progress. In his major work on architecture and geography, Puig distinguished between two European mega-regions: a progressive Mediterranean sphere, including Catalonia, and the area between the Rhine and the Elbe, which Puig classified as "backward" by comparison.[56] The Mediterranean, to which even today Catalans often refer to as *mare nostrum*, provided the opportunities for exchange, trade, and expansion, which cut across the boundaries of modern nation-states such as Italy and Spain. Here, Puig's argument resembles that of later *Annales* historians.[57] The origins of this culture stretched back in time before classical Greece, to ancient Babylon and Mesopotamia.[58] For Puig, the Romanesque era was merely one moment in his *longue durée* model at which the difference between the two spheres became especially visible. The outward manifestation was the proliferation of *décoration lombarde,* yet this was only a symptom.[59] What really distinguished the Mediterranean region was technological innovation. Dramatic deforestation "determined" the character of the region's architecture.[60] Responding to the scarcity of wood, vaulted stone ceilings were invented, technologically superior to the "primitive" flat wooden ceilings of German Ottonian churches.[61] Catalans were at the forefront of vaulting technology, which Puig identified in Ripoll for C.E. 977, Saint-Martin du Canigou in Roussillon, and, crucially, also in what he calls "numerous small rustic churches" in the region.[62] Puig did not write in praise of architects of genius who acted as lone cultural innovators. Rather, he was interested in the objective conditions that fostered technological innovation from the bottom up. Ordinary, or in Puig's words, "somewhat primitive" and "graceless" churches, were particularly revealing examples of such trends.[63]

Puig's classification of the German Ottonian churches as "backward" by comparison is of course rather willful. Under Holy Roman Emperors Otto I and Otto II fifteen cathedrals were erected in Lombardy, a territory which Puig's map shows as part of the *premier art roman* region [fig. 1].[64] Yet Lower Saxony, the imperial heartland of the Ottonians, is categorized as part of the "primitive" region on Puig's map.

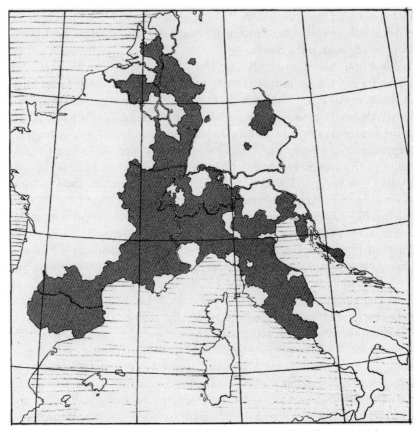

FIG. 5.1. Map from Josep Puig i Cadafalch, *La géographie et les origines du premier art roman* (trans. Jeanne Vielliard), Paris: H. Laurens, 1928.

Almost any conceivable taxonomy would reveal that the monumental Ottonian churches of Cologne were much more highly developed than the simple Catalonia "barns" of the same period. Yet Puig describes Cologne's churches as "simple," "localized," even "retarded."[65] The oddity of this classification becomes immediately apparent even in a superficial visual comparison of Cologne's St. Pantaleon, with a "primitive" flat ceiling [fig. 2], and St-Martin-du-Canigou [fig. 3], one of Puig's favorite Catalan examples. Unsurprisingly, modern scholarship has largely discredited Puig's taxonomy of the Romanesque.[66] Yet it is not historical accuracy that concerns us here. Puig rightly saw his work as revolutionary in implication,[67] and his argument is interesting to us for two reasons. It freed his Catalan medievalism from the suspicion of

FIG. 5.2. St. Pantaleon, Cologne (photograph taken by author in 1985).

political nostalgia, and tied it to an argument that was *structurally modern*. Puig used objective, quasi-scientific arguments, in which architecture became evidence not of aesthetic sophistication, but of technological progress. In doing so, he developed a new political geography that relativized the importance of the nation-state, and focused instead on cultural regions as engines of progress. This gave added legitimacy to modern Catalonia's claim to autonomy from Spain, and tied its advanced industrial development to the region's *longue durée* character. Against this background, we can now better appreciate Puig's other contribution to the re-invention of the Catalan cause as a brand of modernist revival of place: his architectural transformation of Barcelona's *Eixample* district.

FIG. 5.3. St.-Martin-du-Canigou, Upper Church (photograph taken by author in 2003).

4

As the nineteenth century drew to a close, Barcelona had established its reputation as a modernist metropolis par excellence. It was not only a major industrial center; it had also undergone a remarkable physical transformation. The 1860s saw the razing of Barcelona's medieval fortifications. This move was followed by the construction of a massive urban extension, which became a showcase of progressive, rational urban planning. Planned by Ildefons Cerdà in 1859, the *Eixample* was an exercise in applied futurism. Cerdà, who was trained as a civil engineer, prided himself on his scientific as well as his progressive outlook.[68] He planned the *Eixample* for a "new man," whom he prophetically defined as "active, daring, entrepreneurial [. . .] that man who in a few brief instants travels vast distances; the man who in just minutes transmits and circulates his news, his instructions, his commands right around the globe."[69] The square grid would provide the perfect habitat for this new man. It would distribute "with total equality and perfect justice the benefits of 'vitality' [. . .] among all streets," was the "antithesis of privilege and monopoly," and would meet not only the needs of the present, but also all those needs that "may arise" in the future which Cerdà embraced with such optimism.[70] On the one hand, Cerdà's "scientific" planning fitted well into the Catalans' view of themselves as the most industrious and rational of the Iberian peoples. On the other hand, it failed to connect with the discourse of Catalan separatism: the grid was a universal, not a culturally specific shape. As Cerdà himself suggested, his vision was one that would eliminate the particularism of place: "everything in this century is leading towards the disappearance of limits, towards a general merging."[71] Moreover, the grid plan had been superimposed on Barcelona by a *Spaniard*. Puig voiced his protest against this when, in 1891, he announced that "those modern cities with straight roads, rectangular crossings and houses of equal height, which the past century regarded as great inventions— modeled on ancient Rome—embody, when we examine them more closely, ultimately little more than a spirit of uniformity."[72] In a similar vein, he had criticized Cerdà's General Theory of Urbanization as a "work completed by Royal Decree, declared of Public Utility by Royal Decree, published, again, by Royal Decree, the consequences of which were imposed on Barcelona, like it or not, by orders from Madrid."[73] Of course, non-Catalans had made similar points about modern urban planning, and Puig's sentiments resembled those of his more famous contemporary Camillo Sitte.[74] Similarly, Puig's claim that the beautification of cityscapes would "strengthen the soul" of the people, echoed themes that were common currency in the so-called life reform movement of the fin de siècle.[75] Yet through his architectural designs for this district, Puig added a specifically Catalan element to the rejection of uniformity in urban planning.

It is to misunderstand his architecture if it is simply seen as adding an element of color, variation, and playfulness to the city—a reading that has often been applied to the even more idiosyncratic designs of Puig's famous Catalan contemporary, Antoni Gaudí i Cornet.[76] To appreciate what was original about Puig's contribution to Barcelona's urban fabric and, by extension, to the modernist re-enchantment of place, we need to take a brief look at the "Catalanization" of the *Eixample* in the preceding decades. In 1888, Rius i Taulet, sometimes referred to as the "Haussmann of Barcelona," and his liberal colleagues in the municipal government chose the section of the new ring around the medieval core which bordered on the recently razed Bourbon Citadel as the site for the Barcelona World Fair.[77] Although most exhibition pavilions were temporary structures, the event set the tone for urban development in years to come, which would undermine the universalist pretensions of Cerdà's grid. Landmark buildings included the *Palau de Justícia*, commissioned by the city's supreme court, and executed under the direction of Enric Sagnier on the site of the World Fair.[78] Its iconography presented a skillful synthesis of Catalanist and Spanish elements, both architecturally and in terms of the historical figures and episodes that were represented in its elaborate program of statues, friezes, and murals.[79] The work of Lluís Domènech i Montaner was even more influential. Born eighteen years before Puig, Domènech was a typical product of the Catalan *Renaixença*. The café he designed for the Fair contained not only allegorical references to Catalonia's medieval past, but it also gave such memory tropes a decorative and eminently accessible sensual texture.[80] Key to this was the material: as in many European regions, red brick, made from local soil, came to be considered the vernacular material par excellence.[81] In addition, Domènech's building featured mock medieval turrets, crenellation, and decorative bands of ceramic crests, conjuring up a fanciful memory of Catalonia's medieval heritage. Domènech's other landmark building in Barcelona was the *Palau de la Música Catalana*, commissioned by the *l'Orfeó Català*, a choral society founded in 1891 for the cultivation of authentic Catalan music in the spirit of the *Jocs Florals*. The sculptural frame around the stage depicted, on one side, the roots of rustic music, represented by dancing Catalan maidens, and on the other side, the supposedly Nordic quality of the Catalan spirit (represented by Wagner's Valkyries riding out of a "thought-bubble" above a bust of Beethoven).[82]

Puig i Cadaflach's buildings can be seen as a further development of this trend, yet they also marked a new departure toward a more unequivocally modernist approach to the themes of memory and place. Puig, who had placed so much emphasis on archaeological accuracy in his restoration projects, as an architect invented a visual vocabulary that not only took liberties with such precedents, but transposed them into an entirely new idiom. With their rich ornamentation and hybrid historical allegories, his commissions for the *Eixample* were a far cry from the rural archaism of the Romanesque churches he reconstructed. This is already apparent in the first apartment building, the *Casa Martí* of 1896 [fig. 4]. The top floor windows were neo-Romanesque, yet neo-Gothic and plataresque ornaments dominate in the other floors. Moreover, in all Puig's works from this period, Catalan references were mixed with elements of Spanish as well as Dutch and German Gothic, and even Moorish elements in the *mudéjar* ornaments. As restorer and archeologist, Puig was particularly well versed in the intricacies of different historical styles, and not likely to take liberties with such precedents unless he had made a conscious decision to do so. Puig's hybrid iconographies thus require a different kind of decoding. It is instructive to compare his neo-gothicism with the gothicism of Eugène Emmanuel Viollet-le-Duc. Both men rejected the backward-looking medievalism of the Romantics, from whom the Gothic was a deeply spiritual architecture.[83] Yet their modernist trajectories were fundamentally different. Viollet-le-Duc, the chief *Inspecteur général des Edifices Diocésains,*

FIG. 5.4. Puig i Cadafalch, *Casa Martí* (photograph taken by author).

saw the Gothic as the triumph of structural rationalism, which could be compared to the cast-iron architecture of his own day. For Viollet-le-Duc, Gothic cathedrals embodied a new form of logical thinking, which overcame the orthodoxies of Romanesque architecture—a process analogous to burgher cities replacing monasteries as cultural centers.[84] For Puig, by contrast, the Gothic's modernity lay in its ornamental quality. Singularly uninterested in tectonics,[85] Puig helped develop the visual language of *modernisme*, which took the surface, not the three-dimensional form, as its point of departure.[86]

Nothing could be further from the truth, though, than to assume that this surface had no meaning.[87] On this surface, memory could be inscribed, not as a logical reconstruction, but as an enchanted program of playful allusions. The plain brick walls of the *Casa Martí* were a backdrop, a museum wall, an ornamental tapestry, on which Puig's ornaments could tell their stories. These stories, as we have seen, reached back beyond the realms of academic (and state-centered) history. For Puig, the Mediterranean cultural sphere that he identified with his *premier art roman* originated in Mesopotamia. These roots predestined Catalan culture to a particular affinity with ornament, in particular, with ornamental tiles and brick.[88] Thus, rather than contradicting the simplicity of the Catalan Romanesque, Puig's elaborate ornamentation was reminiscent of these earlier roots. On another level, these ornaments told allegorical stories. A leitmotif in Puig's art, as in Gaudí's, is the dragon, which featured as a plaster ornament, on painted tiles, and in wrought iron. Symbol of the Catalan patron saint St. Jordi (St. George), the dragon alluded to the mythical, not the verifiable historical origins of Catalonia. Moreover, the fact that the dragon itself, not the victorious knight who slays the beast, became *pars pro toto* in Puig's and Gaudí's ornaments gave this old iconography a new, vitalist, and almost pagan twist. Again, we encounter a Catalan spirituality which goes "back to nature," in opposition to the scholastic traditions of Castilian Catholicism.

If place-based identities were imaginatively reconstituted in this way, they could also be related to other, equally ideal typical places. Throughout this period, Catalanists had emphasized their alleged affinity with Germanic culture: not the culture of the German state (or its predecessor, the Holy Roman Empire), but rather, the culture of German free cities, with their strong traditions of local patriotism, political particularism, and trading empires.[89] Puig's facade of the *Casa Amatller* from 1900, with its stepped gable [fig. 5], or the *Casa Terradas,* an apart-

FIG. 5.5. Puig i Cadafalch, *Casa Amatller* (photograph taken by author).

ment complex from 1905 [fig. 6], where the red-brick facade was subdivided into slender vertical units, were reminiscent of burgher houses in cities such as Amsterdam, Brügge, or Nuremberg.[90] Such references served not as literal evocations of political models, but as poetic allusions to ideals of old burgher culture and civic liberties. Materials had a similar function. The conspicuous display of wood- and stonework, ceramics, the sgraffito techniques, wrought iron, and so forth recalled a world of craftsmanship and notions of expertise which had a long historical trajectory, but could also be connected to the industrial

FIG. 5.6. Puig i Cadafalch, *Casa Bartomeu Terradas i Brutau* (photograph taken by author).

success of the modern city.[91] In such ways, the surface replaced the structural grammar of architecture as the principal carrier of meaning. The meaning itself was transformed by the process. Where conventional historicism had made learned references, which were to be decoded with the rational mind, and against the backdrop of historical knowledge, Puig conjured up memories that worked more like poetry. This was, after all, the epoch in which, throughout Europe, modernists experimented with new media with which to capture the workings of memory. Philosophers such as Henri Bergson explored the past as duration.[92] Duration itself, not the succession of distinct moments narrated by academic historians, was the foremost characteristic of memory. Avant-garde literature explored ways of mobilizing intuition as a key to accessing this duration: the sights and smells of Marcel Proust, or the free-floating association of Virginia Woolf's and James Joyce's streams of consciousness, served as "architexts of memory."[93] The non-linear structure of such narratives functioned in ways that closely resembled the ornamental textures of Puig's facades. Both were also characterized by an emotional, rather than a rational, approach to the past. In the early twentieth century, Aby Warburg was one of the champions of this approach to memory, which, he suggested, operated through the sub- or semiconscious. Warburg invoked the allegorical figure of Mnemosyne, patron goddess of memory, and his symbolic cosmos, in which astrology and pagan rituals took center stage, revolved around the irrational and shamanistic elements of human culture.[94] The parallel with Puig's fantastic dragons is apparent. Perhaps the clearest evidence of Puig's engagement with a modernist discourse of memory is the final building to be considered here, the *Palau Baró de Quadras* of 1906, a commission by a nouveau riche industrialist of the same name, who had only very recently received his aristocratic title. The facade features many of Puig's trademark elements: Romanesque arches (above the top floor windows), rustic tropes (such as the steep wooden gables above the four dormer windows), and rich plataresque ornamentation contrasting with an otherwise very plain stone surface. Yet the most remarkable feature of this house was a large bay window on the first floor, which featured eight large relief plates [fig. 7]. Each shows a couple in conversation: a man and woman, both in medieval dress, leaning from the frame as if on a balcony, with varying gestures and expressions from relief to relief. It is as if the inhabitants of the house had dressed up in period dress, and were telling each other stories about the Catalan Middle Ages which their home so fancifully recalled. Not only the content, but the act of the conversation is cast in stone: architecture has become a text, it records not a precedent, but the very act of invoking it. It *is* a three-dimensional *recherche du temps perdu*.

5

Puig's architectural contribution to the *Eixample* can be read as a chronicle of a new idiom of memory that was, albeit historical in content, thoroughly modern in structure. It was the logical corollary of the argument Puig had first developed in his art historical research on the Romanesque. In both genres, he helped invent a Catalan sense of place that was simultaneously rooted in the past, and celebrated progress.

FIG. 5.7. Puig i Cadafalch, *Casa Quadras* (photograph taken by author).

Puig reconciled the archaism of a "communitarian" history, which resisted the dominance of the central state, with the portrayal of Catalans as an industrious and innovative people, whose collective character provided the fuel for Catalonia's industrial revolution. This was his analytical contribution to the debate. He also reconciled the centrality of the medieval for defining what was Catalan with the desire to break away from the shackles of conventional historicism. To achieve this, Puig developed a radically new visual vocabulary for expressing the self-consciously fictitious memories of a modern society. This was what could be dubbed his poetic contribution to the debate. Combining the two, a modernity took shape which, rather than embracing spatial abstraction, re-enchanted the notion of place, and made it useable in the world of modern politics. For the Catalan sense of place, history was the point of departure. But far from invoking history to recapture a premodern and anti-urban "authenticity" of place, liberal Catalanism conceived of place, and memory, as something that is located, above all, in the imagination. What this case study demonstrates, then, is not simply that the modernist re-enchantment occurred in early twentieth-century Europe. It also explains why we need to conceptualize instances of resistance to the hegemony of the nation-state in ways that depart from the model offered by modernization theorists. For the modernization paradigm is traditionally invoked to characterize regions as agrarian and traditionalist backwaters, which were forcefully modernized by centralizing nation-states. Catalonia around 1900 was quite the opposite: not only culturally vibrant, but also among the most economically dynamic areas in Europe.[95] Here, a distinctly modernist imagination of place became the basis for an equally modern form of subnational politics.

CHAPTER 6

Modern Magic: Jean-Eugène Robert-Houdin and Stéphane Mallarmé

JOSHUA LANDY

> The world is disenchanted. One need no longer have recourse to magical means in order to master or implore the spirits, as did the savage, for whom such mysterious powers existed. Technical means and calculations perform the service.
>
> —Max Weber

> Third Law: Any sufficiently advanced technology is indistinguishable from magic.
>
> —Arthur C. Clarke

"WHETHER SCIENCE CAN FURNISH goals of action after it has proved that it can take such goals away and annihilate them": this, insists Nietzsche, is "the most insidious question of all."[1] What, indeed, is left when science has disenchanted the world? At one time we considered rainbows mysterious phenomena, divine perhaps in origin (Iris's scarf, God's covenant), but then science came along and taught us about prismatic refraction.[2] We used to believe that the cosmos had—as its etymology suggests—an intrinsic, humanly apprehensible order, with the earth firmly set at its center; after Copernicus, we thought differently. And though we fondly imagined for a while that we were placed on earth for a purpose, we now know that our evolution involved a considerable degree of contingency, and might just as well not have happened at all.[3] Little by little, science has stretched its tentacles into more and more corners formerly occupied by religion and myth.[4] It has removed the persuasion that there is something beyond what is offered by the evidence of our senses; it has uprooted the conviction that things are what they are, and where they are, for a reason; it has eradicated mystery, order, and purpose—and in their place, it has put nothing at all, simply leaving a gaping void. Can science, then, redress its own wrongs? Can it restore mystery and wonder to experience? Can science itself re-enchant the world it disenchanted? Or if not, what can?

Nineteenth-century answers to Nietzsche's question were varied. Many, of course, refused so much as to feel its force, either because they had never sacrificed their beliefs—it is still the case today that thoroughgoing disenchantment affects precious few, even in the "enlightened" West—or because, at the other extreme, they did not see the need to replace them. (These, and not the Christians as is commonly thought, are the target of Nietzche's madman who, in *Gay Science* sec. 125, urges his fellow atheists to face the consequences of the "death of God.")[5] Others, however, took the task very seriously. Nietzsche himself sought to restore a sense of purpose to life, even if this purpose had to be invented and autotelically endorsed by each individual; Jean-Eugène Robert-Houdin, the stage magician, disclosed a mystery at the heart of science; and Stéphane Mallarmé, the magician of words, offered his intricately crafted miniature masterpieces as both models of and training grounds for a new principle of order. The burden of the present essay will be to explain how Robert-Houdin and Mallarmé, two self-described magicians, helped pull off the greatest trick ever performed in the modern age: nothing short of the re-enchantment of the world.

Part One: Jean-Eugène Robert-Houdin

1

It might, at first glance, seem counterintuitive to begin with Robert-Houdin. After all, his chief achievement is to have turned the rejection of supernatural forces and the exposition of frauds into a staple of stage magic. Robert-Houdin called himself a *prestidigitateur*, not a *magicien*; his handbills spoke of illusions (and "experiments"), not of enchantments; he dedicated volumes (*Les Tricheries des Grecs dévoilées*, 1861, and *Les Secrets de la prestidigitation et de la magie*, 1868) to the unmasking of ancient and modern humbuggers; and he was even employed by the French government in 1855 to reproduce each of the feats performed by the Marabout sorcerers, like a latter-day Moses, so as to forestall an impending coup in Algeria.[6] In short, Robert-Houdin made good on his determination, explicitly stated in the 1858 autobiography *Confidences d'un prestidigitateur*, "to offer new experiments divested of all charlatanism."[7] And his successors followed suit, quite literally in fact. Following Robert-Houdin, the choice of sober evening dress was adopted by more or less every magician, and more or less every magician took a swipe at something while on stage, whether past impostors, present spiritualists, or even his own tricks.[8]

The demolition of lingering belief in actual sorcery became, thanks to Robert-Houdin, a primary function of the magic show at large. For belief did coninue to linger, with three factors co-responsible for its dogged persistence. First of all, there was the charlatanism Robert-Houdin was complaining about: even at the end of the eighteenth century, conjurors like Andrew Oehler and Giovanni Pinetti were claiming, letting it be known, or simply not denying that their feats required divine or diabolical intervention. Giovanni Pinetti's antics brought condemnation from Henri Decremps in the form of a treatise, *La magie blanche dévoilée* of 1784; some fifty years afterwards, Jean Julia de Fontenelle found it necessary to publish a book under the same title, this time exposing Louis Comte. The second factor was education. In rural Switzerland, during the second decade of the nineteenth century, Louis Comte was set upon by townspeople armed with cudgels who wanted to burn him alive; Comte escaped, appropriately enough, by ventriloquizing the voice of a demon, causing his terrified assailants to scatter.[9] And in Cornwall a decade later, Antonio Blitz was "arrested and brought before the magistrate of the borough, a Colonel Tremain, and openly charged with being engaged in the 'Black Art.'"[10] "The poor Cornish miners," he explained, "looked upon me as a being not all of human make."[11]

The third and final contributor to the survival of superstition was, perhaps surprisingly, Christianity. While the French legal system had long since abandoned witch trials, an edict of Louis XIV in 1690 decreeing that the relevant criminals were merely guilty of fraud,[12] the eighteenth century witnessed a powerful counter-Enlightenment reaction inside and outside the country. A. Boissier's *Recueil de diverses lettres au sujet des maléfices et du sortilège* (1731) and Antoine Daugis's *Traité sur la magie, le sortilège, les possessions, obsessions et maléfices* (1732) both reaffirmed the existence of real enchanters, as did the abbé Fiard's *De la France trompée par les magiciens et les démonolâtres du dix-huitième siècle*, published—hard to imagine—in the nineteenth century (1803).

Meanwhile, the Vatican, having enacted the Inquisitorial Code of Pasquelone in 1730, helpfully offering a definition of magicians (as those who cause other human beings to be possessed by demons) so as to facilitate their prosecution, went on in 1795 to put the legendary Cagliostro on trial as "a freemason, a heretic, and a sorcerer." (Under torture, Cagliostro confessed.)[13] The Vatican's Code actually remained on the books until 1870, prompting Stéphane Mallarmé—only slightly behind the times—to speak in 1893 of "practices that the preservation, at the papal court, of a law intended to defeat them indicates to be alive and well."[14]

It is, of course, unlikely that *all* nineteenth-century clergymen, and *all* nineteenth-century country dwellers, gave credence to diabolical possession. Reported cases may, on occasion, have been the product of a tacit alliance between members of the Church who did not believe in it and members of the uneducated classes who did not believe in it either. In 1816, for example, a young girl, having become pregnant, understandably chose to blame it on supernatural forces; a Jesuit, equally happy to connive with her in this, exorcised her demon, who, it seems, "ended up stationing itself in the young lady's *pudendum*."[15] The "exorcism" took place on regular occasions for several days—until, one assumes, they finally caught him at it.[16] Nonetheless, plenty of priests and preachers were willing to take the matter extremely seriously, to the point of putting itinerant performers in the dock. In 1826, the ecclesiastical court of Exeter charged Antonio Blitz with "deceiving honest people by base acts, and tempting them to look for riches, by giving themselves over to his master,—the arch-enemy of mankind"; a Manchester clergyman, for his part, called Blitz "a necromancer—at war with religion and morality."[17] And perhaps we should be less astonished at such attitudes, which many Christians today consider almost inconceivably archaic, than at the fact that they ever died out. For as Augustine points out in *The City of God* (bk. 21, ch. 6), "such marvels we cannot deny without impugning the truth of the sacred Scriptures we believe"; the cost, for the Church, is nothing less than the rejection of Deuteronomy 18:10-12, in which God lays out punishments for practitioners of the secret arts, and of Mark 5:1-20, in which Jesus transfers demons from man to pig (to cite only one example from the New Testament).[18]

Thus the cleric preached, the uneducated trusted, and the charlatan profited, all the way into the middle of the nineteenth century. Worse still (from Robert-Houdin's point of view), even the gentry were not immune to mystification.[19] Blitz met with the same behavior in London as he did in Exeter and Cornwall: "even here," he wrote, "there were many to be found with the same feelings of credulity, as ignorant respecting my character, and profession, and performances, as were those in the most remote and benighted districts."[20] In 1830s England, according to Charles Mackay,[21] it was not just the poor who summoned witch doctors to cure diseases inflicted by the Devil, but also "ladies who rode in their carriages." And Robert-Houdin himself, towards 1846, fell victim to an "elegant" female visitor who considered him an actual necromancer.[22] Looking suitably tragic, a veil covering her fine features, this young woman begged him to help her take revenge on a wayward spouse; when Robert-Houdin vociferously denied any connections with the forces of darkness, she simply changed tactics and pulled out a knife. She would not leave until Robert-Houdin had taken down a dusty book from a high shelf, stuck a pin in a candle, and mumbled an impressively incomprehensible incantation. He should, presumably, have checked in advance to see that she had nothing up her sleeve.

2

Robert-Houdin may have played the part when his life was at stake, but as we have seen, he generally considered himself an active force for *dis*enchantment, a champion of enlightenment in its continuing struggle against credulity. And so his theatre seems, to repeat, an unlikely place to look for answers to Nietzsche's "most insidious question." Did its audiences not split down a simple fault line, that of the mid-century at large, with faith (in traditional religion, ancient magic, or recent options such as spiritualism) on the one side and doubt (originated by science, reinforced by prestidigitation) on the other? Were believers, like the dagger-wielding avenger we just met, not free to preserve their beliefs, skeptics their skepticism, throughout the performance? These questions are, it turns out, not entirely rhetorical. To understand why, we need to consider the trick which made Robert-Houdin's reputation when he débuted it in October 1847, the one for which he was best known and most widely copied: The Ethereal Suspension.

Imagine a forty-one-year-old Jean-Eugène Robert-Houdin, dressed in the evening wear he is in the process of making de rigueur, accompanied on his simple and well-lit stage by six-year-old son Joseph, and starting to spin out his patter "with all the seriousness," as he put it, "of a Sorbonne professor." "Gentlemen," he begins, "I have just dis-

FIG. 6.1. Jean-Eugène Robert-Houdin, "The Ethereal Suspension," from *Confidences de Robert-Houdin*, 1861.

covered a new, truly wondrous property of ether. When this liquid is at its highest degree of concentration, if a living being breathes it, the body of the patient becomes in a few moments as light as a balloon."

This exposition being complete, I proceeded to the experiment. I placed three stools on a wooden bench. My son climbed onto the one in the middle, and I made him stretch out his arms, which I held up in the air by means of two canes, each of which rested on one stool.

Then I simply put an empty bottle, which I carefully uncorked, under the boy's nose . . . My son immediately fell asleep, and his feet, having become lighter, began to leave the stool.

Judging the operation a success, I removed the stool, so that the child was no longer supported by anything except the two canes.

This strange equilibrium already elicited great surprise among the audience. The surprise only grew when I was seen removing one of the two canes and the stool which supported it; and finally it reached its peak when, having raised my son to a horizontal position by means of my little finger, I left him thus asleep in space.[23]

What matters here is not that Robert-Houdin succeeded in creating the illusion of levitation, however influential the trick may subsequently have been. What matters is, instead, that Robert-Houdin presented it as a miracle of *science*, with himself acting the role of *professor*, and his performance gaining the feel of an *experiment*. "In 1847,"

Robert-Houdin would later explain, "the insensibility produced by in-haling ether began to be applied in surgical operations; all the world talked about the marvellous effect of this anaesthetic, and its extraordi-nary results. In the eyes of many people it seemed much akin to magic."[24] In order to be enthralled, then, audience members did not have to believe Robert-Houdin possessed of mystical powers, or even particularly skillful. They had only to believe in the mysteries of sci-ence.[25] And believe they did: many of them, misled by a combination of Robert-Houdin's patter, a smell of ether coming from offstage, and their own faith in science, took Robert-Houdin to be actually etheriz-ing his son every night, and wrote to scold him for this appalling mistreatment.[26]

Robert-Houdin's befuddled patrons have, it seems to me, unwit-tingly furnished a partial answer to Nietzsche's question. Science *can* re-enchant the world, after having so mercilessly disenchanted it. For modern science, when presented in the right way, can itself be awe in-spiring.[27] And performers like Robert-Houdin, even as they demysti-fied old superstitions, were simultaneously replacing these with new sources of enchantment—indeed disenchanting *by* re-enchanting. Like Antonio Blitz, Robert-Houdin could have said that his performances had as their aim "to remove the long-prevailing impressions attached to the history of magic, by demonstrating to the mind that the rapidity of the hand, and the mechanical inventions of the nineteenth century, were more wonderful in effect than the mysteries of the ancient magi-cians."[28] Mid-century prestidigitation was a legerdemain in which what was taken away with one hand was, simultaneously, restored with the other.

Nietzsche, of course, asked for more than just wonder; he asked "whether science could furnish goals of action." The answer, surpris-ing as this may be, was again in the affirmative for a segment of Robert-Houdin's audience. A mere two years after the first performance of the Ethereal Suspension, Ernest Renan addressed Nietzsche's question head on, in *L'avenir de la science* (*The Future of Science*). "Since science has barely appeared up till now except in critical form," he wrote, "people do not imagine that it can become a powerful motive for ac-tion. That will change, however, as soon as science has created in the moral world a conviction equal to that which religious faith once pro-duced."[29] And three years after that, Auguste Comte published an ac-tual "Catechism of Positive Religion," offering a new God, a new faith, a new Providence, a new way of explaining the world, a new type of immortality, a new (grounding for) morality, a new set of rituals, and even a prayer, to be repeated "whilst placing the hand in succession on the three chief organs of love, of order, and of progress."[30] Flaubert's Homais, with his absurd devotion to science, is often seen as a caricature; this, however, is only because those on whom he was based, like Ernest Renan, were already caricatures of themselves.[31]

3

We could sum everything up by saying that in mid-nineteenth-century France, religion, science, and magic stood in a curious relationship to one another, as though in a circular relay race. Religion remained stubbornly tinged with magic; magic, for its part, became increasingly scientific; and science took on, for some at least, the appearance of a new religion. As a result, in performing his onstage "experiments," Robert-Houdin was simultaneously contributing to the disenchantment of the world—attempting, via the nonillusionistic aspects of his performance, to extirpate the residuum of superstition—and to its re-enchantment, both via wonder and via the nascent hope in science itself as a "motive for action."

Yet even this précis is not entirely accurate. What we should say, rather, is that when Robert-Houdin performed his experiments, he contributed to the re-enchantment of the world via the *illusion* of wonder and the *illusion* of science itself as a motive for action. For the "ether" in his bottle was, let us not forget, nothing more than air. To be sure, Robert-Houdin wafted the scent of ether across the theatre, and a *part* of the audience—the Renan type—must have taken the act for an actual experiment, just as a second part of the audience (children, Fiard-style clergymen, and dagger-wielding noblewomen) must have taken it for a palpable demonstration of diabolical dealings. But for every believer (in science or religion) there was a thoroughly urbane and disabused spectator, interested only in beating the magician by refusing to be duped; and for every cynic, lastly and most importantly, there was an "homme d'esprit," an individual who asked for nothing more than to be deceived by an artful prestidigitator. "The ordinary man," explained Robert-Houdin,

sees in conjuring tricks a challenge offered to his intelligence, and hence representations of sleight of hand become to him a combat in which he determines on conquering. . . . The clever man [*l'homme d'esprit*], on the contrary, when he visits a conjuring performance, only goes to enjoy the illusions, and, far from offering the performer the slightest obstacle, he is the first to aid him. The more he is deceived, the more he is pleased, for that is what he paid for.[32]

In other words, the capacity crucially required for the full appreciation of a magic show—that which separated the "ordinary man" from
the "homme d'esprit"—was, in Robert-Houdin's estimation, the capacity to let oneself be deceived, knowingly and willingly. (As would
be said about one of Robert-Houdin's immediate successors, "He de-
ludes the most watchful spectator, [even] as he lucidly explains, 'that is
how it is done.'")[33] Demon-hunting clerics and dagger-wielding noblewomen did not possess this capacity, since in their eyes magic was simply a reality; adherents to the religion of science did not possess it
either, since for them the miracle of *science* was real; and cynics lacked
it just as thoroughly, since, as they saw it, being deceived was the worst
imaginable fate. Only those who were beyond universal cynicism had
what it took to allow their world to be re-enchanted by Jean-Eugène
Robert-Houdin. Only those spectators who, with a mental agility equal
to his manual dexterity, were ready to don and doff their lucidity repeatedly throughout the show could respond appropriately to the
Ethereal Suspension—could respond, that is, by entertaining the conscious fantasy that science "can resolve for man the eternal problems
whose solution his nature imperiously demands," indeed that science
"can become a powerful motive for action." What Robert-Houdin required was, so to speak, an ethereal suspension of disbelief.[34]

Robert-Houdin sought out, and sought to create, such spectators not
just because they helped him (by actively contributing to the illusions)
but also because he felt able to help *them*. For his performances did not
merely require the capacity for simultaneous (or quasi-simultaneous)
conviction and distrust; they also offered the opportunity to *hone* that
state of mind, to reinforce an aptitude for detached credulity—that
very aptitude which would make it possible for everyday life to be re-
enchanted. In the Ethereal Suspension, Robert-Houdin provided his
audience with a *model for the construction of a belief system that recognizes
itself as illusory*; even science can be a religion, he seems to have been
hinting with a sly wink to those in the know, if you lucidly wish to believe it one.

Part Two: Stéphane Mallarmé

4

If, as I have suggested, Robert-Houdin viewed nineteenth-century
France as insufficiently enlightened, as being in need simultaneously

of magical demystification and of new, non-magical models for re-enchantment, then later developments surely proved him right. On January 3, 1893, nearly fifty years after Robert-Houdin first took to the stage, the *abbé* Joseph-Antoine Boullan died suddenly at the age of 68. What had been the cause of death? According to the medical establishment, Boullan had suffered a simple heart attack.[35] But according to some members of his sect, a splinter group of the decidedly unorthodox Church of Carmel,[36] foul play had been involved—indeed, metaphysical foul play. For only a few years earlier, the co-founder of the French Rosicrucians, Stanilas de Guaïta, had written to Boullan in threatening terms, condemning him to "death by the fluids" for misusing cabalistic rites.[37] So had de Guaïta murdered Boullan by magical means?

Some otherwise highly intelligent individuals believed that he had. In the pages of the *Gil Blas*, Jules Bois directly accused de Guaïta of having cast fatal spells on Boullan. "It is now an incontestable fact," wrote Bois; "the abbé Boullan, who has just died suddenly in Lyon, was struck down by invisible wrath and criminal hands armed with occult thunderbolts, with formidable and unknown forces." One day later, in the *Figaro*, Joris-Karl Huysmans came out in support of Bois, adding that the Rosicrucians were trying to kill him too (one can only speculate that his "pâte à exorcisme," a present from Boullan, had spared him the same fate). "They have done everything they could," said Huysmans, "to harm yours truly! Every evening, at the precise instant when I am about to fall asleep, I receive . . . how shall I say? . . . fluidic punches on my skull and on my face. I would like to think that I am quite simply the victim of false sensations that are purely objective and are caused by the extreme sensitivity of my nervous system; but I am inclined to think that it is well and truly a case of magic. The proof is that my cat, who for his part is hardly likely to be a hallucinator, is gripped by spasms in the same way and at the same time as me."[38]

In the light of such strong and public statements, and of the duels that ensued,[39] Stéphane Mallarmé decided that something needed to be said. Mallarmé was, after all, a friend of Huysmans: Duc Jean des Esseintes, protagonist of Huysmans's 1884 novel *A rebours*, ranked Mallarmé above all other living poets;[40] a year later, Mallarmé returned the favor by dedicating a poem to des Esseintes (kindly overlooking the latter's fictional status). Mallarmé's article for *The National Observer*, published on January 28, 1893, and titled "Magie," was not so friendly.

Here Mallarmé chided both Huysmans and Bois for continuing, at the very end of the nineteenth century, to believe in the medieval world of wizards and enchantments. He did, however, make a crucial concession to the lovers of magic. For while it is true that spells and sorcerers do not exist in the real world, he argued, still they are to be found in poetry, indeed they are the very source and essence of poetry. "I claim that between the old procedures and the Enchantment that poetry continues to be, there exists a secret equivalence," wrote Mallarmé;

> to evoke, in a deliberate obscurity, the unspoken object, by means of allusive words, never direct, reducing themselves to an even silence, constitutes an effort close to creation, one which gains plausibility by confining itself within the sphere of the idea. Now only the idea of an object is put in play by the Enchanter of Letters, with such aptness, to be sure, that it dazzles, in the eye's imagination. The verse, that incantatory stroke! Who among those who have followed thus far will deny me a similarity between the circle perpetually opened and closed by rhyme and the circles, in the grass, of the fairy or magician?[41]

Poetry, that is, resembles magic by setting up a protected space—in the case of poetry, that delimited by end rhymes—and by using it in order to create something out of nothing. The difference is that poetry evokes the *idea* of an object (presumably its essence, since ordinary language already evokes its concept), whereas magic ostensibly brings forth an *actual* object. Like an alchemical combination of solutions, a poem's words yield clear silence, with *Idée* as their by-product. Poetry thus remains what it has been since its origins: incantation. Poetry has the power to re-enchant the world.

Most of us would presumably agree with Mallarmé in denying the existence of actual magic and insisting on a diagnosis of natural causes for the ill-fated Boullan. But what of the claims about poetry? What would it mean, exactly, for poetry to be magical? If poetry were to re-enchant the world, it could surely not do so by *communicating* something: in a disenchanted world, enchantment could have nothing to do with knowledge. A redemptive poetry would have not to *say* something but to *do* something, to do by saying. Or rather, it would have to permit *us* to do something by its means, just as books of spells permit their users to transform friends into gods, and foes into frogs. And in that case it would have to say something after all—namely, what the spell is, what it is for, and how it is to be used. Redemptive poetry would, then, be an effective spell, *complete with instructions for its use.*

5

Mallarmé's most famous sonnet is, I wish to argue, just such a spell.

Ses purs ongles très haut dédiant leur onyx,
L'Angoisse, ce minuit, soutient, lampadophore,
Maint rêve vespéral brûlé par le Phénix
Que ne recueille pas de cinéraire amphore

Sur les crédences, au salon vide: nul ptyx,
Aboli bibelot d'inanité sonore,
(Car le Maître est allé puiser des pleurs au Styx
Avec ce seul objet dont le Néant s'honore).

Mais proche la croisée au nord vacante, un or
Agonise selon peut-être le décor
Des licornes ruant du feu contre une nixe,

Elle, défunte nue en le miroir, encor
Que, dans l'oubli fermé par le cadre, se fixe
De scintillations sitôt le septuor.

Her pure nails very high dedicating their onyx,
Anguish, this midnight, upholds, a lamp-carrier,
Many an evening dream burned by the Phoenix
And gathered by no funereal urn

On the credenzas, in the empty room: no ptyx,
Eradicated knicknack of sonorous inanity,
(For the Master is gone to draw tears from the Styx
With that sole object in which Nothingness takes pride).

But near the vacant window to the north, something gold
Twists in agony according perhaps to the décor
Of unicorns hurling fire against a nixie,

Her, the naked corpse in the mirror, while, in the
Forgetfulness enclosed by the window, immediately
The septet of scintillations fixes itself.

Let us begin by trying to understand what is going on in these four-teen lines. (I must here crave the patience of readers unfamiliar with Mallarmé, assure them that perplexity is the natural initial state, and promise them that the gains will reward their investment.) At first, second, and third glance, Mallarmé's midnight sonnet appears irreme-diably (and notoriously) opaque: submerged beneath a torrent of scin-tillating, cadenced, harmonious phonemes, we hear plenty, see nothing, and understand still less. The speaker must know where (and when)

we are, and pretends to assume that we do too, since he deploys, perhaps exasperatingly, any number of definite articles and demonstrative
adjectives—*the* Master, *the* room, *this* midnight, *that* object—but the result is, if anything, an even greater sense of confusion. The actors in
the drama are in the main mythical or semi-mythical figures (the unicorns, the nymph), some of which even command a capital letter (the
Phoenix, the Master, Anguish, Nothingness). And the background consists in part of objects that do not exist (no amphora, no "ptyx") and in
part also of objects whose connection to elements in the real world is
uncertain (the "ptyx" again, the "something gold" [*un or*], the "forgetfulness" [*oubli*]). Gradually, however, our eyes grow accustomed to the
darkness, as one or two objects begin to detach themselves from the
void. We receive with gratitude a handful of concrete, present, everyday nouns dispensed from the second stanza onward, reassuring fragments of a tangible scene, stable landmarks by which we may hope to
find our way.

    We can see, at least, that we are in a room ("[le] salon," l.5). We can
also see that the room, otherwise empty ("vide," l.5), contains three
things, (1) tables ("les crédences"), (2) a mirror ("le miroir"), and (3) a
window ("la croisée"). (See lines 5, 12, and 9, respectively.) And then,
as illumination spreads over the scene, it transpires that each of these
objects is the site of further entities, this time more ethereal, whether
vanished, hallucinatory, or intangible. The tables once housed a *ptyx*
(whatever a *ptyx* is: we sense we will have to suspend that question for
the time being); the mirror seems to contain the image of a dead nymph
("nixe," l.11), murdered by unicorns, as in a medieval legend; and a
septet of scintillations is suddenly forming within the frame of the window ("le cadre," l.13). Since it is midnight—this may be the only piece
of solid information retained from stanza one—we may reasonably assume that the scintillations are stars, and that the septet is a constellation. And since the nymph is in a mirror, we may even speculate that
she is the reflection of something, presumably of these very stars, there
being no other source of light.

    If we make it thus far, we have arrived at Mallarmé's own synopsis
of the "subject" of his poem: "An open night window, . . . no furniture,
except the plausible outline of vague consoles, the warlike and dying
frame of a mirror hung in the back, with its reflection, stellar and incomprehensible, of the Great Bear, linking this dwelling, abandoned
by the world, only to the sky."[42] And we may be emboldened enough
to return to the enigmatic opening stanza, still relying on our spatial

sense alone. We may not know *what* the nails of Anguish are, but we can tell *where* they are, namely "very high" ("très haut," l.1). We may thus begin to perceive a gradual downward movement in the first part of the poem, from a point of maximal elevation to the depths of Hades via the intervening empty room; and a counterbalancing movement back up in the second part of the poem, from Hades (implicitly) to the room and thence up to the stars, to the shimmering septet of scintillations. And we may begin to conclude, quite reasonably, that the fingernails are not merely as high as the stars but *identical with* the stars; the pure nails of Anguish in the first line *are* the gleams that appear in the mirror of the final line. *Ses purs ongles très haut* and *le septuor,* so closely related in sound, turn out to be one and the same.[43]

And just as the downward spatial movement of the first half is counterbalanced by the upward movement of the second half, so too, we notice, the *temporal* structure presents us with a pair of mirror images. The quatrains begin at midnight, before flashing back to evening dreams ("maint rêve vespéral," l.3); the tercets, for their part, open with empty skies ("croisée . . . *vacante,*" l.9) and conclude with the sudden emergence of a constellation. (This, indeed, is the force of the word "immediately" [*sitôt,* l.14]: our attention is drawn to the fact that the appearance of the stars is an *event.*) On either side of the Master's removal from the room, which occupies the very center of the poem (lines 7–8), we perceive a pair of parallel events given in opposite spatial, temporal, and indeed evaluative order, like two panels of an almost symmetrical diptych.[44] To the left, a constellation preceded by an anguishing death by fire; to the right, an agonizing death by fire followed triumphantly by stars.[45]

6

If, then, we wish to find an allegorical meaning in the sonnet—and all the capitalized nouns are loudly urging us to do so, albeit only as a temporary measure, as a stepping-stone toward an overall appreciation of the poem—we must clearly start here, from this twice-told tale: *a nymph dies in fire, and a constellation is born.* The flavor is clearly Ovidian, and there may in fact be a direct, if partial, allusion here to the story of Callisto, a beautiful nymph turned by Jupiter into the constellation Ursa Major, after having been changed into a bear by a jealous Juno[46] (this would account for the stars appearing *immediately* following the death of the nymph [l.14], and for them appearing in a *North*-facing window [l.9]).[47] But since Mallarmé's incinerated *nixe* is the counterpart of the incinerated *rêve* in the first panel of the diptych, we should rewrite the story as follows: a *dream* dies and a constellation is born.

We can go further. Based on the contrastive "encor que" (ll.12–13) in the second half of the poem—unicorns kill the nixie, *yet* the constellation appears—and based on the dual action of Anguish in the first half, literally holding up stars and figuratively upholding murdered fantasies, we can infer that the constellation does not only follow but somehow *replaces* the dream. And the poem is generous enough to offer us, at strategic intervals throughout the first three stanzas, further indications as to how to understand the latter. For the tables are not just tables, or "consoles" as they were in the 1868 version, but *crédences*, connoting faith; the windows are no mere *fenêtres*, but instead cruciform *croisées*;[48] each lost dream is a *rêve vespéral* (as in vespers), not just a *rêve du soir*; Anguish is not just holding up its nails but, like a lamp carrier in a sacred ritual ("lampadophore"), *dedicating* ("dédiant") them to the night. And so we should rewrite again: what the constellation replaces is *religious* faith, faith in what Mallarmé, in a famous letter describing an epiphanic night one year before writing the first version of the sonnet, called "that old and nefarious plumage, fortunately floored, God."[49]

If a constellation is capable of replacing religious faith, this is because a constellation is more than simply a collection of stars. It is a set arbitrarily carved out from among the dense cluster on view, deemed to belong with each other and not with the rest; a set, furthermore, on which a *shape*—perhaps even a meaning of sorts—has been imposed, by a doubly bold act of human intervention into the nonhuman world.[50] What before was chaos now comes forth as order; where contingency reigned, now there is a certain internal necessity, as each point of light has to be just where it is for the posited shape to hold. The constellation confers upon each of its members a raison d'être, and all by an act of human will. Unlike the theological *kosmos* it replaces, then, a constellation is *an ordering which tacitly admits its own arbitrariness*.

Once we recognize this, we can see that the poem is a three-act drama of enchantment, disenchantment, and re-enchantment:[51] evening faith in an external source of transcendence, in a suprahuman source capable of delivering an oracular message that would make sense of everything; the death of such dreams, as sunset gives way to darkness; and the emergence of a new, secular, minor-key hope, a principle at least of organization and necessity, even if meaning has been lost.[52]

Like Nietzsche, Mallarmé leaves us with the hope that "one can endure to live in a meaningless world because one organizes a small portion of it oneself" (*Will to Power* 585A).

7

As I suggested earlier, however, merely to *say* this would not be to reenchant the world. Mallarmé's poem must also *do* what it says, *enact* the organization of which it speaks. It must, in fact, live up to its earlier title, "Sonnet allégorique de lui-même" ("Sonnet allegorical of itself"),[53] by working a spell and, at the same time, indicating how the spell operates, showing where to look in order to see the results of its magic. And this, it turns out, is exactly what the poem does. It is indeed its own allegory—not just an allegory of poetry in general, nor yet an allegory of Mallarméan poetry, but an allegory of *itself*—in that its surface stands for its depth, which is to say, in that its visible drama stands for what the poem is quietly doing behind the scenes. For just as the visible drama presents the demise of old forms of enchantment (superseded evening dreams, archaic spirits) and their replacement by newly forged patterns, so too the action of the poem operates by preliminary destruction of the reader's expected expectations and subsequent compensation in the shape of immaculate formal perfection. Everything inessential is removed: no funereal urn; no furniture (other than *crédences*) in the "empty room"; no ptyx; no clothing on the nymph; nothing in the "vacant" window;[54] not even the Master of the house, figure presumably for the poet. The Master has left the room, and left it, what is more, in order to fetch water from the Styx, principle of Nothingness ("Néant"), as though further destruction may be on its way.

It is not that the poet is *entirely* absent, as some critics have suggested.[55] Mallarmé's oft-quoted statement to the effect that "the pure work implies the elocutory disappearance of the poet, who cedes the initiative to words"[56] is actually somewhat misleading. The poet's presence is in fact directly on show here, in the telltale qualifier "perhaps" (*peut-être*, l. 10): clearly *someone* is looking at this scene, *otherwise there would be no one to doubt what is being witnessed.*[57] More importantly, the words are not simply allowed free rein, to generate infinite connections, all equally arbitrary, among themselves.[58] On the contrary, the poet's control over structure is, as we are about to see, so vice-like in its grip as to be felt on every line. What is missing is not the poet per se, but the individual *personality* of the poet. Nothing here about his private life, as we might expect from a sonnet. No mention of love affairs, either celebrated or mourned. Nothing even about his struggles as a writer, whatever a second line of interpretation might suggest.[59] Not so much as a first-person pronoun, in contrast to the other three *Plusieurs sonnets*.[60] The poet has become, as Mallarmé would say, impersonal: "I am now impersonal, and no longer the Stéphane you have known,—but a capacity the Spiritual universe has for looking at itself and developing itself, through that which was me."[61]

If there is a subject here, it is something like the transcendental subject, not reducible to any particular observer. Just as the tears well from the Styx rather than the Master's eye, so the anguish is not Mallarmé's in particular but capital "A" *Angoisse,* aspect of the human condition at large. We may come to the poem expecting it to yield insight into nature (what the night sky looks like, when poetically seen), into the poet's soul (what powerful emotions look like when they are "recollected in tranquillity"), or at the very least into the poet's mind (what the human condition looks like when filtered through the lens of genius). What we find instead is an impeccable structure enclosing almost nothing, "an empty sonnet, reflecting itself in every way":[62] no divine voice from beyond the poem, just a man-made principle of order imposed upon chaos.

8

And man-made order is absolutely ubiquitous. We have already seen how the events in the poem find themselves neatly mirrored from one panel to the other. But the highly unusual rhyme scheme forms its own brace of mirror images, again preserving the pairing while reversing the polarity (the *-yx* rhymes become "feminine," the *-or* rhymes "masculine," in the second half of the poem).[63] The poem's visual dimension even motivates its overall form. It has to be a sonnet, so that it can contain twice seven lines—a quatrain plus a tercet set outside, in the realm of the real stars; a quatrain plus a tercet set inside, in the realm of the reflections—just as the scene it depicts shows us seven stars reflected in a mirror.[64]

Indeed everything, one wants to say, has its immovable place in this poem; everything is exactly what and where it has to be. The starlight *has* to precede darkness in the first half and follow it in the second; the tercets *must* begin low, the quatrains high. The tables, as we saw above, have to be *crédences*, the windows *croisées*, the fingernails *dedicated* to the night. The unicorns must be unicorns, rather than say griffons, because the unicorn is related to the real-life oryx, and "oryx" is the only possible combination of the poem's two ubiquitous rhymes.[65] So too the ptyx can be nothing else if it is to be a container and to rhyme as fully as possible with Styx (as well, presumably, as summoning to religious minds the *pyx*, container for the eucharist).[66] And then, the second line of the quatrains calls to mind the second line of the tercets—not only is "agonise" a near-anagram of "Angoisse," but each is followed by the identical phoneme [s ə]—just as the third calls to mind the third, "feu . . . nixe" almost bringing a departed "Phénix" back to life.[67]

This general principle of overdetermination builds, as it happens, to a stunning climax. The poem's concluding clause—"se fixe/de scintillations sitôt le septuor" (literally, "there fixes itself of scintillations immediately the septet")—is tortured by hyperbaton, that is, by rearrangement of the normal syntactic order, with the express purpose of keeping *scintillations* before *sitôt* and *sitôt* before *septuor*. For only in this way will the last two lines count out, almost subliminally, the appearance of seven stars in the sky: *cadre* (quatre), *scin*tillations (cinq), *sit*ôt (six), *sept*uor (sept).[68] By the time we reach the final word, we are more than prepared for it. We know, of course, that it has to rhyme in "*-or.*" We know that it must point again to the constellation of stars evoked in line one; and it makes sense for the constellation to have seven stars, in part because of the Callisto allusion, in part because only a reflected constellation of seven stars can stand, allegorically, for a sonnet. But then *septuor* is itself a word of seven letters, indeed of seven *distinct* letters; as septet, it connotes music, another man-made form indifferent to content, and thus picks up on the sonorous vacuity of the abolished ptyx; and then, it sends us all the way back to the beginning, since every last phoneme of *le septuor* is contained within those of *ses purs ongles très haut.*[69] No other word would do anywhere near as well.

In all these cases, a word ends up (at least) doubly motivated, finding itself at the point of contact between two (or more) intersecting lines. As though each term were the solution to a cryptic crossword clue,[70] we know it is right—we know it is the only possible choice—not only because its meaning is appropriate but also because its phonetic substance fits. Every single piece of the Mallarméan world acquires an aura of indispensability, almost inevitability, not because it captures adequately some mystical truth about the world, or some emotive truth about the poet,[71] but because it *is the only logical outcome of a self-imposed puzzle.* It gains legitimacy by virtue of its place within the poetic system, not just by virtue of what it points to outside it; each piece, as Proust would put it, receives its raison d'être from all the others.[72]

9

In other words, the poem forms a magic circle from within which all contingency is banished. That is what Mallarmé means, in "Magie," when he speaks synecdochically of the magic circle opened and closed by rhyme: if the first rhyme word appears random ("opening" the circle), the second becomes necessary ("closing" it), and—strikingly— *ends up imparting a type of retrospective necessity to the first.* There is, a priori, no reason why Mallarmé should use the word *onyx* rather than, say, *opale* at the end of line one, but once *onyx* is in place, *Phénix* makes sense, *Styx* appears obvious, and *ptyx* itself somehow feels as though it belongs, even before we know what, if anything, it means. (It is almost as though, in Mallarmé's famous and disingenuous remark, the word had been generated *ex nihilo* "by the magic of rhyme.")[73] But then in turn *Styx, ptyx,* and *Phénix* force us, on rereading the poem, to accept *onyx* as the sole and only possible choice of initial rhyme. Rhyme, as Mallarmé puts it, repudiates chance.

And rhyme, though of primordial importance for Mallarmé, who often knew the ends of his lines before he knew anything else, is synecdochic for aesthetic practice more generally. Literature at large is nothing other than the relentless elimination of chance, the construction of a protected space over which randomness has no hold. The real world is full of haphazard, happenstance objects, people, and events; the created world, by contrast, is one in which everything has a necessary place. And ordinary *language* is made up of haphazard, happenstance *words,* whose connection to ideas is in every case contingent—"next to *ombre* [shadow]," Mallarmé famously complains, "*ténèbres* [darkness] isn't very dark; what disappointment in the face of the perversity that confers on *jour* [day] and *nuit* [night], contradictorily, a sombre tone for the one, a bright for the other!"[74]—whereas poetic language is made up of *lines,* units designed precisely to compensate for this insufficiency. The line of verse, a "total word, new, outside of language, almost incantatory," overcomes the contingency inherent in the separate terms;[75] in verse, things are what they are, and where they are, for a reason. Thus Mallarmé's sonnet does not merely *speak* of constellations; it *is* a constellation, a man-made imposition of order onto an unruly universe. To immerse oneself in *Ses purs ongles* is, for a space, to breathe a different, and purer, air.

To put it another way, to immerse oneself in *Ses purs ongles* is to live, for the first time, in a world of silence. In the ideal poem, we recall, "allusive words, never direct, reduc[e] themselves to an even silence." For, paradoxical as it may sound, silence is never a given; silence is, instead, always to be *created*. While there is, admittedly, such a thing as a stillness that precedes poetry, this stillness is full of virtual noise, of arbitrary speculations and competing hypotheses. After poetry, by contrast, "chance having been defeated word by word, without fail the white space returns, gratuitous a moment ago, certain now, in order to conclude that nothing [lies] beyond and to authenticate the silence."[76] The Stygian silence that follows poetry is authentic, unlike the uneasy peace preceding it, because the former has been produced by a form of speech that expressly targets noise, cancelling it out. Chance must be defeated word by word. Music, which might at first appear to have the edge over poetry, since from start to end it is purely abstract, reveals itself to be poetry's inferior for precisely the same reason. Content cannot simply be avoided; it must be *destroyed*. Just as we can only reach an idea of nothingness by continually imagining objects and then their absence[77]—which is exactly what happens when we are presented with the nonexistent amphora and the nonexistent *ptyx*—so too all false hopes, all evening dreams, all personal feelings must be summoned in order to be eliminated one by one, leaving just silence, white space, and absolute order.

10

Does this count, however, as a genuine re-enchantment of the world? It could easily be argued that *replacing* the world is hardly the same as re-enchanting it. Quite the contrary, it might seem that we are being offered a mere *evasion* from the world, a refuge within a cosmos that is perfectly ordered but that does not exist. Perhaps poetry leaves the world itself just as it is; perhaps the latter's inadequacies become, if anything, all the more glaring as a result of our immersion in an ideal environment. (This is, after all, Nietzsche's verdict on all two-world systems.) Wherein would reside the superiority of such escapism over earlier forms of illusory enchantment?

The answer is, first of all, that the sonnet does more than produce an alternative world. It provides, at the same time, a set of implicit instructions as to how to bring aesthetic ordering techniques to bear on the *real* one. The sonnet does not offer itself as a lesson on the truth of existence—does not seek to teach us that, say, God is dead—but offers itself, instead, as a potential *formal model* for emulation. Rather than gaining a set of *facts* about human life, we stand to learn a *method* for coming to terms with them, a method for projecting a network of connections onto the raw data of experience. ("Things exist, we do not have to create them; we have only to seize the connections among them," writes Mallarmé, "and it is the threads of these connections that form verses and orchestras.")[78] Our engagement with a microcosm in which connections are drawn as tightly as they can possibly be is, if we wish it to be, a *training* for re-engagement with the macrocosm, for an engagement in which we ourselves can find and invent connections, forging a world which, *even though each of its elements remains untouched,* suddenly acquires order, and thus suddenly becomes livable.[79] We should, in other words, understand Mallarmé's entire project of overdetermination as a figure for the importation of apparent necessity into objects and events in the extrapoetic universe; if, like Mallarmé, we experience "a rather cabalistic sensation"[80] on repeating the poem to ourselves, it is not just by virtue of being transported to another realm. The spell works, if we wish it to, on ours as well.

What is more, there is something *sublime,* in the Kantian sense, about the experience of *Ses purs ongles.* In the space of a mere fourteen lines, comprising exactly one hundred words, Mallarmé has set up a network of such complexity that it feels almost impossible for any reader to hold all of its filaments in his or her head at once—let alone for any *writer* to have deliberately *produced* them.[81] We are overwhelmed by the cosmic magnitude of this tiny poem. And the author-figure we are forced to postulate in order to account for all its effects is something more than human, something more than the empirical Stéphane Mallarmé, burning the midnight oil in Tournon. Our universe is enriched by contact with an intelligence of a different order from ours.

11

We should not forget, however, that Mallarmé has promised more than just this for his poetic magic. Out from the silence of absolute necessity, against the background of constructed darkness, something luminous and musical is supposed to emerge, something which Mallarmé, in the article on Magic, calls the idea of an object.[82] Like the constellation, it shimmers ("scintille") before our credulous gaze. And indeed, something more than order attaches to Ursa Minor after we have made *Ses purs ongles* our own. From now on, we will see it differently: no longer as a collection of bright objects in the night sky, but as the symbol for poetic hope, for the capacity of the human imagination to re-enchant the world by giving it an order of our own making. The constellation turns, so to speak, into the symbol of symbolism; the stars, having already been granted structure, now acquire a *meaning* into the bargain. Mallarméan poetry becomes a formal model for the imposition not just of form but of *idea.*

Perhaps we will even start to imagine these stars sending such signals on their own initiative, fixing *themselves* in the mirror (the middle voice of l. 13), as though they really did incarnate the nymph Callisto. Perhaps, in other words, we will begin to believe, animistically, that enchantment is something we may discover in the world around us, not something we are required to create. This, as the *Magie* passage clearly indicates, would of course be an illusion ("cela scintille, à *l'illusion* du regard"). Yet it would be an illusion that one could sustain *even in the face of the knowledge that it is one.*[83] And that brings us to the final, and most important, function of Mallarmé's poem, the function which requires us at last to address the enigmatic *ptyx.*

What exactly *is* a ptyx? The question has been hotly debated,[84] in a way and to an extent that is frankly baffling. For Mallarmé makes it quite plain, in "Le Mystère dans les Lettres," that obscure lyrical works must be ultimately intelligible, and that the guarantee of intelligibility is *syntax.*[85] And the syntax around *ptyx* is, in fact, rather indicative. From the conjunction in line 7 ("car") and the demonstrative adjective in line 8 ("ce"), we can be absolutely sure that the ptyx is identical with the object used to draw water from the Styx. Whatever it is, then, it must be capable of holding water (which would rather rule out Graham Robb's "writing tablet").[86] But we can also tell that its absence is logically linked to the absence of funereal urns; the lack of urns and the lack of ptyx are, after all, connected by a colon ("gathered by no funereal urn . . . : no ptyx"). It is not just that there is no urn *and* no ptyx, as it would be if the two were separated by a semicolon. Instead, it is that ptyxlessness *explains* urnlessness. And this can happen only if the two are identical. No urns *because* no ptyx: ptyx, in this poem at least, is simply a synonym for urn.[87] Syntax guarantees intelligibility; the context of the poem is, and is designed to be, sufficient, without recourse to any sophisticated Greek lexicon.

We are left, in short, with a word which has a clear meaning, *but one given entirely by the surrounding context*. And stranger things are to follow:

Sur les crédences, au salon vide:	On the credenzas, in the
nul ptyx,	empty room: no ptyx,
Aboli bibelot d'inanité sonore	Eradicated knicknack of
	sonorous inanity

An extraordinary set of shifts takes place here within the space of twelve words, shifts not in plot or even in meaning but in *the way the poem is to be read*, shifts not in *what* words mean but in *how* they mean, indeed in *whether* their function is to mean at all. The stanza begins reassuringly, with solid, familiar, and present objects (credenzas). But this referential use of language gives way to what we might call an *anti*-referential use of language: *nul ptyx*, two words whose effect is at once to summon and to eradicate the same mental representation. And from there we move, even more daringly, to what is almost a *non*-referential use of language: the assonance in "aboli bibelot" is so rich, it is barely possible to hear a meaning underneath the flow of sounds. "Aboli bibelot" is practically nonsense poetry; to be sure, it can be understood, but what it says is redundant (we already know the ptyx is not there), and its powerful harmonies simply drown out sense.

Nor do we stop here. Instead we end up in a *self*-referential use of language. It is not the *object* ptyx that is of "sonorous inanity"; it is instead the *word* "ptyx," a word which functions semantically as a placeholder, but which fits the rhyme scheme perfectly.[88] Or perhaps it is the phrase "aboli bibelot" which is sonorously inane, for reasons we have just given; perhaps the second half of line 6 refers to nothing other than the first half of line 6. Either way, reference to the external world is suspended. And our attention is divided: we imagine perceiving real objects; we imagine perceiving the absence of objects; we hear the musicality of consonant phonemes; and we catch the poem in the act of producing those phonemes. Our oscillation between states—an oscillation continually repeated as the poem forces us to reread it multiple times—is, if we use the spell correctly, a training in the two skills that make life bearable: generating fictions, and persuading ourselves that they are true.

Postscript: The Birth of Modernism from
the Spirit of Re-Enchantment

The ultimate function of Mallarmé's poetry is, then, identical to that of
Robert-Houdin's magic performances: to offer us an opportunity to
hone our innate capacity for lucid self-delusion. For Mallarmé, there is
nothing beyond the world we know—"certes, n'est que ce qui est" ("to
be sure, there is only what is")—yet at the same time no escape from
the need to believe that there is something more.[89] We human beings
require illusions in order to live, and the only dignity left us is the capacity to choose our own illusions, and to acknowledge them for what
they are. "Yes, I know," wrote Mallarmé to Cazalis,

> we are but vain forms of matter, but quite sublime for having invented God
> and our soul. So sublime, my friend! that I wish to offer myself this spectacle
> of matter, conscious of being and yet frenetically throwing itself into the Dream
> that it is able *not* to be, singing the Soul and all those similar divine impres-
> sions which have accumulated in us since the dawn of time and proclaiming,
> before the Nothing that is the truth, these glorious lies![90]

We are back, once again, in the three-part drama of re-enchantment.
We began with belief in the "divine impressions" accumulated over
the millenia of early human history; we had a moment of insight, suddenly seizing the truth in ourselves ("vain forms of matter") and the
world around us ("Nothing"); finally, however, we rejected even this
rejection, understanding that the illusion is evidence not just of our
credulity but also of our *creativity*,[91] that God and the soul are therefore not just lies but *glorious* lies, and lies—most important of all—of
which we can and should be *conscious*, even as we believe in them. Mallarmé's key intuition is that a maximally constructed, maximally self-
conscious poetry is the ideal site for spiritual exercises in this domain.
It is by reading such writings, by spending time in their world, that we
may hope to develop the capacities we have for seeing our own world
as orderly, while taking a distance, at the same time, from any given
structure we impose.

One of the defining features of modernist (including "postmodernist")
literature is its tendency towards "reflexivity," towards the establishment and simultaneous undermining of referential illusion,[92] in comic
and non-comic genres alike. Thus James Joyce, after giving very believable life to Molly Bloom, has her beseech him in the middle of her
monologue "O Jamesy let me up out of this" (*Ulysses* 769); Marcel

Proust constructs an extraordinarily elaborate fictional world, only to let a narratorial voice announce that "everything has been invented by me in accordance with the requirements of my theme [*ma démonstration*]" (*Time Regained* 225); on the first page of Gide's *Paludes*, the narrator blithely mentions that he happens to be writing a novel called *Paludes*; M. C. Escher depicts a pair of hands, each impossibly drawn by the other; close to the conclusion of Samuel Beckett's tragedy *Endgame*, Hamm announces "I'm warming up for my last soliloquy" (78); Eugène Ionesco's king, in *Le Roi se meurt*, is told he will die "at the end of the play"; Bertolt Brecht's actors deliberately show that they are actors, rather than attempting to disappear behind the characters they are playing; Italo Calvino's novel *If on a winter's night a traveler* begins "You are about to begin reading Italo Calvino's new novel, *If on a winter's night a traveler*"; and so on, and so on.[93] Serious, representation-undermining self-reflexivity, which until then had been something of a rarity (the German Romantics had theorized it, but few major works instantiated it in recognizable ways),[94] now becomes the dominant literary mode.[95]

But why? So far three main theories have been advanced, which I shall call the *symptomatic,* the *strategic,* and the *informative* hypotheses. According to the symptomatic hypothesis, reflexivity in modernist literature is simply a sign of authorial self-doubt (Furst 1988:308), itself in turn an index of a more general cultural tendency toward self-consciousness: when subjects of knowledge become increasingly aware of their own activity as knowers, as well as of the objects known, it is inevitable (so the symptomatic account runs) that literary artifacts should be infected with the same disease.[96] On the strategic view, by contrast, reflexivity is something deliberately, not unconsciously, deployed by writers, and something deployed precisely as a strategy for *bypassing* the critical spirit of the age. Legitimately anticipating skepticism on the part of the average reader, authors permit themselves a moment of pathos by pre-emptively ironizing it, or at least by ironizing almost everything else. Only one who, like Proust's narrator, has treated love and friendship with the utmost suspicion has the right to move us by recounting the death of his grandmother.[97] For we no longer trust naïve, spontaneous outbursts of enthusiasm; what we trust is, instead, the passion of a cynic.

In a second variant of the strategic approach, self-reflexivity is seen as a way of *controlling* the critical spirit. Consider the predicament of Denis Diderot, author of *Jacques le fataliste,* one of the most reflexive works of the eighteenth century (rivalled perhaps only by its forebear, *Tristram Shandy*). There is a voice within Diderot that loudly pronounces free will to be an illusion, since humans are a part of nature, and nature ruled by iron laws of cause and effect. Another voice, however, just as firmly maintains that this cannot (and had better not) be true. The result: "I fume at being entangled in a devilish philosophy that my mind cannot keep from approving and my heart from denying."[98] Who, then, actually speaks for the conflicted Diderot in *Jacques*? Is it the fatalist title character? The latter's voluntarist master? Or the narrator, who repeatedly insists on his freedom to tell whatever story he likes? The answer is that it cannot be any of them—not least because none of them even speaks (unequivocally) for himself: the ostensibly fatalist Jacques is incapable of sticking to his beliefs, the ostensibly voluntarist master behaves like an automaton, and the ostensibly freewheeling narrator is fully controlled by Diderot. On the contrary, the novel as a whole is what enables Diderot precisely *not* to take a stand, to identify himself neither with the cynical voice within him that declares all action to be determined in advance nor with the credulous voice that proclaims a continuing faith in the *libre arbitre*, but instead with the observer who coolly and amusedly registers the internal debate. In cases of intractable inner conflict, when it is impossible to synthesize both positions and just as impossible to jettison either, the choice is only between denial and an ironic ascent to Olympian detachment; Romantic irony is the only road to equanimity.[99]

It is also, to draw on the third and final variant of the strategic view, a path to freedom. Not just freedom from inner division, and not just freedom from excessive emotion, but freedom from everything that we are and everything we have been. "We must rise above what we love and be able to destroy in our thoughts what we adore," writes Friedrich Schlegel, for "whatever does not annihilate itself is not free."[100] Why? Because freedom, when understood as Gidean *disponibilité*—the capacity to do anything at any time—requires a thoroughgoing unmooring of commitments. If I am to be completely *disponible*, it is not enough for me to stand clear of my attachments to religion, family, state, and community: I must also stand clear of my own most cherished achievements, beliefs, and capacities. I must, in short, attain freedom from *myself*. And thus Romantic irony, as a disparagement of the very work to which so much energy and love is being devoted, becomes, in some hands, a strategy for liberation.

In spite of the power of the strategic hypothesis in its three variants, the most prominent hypothesis today is no doubt the informative, which holds that the function of modernist reflexivity is to *tell us something*. Thus Malcolm Bradbury and James McFarlane, in their authoritative book on Modernism, define the latter as "a new era of high aesthetic self-consciousness and non-representationalism, in which art turns from realism and humanistic representation towards style, technique, and spatial form *in pursuit of a deeper penetration of life*."[101] In other words, reflexivity permits the discovery, and subsequent transmission, of something that had not been seen before. And that something is usually taken to be what Astradur Eysteinsson calls "the social 'fabrication' of reality,"[102] or what Patricia Waugh calls the "fictionality of the world." As Waugh puts it, self-reflexive works "explore the possible fictionality of the world outside the literary fictional text"; "in showing us how literary fiction creates its imaginary worlds, metafiction helps us to understand how the reality we live day by day is similarly constructed."[103] Just as we allow ourselves to believe in the existence of Pip, Estella, and Magwitch while reading *Great Expectations,* so we allow ourselves to believe in the existence of our life and everything it contains. A self-reflexive text like *Paludes,* on the other hand, continually reminds us that it is made up—and asks us to see that the same is true outside the novel.[104]

Stéphane Mallarmé would, it seems to me, reject the premise that the world is a fiction. "Les choses existent" ("things exist"), he is entirely happy to acknowledge. For him as for Nietzsche, the problem with life is, if anything, precisely the opposite: reality is *all too real*; deadly truths are all too easy to come by. What we need in response is not a mechanism for seeing through illusions but, quite the contrary, a technique for producing and sustaining them. And it is this technique, as I have argued, that readers stand to practice when they engage with Mallarmé's writings. These writings undermine the referential illusion they set up not because they reflect, willy-nilly, a tide of self-doubt, and certainly not because they have something important to tell us about the "fictionality of the world"; they do not even have as their primary function the removal of Mallarmé from his own inner divisions, however powerful a by-product this may be. No, the explanation for Mallarméan reflexivity does not reside in the informative hypothesis, or in the symptomatic, or in the strategic. Rather, Mallarméan reflexivity must be understood as *formative,* as designed to offer practice in an increasingly vital skill. It is no coincidence that aesthetic self-consciousness becomes dominant just when philosophy begins to recognize the inescapability of "necessary illusions" (Nietzsche, Vaihinger, and company); works like *Ses purs ongles,* performances like that of Robert-Houdin, and all of their poetic, novelistic, and dramatic relatives are *training grounds for lucid self-delusion,* for the tenacious maintenance of fantasy in the face of the facts. They are what makes possible the re-enchantment of the world.[105]

Appendix: The 1868 Version

<table>
<tr><td>Sonnet
allégorique de lui-même</td><td>Sonnet
allegorical of itself</td></tr>
<tr><td>La Nuit approbatrice allume les onyx
De ses ongles au pur Crime, lampadophore,
Du Soir aboli par le vespéral Phoenix
De qui la cendre n'a de cinéraire amphore</td><td>The approving night lights up the onyx
Of its nails by the pure Crime, lamp-bearer,
Of the Night abolished by the evening Phoenix
Whose ash has no funereal urn</td></tr>
<tr><td>Sur des consoles, en le noir Salon : nul ptyx,
Insolite vaisseau d'inanité sonore,
Car le Maître est allé puiser de l'eau du Styx
Avec tous ses objets dont le Rêve s'honore.</td><td>On some tables, in the dark Room: no ptyx,
Curious vessel of sonorous inanity,
For the Master is gone to draw water from the Styx
With all his objects on which Dream takes pride.</td></tr>
<tr><td>Et selon la croisée au Nord vacante, un or
Néfaste incite pour son beau cadre une rixe
Faite d'un dieu que croit emporter une nixe</td><td>And to judge by the vacant window in the North, something gold
And baleful incites for its beautiful frame a brawl
Made by a god whom a nixie thinks she is carrying off</td></tr>
<tr><td>En l'obscurcissement de la glace, décor
De l'absence, sinon que sur la glace encor
De scintillations le septuor se fixe.</td><td>In the cloudiness of the mirror, decor
Of absence, except that on the mirror still
The septet of scintillations fixes itself.</td></tr>
</table>

CHAPTER 7

The Rocambolesque and the Modern Enchantment of Popular Fiction

ROBIN WALZ

AT THE DAWN OF THE TWENTIETH CENTURY, economic and social historian Max Weber lamented, "The fate of our times is characterized by rationalization and intellectualization and, above all, by the 'disenchantment of the world.'"[1] The accretion of capitalist economics, technological control, and social efficiency gained through bureaucratic administration and professional careers had, Weber believed, encased the contemporary world within an "iron cage of reality." Inhabiting a world without wonder, modern humans were psychically impoverished. By the end of the century, Weber's gloomy prognosis seemed common sense. As political and social philosopher Susan Buck-Morss has noted, it is "a shibboleth in social theory that the essence of modernity is the demythification and disenchantment of the social world."[2]

Yet Weber's prediction may have been more apocryphal than prophetic. In the realm of commercial mass culture, modernity has proliferated enchantments. The "magical" qualities of industrial commodities were noted as early as the mid-nineteenth century: Marx castigated them as fetishes, while Baudelaire celebrated such ephemera as one of the sources of modern aesthetics. In the early twentieth century, surrealists André Breton declared the omnipotence of the dream in modern life, and Louis Aragon discovered a modern mythology in the urban landscape of Paris. In recent decades, cultural theorists have rallied to Walter Benjamin as the major twentieth-century philosopher to combine Marxism, modernism, and surrealism towards the "remagicification" of the world. As Buck-Morss notes, Benjamin found that "under the conditions of capitalism, industrialization had brought about a *r*eenchantment of the social world, and through it, a 'reactivation of mythic powers.'"[3]

Still, ideology critique, modernist aesthetics, and surrealist practices are reserved for the intellectual elite, those who possess sufficient critical rigor and artistic creativity to stand above everyday reality and reconstruct its elements into superior forms. But what of modern enchantments for the ordinary person? A critical challenge for the cultural historian is to chart how the processes of modernity that yielded Weber's iron cage of reality have also generated new forms of enchantment for direct consumption by mass audiences, without the need for theorists or an avant-garde.

One of the modern enchantments to emerge from the industrial output of commercialized nineteenth-century popular fiction was the *rocambolesque*. The term is a French adjective of modern origin meaning "fantastic, incredible, resembling by its astonishing improbabilities the adventures of Rocambole."[4] The reference is to author Ponson du Terrail's criminal-turned-avenger protagonist, whose exploits constituted thousands of pages of adventures serialized in French newspapers, 1857–1870. The term *rocambolesque* remains current in France today and generally applies to any story filled with hyperbolic scenarios and fantastic elements. As articulated by *paralittérature* critic Jean-Luc Buard, "The 'Rocambole style' is a kind of quasi-automatic writing. It is hypnotic writing that continually achieves marvelous, impossible, and unreal proportions."[5] The rocambolesque is not just a description, but dynamic process that generates cultural meaning.

A prominent element at work in the rocambolesque is the *parodique*. In addition to actual parodies, literary and media critic Charles Grivel refers to rapid modes of literary reproduction as "parodic" when they generate confabulated stories. Through a pastiche of repetition and hyperbole, parodic stories yield an attenuated imitation of reality. To some degree, Grivel asserts, all texts are potentially parodic, but those that display an excess of hyperbole more readily lend themselves to a parodic reading, and he notes the Rocambole series as exemplary in this regard.[6] Ponson did not plot out and craft his novels so much as he rapidly copied and pasted them together from other works of fiction and *faits divers* (sensationalist newspaper accounts). According to the historical sociologist of media, Gabriel Thoveron:

He didn't invent anything; he copied. He copied everything, sentimental novels, horror novels, historical novels (they called him the "Alexandre Dumas of the Batignolles"), the *Mystères de Paris,* and more. He borrowed from everywhere—and could write as many as five novels at the same time, keeping track of each. Imagine the sources it took to keep that level of production afloat! He knocked off 10,000 pages a year, for twenty years; editing his "complete works" is inconceivable. His feuilletons were written from one day to the next, without a plan, and sometimes without coherence.[7]

Ponson employed a slapdash method of cultural production, and its industrial motor was fueled by the commercial demands of the marketplace. Although not intended as parody, Ponson's writing technique of indiscriminately copying from a wide variety of literary and newspaper sources, and then giving them his own hackneyed and hyperbolic imprint, rendered a popular oeuvre littered with parodic effects.

In addition, mass readership influenced Ponson's development of the Rocambole series. According to literary biographer and *argotier* (specialist in French slang) François Caradec, "The pastiche-author is not alone: The complicity of his readers is required in order to be believed."[8] Hastily constructed and voluminous, serials are padded with extraneous filler material, and it becomes the task of the reader to find the gems among stones. Further, multiple serials are available for consumption at any given moment, so the modern reader must negotiate the overabundance of serialized culture to develop a taste for a particular series. Given the parodic construction of serials, often that appeal is not based on veracity of the work, or its "literary" merit, but upon the reader's immediate connection to the attenuated aspects of the writing. That is, readers respond directly to the pastiche copy because its elements are both drawn out of and slightly differ from their own perceptions of normative reality.

What makes the rocambolesque a specifically modern enchantment is its historical emergence during an era of rapidly expanding capitalist and industrial modes of production and consumption. While it is not altogether incorrect to characterize the contemporary world as encased in an iron cage of reality, what Weber may not have fully considered are the ways in which new enchantments emerge from the same practices of modernization that have rationalized contemporary life. The rocambolesque serial epitomizes such an unleashing of fantastic sensibilities resulting from "industrial" literary production and its marketplace mass consumption. Rocambole did not spring from the pen of Ponson fully formed, but was conjured up by him in response to dual pressures exerted by newspaper publishers for increased sales on the one hand, and the preferences of a mass reading audience on the other.

Precisely because rocambolesque fiction is mass consumed, its enchantments invigorate the quotidian modern world. Its topsy-turvy delights do not oppose modernity, but unbridle its locked-up humor. As *paralittérature* ("para-literature"), the parodic structure of popular fiction runs parallel to normative reality while remaining slightly out of synch with it. Rocambolesque fiction pushes the play within this fissure to the extreme. From the start, disposed readers must be willing to make leaps of the imagination in order to enjoy such fiction. In turn, a mass readership leverages a rationalizing effect upon the publishing industry through the commercial demand for even more rocambolesque stories. In response, authors must continually adapt by producing even more astonishing, marvelous, and outrageous fiction to satisfy, yet never fully satiate, reader desires—"to be continued." With slight regard for established cultural hierarchies or conventions, the rocambolesque continually metamorphoses its fantastic pastiche of reality as mass consumption demands. The magic occurs between the bars of the iron cage.

> *Q:* Who or what is Rocambole?
> *A:* Rocambole is the son of Ponson du Terrail, who created and gave birth to Rocambole.
> *Q:* Why did Ponson du Terrail create and give birth to Rocambole?
> *A:* Ponson du Terrail created and gave birth to Rocambole to terrorize the dreams of readers, stupefy the affected population with shock treatment, and render watch guards total idiots.
> *Q:* Will Rocambole have an end?
> *A:* No, Rocambole will never come to an end.
> *Q:* Why won't Rocambole ever come to an end?
> *A:* Rocambole will never come to an end, because Ponson du Terrail doesn't want to bother with the dolts who wouldn't be able to live without Rocambole. [A. H., *Le Bonnet de coton* (4 August 1867)][9]

Although largely unknown today outside the francophone world, and within it primarily by those with antiquarian tastes, Pierre Alexis Ponson du Terrail was one of the most successful novelists of nineteenth-century France. A *feuilletoniste,* an author whose novels were published by installment in daily newspapers before being reissued as complete volumes, his most popular and enduring series featured Rocambole, a criminal-turned-avenger hero. The principal adventures of Rocambole traverse four serials—*Les Drames de Paris, Les Exploits de Rocambole, La Réssurection de Rocambole,* and *Le Dernier mot de Rocambole*—although he appears as a tertiary figure in three other series as well, *Les Chevaliers*

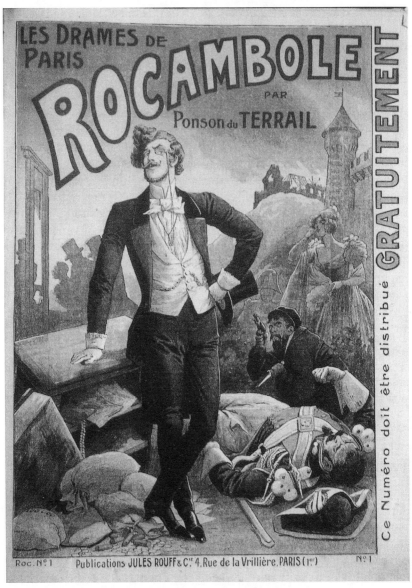

FIG. 7.1. *Les Drames de Paris: Rocambole.* Reissue feuilleton in 157 weekly installments. Cover by Kauffmann. Paris: Jules Rouff, 1883–1886. Courtesy of the Bibliothèque des Littératures Policières, Paris.

du clair de lune, Les Misères de Londres, and *Les Démolitions de Paris.* Concurrent with the Rocambole series, Ponson authored at least seventy-five additional feuilletons, rendering him by far the most prolific novelist of the French Second Empire.[10]

While biography provides a suspect key to interpretation, it is a good point of departure for there is a strong sympathy between the confabulations in Ponson's life and literary production.[11] Pierre Alexis Ferdinand Joseph de Ponson was born on July 8, 1829 into a family of parvenu aristocrats. The paternal side of the family bore military credentials, but Pierre Alexis identified with his maternal lineage, which claimed ancestral ties to the legendary sixteenth-century Pierre Terrail, Lord of Bayard and "knight without fear and above reproach." Pretensions to aristocratic grandeur hit a wall of reality, however, when he was refused admission to the Naval Academy of Marseille due to insufficient proof of his pedigree. Therefore, at age eighteen, Ponson abruptly changed his life direction and headed to Paris to become a writer. He arrived in the capital during the revolutionary days of June 1848, was immediately conscripted into the National Guard, and earned officer's rank for his participation in the suppression of the insurgency. After the end of hostilities, in 1849 publisher Alfred Nettement commissioned Ponson to write a serialized story for his legitimist newspaper, *L'Opinion Publique.* Ponson obliged with *La Vraie Icarie,* a politically reactionary rejoinder to Etienne Cabet's 1842 socialist utopia, *Voyage en Icarie.*

Ponson became a writer during an era of historical transition within the publishing industry, which transformed the feuilleton from a mode of middle-class consumption into a common denominator of mass-cultural literacy.[12] In the early nineteenth century, a gulf existed between the popular and elite presses; colporteurs peddled broadsides and *bibliothèque bleue* chapbooks to rural populations and the urban poor, while the urbane bourgeoisie purchased books (with bindery at an additional expense). Newspapers, at an annual subscription of 80 francs, were prohibitively expensive for the average Parisian worker in the first half of the nineteenth century, who earned about three francs a day (or 1,000 francs annually), or even for civil servants, whose annual salary was two to three times that amount. However, under the Restoration, fundamental changes in the distribution and consumption of printed material began to pave the way toward a mass reading audience. *Cabinets de lecture,* or subscription libraries, provided access to books, magazines, and newspapers to those who could not otherwise afford them, and in Paris their numbers rose sixfold between 1820 and 1840. Some journals began to specialize in compiling newspaper stories and serialized novels, beginning with *Le Voleur, gazette des journaux français et étrangers* in 1826. In 1836, two new newspapers, *Le Siècle* and *La Presse*, slashed their annual subscription rate in half to 40 francs and shortly thereafter began to sell individual issues at ten centimes. Over the next decade, Parisian newspaper sales more than doubled, from 80,000 to 180,000 issues daily.

A mass readership was finally achieved during the Second Empire of Napoleon III. While the population of France increased at less than 1 percent annually, the percentage of bookstores grew more than 50 percent, over 3,500 in total, mostly in commercially vibrant, metropolitan centers. The distribution of printed matter by colporteurs was sharply curtailed, and newspaper and magazine kiosks became ubiquitous upon the boulevards of Haussmann's Paris. Book publishers began to market directly to consumers, starting with Hachette's *Bibliothèque des Chemins de Fer* train station bookstalls in 1853. Weekly magazines, such as *Le Journal pour tous, Les bons romans,* and *Les Romans choisis,* began to publish feuilletons and short stories in compilations at prices as low as 10 centimes per issue. But it was through changes in the marketing of the daily newspaper, with its *rez-de-chaussée* (the horizontal column running across the bottom of the front page) daily installment of a feuilleton novel, that a mass readership for popular novels really developed. In 1863, publisher Moïse Millaud launched *Le Petit Journal,* a daily newspaper designed from the outset to be sold by the issue for a *sou* (five centimes, roughly a penny), rather than by annual subscription. Within two years, *Le Petit Journal* sold over 250,000 issues a day. For the cost of a serving of bread, the newspaper had become daily fare.

It was Ponson's ability to respond quickly to the changing circumstances of the publishing industry, more than his literary talent, that would eventually bring *Rocambole* into being and make it a resounding success. Belonging to the second generation of *feuilletonistes,* Ponson and his contemporaries, such as Paul Féval, Paul de Kock, and Gustave Aimard, had to "learn the ropes" rather than invent the techniques of serialization, developed over the previous decades by such renowned authors as Honoré de Balzac, Eugène Sue, and Alexandre Dumas. With entrepreneurial vigor, Ponson began writing for multiple newspapers, including *Le Journal des Faits*. Launched in 1850, the *Le*

Journal des Faits was designed as a marketing tool whereby installment novels by popular authors were used to boost newspaper sales. Ponson's first major feuilleton, *Les Coulisses du monde*—literally "The Stage-Wings of Society," but figuratively "The Secret Lives of the Rich and Famous"—appeared in it as a 95-part feuilleton in 1851–52. The serial was so popular that *Le Journal de Faits* began to feature Ponson as one of its anchor writers.

The commercial benefits for publishers, *feuilletonistes*, and readers were multiple and reciprocal. Publishers realized that the celebrity of popular authors could boost newspaper sales, and major publicity campaigns were launched to promote new feuilletons. In turn, successful *feuilletonistes* could negotiate their by-the-line salaries, which ranged from five centimes to one franc per line and might vary in length from several hundred to thousands of lines. In addition, commercially successful authors would write several feuilletons simultaneously, some by subcontracting uncredited *"nègres"* (ghostwriters) to write anonymously under the renowned author's signature. Such accelerated modes of commercial literary production were matched by a rapidly growing reading public. In the 1840s, less than half of the French population knew how to read, but by the end of the nineteenth century more than ninety percent could, leaving only the elderly illiterate. In advance of a nationalized education system, the cheap daily feuilleton and weekly fiction magazines created a popular reading audience.

The timing of Ponson's first Rocambole feuilleton, *Les Drames de Paris*, was fortuitous. Following Louis Napoleon's coup d'état in 1851, some of France's most popular authors, among them Eugène Sue, Alexandre Dumas, and Victor Hugo, had gone into exile, fearful of political repression. In 1857, Sue died and his current feuilleton, *Les Mystères du peuple*, was officially suspended for reasons of "inciting hatred and disrespect against the government." The same year, Gustave Flaubert and Charles Baudelaire were each put on trial for "offense to public and religious morality and to good morals" for *Madame Bovary* and *Les Fleurs du mal*, respectively. The entire decade following Napoleon III's proclamation of the Second Empire is generally regarded as an era of political authoritarianism, at the cultural level expressed through decreased public liberties and the increased censorship of the press.

Yet for Ponson du Terrail, November 1857 marks the ascendancy of his popularity with the serialization of *Les Drames de Paris* in the daily, *La Patrie*. At the outset, it was not evident that Rocambole would become the centerpiece of the series. Some years later, in *La Vérité sur Rocambole*, Ponson proffered a latter-day explanation of events.[13] In this highly embellished autobiographical sketch, Ponson recounts how he met Rocambole, formerly the leader of a criminal band called *Les Valets de Cœur*, in the fall of 1857, and how over the years the ex-criminal would write to him and provide details about his adventures. Yet despite Ponson's claim to provide his readers with "the truth about Rocambole," the account is rocambolesque confabulation; no character named Rocambole appeared in *Les Drames de Paris* until several months after the feuilleton was under way.

Charting the development of the feuilleton illuminates how the rocambolesque functions as re-enchantment, beginning with the parodic imitation of previously successful serials. At the publisher's request, Ponson called his feuilleton *Les Drames de Paris*, hoping to cash in on the success of Eugène Sue's *Les Mystères de Paris*. He was not alone in the "something of Paris" formula, which was used by many popular novelists during the Second Empire: *Les Viveurs de Paris* by Xavier Montépin, *Les Mansardes de Paris* by Pierre Zaconne, *Les Bas-fonds de Paris* by Lucien Guéroult, *Les Mendiants de Paris* by Clémence Robert, and *Les Esclaves de Paris* by Émile Gaboriau, among others. Ponson also made use of Sue's basic plotline and protagonist: *L'Héritage mystèrieux* revolves around the restoration of a lost familial inheritance and the defeat of evil characters who are after it. Even his hero, Armand de Kergaz, was loosely modeled after Sue's avenger, Rodolphe. Yet within short order, Ponson's feuilleton began to display a rocambolesque life of its own.

L'Héritage mystérieux, the first novel in *Les Drames de Paris*, opens with a prologue about three members of Napoleon's Grand Army—Colonel Armand de Kergaz, Captain Paolo de Felipone, and a cavalryman named Bastien—who are suffering through the bitter winter retreat from Moscow in 1812. Kergaz is a true aristocratic, "a real man and noble figure" whose blue eyes conveyed his "courage and goodness," whereas the Italian Felipone, "possessing all the vices of degenerate peoples," is a soldier of fortune.[14] Believing he will not survive the frozen march, Kergaz leaves his last testament with Felipone, promising half of his inheritance to him upon the condition that he marry his widow. The treacherous Felipone responds by firing a pistol into his comrades, and he sets off to claim his ill-gained fortune in Brittany. He marries the Countess de Kergaz three years later and, to gain full control over the estate, tosses her son, Armand, into the sea. However, Bastien, who survived Felipone's gunshot wound, suddenly reappears and tells the countess the truth about her nefarious husband. At this moment, she gives birth to a second son, Andréa de Felipone.

Jumping ahead to 1840, Armand, who had survived the intended drowning, is an art student in Rome. Learning of his mother's fate, his stepfather's treachery, and his half brother's usurpation, he returns to Paris in 1843. Armand confronts Andréa at a masked ball in Montmartre and the two prepare to duel. At that moment, Bastien intervenes to lead the half-brothers to the deathbed of Count Felipone. Filled with remorse in his dying moments, Felipone tells Andréa that Armand is the true inheritor of the Kergaz fortune. Refusing to accept this, Andréa declares: "So, virtuous brother, it's between the two of us! We'll see who carries the day, the philanthropist or the bandit, hell or heaven . . . Paris will be our battlefield!"[15] Shortly thereafter, a figure from the criminal underworld of London, the Irish baron Sir Williams (an alias of Andréa), appears in Paris. Assisted by a conniving and seductive courtesan named Baccarat, Sir Williams, the "genius of evil," commences upon a complex set of plans to destroy the lives of Armand and his friends.

Over the course of several hundred pages, fantastic and incredible events occurred in Ponson's astonishingly improbable feuilleton, but the character of Rocambole had yet to appear. As Régis Messac first noted in his magisterial study, *Le "Detective Novel" et l'influence de la pensée scientifique*, the emergence of Rocambole as the protagonist of *Les Drames de Paris* was an accidental and contingent evolution. Toward the end of *L'Héritage mystèrieux*, the story shifts to the village of Bougival, west of Paris, where a bitter old woman named Maman Fripart runs a low-life bar. She had adopted a "malicious and insolent" twelve-year-old orphan known by the sobriquet, Rocambole. At this point, Rocambole was less a character than a set of borrowed characteristics. The etymology of the name comes from the German *Rockenbolle,* a variety of garlic with a large bulb and a piquant-yet-sweet flavor. By the early eighteenth century, in French *rocambole* had taken on the connotation of anything with a "spicy attraction."[16] During the French Revolution, *La Rocambole des journaux* was a satirical political broadsheet that lampooned the revolution's principles and leaders. Insolent, malicious, and piquant were rocambolesque attributes that predated the introduction of Ponson's character.

That Rocambole would become the popular hero of the series was unforeseen. Messac notes, "The feuilleton novel is a fishing line with multiple hooks, one for each day. This is how the process '*la suite au prochain numéro*' ('to be continued in the next issue') works."[17] The *feuilletoniste* does not know in advance which twists in the story will be popular with readers, nor does he have prescience about which episodes will have the greatest effect. For this reason, a large daily circulation is invaluable, for a sudden rise or drop in sales has a direct impact upon revenue. The *feuilletoniste,* whose income is earned by the line, cares little which hooks catch his readers, merely that they return to purchase the next installment. One of those hooks was the incidental character of Rocambole.

Six chapters after the Rocambole's introduction, inexplicably Ponson transformed the orphaned child into a swashbuckling sixteen-year-old rogue. Ponson characterized this young man as a "child of Paris," expertly skilled without effort—"an accomplished horseback rider within a week, swordsman by instinct, crack shot with rifle and pistol, swimmer like a fish to water."[18] When one of Sir Williams's criminal accomplices is shot during a tussle with Armand, the genius of evil recruits Rocambole to take his place. Within a few chapters, however, Rocambole betrays his criminal master, and Sir Williams's evil plans are foiled. At the end of this first novel, Armand emerges victorious, the courtesan Baccarat repents and enters a convent, and Sir Williams flees.

Literary and media critic Charles Grivel asserts that the popularity of a series is typically strongest at the launching of the serial and, as formulaic sequels and knock-offs follow, tends to diminish over time.[19] Yet in Ponson's case, the apex of the series came later, with *La Résurrection de Rocambole* and *Le Dernier mot de Rocambole,* several years after *Les Drames de Paris.* The enchantments of the rocambolesque, the ability to continually delight and astonish readers with outrageously improbable scenarios, provides a key to understanding why this is so. As Messac notes, "it is more important to pique the curiosity than to satisfy it."[20] After the introduction of Rocambole, *Les Drames de Paris* began to develop in new and surprising directions. In 1858, *La Patrie* continued Ponson's feuilleton with *Le Club des Valets de Cœur.* Believing that his half-brother has repented, Armand pardons Andréa and hires him to head a private police force to defeat a mysterious band of criminals, Le Club des Valets de Cœur. The leader of the gang is, in fact, Andréa/Sir Williams himself. However, in this novel Sir Williams is reduced to a behind-the-scenes criminal mastermind. Rocambole, as the Vicount de Cambolh, a handsome and blonde Swedish aristocrat, becomes the dynamic antagonist.

FIG. 7.2. *Rocambole: La Maison de Fous.* Series "Livre Populaire." Cover by Gino Starace. Paris: A. Fayard, 1913. Author's collection.

Again, ultimately Sir Williams's nefarious plans are foiled. Toward the end of the novel, Rocambole is seriously wounded during a sword fight with Armand. Believing he is dying, Rocambole reveals that Andréa is the head of the Club des Valets de Cœur. Baccarat (now transformed as the Countess Artoff) intervenes, captures Sir Williams, and assembles a tribunal of his former victims to punish him. To assure that no one will ever again fall prey to his hypnotic magnetism or evil eloquence, Sir Williams's eyes are gouged out, his tongue sliced off, and his face disfigured, and he is exiled to Brazil to live among savages. Rocambole recovers from his wounds, is pardoned by Armand, compensated 200,000 francs for his assistance, and takes flight for England.

The rocambolesque hooks Ponson threaded across his feuilleton had multiplied over the course of *Le Club des Valets de Cœur*. Manichean oppositions of good versus evil persist, but goodness does not guarantee victory; Armand, ostensibly the hero, is easily duped. Characters switch sides; the criminal prostitute Baccarat is now the noble avenger the Countess Artoff. New and exotic characters are added to an already familiar cast, notably Daï-Natha, an Indian femme fatale who resides in an oriental harem cached within Paris. Physical violence is further sensationalized. Vengeance is elevated above the law. And Rocambole is rewarded for having opportunistically played both sides for personal gain. Increased public demand for the rocambolesque meant that Ponson would make even more astonishing changes to the series.

The criminal Rocambole takes center stage in *Les Exploits de Rocambole*, the continuation of the feuilleton in *La Patrie* at the end of 1858. Following a shipwreck off the coast of northern France, Rocambole steals the identity papers of a young marquis, Albert de Chamery, and leaves the unconscious aristocrat to drown on the rocks. Bearing a physical resemblance to the marquis, Rocambole installs himself in the de Chamery apartment in Paris and sets out to steal the family inheritance. Sir Williams, bearing tattoos and scars from burns inflicted upon him by Australian aboriginals (instead of Brazilian savages), reappears, but the once "genius of evil" has been reduced to a pathetic blind, deaf, and mute figure. Rocambole emerges as a criminal antagonist so violent and immoral that he kills everyone who might be able to expose him as the false Albert: the Marquise de Chamery, the family butler, and even Maman Fripart and Sir Williams.

A proposed marriage between the false Marquis de Chamery and the Spanish princess Conception de Sallandrera forms the basic plot of *Les Exploits de Rocambole*. When the Countess Artoff/Baccarat catches wind of de Chamery's activities, she suspects the hand of Rocambole in it. After discovering the real marquis wrongly imprisoned in Cadiz, Baccarat lures Rocambole to Spain under the pretense of an impending marriage to Conception, and she captures him. She orders her vigilante executioner to disfigure Rocambole's face with acid. The defeated criminal is imprisoned, and the real Marquis de Chamery and Princess de Sallandrera properly marry. While the form of the happy ending, with its restitution of social order, had been preserved, the feuilleton's pages were filled with the outrageous criminal and murderous exploits of Rocambole, more popular than ever with a mass-reading audience.

At this point, however, Ponson misstepped with *Les Chevaliers du clair de lune,* the continuation of the feuilleton in 1860. While continual metamorphosis is a rocambolesque imperative, the simple act of changing characters and plots does not guarantee reader popularity. In this new serial, Ponson cached the criminal Rocambole in the shadow of a group of avengers, the "Knights of the Full Moon." Like Sir Williams previously, Rocambole is scarred and reduced to being a criminal schemer. Yet readers of *La Patrie* soon made it clear, through diminished sales, that they preferred a handsome and energetic Rocambole to a disfigured and crippled one. *La Patrie* discontinued the series, and Ponson's relationship with the newspaper ended. Over the next few years, Ponson developed new series—*Le Paris mystérieux, La Jeunesse du Roi Henri, Les Mystères du temple,* and *Les Masques rouges*— and he reissued *Les Drames de Paris* and other early works in weekly feuilleton magazines.

The issue was not that Rocambole had become less popular with readers. The problem was how to continue to make the series rocambolesque. Ponson responded to the challenge with *La Résurrection de Rocambole* in 1865, serialized in *Le Petit Journal,* a leading Parisian daily that heralded the serial's release with a massive advertising campaign. In this new set of adventures, Rocambole is transformed from a malevolent criminal into a *justicier,* an avenger-hero. Five years of hard labor as prisoner "one hundred seventeen" in a Toulon (rather than Cadiz) jail have reformed him, and he has become a champion of the falsely convicted. He is also fair, blonde, and handsome once again, a physical ennoblement to match his moral redemption. New companions assist him—Milon, a good-hearted though dull-witted ex-convict, and Vanda, a scorned Russian woman with an avenging spirit of her own—and the Countess Artoff/Baccarat returns, all of whom are fiercely loyal to the *Maître* ("Master"). Rocambole the avenger proved to be even more popular with the reading public than the criminal, gaining the newspaper around 50,000 new readers.[21]

The plot of *La Résurrection de Rocambole* revolves around two wealthy orphans, Antoinette and Madeleine, who are being pursued by evil brothers, the Barons Karle and Philippe de Morlux, for their inheritance. Adopting the alias Major Avatar, Rocambole and companions combat the Morlux brothers. Antoinette's story takes place in Paris, where the Morlux are aided by a corrupt private detective, Timoléon. The plot against Madeleine occurs in Russia, between Moscow and St. Petersburg, with the nefarious barons assisted by the treacherous Countess Vasilika. With the resurrection of Rocambole, Ponson's feuilleton appeared interminable.

In the novel's cliff-hanger ending, the Countess Vasilika mortally wounds Rocambole during a duel by thrusting a sword into his chest, clear up to the hilt. At the same moment, Vanda bursts into the room, draws a pistol, and blows out Vasilika's brains. With blood gushing from his chest wound, Rocambole rushes out the door. Milon and Vanda follow the trail of blood to the bank of a river:

"Ah!" Milon cried out. "Once more, he is dead!"
But Vanda straightened herself up, seething, furious, fire in her eyes:
"No!" she said. "No, it's not possible, no, God doesn't want it . . ."
"No, ROCAMBOLE IS NOT DEAD!"[22]

Indeed, the avenger-hero was not dead. In 1866, *Le Dernier Mot de Rocambole* followed in *La Petite Presse*, to even greater commercial success, attracting nearly 100,000 new readers. Over the next three years, the newspaper carried the subsequent Rocambole adventures, *Les Misères de Londres* and *Les Démolitions de Paris*. Plots were as convoluted as ever. A gang of stranglers from India terrorizes Paris, a fortune is restored to a disinherited Irish Lord, a villainous English Lady falls in love with Rocambole. His character continued to adopt multiple and unlikely aliases, as a Scotland Yard detective, a German doctor, an English alienist, a Scottish evangelist, a prison doctor in charge of executions, a sixteen-year-old peasant lad, an eccentric English Lord who keeps a scrapbook of "curious crimes," and others.[23] Ponson's rocambolesque series only came to an end with the Franco-Prussian war of 1870 and his coincidental, premature death by smallpox in January 1871.

Despite Ponson's success as an author, or perhaps due to it, he received little critical praise. Perhaps more than any other popular series

FIG. 7.3. André Gill, "True Portrait of Rocambole." *La Lune,* 11 November 1867. Courtesy of Special Collections, University of Michigan Library.

of the era, *Rocambole* represented what the early nineteenth-century literary critic Sainte-Beuve had decried as "industrial" literature. Official pronouncements against Ponson abounded, the general consensus being that he was a hack writer who played to the basest instincts of his popular readership. Pierre Larousse's *Grand Dictionnaire universel du XIXe siècle* noted, "His work is based on a series of extraordinarily improbable adventures, and the vulgarity of its characters, mostly populated with hardened criminal types, is nauseating." The Abbé Louis Bethléem's entry on Ponson in *Romans à lire et romans à proscrire* added, "He published dismal and unbelievable novels full of impossible plots in newspaper installments. In them, one could find phrases such as, 'This man's hand was as cold as a snake's.'"[24] Both Larousse and Bethléem judged that Ponson's prolific output of vulgar fiction had a deleterious effect upon the public.

Ponson was savagely parodied in the press as well, in such lampoons as *La Dernière Mort de Rocambole* ("The Final Death of Rocambole"). Gustave Flaubert lambasted the popular author in a satirical fragment from *L'Album de la marquise:*

It was the year 185?, October was coming to an end, an amazon mounted on a handsome black horse of the Irish race galloped along the sheer route of Elberstein manor.

This amazon was the marquise.

Some distance behind her, driving an elegant Ehrler carriage harnessed to a magnificent horse, followed a thoroughly young man with extremely fine manners.

This man was the viscount . . .

"Oh!" He said, lighting his cigar with lightning flashing from his eyes . . . "Let me kiss your forehead, even if it means taking a bullet to the chest."[25]

Such caricatures abounded in newspapers and literary magazines in the 1860s, poking fun at Ponson's excessively redundant and fantastically incoherent "style."

But others recognized that, as far as *Rocambole* was concerned, literary style was beside the point. The rocambolesque enchanted the public, and that was enough. Émile Gaboriau, author of the Monsieur Lecoq detective novels published during the same era, noted Ponson's skill in attracting readers: "Every evening, one of my friends rushes out to get the newspaper that carries the exploits of Rocambole: 'God!' He exclaims, 'How Ponson gets on my nerves! He makes up the most absurd stories, and he doesn't even know how to write proper French!' But the following day, he buys the next installment."[26] A *feuilletoniste* himself, Gaboriau understood well that *la suite au prochain numéro,* "to be continued in the next issue," was the thing in itself, the symbiotic relation that nourished newspaper sales, the writer's income, and the readers' pleasure. In this "age of mechanical reproduction," as Walter Benjamin later observed, any sense of literary aura was surpassed by commercial cult value in popular works such as *Rocambole.*

Yet it was precisely disregard for artistic pretense that permitted the rocambolesque to flourish. According to symbolist author Villiers de l'Isle Adam, Ponson was a prophet of modernity:

His is the most sure and prolific pen in our magnificent land, and everybody who is anybody talks about his stuff, whatever they think of it.

I forget his name: But his is the kind of talent that cleverly *singes* his erstwhile colleagues with the most obscene situations! . . .

His heroes are most interesting, in that they are killed on one page, and then resurrected when the page is turned over. On these pages, feverishly scanned by the eye, the true shadows of Orpheus, Homer, Virgil, and Dante are silhouetted. To sum up, this man, this moralist, already represents *the pure expression of modern Art in both its Renaissance and its maturity.*[27]

For Villiers de l'Isle Adam, Rocambole conjured up a new art from ephemeral commercial culture, consumed one day and discarded the next, constantly changing yet fundamentally remaining the same. The rocambolesque was a uniquely modern metamorphosis of the carnivalesque, rude popular culture that is scorned by social elites while nonetheless being consumed by them along with the rest of the population. Yet the rocambolesque did not recapitulate traditional culture and festivals, rooted in agricultural and liturgical cycles. Instead, it was fueled by the feverish popular demands of the commercial marketplace. The modern world is not turned upside down, for in the endless repetitions and exaggerations of the rocambolesque feuilleton there is neither up nor down, only seriality—"to be continued." Although critics and the literary establishment lambasted *Rocambole,* Villiers de l'Isle Adam caught glimpses of a new, modern aesthetic beyond its shadows—marvelous, insolent, impossible, and in perpetual motion.

The popularity of Rocambole continued after Ponson's death.[28] By the end of the century, Constant Guéroult had written *Le Retour de Rocambole* (1874), Pierre Zaccone *Maman Rocambole* (1881), and Jules Cardoze *Les Bâtards de Rocambole* (1886). In 1911, the daily *Le Matin* published an anonymously authored feuilleton, *Cadet Fripouille: Rocambole, aventures inédits,* and Ponson's original Rocambole series was reissued in "Le Livre Popularie" series by publishing magnate

Arthème Fayard II shortly thereafter. In the 1920s, Frédéric Valade wrote seven new Rocambole adventures, beginning with *Le Petit-Fils de Rocambole* ("Rocambole's Grandson"). Across the twentieth century, Rocambole novels have been reprinted in France and adapted for theater, film, radio, and television.

Numerous popular French avengers and villains descended from Rocambole as well: Arsène Lupin, Fascinax, Zigomar, Fantômas, Rouletabille, Chéri-Bibi, Judex, Belphégor.[29] A French taste for the rocambolesque played into popular enthusiasm for crime fiction generally, culminating in the *roman noir* or *polar* of the postwar era. As a historical trend, the nineteenth-century industrial culture industry that generated the rocambolesque feuilleton novel was supplanted in the twentieth century by a dazzling array of mass culture, not only within France but internationally. Pulp magazines, dime novels, and comic books have multiplied in mass print culture, while film serials, blockbuster movies, television series, and home video have dominated popular visual culture.

The adjective *rocambolesque* remains in common French usage today, referring to any fantastic, over-the-top story, whether fictional, "true life," or even newspaper reportage. While the world is being routinized by a global capitalist economy, mass culture generates materials for its popular re-enchantment as well. Seemingly echoing Weber, as the mid-twentieth-century surrealist Pierre Mabille stated, "A definite antinomy seems to exist today between the ways of the marvelous and those of science."[30] But as a physician who believed in both science and in magic, Mabille understood how popular fiction could function as a "mirror of the marvelous" that animates a disenchanted modernity. The rocambolesque revives an otherwise sterile reality with irrepressible enchantments for popular audiences throughout the modern world.

CHAPTER 8

"Lost in Focused Intensity": Spectator Sports and Strategies of Re-Enchantment

HANS ULRICH GUMBRECHT

SOMETIMES, REACTIONS FROM practitioners become particularly inspiring moments in the lives of professional humanists. For only practitioners can confirm that our tentative conceptual constructions are on target and, at the same time, only they have an authority to justify the effort of pushing further certain thoughts that have begun to emerge in our minds as bold and therefore often vague intuitions. Such a decisive intellectual moment had arrived when, during a colloquium on "The Athlete's Body" organized by the Athletic Department and the Department of Comparative Literature at Stanford University in 1995, Pablo Morales, a three-time Olympic gold medalist in the butterfly swimming events and a Stanford alumnus, explained, as if in passing, how the addictive desire of "being lost in focused intensity" had brought him back to competitive sports after a first retirement and at an age that simply seemed to exclude any world-class performance in his sport.

Quite explicitly, Morales's complex concept referred both to the spectator's and the athlete's experience. For what had brought the impression of "getting lost in focused intensity" back to him as something he could not yet live without, was the television broadcast of a track-and-field event at the 1988 Olympics:

I will never forget watching the great sprinter Evelyn Ashford run as, in the anchor leg, she came from behind to win the gold medal for the United States. The race was shown through to its conclusion, after which a replay was run but this time with the camera focused on Ashford's face before, during, and after her sprint. Her eyes first panned the oval, then focused on the baton, then on the curve ahead. Oblivious to the crowd, oblivious even to her competition, I saw her lost in focused intensity. The effect was immediate. I had to remove myself from the room. But when I thought about my reaction in the ensuing hours, I came to realize what I had lost; that special feeling of getting lost in focused intensity.[1]

Pablo Morales's narrative helped me distinguish three different dimensions in the experience of sports. First, the words *being lost* point to a peculiar isolation and distance of athletic events from the everyday world and its pursuits that is comparable to what Immanuel Kant called the "disinterestedness" of aesthetic experience. Second, what athletes and spectators "focus" upon—as something already present or something yet to come—belongs to the realm of epiphanies, that is to the events of appearance, more precisely to events of appearance that show moving bodies as temporalized form. Third, both the experience and the expectation of epiphanies are accompanied by—and then further enhance—halos of intensity, that is, states of a quantitatively higher degree in the awareness of our emotions and of our bodies.

To describe the experience of sports as "getting lost in focused intensity" suggests that sports can become, both for athletes and spectators, a strategy of secular re-enchantment. For "being lost" converges with the definition of the *sacred* as a realm whose fascination relies on being set apart from everyday worlds; *epiphanies* belong to the dimension of re-enchantment precisely because modernity's drive towards abstraction had always tended to replace them through "representations," that is, through nonsubstantial modes of appearance; likewise, *intensity* marks a level in our reaction to the world and to ourselves that is normally bound to fade on the trajectory of disenchantment (which has become so strangely normative to us)—and that, by the same logic, thus turns into a predicate of re-enchantment. Even more so than in some other cases of secular re-enchantment, it seems evident that we can refer to practicing sports and to watching sports as social *"strategies."* For while it is not clear what exactly those practices may replace in contemporary culture, and while we do not associate a single purpose or a generalized function with them, there is an impression that the presence and the growing importance of sports today stand for something—and should indeed stand for something—that we have lost.

In four brief reflections, I try to retrieve some of those features from a formerly "enchanted" world that, most of the time half-consciously, we recuperate when we watch and practice sports. First, I concentrate on the athlete's performance as an event that allows for (the equivalent of) miracles. Second, I then try to identify components of re-enchantment, above all effects of "epiphany," in the spectator's experience. Third, I talk about the stadium as a "sacred" place. Fourth, I conclude by describing a specific kind of "gratitude" that ties many spectators to the presence and to the memory of their favorite athletes.

1

Thanks to their complex theological content, reading only a few of Pindar's Odes is enough to understand how victorious athletes were considered to be "heroes" in Greek antiquity, *heroes* without the distance or the irony that we normally imply today when we use this word—and how heroes were demi-gods. For there was no doubt that in the athletes' great moments of performance the power of gods—and indeed the gods themselves—became present, present in the athletes' flesh and present in space. Watching athletes compete gave their spectators the certainty to be close to the gods. The expectation that gods would be willing to engage in athletic competition was consistent with what the Greeks believed to know about most of them: think of Hermes and of Aphrodite, of Hephaistos, Poseidon, and above all of Zeus, and you will realize how the identities of those gods were built on different types of physical prowess. Both the *Iliad* and the *Odyssey* made it clear that, based on their physical strengths, these gods were constantly competing with each other, that *agon*, that is fight and competition, was their central life form—and often indeed the only reason for them to become interested in humans at all.

The closeness of the gods whose actual presence the athletes' *agon* was supposed to help conjure up and to embody became the reason why all Pan-Hellenic games, most visibly the games at Olympia and at Delphos, were organized around religious sanctuaries. For the appearance of the gods was a type of event supposed to become real in space—and it may well be from this premise that Martin Heidegger took the inspiration to describe what he calls "the unconcealment of Being" and the "event of Truth" through a spatial topology—that is, as "sway," as "coming forth," and through his etymologizing interpretation of "objectivity" as getting closer in a horizontal movement.[2] At the same time, a culture that counts on the gods' presence as a permanent possibility, as ancient Greek culture seems to have done, will not be prone to use words such as *miracle* and to single out a specific dimension of the "miraculous." Once again, however, Pindar's Odes make it clear to us that the great Olympic victories were seen as events of divine presence—events that exceeded the limits of the humanly possible. One might even go so far as to speculate that the Greeks didn't care about keeping records—about how far a discus had been thrown or by how much a runner had distanced his opponents, because divine powers will ridicule any kind of measurement.

Obviously, and for many good reasons, it is considered a symptom of bad intellectual taste in present-day culture to find an athlete's performance "divine" or to appreciate its potentially record-breaking dimension as "miraculous." For several decades now, different sports have triggered the development of scientifically based practicing methods—and in a number of countries this has led to the emergence of an academic discipline well capable of explaining away, rationally, what the Greeks took to be divine inspiration in athletic performance. Successful athletes today are all too well aware of how much they depend on the progress of highly specialized research, and they have also learned to draw a clear border between this necessary basis of their performance and what they consider to be remnants of personal superstition. How they personally live and remember their most inspired moments strongly converges with the tradition of thinking enchantment as divine presence. From this perspective, I find it telling that "being in the zone," a spatial metaphor, has become a conventional way among athletes today to invoke particularly inspired moments, moments that defy all rational explanations. Here is a description of how it feels to be "in the zone" written by J. R. Lemon, one of the better runningbacks in the history of Stanford football:

When a player has entered the zone, a state of hypersensitivity and tension has taken place. This explains the apparent ease during my run toward the end zone. It is not that I am not working as hard as the other players on the field. It is just that in this state of hypersensitivity, things are moving so much slower than they are for the rest of the players on the field. My senses are much more aware of what is going on around me and that enables all of the triggers inside of me to react a little faster than the other players, making me appear more fluent.

Obviously J. R. Lemon avoids religious language in these sentences, although he certainly does not imply that "being in the zone" is a state completely under the control of his intentions. A player must be physically and mentally well prepared to be open for it—but this will not be enough. What else needs to happen for a player to be in the zone will depend, as we would say today, on whether he is "on," whether a specific game is "his" or not—it will depend on what the Greeks would have called divine inspiration.

2

If, for an athlete, "being in the zone" is a state whose arrival he or she is expecting "in focused intensity," the spectators' focus, especially in team sports, is on the emergence of beautiful plays. Beautiful plays are the epiphany of form. Yes, ultimately most spectators do want "their" teams to win—but if winning were all, it would be enough for them, every game day, simply to check the final scores. A beautiful play, for example J. R. Lemon receiving the ball from his quarterback and finding a hole in the other team's defensive line through which he will run with the ball for another first down, is an epiphany of form because it has its substance in the participating athletes' bodies; because the form it produces is unlikely and thereby an event, achieved against the resistance of the other team's defense; and finally and above all the beautiful play is an epiphany because it is a temporalized form, a form that begins to vanish in the very process of its emergence.

For each individual spectator, such a beautiful play performed by his or her team produces an instant of happiness. We breathe deeply and for a moment we realize how the players' achievement and confidence become contagious and seem to carry us. This at least is what most spectators hope will happen to them, most precisely—and unknowingly—all those spectators who have interiorized the game's rules and its rhythms, and who do not have a professional stake in analyzing what is happening on the field, as coaches or journalists do. These spectators, we might call them "the common spectators," who can afford to let their emotions go, will soon feel how they are becoming part of a larger, communal (rather than collective) body. It is within this communal body that spectators who have never met before nor will ever meet again feel comfortable embracing each other, and it is this communal body that likes to become the movement of "the wave." Seeing itself perform such a movement and listening to the noise that it can produce at certain moments of the game provides a self-awareness that adds cohesion to the spectators' body. The spectators' communal body can become the basis for the fans to feel united to the players of their own team and may, at some rare and glorious occasions, even conquer the other team and its spectators. This was the mood when, for the opening night of Stadium Australia in Sydney, New Zealand's rugby team snapped a sensational winning streak from its archrival Australia—in what the morning newspapers, even in Australia, would unanimously celebrate as "one of the greatest matches played in the history of rugby."

There seems to be a level of participation where the enjoyment and appreciation of beautiful plays exceeds the desire for victory, where communal convergence overcomes the dynamics of rivalry. The ambiguity inherent in such moments certainly appears in other types of communal bodies, above all in those shaped by religious experience. It must have been the promise to overcome individual reclusion that motivated one of the most canonical interpretations of the Christian church as "Christ's mystical body." But history shows us how, in certain moments, the "bodies" of different denominations took shape against each other, leading into devastating religious wars whereas, at other moments, religious communities have enthusiastically opened up for ecumenical fusion and happiness. If today the divisions separating the different interpretations and forms of Islam seem to be more irreconcilable than ever, ours is a moment prone to co-celebration within Christianity. And it may not be random that stadiums built for team sports events are used as sites for contemporary religious mass events. As long as religious communities continue to exist, it is banal— and simply inadequate—to say that sports have become "the religion of the 21st century." But it is obvious how sports and a renewed enthusiasm for religious experience are converging today as ways of re-enchanting the modern world.

3

Before this background, it does not take great theoretical imagination to see that stadiums have a status of sacred spaces. For they gain an aura by being visibly dysfunctional, that is by being demonstratively different from spaces and buildings that fulfill predefined functions in our everyday lives. From an economic point of view, no more counter-intuitive gesture exists in contemporary culture than that of building new stadiums in downtown areas where the real estate is extremely expensive. For not only do sports facilities not allow for high-rise construction as it normally maximizes the efficiency of the ground acquired, but above all stadiums are empty during most of the week and often over even longer stretches of time.

This does not only explain why empty stadiums, as sacred spaces, have an almost irresistible appeal for passionate sports fans. Above all, stadiums as sacred spaces are spaces that require and trigger layers of ritualized behavior during those comparatively short moments in which they are filled with action. Being in a stadium, both for athletes and spectators, is not primarily about inventing and showing individualized action. It is about inscribing oneself, physically, into a preexisting order that only allows for narrow spaces of variation. Every event, every country, every moment in the history of sport develops its own rituals, poses, and gestures that open up a dimension for endless individual interpretation. Think of the gradual historical transformations in the uniforms for different sports, of the changing objects of attention for halftime entertainment, or of the signs of tension or mutual respect between the players on rival teams (from archaically "sportsmanlike" correctness via openly mean antagonism to the fake friendship smile of media stars).

Through the multiplicity of such colorful developments, however, there is one structural pattern that imposes itself in any situation of spectator sports—and this form is clearly related to the nature of the stadium as sacred space. It is the contrast between moments of emptiness or inaction and moments filled with the most intense bodily activity, a contrast that, reiterated on many different levels, mimics the relation between the mostly empty stadiums and the busy urban environments into which they are built. When the common spectator enters the stadium, half an hour or ten minutes before the kick-off for the game, he or she will see and be immediately attracted by the empty playing field, which is a promise for the imminent moment, in which the teams will "take the field." It is through the utterly unsurprising and yet explosively exciting moment when the teams take the field that the spectators are conjured into their communal identity and agency.

After this inaugural scene, the central contrast shifts to the constantly repeated difference between slow movements (or stasis) and the speed and power typical of athletic performance. There is probably no other team sport that plays out more forcefully the potential of this structural element than American football. Preceding each play, two times eleven players stand in front of each other, like freeze frames, drawing complicated forms on the field. What can follow, from the second that the center hands the ball to the quarterback to initiate a new play, is not completely covered by the contrast between the beautiful (offensive, negentropic) play or the destructive (entropic) powers of the defense. For American football also provides a type of situation where, after the seconds of the double freeze frame, neither form nor chaos happen, the reasons for this "neither/nor" being "delayed game" or "offside." Following such a call, the players go back to the sidelines to talk to their coaches, before they line up again. Nothing relevant for the game has happened meanwhile. And it is this impression of "nothingness" that matters.

For one might well speculate that players and spectators in a stadium jointly produce, on different levels, an embodiment of what Martin Heidegger, in the opening movement of his "Introduction to Metaphysics," identified as the one primordial philosophical question, that is the question of why there is something as opposed to nothing.[3] This question can well provoke existential vertigo to whoever dares to think through its possible consequences. But embodying a question is different from thinking it through and from exposing oneself to its existential impact. Most certainly players and spectators have no idea of what they may be embodying—and less an intention to do so. It is as if, in the sacred space of the stadium, they fulfilled a religious commandment for which neither words nor a theology is available.

4

In speaking and writing about sports from a historical angle, there is a tendency to overemphasize moments of repetition that suggest continuity, a tendency that probably comes from the—doubtlessly adequate—intuition that our participation in sports, both as athletes and as spectators, resonates with very basic and therefore metahistorical layers of human existence. Against this trend of focusing on historical invariables, it is important to highlight that, on the other hand, the circumstances under which such basic layers of our existence are being activated by sports make up for a history of astonishing discontinuity.[4] There were times, between ancient Greek culture and today, where it would have been difficult to discover any phenomena resembling our present-day notion of "athletics." None of those team sports, for example, whose incomparable popularity in the early twenty-first century tempts us to identify them with sports at large, existed before the mid-nineteenth century. The crowds that they attract, into stadiums and through the media, have been steadily growing over the past one hundred years—and seem to continue to grow. Thus the idea becomes irrepressible (and perhaps even irrefutable) that the—at least quantitatively—triumphant history of team sports as spectator sports points to a new and important function of compensation, a function of compensation and secular re-enchantment that is—in a time when the Western process of secularization and disenchantment of the world (in the sense of Max Weber) may have reached a close-to-perfection stage within our globalizing public sphere. For are there any phenomena left today that are allowed to be publicly nonrational and nonpragmatic?

We may also ask, in this context, why teams and their collectively produced epiphanies of form seem to fascinate us even more today than the most eminent players who are part of those teams, and why we are moving away, if slowly, from that type of almost exclusive concentration on individual athletes that characterized ancient Greek sports or the astonishingly popular world of professional boxing in England during the late eighteenth and early nineteenth centuries (today players who endlessly cultivate individual stardom, like British soccer star David Beckham, clearly diminish their status within the world of athletics). A possible explanation might be that, in its present-day form, the re-enchantment provided by sports (and other phenomena) no longer appears to be a gift granted by the gods to athletes who are demigods but, probably, as an effect of the well-coordinated—perhaps even sacramentally coordinated—behavior of the many. It is difficult to predict where this development will take us. At any rate, sport, with its re-enchanting effects, has conquered a large proportion of the contemporary leisure world. As such, it stands in harsh contrast to a public and professional world that could hardly be more disenchanted. Should one take the most recent conquests of fashion (you can wear baseball caps and Nike sportswear in your office) as an indication for a future where sports will spill over into the rational dimension of our collective existence?

Today, many of us still feel this beneficial effect of sports as compensating for things that we seem to lose and may already have lost irreversibly in the process of modern disenchantment, among them the effect of keeping open a place for the body in our existence. This would explain why so many sports fans (and I am certainly one of them) experience both an intense and a vague gratitude towards their most admired heroes. It is a "vague" gratitude because we somehow know that former athletes or contemporary athletes "as private persons" cannot really be its addressees. Of course there are rare occasions that offer the possibility (of trying) to say, personally: "thank you Mr. Jeter for having been such an outstanding shortstop for the New York Yankees over so many years," or "dear Mr. Montana, I will never forget the soft accuracy of your touch-down passes." But it is (statistically at least) unlikely that our heroes will ever be thankful for such gratitude, let alone engage in a conversation with us. Above all, we feel that ours is a gratitude whose referent, quite literally, "transcends" the level of individuals and of individual conversations. In this sense, ours is a gratitude similar to the gratitude that made the Greeks believe in a spatial proximity to the gods as a condition for great athletic achievements. However, as so many of us have lost, for their private existence, the traditional religious horizons of transcendence, this gratitude gets deflected, so to speak, towards the world that we have. Gratitude for great athletic moments turns into gratitude for those things that we approve of, like, enjoy, and appreciate in our everyday lives. Being thankful for what we have does not necessarily make us "uncritical" and "affirmative." Although this exactly must be a fear that explains why so many intellectuals—even some intellectuals who love to watch or to practice sport—have such a hard time making their peace with it.

CHAPTER 9

Permanent Re-Enchantments: On Some Literary Uses of the Supernatural from Early Empiricism to Modern Aesthetics

NICHOLAS PAIGE

HOW SHOULD WE READ THE *re* in re-enchantment? Straightforwardly, the prefix might be assumed to designate merely a return of enchantment: despite the triumph of instrumental reason that Weber dubbed "the disenchantment of the world," an older superstitious worldview refuses to disappear, and stages intermittent raids—Mesmerism, ESP, Roswell—into an otherwise predictable, quantified world of well-ordered things. Yet *re* carries a powerful hint of estrangement or distancing as well. It cannot simply be that reason and credulity continue to claw at each other's throats, and that we call the residual beliefs of those who persist in thinking unscientifically re-enchanted. If enchantment implies belief, re-enchantment implies something more like the memory of what it might be like to believe. So although the *re* of repetition resonates within the term, it is a repetition acknowledged as such, a reprise or recall in which the disenchanted modern mind experiences enchantments at a remove, usually via art. The estrangement effect can come from cultivated self-consciousness or irony; it can also derive from a sense of enchantment as a historical artifact, a thing of the past. And it can be blatantly obvious or nearly invisible: some of its most potent forms—the literary fantastic, for instance—play at reducing as much as possible the remove with which we experience enchantments, so as to cause our disenchantment to teeter briefly, as if threatening to pull us back down into belief. "It was a thoroughly silly story," Freud wrote of a magazine piece in which carved crocodiles come to life; "but the uncanny feeling it produced was quite remarkable."[1]

Re-enchantment is thus a product of art—Freud himself noted in his essay on the uncanny that its effect was much more pronounced in literature than in life—but not, certainly, of the art of all times and places: because the term designates a dimension of aesthetic experience embedded within the disenchanted worldview itself, re-enchantment must be a modern phenomenon. But how modern? Is it possible to date its apparition? Freud's focus on E. T. A. Hoffmann's "The Sandman" would point toward the romantic fantastic, but we can move back without much trouble to Horace Walpole's 1764 gothic harbinger, *The Castle of Otranto*, whose supernatural represents, in Barbara Benedict's words, "the remnant of superstition converted in the age of reason into pleasure"—a supernatural therefore thoroughly re-enchanted.[2] One goal of the present essay, which uses a limited number of French examples taken from the 1670s to the turn of the century, and then again from the 1770s, is to suggest that a history of re-enchantment must go back further still, so as to account for, say, the earlier craze for fairy tales and *A Thousand and One Nights*.

I wish to emphasize from the start, however, that I will not offer such examples because as an early modernist I am eager to show that re-enchantment starts earlier than commonly thought. It does, I think, but this is only half the story. On the one hand, the remarkably pervasive idea that re-enchantment constitutes some sort of belated critique or subversion of Enlightenment rationality *is* untenable: forms of literary re-enchantment accompany disenchantment from the very beginning, that is, from the latter part of the seventeenth century, or the period conventionally designated as the pre-Enlightenment. On the other hand, a longer view also makes it clear that re-enchantment develops historically within modernity. If early forms of re-enchantment are now customarily downplayed or ignored, this is not without reason: something is in a sense "missing" from them. The second part of my argument is therefore that there is one qualitative shift within this history; it occurs in the second half of the eighteenth century and allows a new and potent type of re-enchanted work to come into existence. The shift is signaled by the appearance of the gothic and the fantastic; but in contrast to most accounts of these genres, which rightly stress their newness, I seek to understand them as a linked—epiphenomenally, as it were—to the development of a powerful mode of aesthetic production that I will call the invention of modern fiction. The gothic and the fantastic are not the "flip side" or repressed other of a literary realism slowly consolidating its dominance; nor are they merely the symptom of various local determinants, such as the growth of consumerism, female literacy, or lending libraries in Britain. Even less should they be considered through reference to real beliefs, as if somehow readers of these new genres were less skeptical than the readers of fairy tales, or more critical of hegemonic Reason. Rather, these genres served as the prime testing ground for a dramatic redefinition of the relation of reality to the imagination, a redefinition integral to what Jacques Rancière calls the modern aesthetic regime, which nineteenth-century realism is part of and not opposed to.[3] To say that modernity is re-enchanted is not to say simply that it abounds in strategies of resistance to instrumental reason: the "re" in re-enchantment marks the specifically modern relationship between art and the world.

The Supernatural Pleasures of the Imagination

Descartes, Pascal, Hobbes, Spinoza: the philosophical work of any or all of them can help us to construct the narrative of our own disenchantment, a narrative that tells how the natural world was shorn of correspondence to the world of humans, rationalized, objectified as pure matter.[4] Yet with intellectual history alone as a guide, disenchantment is difficult to date. After all, these thinkers had their skeptical ancestors: they were not the first unfettered minds. And they had contemporary adversaries: many refused their arguments. If there is some legitimacy to claiming the second half of the seventeenth century as truly disenchanted, this must be because the purging of outdated beliefs had become something of a cultural phenomenon in Western Europe by this time. The purging was in part institutional: in July 1682, for example, the once respected science of demonology is mooted in France by royal edict; sorcerers and diviners, the edict declared, could still be vigorously pursued, but only as all-too-human impostors. More important still, however, is that plentiful evidence exists to suggest that disenchantment was becoming quite simply fashionable. Hence, when in 1680 more bemusement than apprehension greeted the comet appearing in the skies over Europe, northern Africa, and America, a new breed of literature, half philosophy and half entertainment, came into existence: Pierre Bayle took the first steps on the road to becoming an "Enlightenment" thinker with his *Pensées diverses sur la comète* (1682); and among Bernard Le Bovier de Fontenelle's juvenilia was a topical comedy entitled simply *La Comète* (1681).[5] The most notable thing about works such as these is less the skeptical ideas they express than the level on which they operate: the easy banter of Bayle's and Fontenelle's early works suggests that there was a genre to be carved out that had little to do with learned polemics, which in fact continued to rage.[6] They raged elsewhere, however, and the field was open for authors to reprocess such debates as a form of leisure reading. This was, in part, a vulgarization: Bayle and Fontenelle imparted information and scientific discoveries to people who were not what we might call "scientists." But it was also the propagation of an attitude. Natural events such as the comet's return furnished an opportunity for people to narrate and to represent their own disbelief, to understand themselves as being part of a select group for whom the obliviousness of the natural world to humans was now comically obvious.

Hence, it was at this time that stories of disenchantment start to appear in France: the confrontation between credulity and skepticism became a motor for narrative. A fine example would be the piece of literary ephemera that is Thomas Corneille and Jean Donneau de Visé's 1680 hit play *La Devineresse*. Here, a gun-toting marquis unmasks, by sheer threat of violence, a phony deviner who has taken in some provincial nobles and credulous bourgeois with her (literal) smoke and mirrors. Like many prior works, often comedies, that feature bogus magicians or astrologers hoodwinking people (typically in the service of young love, as in Calderón's *El astrólogo fingido* [c. 1632]), *La Devineresse* may be said to tell us something timeless about the propensity of people to be duped. But unlike works like these, and unlike the "literature of roguery" more generally, it is a true debunking narrative: the play presents us, the viewers, with circumstances whose most obvious explanation is supernatural, and encourages us to find the alternate, rational cause; it makes us adopt a skeptical worldview, and congratulates us when we do.[7] The work's brief but intense success (it reputedly enjoyed the highest gross receipts of any work produced on the seventeenth-century French stage), added to its utter lack of literary ambiguity, make of it the perfect transparent symptom of its culture's awareness of itself as disenchanted: things were, after all, just things, able to hold power over you only if the thing in question was a gun pressed to your temple. Like the work of the philosophers of the time, the play enacts what Anthony Cascardi has described as "the rational subject's vision of its own radical emergence from 'mythical' consciousness [and] its break from a 'mimetic' union with the natural world."[8]

The literature of disenchantment, however, was more than a vehicle for skepticism and rationalism: from the moment the first recognizably modern debunking narratives were articulated, writers also used them to think about how the process and pleasure of reading implied a symbiotic relation with superstition. In the fifth book of Adrien-Thomas Perdoux de Subligny's *La Fausse Clélie* (1670), one of a number of *Decameron*-type novels of the period featuring aristocratic storytellers, a fashionable group of men and women wandering in the gardens at the chateau of Vaux-le-Vicomte stumble upon a man who has just fainted. When he comes to, the disoriented man claims to have seen the ghost of his dead and much regretted mistress, whom he had been prevented from marrying years ago on account of a family feud. The elucidation of this mystery is taken up later in the novel, but while waiting to discover the identity of this ghost, characters exchange in round-robin fashion a series of tales of the supernatural. Many obey the standard "debunking" pattern by furnishing a climactic rationalistic explanation: if a credulous woman maintains that in a certain household an apparition visits each time someone is to die, a skeptical gentleman, the Chevalier de Montal, will quickly reveal the story's ancient source (Lucian's second-century *Philopseudes* [*The Lover of Lies*], a key classical compendium of supernatural lore). In that sense, the world of *La Fausse Clélie*, like that of *La Devineresse*, would seem to be thoroughly disenchanted: none of its supernatural claims are ever upheld. Still, it is a basic but not insignificant paradox that all these debunking narratives depend in a very real sense on an initial enchantment, that in order to "dispel" that enchantment they must continually recall it. The result is that the supernatural acquires an odd enunciative status: it is not so much asserted by some characters and denied by others, but admitted hypothetically and temporarily into the fictional world for the emotion it produces. One of Subligny's tales, which gives in a nutshell the formula that will power thousands of gothic narratives, detective stories, and Scooby-Doo episodes, involves a magistrate who is almost duped into selling off his chateau because he thinks it is haunted. Here, listeners are presented with a possibility which is immediately foreclosed: the narrator tells her listeners straight away that the story is designed to illustrate that most supernatural occurrences are only tricks. But, like *La Devineresse*, the story is told from the point of view of the investigator—the magistrate, in this case, who senses something fishy going on and lays a trap. And while a naïve listener is there to protest that she cannot see how the events can be rationally explained, the narrator proceeds to divulge the guilty party, along with his motives and his machinations. Upon which the Chevalier de Montal, who has already demonstrated his knowledge of Lucian, exclaims: "I was just about to say as much, . . . and I suspected it from the very beginning."[9]

This type of narrative, clearly an ancestor of the "supernatural explained" of Ann Radcliffe and others, was destined for solid success: the supernatural, in spite of the fact that it is never precisely *believed*, produces effects in the reader. One effect implicit in the skeptic's "Aha! I knew it!" is the cognitive pleasure produced by devising a rational explanation that fits the data just as well as the supernatural explanation which at first suggests itself. The other effect, which Subligny's characters formulate themselves after the magistrate's tale, involves the physiological effect of fear produced in a listener who nevertheless "knows" the supernatural to be impossible: all present, including the skeptical Chevalier, conclude that such stories reactivate patterns of thought from our childhood, patterns which reason is powerless to disable.[10] Both of these effects—of satisfying cognitive closure and of vicariously experienced fear—imply that the literature of disenchantment cannot really do without enchantment, or more precisely, that it *re*-enchants in the sense that it provides a space to entertain, provisionally and at a knowing remove, a memory of the supernatural that we feel in our bodies even as we attack it with our minds.

The temptation, faced with the obvious skepticism of Subligny's tale, is to foreground its polemical function, as if by necessity he must have been arguing with people who really believed in the supernatural. Certainly, there were such people, and not only the unenlightened masses: many early empiricists maintained an "open-mindedness" that was not the mark of an old credulity, but rather a properly scientific confidence that unseen material causes might make many seemingly impossible things possible.[11] There is, however, a way of understanding literary appearances of the supernatural that does not reduce them to simple statements about the way the natural world is—a way, in other words, to divorce their appearance from the grand narrative of triumphant reason. For we might also say that Subligny is here exploring the precise nature of novelistic reference, and the truth value of fictional utterances. Does the pleasure of reading depend on the truth of literary statements? Or is it independent of truth altogether? Naturally, many had asked similar questions earlier; but for writers such as Philip Sidney, whom I will take up below, the problem concerned the poet's potentially dubious traffic in mythology, legend, and fable. The literary appearance of superstition, however, raised a qualitatively different issue: how could someone else's beliefs—beliefs that did not have the cultural prestige or sanction that belonged to myth or legend—be recycled as our leisure reading?

A further short example is in order, since Subligny's recycling was one of a number of attempts at provisionally entering into or ironically inhabiting referential discourse whose truth was assumed to be doubtful. In 1670, Nicolas Montfaucon de Villars published to considerable interest *Le Comte de Gabalis, ou entretiens sur les sciences secrètes*, a first-person account of a man who undergoes an initiation of sorts in the "cabalistic" sciences.[12] From the very outset, the narrator is skeptical of the supernatural, but he decides to look a little closer by pretending to be a novice in search of occult knowledge. When Gabalis, a renowned German sage, arrives in Paris, the narrator hopes for something a little less absurd than what a number of so-called initiates have so far been able to offer. Yet his bemusement only increases: Gabalis dismisses the teaching of most other occult masters as erroneous, superstitious, even; his own elaborate explanations, meanwhile, are no less fanciful than those he denounces. Unperturbed, the narrator lends his ear to the master, whom he prods with mock-serious questions about matters such as the mating habits of sylphs. The reader expecting a climactic debunking of Gabalis's delirium is disappointed, because the narrator never makes recourse to the voice of reason: the fact that the master is a madman needs no proving, and the book consists entirely of his fanciful doctrine. The work rests therefore on the idea that superstitious belief is imaginatively fascinating. Villars shows that it is possible to enter into the superstitious mind, to reproduce its broken reasoning and faulty modes of inference, all in the interests of readerly pleasure. The *world* may be disenchanted, but its banished enchantments can be retrieved and savored as an enjoyable fancy.

Were these decades a pivotal moment in the evolution of real beliefs about the return of the dead, invisible creatures, and so on? This is the question scholars of supernatural narrative from vastly different periods rush to answer in the affirmative, as if they were witness to the key historical juncture in which the waning of closely held beliefs about reality allows their migration into art. Thus Terry Castle situates a wave of early nineteenth-century debunking narratives about ghosts—and a simultaneous interest in magic lantern shows, whose very fakeness was part of their appeal—"at precisely that moment when traditional credulity had begun to give way, more or less definitively, to the arguments of scientific rationality."[13] And E. J. Clery views the famous Cock Lane ghost case of 1762, and the publication of *The Castle of Otranto* two years later, as signaling the move of the supernatural from doctrinal debate and speculation to the realm of pure spectacle.[14] But modernity's need to return again and again to this feeling of being on the cusp need not be taken for an actual historical transition. "Today half of Europe thinks the other half has long been and still is superstitious," wrote Voltaire in his *Dictionnaire philosophique*; he was referring to Protestant critiques of Catholic dogma, but he might as well have been thinking of the way modern culture defines itself by continually propping up, and then deflating, the specter of credulity.[15] In that sense, disenchantment is not a moment we can locate, be it in seventeenth-century France or eighteenth-century England, or even a long process through which the stubborn bedrock of belief is slowly eroded. Disenchantment involves endlessly resuscitating—or downright inventing—an enchantment of some past, any past, so that a culture may think of itself as disenchanted.

But tales like these are above all laboratories for thinking about what literature does—not what literature does at all times and in all places, but what it was starting to do by the late seventeenth century. Two factors behind this persistent haunting are key. First, the questions superstition raises are properly aesthetic questions: they arose in the margins of neoclassical poetics, which conceived of the arts as a *techne* or a savoir-faire, bounded by the precedent of classical models, by the demands of decorum (the appropriateness of representations to this or that subject), and by the Horatian precept of *utile dulci.* The early uses of the supernatural I have just evoked, by contrast, work through what Joseph Addison soon called "the pleasures of the imagination," pleasures that do not need the sanction of reason or moral usefulness or truth, but that are valued for the peculiar effects they produce in the reader.[16] Hence, when Subligny asked how it was that something we know to be false produces real emotion, he was asking a question that was at the heart of early aesthetic speculation. The second factor, which cannot be entirely separated from the first, involves the assumed referentiality of language, that is, its function as a cognitive instrument with which we make more or less accurate representations of the world "out there."[17] Disenchantment can be described as the process by which discourse that purports to describe the real world is stripped of its referential credentials, after proper inspection of the sort the Chevalier de Montal brings to bear; re-enchantment then attributes to that stripped discourse a new function, aesthetic and imaginative. Superstitious statements possess, then, a mitigated or ironic referentiality: they are referential discourse whose expiration date has passed, but which is still good for something else. When authors beginning in these years returned to a supernatural they did not appear to believe in, this was not because the credulous still needed to be enlightened; rather, re-enchantment provided new possibilities for a literary creation that escaped the constraints both of history and of classical *imitatio*.

The fairy tale was the fin-de-siècle literary phenomenon that put the self-conscious reprocessing of someone else's belief front and center. Subligny had already speculated that tales of ghosts actually reactivated childhood beliefs and fears; many of Charles Perrault's adaptations of well-known tales—"Blue Beard," "Tom Thumb," "Little Red Riding Hood"—seemed to aim for just this retrospective shiver. Re-experienced fear, however, was a relatively minor goal of fairy tale production at the time, a production that was instead unremittingly playful. Unlike Perrault, who limited himself to laconic and elegant retellings of popular favorites, the main practitioners of the genre were women writers who used it to underline the possibility of a literary creation that was entirely fanciful, unburdened not only by the plots and methods of the ancients but even by the precedent of folkloric culture. (Only about half of the eighty tales published between 1696 and 1705 have folkloric antecedents, after which a full 90 percent of the production is invented.)[18] In fairy tales, the very creatures made popular by books like *Le Comte de Gabalis*—sylphs, gnomes, elves, and many more—were set free and allowed to frolic in a discourse no longer framed by the question (spurious as it had often been) of superstition and belief: our world may be thoroughly disenchanted, but the naïve language of the fairy tale allows us to play at being the children we know we are no longer. It is what Susan Stewart has called a "distressed" genre, in the sense that it marks a deliberate return to bygone beliefs, beliefs "pried from a context of function and placed within a context of self-referentiality."[19] In another sense, however, the ironic playfulness of the fairy tales of this particular moment could be said to evacuate the question of belief entirely: it was not only that fairy tales were improvisations based on someone else's beliefs, but also that the imagination could create fictions to which nobody ever lent credence. Inserted into novels whose aristocratic characters tell them to divert or impress or seduce one another, they provided the means to put forward an anti-rhetoric that foregrounded unbounded imagination ("the marvel of imaginations unrestrained by the trappings of truth," says one such narrator) and invention as a sort of creation ex nihilo ("[This tale]," says another, "is absolutely my own").[20] From their first appearance in the early 1690s, fairy tales were recognized as something literally *new*; indeed, they could serve as a kind of "manifesto of modernity" precisely because they owed nothing to the erudition of classical learning, and because they were statements without a history.[21]

The vogue for fairy tales, strongest at the turn of the eighteenth century but reverberating for decades more, was only part of a much larger recycling of superstition into a new marvelous. Fairies invaded the theater, combining with the stage machinery increasingly popular in France to create special effects of a sort that fooled no one but instead displayed in the comic mode their own theatricality.[22] And the literary genre that took off with the publication of Antoine Galland's translation of *The Thousand and One Nights* in 1704, that of the exotic or oriental tale, functioned in parallel with the fairy tale: starting as pseudo-ethnographic appropriation of traditions now deemed enchanted, the exotic tale spawned a huge local production whose attraction lay in the particular concept of the imagination it presupposed—unpedantic, easy, and improvised, as labyrinthine and recursive as Galland's tales within tales within tales. If so much of this production now appears to us irretrievably minor, this is not only because of the expected ratio of mediocrity to genius in any era's literary production: all these genres tirelessly flaunted a frivolity verging on nonsense.[23] This was a permanently ironic, and not absorptive frivolity: spectators and readers could scarcely forget that what they were watching or reading was a fabrication—because the content was unbelievable, of course, but mostly because the mode was calculated to let creators parade their cleverness. (Sheherazade's desperate narratorial predicament, then, appears as convenient shorthand for that facing contemporary authors of fiction—entertain or die.) And as the century wore on, tales of the imagination, ironic from their very inception, were made still more so. Whence, for example, the appearance of parodic fairy tales, in which characters demonstrate their knowledge of the rules of the genre, or behave quixotically, as if they were living a fairy tale—rather unnecessary developments, since, as Jean-Paul Sermain has pointed out, the genre, having stressed its artificiality from its inception, should have been proof to debunking.[24]

Many of these early strategies for taking (or inventing) old enchanted beliefs, stripping them of their referential claims, and recirculating them as ironic food for an unbound imagination persisted and continue to persist. In this light, postmodern recycling appears less a phenomenon made possible only by mechanical reproduction and late capitalism, than part of the widespread modern propensity to deny cultural artifacts their truthfulness or "use value" precisely so that they may become objects of entertainment. More could be said about this— about the way inflatable plastic "reproductions" of Münch's anguished Modernist "The Scream," for example, may well be a rough equivalent of fairy tale recreations of bygone beliefs. Without going this far, however, we can use the parallel to better stress the peculiar depthlessness of early modern re-enchantments: fun and fancy abound, but there is not much in the way of strong claims for the artwork. If early re-enchantment can be said to reconnoiter the terrain of the aesthetic—to assert the rights of the creative imagination against instrumental reason and the burden of traditional literary *imitatio*—that terrain is not yet fully occupied. Notably, the whole Neoplatonic association of poetics with a higher (metaphysical) form of truth, usually acknowledged as entering modern aesthetics via Shaftesbury, has yet to give the creative imagination its Romantic weightiness. Moreover, there was the philosophical problem of thinking the operations of reason and the imagination as something other than oppositional: it was perhaps inevitable that the literature of re-enchantment remain ironic and frivolous as long as the imagination was, as Malebranche had it, a source of sensory error that caused us to see things that were simply not there. But how would strategies of re-enchantment change if imaginative activity was shown to be behind all our mental representations, if the imagination was seen to underwrite each and every operation of the thought process itself, as it would be for writers like Voltaire and Diderot?[25] What if there were another tool besides irony that would guarantee that we not accept literary statements as literally and superstitiously true? In other words, what would be the impact of the advent of a discursive mode that short-circuits the true/false binary that had presided over all previous uses of the supernatural—that is, the discourse of realism, or verisimilitudinous fiction?

The Fantastic and the Re-Enchantment of Fiction

The work of Jacques Cazotte (1719–92), by all accounts the first practitioner of the fantastic, resumes well the shift from the irony fatigue that plagued the early literature of the imagination to a new strategy of re-enchantment that cultivated a type of assertion that was neither naively superstitious nor knowingly fanciful—modern fiction. Fiction of this particular type is distinct on the one hand from a discourse that steadfastly promotes its correspondence to the real world (what Michael McKeon dubs "naïve empiricism"), and on the other from untruth trumpeted as such, a discourse that had abandoned all referential claims (what one might call, with Addison, "fancy," noting in passing its obsolete meaning of "spectral apparition").[26] But modern fiction is distinct, as well, from those seventeenth-century strategies that employed a distancing irony so as to enable the reader to understand purportedly referential discourse as in fact imaginative. For it arises out of what Catherine Gallagher has described as "a massive reorientation of textual referentiality": unlike history, or a scientific report, it does not claim to be literally true, so it does not need to ironize those claims; neither, however, does it revel in its falseness, in the manner of fairy tales.[27] Instead, it conjures in the reader's mind a reality that looks and feels like the real world, but that is understood to be an invention. It is this that permits a qualitatively new type of reenchantment, nonfrivolous and nonironic: fiction can open the door to an heretofore untapped aesthetic exploitation of supernatural effects because it does not pretend to be a statement about the world.

Cazotte began his literary career in the 1740s symptomatically—with fairy tales strongly marked by the self-conscious promotion of imaginative fabulation.[28] But the program of the tale Cazotte is now remembered for—*Le Diable amoureux* (1772), which Romantics such as E. T. A. Hoffmann and Gérard de Nerval knew well—is radically different. For Tzvetan Todorov, *Le Diable amoureux* fulfills the sine qua non condition of the fantastic: Cazotte's story plays with the question of whether the supernatural has really intruded into reality.[29] Has our initially hubristic first-person narrator, Alvare, truly been seduced by the devil? Or was it, as they say, all just a dream? The scene of this foundational hesitation is Naples, the city known, since Salvatore Rosa's proto-gothic paintings of the previous century, for resuscitating in skeptical northern Europeans atavistic thoughts of the supernatural. When, after a smoky evening of idle chatter about the esoteric or "cabalistic" sciences, Alvare is approached and interrogated by a mysterious participant who claims to be an initiate, he quickly accepts his interlocutor's proposal to introduce him to the occult. Led down to a secret chamber beneath the ruins of Herculanum, in the town of Portici, he displays the intrepid, even hubristic, bravery typical of the skeptic. Cazotte's hero is a strange mix: he boasts that he will get the better of the "tricksters" (*mauvais plaisants*) he assumes are setting him

up by tweaking the ears of the Devil promised to appear in the penta-
cle scratched onto the floor of the chamber; but he also discovers that
his awakened "imagination" is producing involuntary effects—sweats,
chills, raised hairs.[30] But then again, perhaps the mix is not as strange
as all that, since we have already encountered it, nearly a century earlier, in Subligny's character's reflections on the fright provoked by
things one does not believe.

However, Cazotte, unlike Subligny, is able to push further: his short
novel will develop once the summoned Beelzebub actually appears, in
the form of a hideous camel's head, and asks, "*Che vuoi?*" What does
the rational, disenchanted subject really want? In the hero's case, he
clearly wants to renounce the tiresome irony that had so long accompanied literary efforts to deal with the supernatural. Immediately, he
orders the apparition to take the form of a spaniel; and the camel vom-
its the specified dog at the narrator's feet. Alvare presses on, demanding that a feast be served up for his cabalist friends, and that the dog
appear there as a page dressed in his new master's livery. All this
occurs—to the amazement of Alvare's group, and no doubt to the
reader's, for the tone of Cazotte's tale has a bracing simplicity absent
from previous re-enchanted discourse: the narrator retains a certain
cocky humor, but gone is the ironic assertion practiced by Villars, gone
too the nonsensical fancy of the fairy tale. Gone, finally, the distanced
perspective of the skeptic who is but temporarily unsure of the all-too-
natural causes he knows to be behind the observed phenomena. The
spirit world is seemingly before us.

As Todorov has argued, and others have shown in detail, the dieget-
ical reality of the events of *Le Diable amoureux* is undecidable: Cazotte
toys with what will become the favored modernist explanation for
apparently supernatural occurrences—it was a dream or hallucination—while at the same time making that hypothesis internally inconsistent.[31] The fantastic, much like Freud's uncanny, is defined by
Todorov as the deliberate cultivation of a hesitation in the mind of the
reader—that is, have the laws of the natural world really ceased to
apply? But what permits *Le Diable amoureux* to offer us a *serious* hesitation, when earlier writers seemed to accept as a given that assertions
of the supernatural had to be false? What makes for the qualitative difference—self-evident for Freud, and explored in depth by Roger Caillois—between fairy tales and fantastic or uncanny narrative?[32] Or,
more basically, why does it become possible to take the supernatural
seriously, when one would expect ever more rationalization? Is *Le*

Diable amoureux a sign that the archaic cause of superstition was making an unwelcome return, as Freud's theory of the uncanny suggested?[33] Or is it the opposite—is it, as Clery has postulated about the rise of the gothic, that the era of superstition is now so far in the past that writers could speak of ghosts and devils plainly because they no longer feared ridicule?

The appeal to the state of actual beliefs in late eighteenth-century Europe, though a tempting recourse, is in fact of little relevance to a question that is fundamentally aesthetic in nature.[34] Clery is no doubt correct to say that by the 1770s, staged ghosts are able to be taken seriously because "the very notion of superstition, let alone the stigma, has vanished as a factor in the audience's reception."[35] That vanishing, however, is not the result of a revolution in people's worldview; it is, rather, the result of a revolution in fiction. For whether or not the Enlightenment saw renewed interest in the supernatural, Cazotte's text is simply not making referential claims. The reader of the fantastic may well ask whether or not natural laws have ceased to apply *in the text;* we do not, however, need to ask that question about the real world, because we know that the novel, though it *seems* to be referring to the real world, does not in fact do so. And this is why Cazotte's *Le Diable amoureux* can recover a seriousness not previously possible: it has internalized the question of whether or not the supernatural exists, made it part of the narrative world, and framed it not by irony but by the fictional contract. Cazotte can approach the question of the existence of the supernatural without irony because it is now advanced within a fiction.

Much the same can be said about the gothic in general, of which the fantastic is just one part.[36] What is noteworthy about *The Castle of Otranto* is not that it recycles old beliefs as entertainment, since by the 1760s that type of re-enchantment was nearly a century old; rather, Walpole's novel stands out because its re-enchantment is surprisingly serious in tone. Initially, in the novel's first printing, Walpole achieved his matter-of-fact tone by professing to reproduce a discovered manuscript, thus distancing its assertions by historical remove rather than irony. Such was, in fact, an important mid-century strategy for undercutting suggestions of the supernatural without the manifest irony Villars displayed in *Le Comte de Gabalis,* and that was pushed to self-conscious heights by the fairy tale. For it was also possible to attribute superstitious assertions to people of the past: as in the ballads of Macpherson and Chatterton, bogus antiquity provided a distancing cover needed by readers of the time in order to re-admit enchantment to literary discourse.[37] But Walpole took the signal step of revealing his own hoax: when a second edition of *Otranto* was published a few months after the first, the author wrote a preface laying claim to a "new route" that managed to blend the discourse of "common life" and "probability" with "the great resources of fancy."[38] The historian's alibi, and the literary hoax, became moot: literature could assert things in a manner that was *realistic* without being *real*. The gothic's literary-historical function was to explore that *-ic*: the gothic was a test case for fictional referentiality, in that it showed that fiction could be literally unbelievable and yet aesthetically effective in the proper sense. For as much as Rousseau's *Julie* (1761), with which it seems to have nothing in common, it produced feeling.[39] But while Rousseau still maintained a maddeningly convoluted posture regarding the reality of his characters, the supernatural enabled Walpole to prove that fiction could produce serious effects even when the reader was sure beyond any doubt that it referred to nothing in the real world.

The fantastic had a slightly different historical function, but also one that policed the boundaries of fictionality just as surely: its trademark hesitations in the mind of the narrator and reader in fact have nothing to do with the reality of the supernatural, and everything to do with showing how aesthetic emotion is produced out of thin air. To return to Alvare, the hero of *Le Diable amoureux,* we must note that the reality of the diabolical apparitions in the cave beneath the ruins of Herculanum is not the source of the hero's hesitation. Strangely perhaps, Alvare immediately grants the apparitions a certain type of reality: yes, there is an order of beings with which man can be in contact, and which have power over the natural world, even though they are not of that world. But what Alvare himself must be brought to believe, and what he really hesitates over for the course of the main narrative, is whether or not the two orders of reality can become confused. The hideous camel's head, the spaniel, the page boy—all these exist for Alvare as "real" apparitions. But is it possible that the page boy Biondetto has actually become Biondetta, a former sylph who has decided to take on flesh out of love for the intrepid Spaniard? Certainly, this is Alvare's fervently expressed desire—that the supernatural become natural, that is, physical: "'Ah! Biondetta!' I said to myself, 'if only you weren't a fantastical being! If only you weren't that horrid dromedary!'" (52); "'Fantastical being, dangerous deception!' I cried, 'is it possible to better assume the form of truth and nature?'" (73); and finally, "'O Biondetta!' I said,

'I am overcome with love, persuaded that you aren't at all a fantastical being, convinced that you love me'" (78). This end to hesitation occurs immediately after Biondetta, seriously wounded by a knife-wielding, true-life jealous rival, lies prone before Alvare, who can at last contemplate her "beautiful bleeding body, cut by two enormous gashes that seemed as if they must both be attacking the wellspring of life" (75). We need not be put off by Cazotte's rather banal morality (after sex with the devil, remorseful Alvare is welcomed back into the fold of humanity by his mother), or his predictable gendering of temptation: the real temptation here is that, in Walpole's terms, the "great resources of fancy" mix with "common life." Reading, in other words, tempts us into forgetting that the uncanny realities of fiction do not exist, that their blood and bodies are fake. The fantastic does not tempt us into regressing into the enchantments of our ancestors; instead, it demonstrates the power of fictive illusions while simultaneously warning us that aesthetic emotion is not real, however tempted our bodies might be to believe it.[40]

Putting Re-Enchantment to Work

The prototypical fantastic temptation of taking the imagination for flesh and blood, and its awakening of real desire through the imagination, must therefore be read as being about the re-enchanted mode of literary delivery that is modern fiction. Alvare's desire that the imagination take on flesh is a translation of the very problem I have been examining—the strange status of fictions that admit they are not real yet, by dint of that very admission, come to acquire a realism previously impossible. The hesitation proposed by the fantastic is none other than a fascination with the propensity of literature to take on the form, shape, and color of reality—indeed, to be *more* beautiful than the real. This is not, however, to say simply that the fantastic warns us away from reference, perhaps in the same way that *Don Quixote* reminds us not to take the idealizations of romance for reality; nor is it to propose that the genre celebrates the literary as pure form. If the realistic is not real, it is not simply a lie, either: it maintains a conceptually fraught but nonetheless very powerful relation with reality. Realism allows us to talk about how the world *works* without obliging us to reproduce how the world *is*.

"The history of Western literary theory can be summed up as a continuous debate on the classical dictum that poets are liars."[41] Hans

Blumenberg's reminder of the vertiginously deep substrata underlying any discussion of "fiction" invites an assessment of the extent to which modern realist fiction does or does not introduce a qualitatively new term to that old debate. How might the concept of fiction that Walpole and Cazotte explore mark a break with fiction as it had been long understood by opponents of Plato? "The poet never maketh any circles about your imagination, to conjure you to believe for true what he writes," affirmed Sidney, against Plato, in his *Apology for Poetry* (c. 1583); poets thus do not lie, and presumably tell another sort of truth altogether.[42] Such a defense is serviceable, but becomes complicated once a species of poets called novelists started to set their fictions in the present day, on a terrain that has been mapped and surveyed and peopled with characters with names like yours and mine. That, after all, is much closer to history than to poetry. Indeed, one of the most persistent and often studied features of the early novel, dating precisely to the first disenchanting (and simultaneously re-enchanting) narratives that appear around 1670, and lasting through to the end of the eighteenth century, is its claim to historical veracity: Sidney's poet may affirm nothing—"and therefore never lieth"—but the early novelist does affirm, emphatically, the literal reality of journal, memoir, or letters. Michael McKeon calls this naïve empiricism—falsely naïve, however, for plenty of evidence suggests that in no sense were readers dupes of such strict referential claims: "I do hereby give notice to all booksellers and translators whatsoever, that the word Memoir is French for a *novel*," wrote Richard Steele in *The Tatler* of October 22, 1709, and Bayle had made similar remarks over a decade earlier in response to a wave of historical fictions.[43] Indeed, most literary historians now seem to agree that secret chronicles, memoirs, letter novels, and journals were not even intended to fool anyone, that the pretense of truth telling was a narrative strategy made necessary by the fact that in the seventeenth and eighteenth centuries there was simply no available mode that would permit writers to set invented stories in the contemporary social world. Barbara Foley, in her account of what she calls the "pseudofactual," has perhaps put it best: the age of the "true story" staked out a territory for prose fiction—making statements about the world—that was distinct from that of poetry, and could do so only by claiming a literal truth that was understood ironically.[44] Modern realist fiction does not make such claims, and does not need the buffer of ironic assertion. Which is not to say that "realism" doesn't refer to the real world—it does, of course, but in a manner understood as abstract or analogous. Old Goriot's lack of historical existence, to take a canonical example, does not for one moment impede Balzac's ability to use him to say something about the historical evolution of French society from the Revolution to the Restoration. On the contrary, one might say that it is because the reader can stop worrying about the novel *as* history that the novel is freed to take history as its subject.[45]

There is thus an unexpected affinity between the fantastic and the dominant prose form of which it is usually seen as the subversion or negation—the realist novel generally conceived. Both forms come into existence once fictional discourse gives up its empiricist alibi: the realist novel can feature characters going about their lives in the world, and aspire to give the reader knowledge of that world, without pretending that it is history; and now the supernatural can function without making claims that conflict with those of science. And just as the abandonment of the pretense to history allows the novel actually to begin its serious examination of the historical process, the fantastic, by avoiding the brand of re-enchantment that simply converted superstitious discourse into fanciful entertainment, is able to produce knowledge—knowledge about the workings of the mind. Cazotte himself describes *Le Diable amoureux* in his epilogue as an "allegory in which principle is locked in a struggle with passion[, and where] the soul is the battlefield" (125); if we follow Todorov, we might update this language a bit and say that the psychological explorations made possible by the fantastic in turn make possible the discoveries of Freud.[46] There are many other ways, moreover, that one might conceive of such a genre producing knowledge. Terry Castle has shown how the supernatural in Radcliffe permits and accompanies a signal shift in the way human memory and imagination are conceived: the wave of cultural interest in ghosts at the turn of the eighteenth century involves the relocation of "the spirit-world of our ancestors" into the human mind, as the boundary between ghost seeing and ordinary thought was eroded in psychological theories of the period.[47] Marshall Brown sees the gothic and the fantastic as Kantian thought experiments that probe the question, "What is the nature of pure consciousness?"[48] And this is only the tip of a large iceberg, of course: it is the very richness of the readings scholars are able to perform that confirms these genres' ability to undertake a brand of cultural work that previous forms of re-enchantment could not.

For many, the fantastic and the gothic constitute "the bad conscience of this positivist era": in place of the rationalized and material world of things and men, they give us the irrational realm of the psyche.[49] Yet the realist novel itself is no less re-enchanting than the genres that appear on the face of things to subvert it. To be sure, realism's attempts at describing the brute reality of the world can be seen as an outgrowth of the empirical use of language; and it is also true that in the way that it debunks the illusions of its characters, the realist novel does have a fundamentally disenchanting function. But in another sense, one of the main illusions dispelled is precisely that social reality is something immutable or given; losing one's illusions in the realist novel usually amounts to realizing that signs can be manipulated to create realities that never before existed.[50] Realism's disenchantment thus does not return us to a manifest and unambiguous real world "out there"; it suggests rather that reality itself, and especially the reality of money, is fabricated, and that the secret to success lies in the mastery of fictions— the deployment of re-enchantments—in which one does not, in fact, believe. This is why Catherine Gallagher and Stephen Greenblatt point out that novel reading is also a species of re-enchantment. If capitalism causes, in Marx's phrase, "[t]he productions of the human brain [to] appear as independent beings endowed with life," so does the novel— only whereas Marx aims to demystify this modern superstition, the novelist's manifest trade in the unreal does nothing to diminish the efficacy of its illusion.[51] (In this, Gallagher and Greenblatt liken novel reading less to Marx's idea of fetishism, which presupposes the possibility of enlightenment, than to Freud's, in which the unmasking of the fabrication does little to reduce its power—*je sais bien mais quand même*.) Such is the re-enchantment of realist fiction, exemplified by Dickens's *Great Expectations*, which "invites us to appreciate the *believable* as such," and convinces us to "extend credit to representations of the social without becoming credulous about their specifics."[52] This is what allows the realist novel to denounce the social world as an imaginary construction, a superstition, without exposing itself, as it would if it asserted its truth, to a subsequent denunciation.

The type of mitigated credence accorded to fiction usually goes by the Coleridgian name of suspended disbelief; it is important to underline, however, the extent to which the fictionality thus described can never be reduced to mere imagination or fancy, for the question of reality refuses to go away. Hence, in Coleridge's famous description of his plan for the *Lyrical Ballads*, the poet sees the work resulting from a double blurring of ontological categories achieved through the work's shared authorship: while Coleridge would busy himself with making the unreal real, Wordsworth would do just the opposite.

[I]t was agreed that my endeavours should be directed to persons and characters supernatural, or at least romantic; yet so as to transfer from our inward nature a human interest and a semblance of truth sufficient to procure for these shadows of imagination that willing suspension of disbelief for the moment, which constitutes poetic faith. Mr. Wordsworth, on the other hand, was to propose to himself as his object to give the charm of novelty to things of every day, and to excite a feeling analogous to the supernatural, by awakening the mind's attention from the lethargy of custom and directing it to the loveliness and the wonders of the world before us.[53]

For Coleridge, it is not so much that aesthetics takes us into an imaginative realm defined by its incompatibility with reality, as had been the case with Addison's "fairie way of writing" that appealed only to the imagination, or even with Sidney's poet who could not lie because he did not affirm; on the contrary, modern aesthetics has great need for reality, with which the creative imagination is caught in a ceaseless *pas de deux*. As Deborah Elise White has put it in her study of the use of superstition in the elaboration of Romantic poetics, "If imagination unbound is merely delusion and imagination bound merely decoration, poets become very minor figures in the life of a nation and its language."[54] For Jacques Rancière, the opposition—commonly taken as foundational of the aesthetic—between the realist, instrumentalist use of language and intransitive poetic language is in fact misleading: the conception of language that underwrites the aesthetic even in its "purest" realization (in Flaubert or Mallarmé, for example) is always one that sees in things themselves an immanent poetic Word.[55] Rancière's rethinking of the modern doctrine of artistic "autonomy" highlights the link, present since at least the German Romantics, between the aesthetic and the real (political and material) world that art is supposed to transform. "[T]he object of [aesthetic] experience," he writes, "is 'aesthetic' in so far as it is not—or at least not only—art."[56]

It is this reckoning with reality that early forms of re-enchantment were unable to perform. If talk about the supernatural is such a constant of disenchanted modernity, this cannot be because people had really not, after all, moved on from an earlier credulity. Rather, it is the odd new referentiality of modern fiction that is plumbed each time the question comes up. In the background of the present study has been the idea that modernity does not so much overcome superstition but invent it: there never was an enchanted world of people who "really believed" in the sense moderns give the term. That is, we tend to think of belief as having a content, or as being an assertion about the way the world is, but in a sense this very conception is derived from an empiricist, scientific view.[57] Although medieval and Renaissance poets, explorers, and naturalists returned again and again to the marvelous, only very rarely did they approach the category from the perspective of "reality." Hence pre-modern wonder, which was thought of a cognitive passion, did not aim to split phenomena into the empirically true and the empirically false, but to stimulate horror, curiosity, awe and admiration.[58] These are, of course, many of the emotions poets targeted, so we could say premodern wonders were, like the modern supernatural, of prime literary concern. Still, literary concerns change, and in a world obsessed about both truthful representation and the reality of the imagination, the supernatural thrived because it was a prime way of thinking about the unliteral yet not purely fanciful nature of fictional reference. The supernatural therefore did not so much survive from an earlier time—though it could certainly rummage around in the premodern attic for bits and pieces of its iconography—as come into existence with the modern: before re-enchantment there was not enchantment, but some other mode of knowledge production that by its very nature could be neither superstitious nor antisuperstitious.

Modern literary re-enchantments are many and varied, and they do deserve analysis that takes account of their local determinants. The growth of magical realism in South America, for example, undeniably has to do with the relation of "peripheral" writers with dominant European realism and modernism; French surrealism might be seen as resulting from the interaction of a specific literary field with the theories of Freud or Henri Bergson. But local trees should not keep us from taking a longer view: re-enchantments continually return because they are the means by which we conceive and reconceive of the aesthetic and of fiction. When early modern authors "attacked" superstition, there was nearly always a pleasure in that attack that they reflected on, and a realization that somehow the disenchanted separation of the true from the false was incompatible with narrative pleasure. I have argued that early re-enchantments were somewhat limited in the effects they could have: in their efforts to skirt the assumed referentiality of prose, and affirm its entertaining potential, they resorted to distancing mechanisms that consigned their utterances to an imaginary realm that by design was insignificant. Only a later discursive modification, whose origin I cannot hope to explain but which is signaled by the appearance of the gothic and the fantastic, would allow a more potent reenchantment to emerge, one that was able to examine the reality of the imagination and the imaginary nature of reality. These genres, which emerge just before the realist novel, as if to prepare its way, have no monopoly on superstition, and do not preclude a host of other possibilities for devising strategies of ambiguous reference—from the way that Hawthorne or Gogol "resort to a variety of narrative devices that leave open the possibility of a rational explanation for seemingly supernatural occurrences even though the 'magic' is never explicitly denied" to the more modernist introjection of explanations through recourse to the psyche, as in Henry James or mid-twentieth-century pulp tales of paranoia.[59]

All such examples can and should be tied to the specific circumstances of their elaboration, while at the same time being recognized—to use the words with which Franco Moretti has described the repeating patterns of generic evolution—as "the same comet that keeps crossing and recrossing the sky."[60] This particular comet, no more than the one Bayle and Fontenelle once converted into an object of literary interest, cannot be simply disenchanted, debunked, and forgotten: the modern necessity of thinking about literature's relation to the world is endlessly vexed because, as Bruno Latour argues in *We Have Never Been Modern,* we both believe in that world's independent existence and hold it to be an imaginary human construct. What makes the supernatural attractive as a subject, and what a genre like the fantastic foregrounds for our pleasure and discomfort, is that the fictional renunciation of truth claims does not, as it could with Sidney, make the problem of the real go away. Rather, the same concept of fiction that allows us to avoid asking whether a text is true also discourages us from thinking that literature is but a frivolous flight of fancy. Or put another way, fiction, through the constant shuttling back and forth between reality and imagination, continues to beat away at the disenchanted barrier between mind and things, the subject and the world.

CHAPTER 10

Gnosophilia: Bloch, Benjamin, and the Authority of Counter-Tradition

DANIEL JIRO TANAKA

IN THE 1998 MOVIE *X-Files: Fight the Future*, an undercover informant meets FBI agent Fox Mulder in a dark alley to reveal a dangerous secret. There exists a powerful clandestine group—a "government within the government"—conspiring to cover up evidence of alien life. More sinister is the suggestion that this shadow government may also be in cahoots with the aliens, whose ultimate goal is colonization of the earth. The informant delivers these details in increasingly hushed tones, until he finally reveals the name of that secret agency in a barely audible whisper: "FEMA!"

Well, now we know. Our laughter at this revelation is the sign of a historical *peripeteia*. If a decade ago it was still possible to suspend our disbelief and go along with the fantasy of an inscrutable and nearly omniscient government agency, now we feel only a bitter irony about precisely that agency's lack of omniscience. Though conspiracy theories of all sorts still abound, and a certain amount of (justifiable) paranoia persists about the extent of wire-tapping, these things are no longer as enchanted as they once were. In other words, it is no longer compelling to fantasize about the supernatural alliances from which political agents (or other historical forces) could have derived their power. Rather, we are now more apt to view political or corporate conspiracy as a product of the more mundane machinations of ordinary, flawed people in positions of extraordinary power.

But why, then, begin a study of re-enchantment with a quintessential moment of *dis*enchantment? Max Weber famously suggested that in a disenchanted age, the incalculability of the world would be consigned to the mere realm of private demons—to a pianissimo far tinier than the grand metaphysical mysteries of earlier times. But what Weber overlooked (and what others after him were quick to point out) was the extent to which rational, disenchanted societies also sanction and even require certain forms of enchantment, precisely in arenas more public than the chambers of our minds. If we accept that societies continue to partake of communal forms of enchantment, then it also stands to reason that re-enchantment is historically specific and contingent. The appeal to magic or the supernatural—no matter how fantastic—is most compelling when it taps into an epoch's anxiety about its own mode of disenchantment. In other words, re-enchantment responds to, and hence often incorporates, the forms of rationality and calculability that dominate a culture at a given moment.

Walter Benjamin and Ernst Bloch came of age in the early years of the twentieth century, when the Weberian terms of modern disenchantment were still being forged. As Norbert Bolz has argued, a generation of young intellectuals at the time of the First World War attempted to explode the "iron cage of disenchantment" that Max Weber had described.[1] Both Benjamin and Bloch devise strategies for transcending that cage without thereby leaving the world; in this, they share the belief that the traces of lost perfection lie indelibly embedded in the muck around us, and that such traces might still be excavated if one looks in the right places and in the right way. The present study examines the historicity of the means at their disposal to resist disenchantment. To understand any attempt to "re-enchant" the world is to historicize that attempt; we must see not only which aspect of the disenchanted world an author resists, but also which traditions he has at his disposal to do so.

One prominent aspect of modernity that both Benjamin and Bloch reject is the exclusively scientific and rational description of experience. As university students, both attempted to overcome Neo-Kantianism, the philosophical orthodoxy of the time. The Neo-Kantians had taken up Kant's central question in the first *Critique*: "How are synthetic a priori judgments possible?" Kant began from the premise that epistemological certainty about the world does in fact exist—as natural scientific knowledge—and then asked how such knowledge is possible. Referring to precisely this question about "conditions of possibility," Ernst Bloch wrote in 1918:

One might just as well ask how Javanese dance rites are possible, or the Indian mysteries, or Chinese ancestor worship, or (to be Western European . . . about the matter), how predestination, the Apocalypse, or other such synthetic a priori judgments are possible; and it would behoove us to do so if we wish to plumb the depths not only of our little corner of the world, but of the entirety of the Spirit [*Geist*] that has been accorded to humans.[2]

Like Bloch, for whom Kant's question epitomizes the moment of Western disenchantment, Walter Benjamin objected that Kant's "one-sidedly mathematical and scientific concept of experience" was "metaphysically barren." However, Benjamin's reservations about Kant are not tantamount to an outright rejection of reason; in fact, Benjamin's early critiques of mythical thinking are often consonant with the Enlightenment project. Rather, what Benjamin and Bloch reject is the reduction of all human and historical experience to the limited sphere described by science. In order to construct an alternative to the positivistic excavation of historical experience, both appeal to an esoteric but malleable counter-tradition—one highly suited to the secular modernity of Weimar Germany.

The counter-tradition to which I refer is Gnosticism, which has its place in discussions of Bloch's early work, but which has, in the case of Benjamin, remained marginal relative to his more well-known engagement with Kabbalah and Jewish mysticism. In what follows, I will explicate some of the central gnostic features of Bloch's early work, *The Spirit of Utopia* (1918), and then argue for the underlying gnostic structure of Benjamin's essay on "Goethe's Elective Affinities" (1921). Given that the scholarly reconstruction of Gnosticism remained incomplete throughout Benjamin's and Bloch's lifetimes, I contend that their creative stance toward it was, necessarily, *a function of that incompleteness.* In other words, it is that incompleteness that renders the Gnostic tradition malleable and eminently suited to the purpose for which first Bloch, then Benjamin, enlist it: the critique of a disenchanted modernity.

Malleable Gnosis

The last decades of the nineteenth century saw a renaissance in scholarly research on the history of religions, particularly in the German academy. Speculation about the Gnostic origins of Christianity was prevalent enough that contemporaneous work on the Kabbalah and Manicheanism needed to be defined in their degree of similarity to, or divergence from, the Gnostic tradition. Thus even Gerschom Scholem, writing in the twentieth century, felt it necessary to refer to Kabbalah as a form of "Jewish gnosis," despite a temporal separation of several centuries between the Gnosticism of late antiquity and the Jewish mysticism of the Middle Ages. Significantly, the question whether Gnosticism was an identifiable movement at all (however murky) seems to have bothered scholars at the turn of the century far less than the question of the role it played in the emergence of Christianity. In short, the existence of Gnosticism was not at stake, but rather that of the *normative* boundaries among Christianity, Judaism, and the Oriental or pagan religions. But the stability of the term *Gnosticism* has been productively challenged by more recent scholarship, which shows that a single, unified religion cannot be neatly discerned behind the diverse doctrines or the variety of ideological interests at play in the attempts to recover it.[3]

The central event that shed light on everything before (and after) it was the discovery, in 1945, of a large collection of lost Gnostic texts. The story of that spectacular discovery, near the town of Nag Hammadi in Upper Egypt, has entered the lore of great twentieth-century finds. An Egyptian farmer engaged in a blood feud to avenge his father's murder stumbled across a clay jar in which he discovered thirteen papyrus books. The books, or codices, contained some fifty-two texts—fourth-century Coptic translations of even older Greek texts.[4] But while the discovery set research on surer empirical footing in the latter half of the twentieth century, paradoxically, the sheer diversity of "heretical" Gospels (many of them previously unknown) simultaneously began to cast doubt on the existence of Gnosticism as a single religion with a unified canon. In comparison with this sudden proliferation of available source material, the number of primary sources on which earlier interpretations had been based was extremely limited. Previous knowledge was based almost exclusively on early Christian refutations of Gnostic heresies. With the exception of two Coptic manuscripts discovered in the eighteenth century and a third recovered at the end of the nineteenth, representations of "Gnostic" creeds and practices derived from the polemics of Christian authorities writing in the second and third centuries. Plotinus, the third-century Neoplatonist philosopher who exerted considerable influence over the young Georg Lukács, devoted an entire chapter of his *Enneads* to a refutation of Gnosticism ("Against the Gnostics; or against those that affirm the Creator of the cosmos and the cosmos itself to be evil"). Thus the dearth of primary sources before 1945 and the mystique that accrued to this lost tradition added to the allure of a secret canon suppressed by orthodoxy. Furthermore, the relatively meager empirical basis for this canon meant that it afforded a small repertoire of unsystematized but malleable heterodox eschatologies.

The feature most typically identified with Gnosticism is its dualism. According to this view, the true divine being resides utterly beyond our world, an "alien God" or "the Alien" in the terminology of the second century Gnostic writer Marcion. Similarly, the Mandaeans, whose name derives from the Aramaic word for knowledge, refer to "alien Life."[5] The corollary to the true God's transcendence is the notion that Creation itself—the world—is fallen and corrupt, and its Creator evil: "The cosmos is the handiwork of inferior beings, of a jealous demiurge called Jehovah, of petty gods or demons, or else it is a delusion, the result of a fall, the self-estrangement of God from Himself."[6] This dualistic theology is the object of Christian attacks, not least of all because it challenges the unity of Savior and Creator and the continuity of the Old and New Testaments. Even Plotinus, whose Neoplatonism at times resembles the speculative cosmology of some Gnostic systems, rejects the notion of an evil Creator. The material world in which we exist is "error," the result of the true divinity's estrangement or even "defection" from itself. Though this alien God resides entirely beyond the natural world, shards of his essence have been trapped in the cosmic prison that is our world. Knowledge, or *gnosis,* is a revelatory perception of these "sparks" of the divine essence within our souls, or *pneuma.*[7] The esoteric knowledge called gnosis, then, is at odds with the paradigm of rational knowledge that has been handed down in Western thought. According to Hans Jonas, rational knowledge in the Greek sense of *theoria* is universal and pertains to a knowing subject that is "informed," whereas gnosis is particular and mutual: the known divulges itself and the knower is "transformed."[8] The Egyptian poet Valentinus, writing in Rome in the second century C.E., contended that true knowledge is not only the instrument of salvation but itself represents the restoration of the alienated divinity within us. And just as true knowledge is either the medium or the very end of salvation, ignorance of the divine spark within us is the root of our fallenness.

Before proceeding further, it is useful to make the distinction, as many commentators have done, between *Gnosticism* and *gnosticism.*[9] Though recent research has deconstructed the unitary stability of Gnosticism, I retain this spelling provisionally to refer to the phenomenon of late antiquity that many modern writers imagine to be a unified movement. This is to be distinguished from gnosticism (with a small *g*), which designates the family of modern recoveries and re-figurings of that ancient "religion." This latter sense of the term is compatible with Hans Jonas's contention that gnosticism represents an existential sensibility that tends to flourish during periods of extreme alienation.[10] Furthermore, it accepts the variety of ideological and polemical interests at play in the modern attempts to recover or enlist Gnosticism; it is defined as much by the use to which one puts it as it is by the set of ancient doctrines or images. Finally, gnosticism extends, as we will see, to the hermeneutic stance taken by many of its modern exponents; in their hands it becomes a mode of writing, or a technique of reading, or both.

Given this more expansive definition, we become witnesses to the veritable *gnosophilia* of modern thought, the ubiqitous penchant for redeploying gnostic structures and images. But this apparent ubiquity leads us to a curious paradox. As we have seen, the majority of the primary texts of Gnosticism were not discovered until 1945. Modern gnosticism has therefore been a remarkably fecund tradition despite—or because of—the incompleteness of its source material. The periodic resurgence of gnosticism, then, suggests that it is *simultaneously malleable and conservative*. On the one hand, its fundamental, mythic dualism has been employed both to describe and to escape a variety of cages, each particular to its unique historical situation. On the other hand, successive reenactments of the gnostic dilemma seem to draw on a relatively limited repertoire of structures and images, despite the fact that scholarship after Nag Hammadi has uncovered a vast array of diverse and even competing canons. This relative conservatism within literary and philosophical gnosticism is, at least in part, a function of the usefulness of its status as a heresy.

It is not difficult to imagine how one might wield the gnostic dualism against various orthodoxies that have emerged in the process of modernization. For this reason, considerations of modern gnostic thought tend to begin with the Enlightenment. In his commentary to the English translations of the Gnostic Library, Richard Smith writes:

The Enlightenment writers created a sympathetic picture of the Gnostics because heterodoxy suited their anti-orthodoxy. They emphasized the dualist critique of the world, but ignored the dualist promise of transcendent escape. The *philosophes* thus created a version of the Gnostics that was, like themselves, secular. [. . .] The eighteenth century *philosophes* regarded Gnosticism as a counter-tradition and wielded it as a weapon in their outflanking tactics to overthrow the received tradition.[11]

Smith goes on to consider the various incarnations of modern gnosti-cism, from Blake and Melville to Jung, Heidegger, and more recently, Harold Bloom. In such cases, modern thinkers offer a kind of secular soteriology: recognizing the error of the manifest world ends not in an irruption from that world, but in a world-immanent, self-salvation of humankind.

Mystical language saturates the work of many secular thinkers of the twentieth century. Furthermore, it would be inaccurate to expunge all elements of theology from Bloch and especially Benjamin. How-ever, both thinkers combine their respective theological philosophies with more secular strategies of consciousness-raising. In practice, Ben-jamin's profane illumination is a kind of "paying attention to," exe-cuted with mystical intensity. It is the attention to secular aesthetic traditions, and to the broken pieces of lost perfection that constitute the historical and post-lapsarian world. Thus Benjamin is drawn to the consciousness-altering aspects of Surrealism, and Bloch experiments with the liberating potential of Expressionism—in order to burst our specifically modern form of entrapment. In this respect, Benjamin and Bloch take up the mantle of their world-immanent eighteenth century predecessors. If the *philosophes* focused on countermanding the author-ity of received tradition, Benjamin and Bloch avail themselves of the gnostic counter-tradition in order to critique the disenchanted moder-nity that Weber had described.

The drive to impart secret, esoteric knowledge becomes an essential part of the tone of many literary and philosophical texts (this is partic-ularly true of Bloch's *Spirit of Utopia*). As a literary technique, it is a strategy that often aims at divorcing language from its use as a mere instrument or tool for representing the world around us or the contents of our minds. Benjamin, writing in a Kabbalistic vein, calls this instru-mental understanding of language the "bourgeois view." Rather, gnos-tic writing, considered as a technique, is unremittingly evocative, often figurative and lyrical; it is the struggle to awaken something within us that has been deadened by our entrapment in a network of inexorable causality. Bloch's language, as we will see, strives to reveal a secret, utopian self—not through reasoned argument but through tonality and the reverberations of homophonous associations and synesthetic turns of phrase. Similarly, Heidegger's language, though by no means lyri-cal or subjective, strains the common usage of everyday words in order to get at the forgotten meaning of "Being." (It is no coincidence that Hans Jonas, who emphasized the existential sensibility of gnosticism, was a student of Heidegger.)

The language of gnosis is also dissonant, since to intuit the secret knowledge of one's divine origins is to suffer one's own foreignness in the world. Thus the poet Rilke, in the elegiac mood of his mature work, writes that even "the shrewd animals notice that we're not very much at home in the world we've expounded" (*und die findigen Tiere merken es schon, dass wir nicht sehr verlässlich zu Haus sind in der gedeuteten Welt*).[12] But perhaps the greatest modern minstrel of discomfort is Kafka, whose writing is so often a struggle against his mooring to the abjection of corporeal existence. According to Walter Sokel, Kafka's gnostic mood is a double bind: it is both recognition of the part that resides in Paradise and necessary subjection to the worldly powers around him. "[W]hile alienating him completely from the world that he knows, writing opens another world to him. This strange unknown world dwells in his depths. It is inchoate, immaterial, indescribable. [. . .] Kafka is able to say of it only *that* it is, that it dwells inside him, urging to be revealed."[13]

Although Max Weber rejected the possibility of transcending our rational modernity and preached instead an acceptance of its conditions, the "iron cage of disenchantment" remains a deeply gnostic image, reminiscent of the dungeon in which the malicious God, or Demiurge, has imprisoned the *pneuma*. The canonization of Weber's image as the quintessential emblem of disenchantment suggests that the modern affinity for gnostic tropes—our "gnosophilia"—does not belong solely to the realm of mystics and prophets seeking to escape an all-too rational modernity. Rather, to interpret the world as disenchanted is also to point to our entrapment, a revelation that revives precisely the forms of transcendence that disenchantment claims to have abolished. In short, disenchantment cannot be articulated without invoking its "Other." For the critical contemporaries of Weber, the act of articulating the conditions of the modern cage necessitates the attempt to grasp all that is not encompassed by those conditions. (The citation from Bloch at the outset of this essay is a prime example.)

For writers in the early part of the twentieth century, the existence of a suppressed and secret canon of wisdom promised not only a means by which to capture the general apocalyptic mood of the First World War, but also a source of heterodox authority with which to oppose modernity's rationalized institutions—not least of all, the academy. Like Walter Benjamin, Ernst Bloch maintained a cautious distance from what he perceived to be the orthodoxies of academic philosophy. But unlike Benjamin, who abandoned his plans to write a dissertation on Kant, Bloch did produce a doctoral thesis on a major strand of Neo-Kantian thought. Both rejected the ahistorical idealism of the Kantian tradition, but sought in different ways to make up for that lack. As Anson Rabinbach writes, "After 1914 we see in both Bloch's and Benjamin's writings an attempt to find a secular and theological philosophy that can embody the messianic impulse in relation to a real apocalypse and to translate the promise of European culture into the promise of political redemption."[14] For Bloch, the gnosticism he received from Georg Lukács, Neoplatonism, and German Romanticism provided the language and conceptual architecture with which to express this impulse.

3. The Gnosis of Self-Encounter in Bloch's *Spirit of Utopia*

The Spirit of Utopia, Bloch's first long work, was composed in the years from 1915 to 1917 and appeared in its first edition in 1918. Bloch revised the book for a second edition, which appeared in 1923 and contained modifications to the organization of its chapters, as well as a revised preface that invoked the spiritual condition of postwar Germany. But the mood of the First World War and its aftermath accounts only in part for the prophetic, apocalyptic tone of the text (in either edition). Most pertinent to an understanding of its intent is Bloch's comment, in an afterword of 1963, that the book represented an act of "revolutionary gnosis."[15] In fact, the gnostic eschatology of the work as a whole is the metaphysical scaffolding into which Bloch's diverse reflections on art, music, and philosophy fit.

From the outset, we are within the figurative language of *The Spirit of Utopia*. It is a deliberate, at times severe, interiority from which the reader never emerges into the gentle repose of expository distance. "How now? It is enough. Now we must begin. Life is delivered into our hands." And in the second edition we read: "I am. We are. That is enough. Now we must begin." The "I" and "we" of the later version capture the trajectory of the whole: the work aims at an unprecedented experience of self-encounter (*Selbstbegegnung*) that culminates in a socialist utopia. Or, to remain with the opaque pronouns that greet us in the opening line, the self-realization of a not-yet-conscious "I" entails the realization of a still inchoate and latent "We." The progression is reminiscent of Hegel, but only in a limited sense, for in Hegel even Absolute Spirit remains in the orbit of Mind (*Geist*), an objective feature of the historical world. The knowledge that the self gains in Bloch's text is neither mental nor theoretical; it is *gnosis*—which signifies an immediate acquaintance or familiarity with (divine) essence, over and against any form of cognitive knowledge or consciousness. If true knowledge is an encounter that transforms us, the overarching "narrative" of Bloch's text is the ongoing process of a transformative self-encounter—one that contains the promise of salvation. Beyond the seeming aestheticism of Bloch's arguments or the prophetic cadences of his prose, it is this soteriological aspect that early readers identified as "expressionistic." The gesture of heralding a new future bears the stamp of Nietzsche's Zarathustra, whom Expressionist poets of the time had invoked, if not always by name, then in tone and manner.

As Michael Pauen has convincingly shown, the gnostic idea that knowledge is the key to salvation not only informs the general trajectory of *The Spirit of Utopia*, but also structures the progression of its argument.[16] For Bloch, art is the object of contemplation through which we encounter our true selves, and in this, he diverges from the nineteenth-century aestheticism that advocated "art for art's sake." The aesthetics of *The Spirit of Utopia* unfolds in a series of essay-like chapters that proceeds from simple to more complex plastic forms (pottery, architecture, painting) and finally to music, the most abstract and metaphysical form. Thus we begin in contemplation of a simple clay jar (*Krug*): though it is childlike in its simplicity, we become richer and more present to ourselves if we overcome a merely "empathic" (*einfühlend*) or imitative relationship to the object. By encountering the "brown, peculiarly grown, Nordic and amphora-like" object, Bloch writes, "I [. . .] thereby grow richer and more present for my part (*als mein Teil*) upon this thing that takes part in me (*mir teilhaftig*)."[17] Here, the wordplay conveys the aspect of mutual participation between subject and object: we are to take part in the aesthetic object as something that is already a part of us by virtue of its history. Bloch begins with the simplest of objects in order to show how it, too, partakes in our awakening. The goal of this process, as we discover at the end of the following chapter, is "the fullness of appearing to oneself"; or in other words, the "self-presence of that which is eternally intended, the I and the We," and "the self presence of our hidden divine existence."[18] The self-knowledge we attain through the contemplation of the aesthetic object is not that of the traditional sort, the *nosce te ipsum* of classical and Christian thought. Rather, it is the secret knowledge of Valentinian gnosis, according to which the knowledge of what is hidden in us *is* itself salvation.[19] Put another way, to cast off ignorance of the spark within us (the *pneuma*) is to liberate and restore the divine essence to itself, but also to effect the full realization of the human.

In his chapter on "The Production (*Erzeugung*) of the Ornament," Bloch turns to architecture, sculpture, and painting across a variety of epochs, from Greek antiquity to European modernism. Here, he appeals to Alois Riegl's concept of *Kunstwollen,* or "aesthetic volition." Riegl, a founding member of the Vienna School of art history, had argued that the aesthetic sensibilities of a given culture were more than simply a passive reflection of its worldview; rather, a culture attempts to shape its relationship to the world actively through its art. Art therefore reveals a culture's collective "desire," its volitional impulse to shape the world around it.[20] Thus Bloch sees in the monuments and crypts of ancient Egypt a nameless fear of death that produces only an affirmation of death, a desire to become like stone. Whereas this Egyptian "immanence" signifies the sovereignty of inorganic nature over life, the Christianity of Gothic architecture introduces what Bloch calls "the spirit of resurrection"—a desire to burst stone and point to a life beyond. (A Hegelian form of Orientalism is clearly discernible here: the older, Egyptian form of immanence is required to articulate the later, Christian mode of transcending inorganic material.) Modern painting realizes an active and creative relationship to space that was latent in the Renaissance: in Raphael and Leonardo, Bloch argues, things no longer merely inhabit space; space inhabits things. Cubism most fully realizes this tendency in an active and constructive relationship to space that Bloch calls "spatial magic" (*Raummagie*).[21] In this sweeping survey, plastic art forms strive against mere materiality; things become mere "masks," as the hidden human interior (*das menschliche Innere*) approaches the secret interior of the world (*das Innere der Welt*).

The abstract, subjective language with which Bloch describes plastic art is only half of a textual strategy that we might call "chiastic." Just as external objects grow increasingly interior and lose their materiality, so do the "sounds" (*Klänge*) of the invisible world grow increasingly plastic and imagistic (*bildhaftig*).[22] As becomes clear in the expansive "Philosophy of Music," sound is identified with an awakening interiority, a hidden and as yet unknown "Self" that has little to do with the traditional self or subject of philosophy. Yet even as Bloch's language aims at a metaphysical register of the aural sensorium, he also marshals a plastic image to concretize the interweaving themes of his music theory. Bloch borrows the image of the carpet from Lukács, who employed the image as a "heuristic concept" (*Hilfsbegriff*) in his *Soul and Form* of 1911. (The appearance of the carpet in Lukács again shows the influence of Alois Riegl. In his *Problems of Style* of 1893, Riegl had described the "Oriental spirit of abstraction" evident in the antinaturalism of ornamental arabesques in Near Eastern art—an interpretation he also extended to tapestry and carpets.)[23] For Lukács, the arabesques of the carpet signify an absolute interpenetration of form and content: they are not merely form in the sense of an abstract template or container for the "real content" of the artwork; rather, they are the very threads that constitute the materiality of the object. In Bloch's text, this highly metaphysical notion of the carpet serves a regulative and teleological function. In other words, the carpet represents an ideal interpenetration of sensible and supersensible form—an ideal against which Bloch measures the relative degree of perfection attained in works throughout the history of music.

The image of the carpet not only represents the methodological goal of Bloch's theory of music, it is also an emblem for the style of his writing. The word *tone* (*Ton*) is a thread that grows progressively entangled in the gnostic argument of *The Spirit of Utopia*, gradually accruing a variety of meanings. Bloch exploits the multiple meanings of *Ton*, which in German can mean both clay and "tone" in all the senses of the English word. Thus the clay of the earthenware jar in the opening chapter resonates both with the tones of color in Bloch's discussion of modern painting, and with the aural sense of the word developed in the later chapters on music. There, tone emerges in a variety of incarnations, as Wagner's "(en)toning gestures" (*tönende Gebärde*),[24] a tone that "does not yet speak,"[25] and an "intonation" (*Tonfall*) that puts us in touch with "a silence more eloquent than speech."[26] This proliferation of meanings points to a significant aspect of the function of tone in Bloch's text. Though it is essential to the work's eschatology, the term is not purely conceptual in any rational sense; rather, it is essentially evocative and resonates with all other stages of the argument. Indeed, it effects an associative "tonality," an ecstatic interconnectedness of all the aesthetic objects under consideration, such that these objects are liberated from the phenomenology of traditional aesthetics.

But Bloch does not merely advocate a return to theology after the fact of disenchantment. It is clear from his earliest writings that an inward turn toward a subjective eschatology is necessitated by the incompleteness of a rationally expounded, disenchanted world. Despite their excavation of anti-rational and esoteric forms of knowledge, neither Bloch nor Benjamin is interested in "turning back the clock" to a mythical time before the disenchantment of the world; rather, they attempt in their writing to tap into the remaining "other" of modern rationality. This aspect of Bloch's project is evident in his stance toward the Kantian tradition—in particular, to the negative, limiting moment of the Kantian critique. (It was this aspect of Kant's philosophy that led Moses Mendelssohn to call him "The All-Destroyer.") As Bloch's early work amply shows, his primary impulse is not to reject the natural sciences, but to harness and articulate a utopian energy that the rational interpretation of the world cannot address.

Bloch's utopian philosophy aims at the recognition of an unexamined and "unnamed mystery" that resides within the given, empirical world. Thus in his 1908 doctoral dissertation on the Neo-Kantian philosopher Heinrich Rickert, Bloch writes: "Not until time's line no longer lies in the merely sensuous shadow of an eternal present will the night of existence be illuminated by a comprehended past and future."[27] This argument, left hanging in the dissertation, finds its fullest expression in the notion of the "darkness of the lived moment" in *The Spirit of Utopia*. It calls into question the very idea of self-presence. Whereas the positivistic view of history relies on an insufficiently problematized concept of the present moment, Bloch argues that this moment is shrouded in darkness: we do not have unfettered access to the lived moment, and thus we live in ignorance of the true aspect of full self-presence. Here, his philosophy approaches negative theology: the metaphysical fullness at which it aims can only be described negatively—that is, as the negation of the incomplete reality in which we live. The point is to grasp the fact *that* we are not present onto ourselves, *that* our being is divided and that the accessible face of our experience is not the whole story. (Heidegger's existential ontology begins with a similar gesture: we have forgotten the meaning of Being, and we are unaware that we've forgotten it.) Thus recognition of our own ignorance is itself a kind of gnosis; to see that the accessible face of our experience is incomplete is also to intuit the greater fullness from which we have fallen. This recognition is not Socratic, since Socratic self-knowledge is conscious and proceeds through dialectical reason, whereas gnostic recognition implies a non-cognitive familiarity with the divine spark in us. The gnostic redeemer, then—the agent that pulls us out of this "night of existence"—is not divine but *human*: by recognizing his own fallenness, man initiates the restoration of his own divinity. As Michael Pauen has suggested, the human subject is both the agent and the goal of this process, a process that results in Bloch's "apotheosis of the subject."[28]

Bloch's turn toward the subjective is aimed at an overcoming of philosophy's rational, knowing subject, and toward the articulation of a new self that belongs to the utopian future. His apocalyptic tone throughout the work is clearly a reference to the Russian Revolution, whose ideal potential Bloch initially embraced before eventually growing disillusioned with Stalinism. Benjamin, however, diverges significantly from Bloch's commitment to the subject as the site or agent of salvation; for Benjamin, the world can only be saved through the surrender of subjectivity.[29] As Adorno later wrote, "In all phases Benjamin thought of the demise of the subject and the salvation of mankind as one thing."[30] Benjamin studied *The Spirit of Utopia* carefully in 1919 but remained ambivalent about its subject-centered eschatology. In a now famous short piece titled "Theological-Political Fragment," he wrote that the merit of Bloch's work lay in its repudiation of the political validity of theocracy. While offering a vision of human perfection, the work's gnostic eschatology cannot, for Benjamin, be the basis of a political program.[31] What he does share with Bloch, however, is the search for "profane illumination"—that is, a messianic impulse to interpret modern experience as consisting of fragments of an ideal state of perfection.

4. Critique as Gnosis: Benjamin's Reading of Goethe

If Bloch is a gnostic writer in his use of expressionistic dissonance, Benjamin is a gnostic *reader*. In his lengthy essay on Goethe, Benjamin attempts to explode the false world posited by Goethe's novel, *Elective Affinities*. His aim is to reveal the absolute interpenetration of fictive elements in that novel, ultimately to show that such interpenetration is the cage of man's "entrapment in nature." He employs the Romantic notion that to critique a work of art is to complete it; unlike the Romantics, however, Benjamin contends that doing so also means showing the way out. As we will see, this act of rupturing the enclosed sphere of Goethe's novel entails a powerful misreading—one that reveals Benjamin's gnostic intentions.

Scholarship on Benjamin's early work has traditionally focused on his theory of language and its roots in Jewish mysticism. Like Bloch, Benjamin strives in his writing against the view of language as a mere means or tool. In his youthful essay "On Language as Such and on the Language of Man" (1916), Benjamin advocates an anti-instrumental view, according to which language is not a means for communicating mental contents, but a medium of revelation.[32] Though a comprehensive reading of Benjamin's language mysticism lies beyond the scope of this essay, we should note that it informs much of his early work, including his influential essay on translation (1924) and the 1926 treatise on baroque drama. Most relevant to our present concern is Benjamin's focus on language's esoteric dimension: the "bourgeois" view of language as a tool for expressing mental contents is superceded by the notion of language as a medium in which a greater truth is revealed, independently of the intentions of individual speakers.

A similar "double view" appears in the correspondence surrounding the composition of the Goethe essay. In a letter of 1919 to his friend Gerschom Scholem, Benjamin cites the following passage from *The Spirit of Utopia*:

Know that there is a double view for all worlds. One shows its exterior, namely the general laws of the world according to its external form. The other shows the inner essence of worlds, namely the essence of the human soul. Accordingly, there are two levels of action: works and the order of prayers. Works aim to perfect the world with respect to its external face, whereas prayer shows how the one world is contained within the other and lifts this world upward to heaven.[33]

Bloch had mistakenly attributed this passage to the *Zohar*, the major work of the thirteenth-century Spanish Kabbalist Moses de Léon. According to Scholem, the passage appears first in Franz Josef Molitor's *Philosophie der Geschichte, oder über die Tradition*, a work with which Benjamin was familiar by 1919 at the latest. In Benjamin's essay, it is not prayer, but rather critique (*Kritik*) that reveals another world and lifts it out of its containment.

In his doctoral dissertation on early Romantic aesthetics, Benjamin had developed the concept of literary critique that he later put into practice in the Goethe essay.[34] In the dissertation, Benjamin takes up Friedrich Schlegel's notion that to critique a work of art is to complete it. But whereas Schlegel believed that the critic "completed" each individual work of art by showing how it was part of a single, ideal continuum of Art, Benjamin argued that such completion could only be marked by a moment of rupture, not continuity. In the Goethe essay, Benjamin attempts to show that there exists a fragment of the ideal world trapped within the otherwise fallen, mythic world of Goethe's novel.

Goethe's novel *Elective Affinities* (1809) is ostensibly about the end of a marriage between a nobleman, Edward, and his wife, Charlotte. Edward abandons his wife for the younger Ottilie, and Charlotte in turn falls in love with another, Otto. The central simile of the novel is the likening of human attractions to chemical valences: just as elements in a compound often recombine with elements to which they have a stronger chemical attraction, so too do human couples break apart and seek out others with whom they share a stronger natural—"elective"—affinity. (The English translation is somewhat misleading; the German *Wahlverwandtschaft* in this context connotes preference but not free will.) Benjamin's critique of the novel is that it reflects all too well the "metaphysically barren landscape" of the Enlightenment, the same horizon of experience that Kant had described. More precisely, the novel's central trope represents the extent to which humans are trapped in nature. Benjamin calls this entrapment "mythic."

The concept of myth that Benjamin employs here is notoriously murky. The term derives in part from the idiom of German Idealism. Among Benjamin's contemporaries, Neo-Kantians such as Hermann Cohen and Ernst Cassirer had interpreted various mythologies ontologically: the intermixing of gods and humans in the mythological conception of the world implied that they occupied the same plane of existence—a single, monological domain. In his posthumous work, *Religion of Reason Out of the Sources of Judaism,* Cohen argued that the reduction of existence to a single order of being is symptomatic of pantheism, which must be opposed at every turn. (As Franz Rosenzweig and Gerschom Scholem both noted, Cohen opposed "immanentism" in all its forms, from pantheism to Spinoza's rationalism.)

In an early piece on religion, Benjamin had similarly objected to pantheism and its modern incarnations. The most influential of those incarnations during Benjamin's formative years was the philosophy of Monism. The rise of the scientistic worldview called Monism is largely attributed to Ernst Haeckel (1834–1919), the biologist and popularizer of Darwinism in Germany. In addition to his work on morphology throughout the 1860s, Haeckel published in 1899 a summation of his popular philosophy titled *The Riddle of the Universe.* The work was translated into thirty languages, its popular success culminating in the founding of the German Monist League in 1906 and the International Committee of Monism in 1911.[35] Haeckel's proximity to Spencerian Social Darwinism is well documented,[36] but the success of the movement must also be attributed to his indefatigable opposition to the church, his progressive iconoclasm in the face of the "forces of reaction." Above all, what Haeckel promised was not the abolition of religion in general, but rather the founding of a secular religion, a scientific philosophy that would grant the solace that dogmatic religion had traditionally given.

Benjamin makes explicit reference to Monism both in his correspondence and the 1912 "Dialogue on the Religiosity of the Present." His contact with the movement came through the figure of Wilhelm Ostwald, the Nobel Prize–winning chemist to whom Haeckel had handed over leadership of the German Monist League in 1910. Benjamin's early mentor, the educational reformer Gustav Wyneken, had found in Ostwald and in the Monists powerful allies in the struggle for school reform. Wyneken met both Ostwald and Haeckel in Munich in the early years of the twentieth century, and by 1913, Ostwald had gained enough acceptance in Wyneken's circle to publish the lead article in an issue of its journal.[37] In his correspondence, Benjamin voiced strong objections to Ostwald's contribution to the journal, and in the 1912 "Dialogue," we see why. There, Benjamin took issue with any pantheistic religiosity that sees evidence of divinity everywhere and in all things. Furthermore, he objected to Monism's promise of a secular religion, because it falsely posits the unity of matter and spirit—a unity that Benjamin rejected as "hopeless speculation."

If pantheism represents that singular ontology in which divinity and humanity are united in the same order of being, Monism celebrates that unity through science. It is precisely this collapse of the human into the natural order that Benjamin, less than a decade later, exposes as "mythic" in the essay on Goethe. Significantly, Haeckel had argued that Goethe was the poet of Monism, going so far as to cite Goethe's late novel as a prime illustration of the monistic cosmology:

In his classic novel *Elective Affinities*, Goethe famously equated the relationships of the two couples with the chemical phenomenon of the same name [*Wahlverwandtschaften*, valence]. The irresistible passion that draws Edward to Ottilie, or Paris to Helen, and overcomes all obstacles of reason and morality, is the same powerful, "unconscious" power of attraction that, in the fertilization of the egg cell in animals and plants, drives the sperm to penetrate the egg. It is the same prodigious force that binds two atoms of hydrogen to one atom of oxygen in the formation of a water molecule.[38]

Haeckel goes on to call this the "principle unity of elective affinities in all of nature," a unity that reaches "from the simplest chemical process all the way up to the most convoluted novel of love." Monism, then, comprises the philosophical horizon within which Benjamin composes his critique of myth; it sets the stakes involved in unraveling the Goethean entrapment in nature.

Benjamin's interpretation of Goethe's novel exhibits a kind of readerly, hermeneutic gnosticism: the task of his critique is to bring the mythic entrapment to light and ultimately, to rend its enclosure. Early in the essay, Benjamin lays bare the novel's "chaos of symbols," its interpenetration of symbolic motifs. As the reading progresses, it becomes clear that the symbolic economy of the text also represents the degree of human entrapment in nature—that is, the extent to which the protagonists are caught up in its nexus of causality. In the abstract, conceptual register of Benjamin's essay, this entrapment signifies a fateful cross-contamination of the pure, ideal world and the empirical: "If, in this contamination of the pure domain and the empirical domain, sensuous nature already appears to claim the highest place, its mythic face triumphs in the comprehensive totality of its appearances. It is, for Goethe, only the chaos of symbols."[39] But the novel would not be an object of Benjamin's critique if it did not also contain a latent mode of resistance to the enclosure it lays out. We are "in bed" with nature, but this proximity reveals nature's demonic, "supernatural" face. According to Benjamin, even Goethe, who famously studied plant morphology and natural history, recoiled at times from nature's dark magic. "Mythic humanity," Benjamin writes, "pays with fear for intercourse with demonic forces."[40]

But Benjamin's insistence that the novel does latently resist its own mythic content leads him to a startling misprision. Goethe's novel contains an inset novella titled "The Curious Tale of the Childhood Sweethearts," in which an anonymous youth rescues his beloved from drowning in a river. Immediately following the novella, it is suggested that the youth in it is the man with whom Charlotte has fallen adulterously in love. (Upon hearing the story, she is agitated and leaves the room.) Though the novella is thoroughly intertwined with the surrounding plot, Benjamin's reading downplays this continuity, in order to highlight the novella's promise of redemption over and against the fallenness of the novel's characters. "[T]he mythic themes of the novel," we read, "correspond to those of the novella as themes of re-demption." Benjamin's interpretation of literary form reveals his essay's central antinomy: the opposition of redemption to myth. Not only does the novella essentially oppose the order of the novel, where humans remain trapped in nature, it transcends the novel from within it: "With regard to the freedom and necessity that it reveals vis-à-vis the novel, the novella is comparable to an image in the darkness of a cathedral—an image which portrays the cathedral itself and so in the midst of the interior communicates a view of the place that is not other-wise available."[41]

This is the central gnostic moment of Benjamin's essay, which from the start aims at this rupture, this discontinuity between the cage of a fallen existence and the Archimedean glimpse beyond it. The critique of Goethe's novel, then, is the revelation of this hidden moment of re-sistance, this tear in the fabric of our mythic entrapment. Whereas Bloch's evocative prose aims at exhorting the Self to confront the "darkness of the lived moment," Benjamin's form of gnosticism is structural. His critique points at the cage and makes it visible; it at-tempts to reveal the secret at the center of the novel. And if Bloch shakes us into awareness of the darkness of the lived moment through the dissonance of his expressionistic prose, Benjamin's critique of Goethe's mythic novel is imagistic and mute. He does not seek to expose the secret of Goethean entrapment in myth through linear, ex-pository prose; he attempts to show it imagistically. In this respect, Benjamin's Goethe essay anticipates the "dialectical images" of his later work—frozen images of the past that explode what is false about our conceptions of history and time.

We began by noting that the appeal to gnostic structures is historically conditioned, not only by the availability of source materials, but also by the form of disenchantment against which gnosticism is employed as a counter-tradition. I have suggested that the ontology of Monism—the unbroken continuum that binds humanity to the behavior of atoms—comprised the philosophical and historical horizon of Ben-jamin's notion of mythic entrapment. Because of Benjamin's range of interests, even early in his career, it would be incorrect to characterize him as a consistently gnostic thinker. (Ludwig Klages' engagement with gnosticism is more sustained, and Jung's is more explicit.) Never-theless, Benjamin's reading of Bloch's *Spirit of Utopia* yielded, in the Goethe essay, an idiosyncratic rendering of gnosis as a form of critique.

Despite changes in the technological face of modernity that far surpass anything the Monists could have imagined, a veritable canon of gnostic "acts," like those of Bloch and Benjamin, now comprises the critique of rational modernity.

Disenchantment as Max Weber envisioned it meant not only the disappearance of incalculable forces, it also implied the ascendancy of the calculable world. Thus at its most fundamental level, the consideration of modern gnosticism in its aesthetic and philosophical forms is a discussion of disenchantment itself. The more completely we map the causal world and our own implication in its web, the riper that world becomes for gnostic re-envisioning. In other words, the utopian promise contained in scientific positivism's dream of complete knowledge often becomes the site of gnostic anxiety. Moreover, the status of gnosticism as a heresy has been as central to its usefulness to interpreters as any particular doctrine. As a source of heterodox authority, it refigures and recasts the accepted wisdom of orthodoxy as a cage of ignorance. That cage has been reconstructed to refer to various modern forms of entrapment and alienation. Regarding the progressive disenchantment of the world, the modern gnostic is an *ag*nostic—a skeptic who wants to show us the secret way out. In considering the variety of gnostic irruptions from the world, we come to see the forms of transcendence that ostensibly hearken back to a pre-rational world *not* as attempts to escape a world-immanent reality, but as worldly products of the modernity to which they refer. Re-enchantment, then, is not the return to an older form of historical life, but rather an inexpungible part of the disenchanted landscape.

CHAPTER 11

The Birth of Ideology from the Spirit of Myth: Georges Sorel Among the Idéologues

DAN EDELSTEIN

AGAINST THE DISTANT BACKDROP of a smoldering Paris (bombed by the Prussians, pillaged by the Communards, then bombed again by the Versaillais), the Russian nobleman Versilov describes an enchanting dream, in which Claude Lorrain's painting, "Acis et Galathée," strangely came to life. The nobleman, however, remembers the painting as "The Golden Age," and his dream expressed a powerful political urge:

it was exactly as in the painting—a corner of the Greek archipelago, and time, too, seemed to have shifted back three thousand years; gentle blue waves, islands and rocks, a flowering coast, a magic panorama in the distance, the inviting, setting sun—words can't express it. Here European mankind remembered its cradle, and the thought of it seemed to fill my soul with a kindred love. This was the earthly paradise of mankind: the gods came down from heaven and were united with people . . . [. . .] A wonderful reverie, a lofty delusion of mankind! The golden age—the most incredible dream of all that have ever been, but for which people have given all their lives and all their strength, for which prophets have died and been slain, without which the peoples do not want to live and cannot even die! [. . .] A feeling of happiness unknown to me before went through my heart, even to the point of pain; this was an all-human love. It was already full evening; a sheaf of slanting rays came in the window of my little room [. . .] And then, my friend, and then—this setting sun of the first day of European mankind, which I had seen in my dream, turned for me as soon as I woke up, in reality, into the setting sun of the last day of European mankind![1]

This final reference to the shattering of socialist ideals in faraway France underscores the tantalizing allure of this vision: though Versilov recognizes his dream is a "delusion," one which has just been repudiated by a historical process, he still cannot help but desire it. The enchanting beauty of this "magic panorama" draws him in, submerging him under ecstatic emotions ("a feeling of happiness unknown to me before"). These rapturous qualities sweep his more rational doubts and concerns away. Though death, too, is found in this Arcadia ("for which prophets have died and been slain"), the promise of this golden age seems worth any price. But unlike an idyllic reverie, Versilov's dream is brimming with revolutionary passions: it is an expression of the communitarian faith, an "all-human love," that animated nineteenth-century socialist ideologies, most recently at the Commune de Paris. The glorious society of the future that revolutionaries, from 1789 onward, represented as a coming golden age is encapsulated in this tableau of a joyful and just community.

Versilov may be a fictional character,[2] but the psychological process described in *The Adolescent* illustrates the very real power of revolutionary visions and the intricate relation between myths and political ideologies. The inscription of myths in political theories and representations of power goes back to antiquity, but their absorption within revolutionary ideologies is a distinctly modern phenomenon—if only for the double reason that both the concepts of "revolution" and "ideology" emerged at the end of the eighteenth century.[3] A defining feature of modernity, ideology has paradoxically become over the years an increasingly diffuse and nebulous concept, as competing definitions have tugged its referential cover in different directions. The term remains a staple feature of Marxist social criticism, where it retains the pejorative sense of "illusion," yet in the last thirty years, a more anthropological definition (largely derived from the work of Clifford Geertz) has found its way back into historical circles.[4] Neither of these definitions, however, account for the meaning assigned to the term by its coiner, A.-L.-C. Destutt de Tracy, for whom *idéologie* first and foremost designated a specific type of epistemology.[5] I suggest in this chapter that this original meaning can help us appreciate the powerful charm of revolutionary ideologies, but also, by contrast, to recognize a different type of political enchantment, one that does not contradict the twin demands of secularism and rationality.

The distinction between these two types of political enchantment passes through two definitions of myth. The first one encompasses the sort of myth found in Versilov's dream: in this case, the myth is a story about origins, imbued with the authority of the ages, and from which an entire political ideology can seemingly be deduced.[6] As will be shown, when such myths produce effects of political enchantment, it is rarely of a secular or rational sort. The second definition of myth is a much more "modern" one, in the sense that it does not depend on ancientness or tradition; instead, it designates as mythical certain aesthetic, emotional, or moral qualities that attach themselves primarily to images (often in contradistinction to stories). Most importantly, myths of this second type are not the cornerstones of ideologies, in the original, epistemological sense of the term. They can thus provoke enchantment effects that do not contradict rational or secular thinking, or in extreme cases, lead to totalitarian nightmares.

The most elaborate theory for this second type of myth, I argue, can be found in the work of Georges Sorel. This claim will strike many readers as deeply counterintuitive, since Sorel is generally considered to be one of the masterminds behind twentieth-century totalitarian ideologies.[7] While it is true that Sorel did not have the most enviable readers (most notoriously, Benito Mussolini), he nonetheless established a clear and unambiguous distinction between *mythe* and *utopie* in his most renowned work, *Réflections sur la violence* (1908). For Sorel, "myth" refers to the psychological and aesthetic qualities of political (or social) representations, while under the heading of "utopia," he designated the content and epistemological structure of political policies, which he considered irrelevant. Sorel thus indicated how (aesthetic) myths could be separated from (epistemological) ideologies, thereby outlining a model of political enchantment that may be wholly compatible with secular rationality. It is this model that I describe in the final section of this essay.

The Mythical Origins of Totalitarianism

Any discussion of political enchantment must first deal with the dangerous and disastrous dialectic between myth and ideology in modern history.[8] Under the Weimar Republic, Karl Mannheim already cautioned against the irrational "distortions" caused by myths put to the service of revolutionary ideologies.[9] His warnings proved prophetic: with the rise of Nazism, mythology was soon exploited for purposes of political authority, aesthetic purity, and murderous ideology, both in propaganda literature (most notably Alfred Rosenberg's *The Myth of the Twentieth Century*) and within the government itself (with the creation of the SS *Ahnenerbe Forschungs- und Lehrgemeinschaft*, an institute dedicated to the study of "ancestral heritage").[10] This exploitation of myth was clearly, as well as consciously, at odds with rational inquiry, since the Nazis were fascinated (initially at least) with the occult powers promised by theosophists and other mystics.[11] As Max Weber lectured on the "disenchantment of the world," at the University of Munich in 1917, members of the proto-Nazi Thule society were meeting at the Vierjahreszeiten Hotel, only blocks away.[12]

Myths also featured centrally in the Fascist politics conducted at this same time in Italy. In numerous speeches, Mussolini proudly claimed that the Fascist party had given the Italians "their" myth: the myth of the great nation, of a New Rome.[13] This self-conscious emphasis on created myths, in both Mussolini and Rosenberg, was largely inspired by the strong emphasis placed on evocative, inspirational images by Sorel. Describing such images as "myths," Sorel claimed that enabling individuals to picture the future was what gave them the (literal) faith to act.[14] Mussolini in particular took these lessons to heart, famously crediting Sorel for having taught him everything he knew.[15] This overt borrowing by a fascist ideologue and leader of a political theory of myth has reinforced the opinion that myths can only serve, in the political realm, to bury rational deliberation under a wave of passions and spiteful images.

The case against political myths would seem to be closed. The only rational manner in which to conduct political reform after the age of totalitarianism, according to one of its harshest critics, is through "piecemeal social engineering," not visionary tabula rasa.[16] And yet this reformist approach may ignore certain psychological and historical facets of human reality at its own peril. Utopian theorists such as Ernst Bloch have long argued that there is a deep human need for dreams of Versilov's type.[17] Leaving aside the veracity of this psychological judgment, such dreams were certainly widespread in nineteenth-century Europe, when post-revolutionary writers, from Alfred de Musset to Stéphane Mallarmé, railed against the "disenchantment" of a faithless world.[18] Of course, the negative charge of disenchantment could easily be reversed: five years after mocking Alphonse de Lamartine for having meddled in politics, and after urging an ivory-tower detachment from history, Paul Verlaine was fighting alongside the Communards in Paris.[19] This easy reversal in fact harbors an even harsher moral: where disenchantment looms, piecemeal social engineering is threatened. A single ideological tidal-wave (be it in the form of an electoral sweep) can wash away fifty years of progressive measures. Myths may be dangerous as political tools, but might they also be necessary evils?

In order to disentangle myth and ideology, the following section examines how the two were in fact brought together at the end of the Enlightenment by the *philosophe* Destutt de Tracy. Tracy claimed that *idéologie*, as he called his new science, was merely a formalization of the abbé de Condillac's sensationalist epistemology, but in fact modeled this science on another text, Charles Dupuis's *Origin of all Cults* [*Origine de tous les cultes*], a mythographical treatise. The "fundamental ideas" that Tracy argued lay at the basis of all knowledge closely resembled the Ur-myth at the heart of Dupuis's treatise, the sacred myth of the sun. It was at the institutional level, however, that Tracy's science truly helped launch the age of ideology: perceived as the fulcrum of a new Atlantis, the Institut National inspired a crowd of emulators, who all sought ideological solutions of their own for post-revolutionary Europe. These solutions amplified the mythical overtones of *idéologie*, paving the way for the full-blown political enchantments of the twentieth century.

Idéologie as Epistemology: Condillac and Destutt de Tracy

In her study of totalitarianism, Hannah Arendt called attention to how extreme ideologies all seem to attribute an inordinate importance to "one idea:" "Ideologies always assume that one idea is sufficient to explain everything in the development from the premise [. . .] You can't say A without saying B and C and so on, down to the end of the murderous alphabet."[20] Roger Griffin has described this "one idea" more specifically as the "mythic core" of totalitarian ideologies (*Nature of Fascism*, 32–36). While the context for both these remarks is twentieth-century political movements, their analysis in fact applies equally well for the original eighteenth-century theory of *idéologie*. Generally considered to bear little relation to later versions, historians who have studied Destutt de Tracy's "science" closely offer a different assessment, even suggesting that the fundamental signification of ideology may be found in "overlooked elements which its coiner and its contemporaries originally gave the word and the science."[21] Chief among these elements is its particular notion of epistemology, as well, we shall see, as its hidden inscription of myths.

Tracy was a soldier, a politician, and a philosopher of language, intellectually indebted, like many French Enlightenment *philosophes*, to Condillac. This indebtedness is plainly evident in the work that first introduced the term *idéologie*, Tracy's *Memorandum on the faculty of thought* [*Mémoire sur la faculté de penser*]: presented at the Institut National in 1796, this treatise consists in large part of a fine-tuning of Condillac's *Treatise on sensations* [*Traité des sensations*] (1754). As a "science des idées" (Tracy defined his neologism with respect to its etymology), *idéologie* was primarily concerned with the relations between perception, signs, and ideas, that is, the very same relations examined in Condillac's *Traité*.[22] Tracy himself often credited Condillac for inspiring his own work, even writing in his later *Elements of Ideology* [*Eléments d'idéologie*], "he truly created *Idéologie*."[23]

The key epistemological principle for both Condillac and his disciple was the notion of a semiotic chain. According to Condillac, every idea is necessarily a development of simpler and earlier ideas: "All of our needs are dependent on one another; and one can view perceptions as a series of fundamental ideas, to which all our knowledge is attached. Above each idea are other series of ideas, constituting sorts of chains [*des* espèces *de chaînes*]."[24]

A great chain of knowledge thus connects all ideas and sciences back to a series of "fundamental ideas"; these ideas are not only elementary (i.e., basic concepts such as space, movement, or self), but *chronologically* precede all others as well. Philosophy, according to Condillac, should begin at the beginning: "Let us consider a man *at the very first moment* of his existence [. . .] Let us continue to observe the moments where he begins to reflect on what his sensations are provoking with him" (*Essai*, 2–3, emphasis added). His epistemological method rests entirely on a genealogical order: "We must return to the origin of our ideas, understand their generative means, follow them up until the limits prescribed by nature; and in this manner, establish the scope and limits of our knowledge, and renew all human understanding" (xi).

This genealogical order would resurface as the defining feature of *idéologie*. Tracy immediately describes his new science as "the *first* among all others in the genealogical order, since the others derive from it."[25] As Condillac before him, Tracy invokes the metaphor of an epistemological chain: "everything is connected, everything is entwined [*tout se tient, tout s'enchaîne*] by an infinite multitude of relations [. . .] no truth is isolated or different from others."[26] Interestingly, this preference given to the "genealogical order" marks a sharp reversal from the epistemology enshrined in the *Encyclopédie*. In his "Preliminary Discourse," Jean le Rond d'Alembert had rejected precisely this order of knowledge in favor of an "encyclopedic order," which disregarded the chronological order in which sciences and ideas came into existence.[27] By re-inscribing time, or more precisely history, into the order of knowledge, Tracy thus placed a premium on origins and ancientness. *Idéologie* moved epistemology closer to a mythical pursuit.

How mythical was this theory of knowledge? Tracy's description of "primary truths" (*Mémoire*, 129) certainly seems to bestow them with a mythic aura. More than simply appearing first, these initial ideas are described as containing all the future ones to come:

The different parts of our knowledge only appear separate to us because we still ignore the relations that bind them. If they could all be shown, like astronomy, to have all derived from a single unique principle, then it would become clear that the totality of human science was contained in a small number of propositions, and that, *to unite all the branches into a common trunk,* one would only have to discover the prime proposition, from which all the fundamental propositions of each specific science derived: then we would truly have a complete knowledge of all that existed, and it would be patently evident that all secondary truths are but the consequences of a primary truth which implicitly contains them all, and of which they are only partial developments (*Mémoire,* 129, emphasis added).

The genealogical premise that the complexity and diversity of culture can be explained by "a small number of propositions," which can in turn be reduced to a "primary truth," is here developed even further to suggest that the different disciplines are in fact fundamentally identical: "all the branches [are united] in a common trunk." This epistemology of unity had already been described in a work written a year earlier on the history of religions (to which I shall return shortly): "It is the fundamental principle of the entire system of religious ideas that is revealed, and the intimate link, or even, *the identity of all its branches,* that is completely uncovered."[28] The encyclopedic tree can be replaced, according to Tracy, by a generative "primary truth," by the seed for the entire tree of knowledge. The "one idea" that Arendt perceived at the core of twentieth-century ideologies was already visible in their original formulation.

The mythical qualities of *idéologie* were numerous: not only did its epistemology rest on the mythical gesture of a return to the origins, but the ideas believed to lie at this source were pregnant with the totality of knowledge. The "primary truths" truly seemed to possess the

sort of "wisdom of the ancients" (Sir Francis Bacon's expression) traditionally perceived in myths. Michel Foucault drew attention to this
similarity in his celebrated history of epistemologies: "Ideology, by extending its analysis to the entire domain of knowledge [. . .] sought to
readmit in the form of representation that which was being constituted
and was reconstituting itself beyond it. This retrieval could only be accomplished through the quasi mythical method of a singular and universal genesis."[29]

Idéologie and the Mythical Method: Destutt de Tracy and Dupuis

This search for the "genesis" of knowledge, however, may have been
more than just "quasi" mythical. Though Condillac was undoubtedly
the prime inspirer of Tracy's science, he was not alone; his influence
may even be somewhat exaggerated.[30] For instance, the text by Condillac to which Tracy paid the most (and virtually the only) attention was
the Traité des sensations, a much more circumscribed version of Condillac's own epistemological study, the Essay on the Origin of Human
Knowledge [Essai sur l'origine des connoissances humaines]. In the Traité,
using the famous example of a statue that progressively acquires the
five senses, Condillac limited his discussion to how simple perceptions
provide humans with their sense of space, movement, memory, and so
on. Tracy perceived this approach to be fundamentally flawed, claiming that it was insufficiently realistic, and that philosophy must instead
study life in medias res, in order to explain the here and now of confusing reality.[31]

The imperative to impose order on the chaos of life, rather than to
devise a simplified model from the onset, seems to have been a result
of Tracy's revolutionary experience. Disturbed by the turmoil of revolutionary politics, and in particular by the intrigues of his fellow
assembly members, he dreamt of straightforward authoritarian solutions, with a strong police force imposing order on the tumult of society.[32] Though he himself would be imprisoned during the Terror, his
political ideas shared many structural similarities with those of his
jailors: the leading Jacobin politicians ritualistically rooted their arguments in "principles," of which the subsequent points were invariably
"corollaries."[33] This revolutionary experience indelibly marked Tracy's
philosophical outlook: just as the secretive and intricate workings of
government offended his sense of justice, so did the general confusion

of life. [34] The standardization that had been imposed on the weights, distances, months, days, and hours of French revolutionary life should ultimately be applied to "feelings, ideas, knowledge, tastes, and even needs" (*Analyse raisonnée*, v). One can easily detect here the influence of the marquis de Condorcet, one of Tracy's colleagues in the *Société de 1789*, on these political ideas. [35]

But it was religious and cultural otherness that goaded Tracy above all, "that multitude of different religious systems, that have caused so much pain on earth, that have so often led to bloodshed" (*Analyse*, XLIV). His frustration with religious diversity led him to study the antiquarians of his time, notably Antoine Court de Gébelin, the Président des Brosses, and Jean-Sylvain Bailly. His religious curiosity was only satisfied, however, by another antiquarian and future colleague at the Institut National: Charles Dupuis, author of the *Origin of all Cults, or Universal Religion* [*Origine de tous les cultes, ou Religion universelle*] (1794). [36]

Dupuis's book became instantly famous (if not an instant best seller, standing at four gigantic volumes), as his thesis was scandalous in the extreme: all religions, he claimed, are degenerate forms of an original Egyptian solar cult. In itself, this thesis was not new: Court de Gébelin had advanced a similar hypothesis twenty years earlier, also situating the original sun-worshipping society in Egypt. [37] Both Court and Dupuis were in fact echoing the Egyptian thesis of the abbé Terrasson, whose novel *Sethos* (an inspiration for *The Magic Flute*) had already portrayed Egypt as the "mother of sciences and arts," which had "communicated" science and civilization to all other countries. [38] In Dupuis's retelling of this story, however, its central claim was pushed to extremist conclusions, namely that Christianity itself was a solar religion, with Jesus Christ as the sun, and his twelve disciples as the zodiac signs. [39] Even in the religiously confused atmosphere of the Directory, this thesis caused an uproar and would be publicly mocked by Napoleon himself. [40] It nonetheless proved remarkably tenacious: solar mythology became the dominant hermeneutic code of nineteenth-century mythography. [41] For his part, Tracy read Dupuis's summa as soon as it was published, and was enthralled:

At that time (in Year 3) appeared the great Work by citizen Dupuis, on the origin of all cults. I hoped to find what I was looking for, and my expectations were filled beyond hope. I had not imagined that one could shed so much light on such obscure antiquity, and produce such a strong sense of certainty in matters where no-one had previously moved past probabilities (*Analyse*, xlvi).

He immediately set out to write a "rational analysis" [*analyse raison-née*] of Dupuis's studies. As he explains in his "Preliminary Discourse," he did not publish this text until 1799: "I therefore did this Analysis as I finished it years ago" (xlix). The Post-Scriptum specifies, "All that proceeds dates from Year 3" (151). This chronological precision is critical, as it informs us that Tracy's work on Dupuis immediately preceded, and was perhaps co-temporal with, the essay in which he first proposed and defined the term that guaranteed his intellectual fortune, *idéologie*. A brief review of the *Analyse raisonnée* suggests just how influential Dupuis's treatise may have been.

It was the methodology adopted in the *Origine de tous les cultes* that interested Tracy foremost: the purpose of his *Analyse raisonnée*, he wrote, was to "indicate the progress [of Dupuis's work], the chains of its ideas, the series of its proofs and the links of its topics" (xlix). As Tracy's focus on these methodological "chains" (*l'enchaînement, la série, la liaison*) implies, the great achievement of Dupuis's work, in the eyes of his commentator at least, was to have demonstrated the power of the "genealogical order" in organizing human knowledge. Under the cover of a genealogy of religions, Dupuis had in fact written a genealogy of the arts and sciences that clearly illustrated Condillac's theory about the great chain of knowledge.

Tracy summarizes the main stages of this genealogy in the first chapter of his *Analyse raisonnée*. First comes astronomy, the "natural" science whose textbook lies open in the nighttime sky. Astronomy in turn begets logic, which is required to compare empirical observation with theoretical analysis; next comes geometry, for studying the lines and curves of orbits; and then calculus, to determine the future positions of the stars. Astronomy later gives rise to history, as the movement of the heavens is the measure of time; agriculture, by teaching men when to plant (with the zodiac); geography and navigation, since longitude and latitude are determined by the stars. Metaphysics, astrology, poetry, and theology can also be traced back to the science of the stars, as can moral philosophy and, in a word, religion. Astronomy thus constitutes a "fundamental idea," anchoring the great chain of knowledge, and generating the entire range of arts and sciences. As we saw above, the important passage from the *Mémoire sur la faculté de penser* that outlined Tracy's main epistemological principles singled out "astronomy" as his example of a seminal science, from which all others could be derived. Dupuis's treatise on mythology thus seems to have been the trigger for Tracy's epistemological theory. *Idéologie* was literally born from the spirit of myth.

The Myth of *Idéologie*: the *Institut National*, Saint-Simon, and Political Enchantment

The "mythologization" of primary truths and fundamental ideas in *idéologie* clearly mirrors the antiquarian search for the original myths, which lay at the source of later mythologies and cultures. *Idéologie* shared the same structure as Romantic mythography: but was their symmetry merely structural, or did these fundamental ideas and Ur-myths share real properties? More to the political point, were Tracy's "*vérités premières*" myths of the sort that could provoke revolutionary dreams? This is the question whose answer will illuminate the relation between *idéologie* and ideology. As the following section seeks to demonstrate, their relationship is patent and direct.

The enchanting political and spiritual power of *idéologie* is particularly evident in the case of Tracy's model, Dupuis. In his first published text on mythography, Dupuis presented his findings as a return to the true, sacred origins of religion, and not at all as an exercise in disenchantment. His text even began in the vocative, as though it were an ode to the solar god:

The entire universe adores you [o Sun] under a multitude of different names. The universality of this cult should not surprise us; the Sun only had to show itself to command the admiration and respect of men, who sought in it the King and Father of nature. And even when philosophers elevated their thoughts to the idea of an invisible and superior God, they still considered the Sun his first creation and most beautiful image.[42]

Dupuis's stirring invocation was not entirely unusual: Court de Gébelin had already hailed mythology as a "sacred discourse" (*Monde primitif*, 1:68), while Swedenborg claimed that the physical sun corresponded to God in the invisible world.[43] What is most striking about this passage is that it announced the manner in which Dupuis's thesis would be "supernaturalized" by his readers.[44] Where he argued that the gods of mythology represented stars and planets, Dupuis was often read as stating the contrary, namely that the stars and planets were themselves divine. Both Shelley and Keats, for instance, interpreted his thesis in this manner, depicting an enchanted cosmos in their poems.

In Shelley's *Prometheus Unbound*, this supernaturalization is the result of a metaphysical uprising (situated in the wake of the French Revolution), which is sustained by a socialist and spiritualist ideology.[45] A similar combination of astral deification and golden age socialism would be found in France, both among poets (such as Nerval) and revolutionary theorists.[46]

The reception of Dupuis's theory points to the fundamental ambiguity in both his and Tracy's projects. Claiming to seat knowledge on a firmer, more rational basis, Dupuis and Tracy reached beyond the pale of philosophical demonstrability, transforming epistemology into mythical, and even metaphysical, speculation. As the reactions of Dupuis's readers suggest, this epistemological shift contributed to, though was not directly responsible for, a first type of "re-enchantment of the world," through which the universe was repopulated with otherworldly beings, who controlled the political destiny of the Earth. It was this millenarian and, by extension, largely irrational version of enchantment that would persist well into the twentieth century.

In Tracy's case, the connection with later ideologies may seem less evident, as *idéologie* never moved past its initial stages. Tracy sketched the outline of a new epistemology, but did not fill it in to the point of uncovering the "primary truths," which he claimed underpinned all knowledge. In a sense, however, his silence was equally effective in casting a mythological pall over this fount of science: the myth of an original, all-encompassing law was one of *idéologie*'s most important epistemological legacies, as we will see. But if Tracy did not devise many concrete myths himself, he undoubtedly helped fashion the myth of *idéologie* per se. Simply put, this was the myth that a small body of scientists, embodied by the Institut National, could revolutionize human knowledge, provide political guidance to society, and offer a new moral foundation for humanity. These objectives may sound familiar to any student of the Enlightenment, and like a simple rehashing of the myth of progress, but they received a defining twist in their new institutional context and in their relation to an actual myth—the myth of Atlantis.

Tracy presented his new science as inseparable from its institutional home. *Idéologie* was the name for the subject to which his section in the Institut National was dedicated: "the science that preoccupies us is so new that it is still nameless. It is undoubtedly to its progress that is especially dedicated the first section of this class; and this is the *section for the analysis of sensations and ideas"* (*Mémoire*, 70). This section was the first of six in the Institute's second class, and Tracy perceived its primacy in typical genealogical terms.[47] *Idéologie* constituted the basis for the other five sections in the second class, and Tracy even suggested that ideology could extend to the first class (dedicated to the sciences) as well: "it seems to me that *idéologie* can be either physiological or rational."[48] The Institute's organization thus mirrored the epistemology of Tracy's science. One was simply the materialization of the other, a fact which may explain why the members of the Institute came to be known collectively as *les idéologues.*

On the surface, the Institut National was founded to replace the royal academies, which had been abolished in 1793. But as Emmet Kennedy remarked, "[t]he Institute was a substitute for, not a restoration of, the royal academies."[49] Its organic structure and political purpose differed drastically from the isolated, disaggregated nature of the earlier academies, as did its installment at the top of the French educational system. In fact, the closest model for the Institute was not so much the academies, as another, albeit fictional, scientific body—"Salomon's House," the research institute that governed Francis Bacon's utopian society, *New Atlantis.* This group of scientists and scholars had discovered all sorts of technological wonders, from refrigerators to airplanes, and expressed equal interest in the *arts et métiers* as in science and engineering.

This scientific corporation had understandably caught the imagination of the *philosophes*: in his own utopian *El Dorado* (situated like Bacon's New Atlantis in South America), Voltaire included a "palace of sciences" whose mission was to advance science and technology.[50] Toward the end of the century, Bacon's text inspired Condorcet to write a commentary on this institution, the *Fragment on Atlantis, or Combined Efforts of the Human Race for the Progress of Sciences* (a companion piece to the better-known *Draft for a historical table* [*Esquisse d'un tableau historique*], both of which were written in hiding). The *Fragment* explored the pragmatic means for ensuring scientific and, by extension, human perfectibility, taking as its point of departure the council of scientists in the *New Atlantis*: "Bacon had conceived the idea of a society of men dedicated solely to the pursuit of truth. His project encompasses all aspects of human knowledge."[51] Condorcet then outlined his own plans for a new scientific academy, summarizing and developing ideas that he had been advancing for the past twenty years. Through the intervention of F. -A. Boissy d'Anglas, A. -F. Fourcroy, and P. -C. -F. Daunou, these ideas ultimately served as the detailed blueprint for the decree founding the Institute in 1795.[52]

The sway that the Atlantis myth held on the members of the Institute is difficult to evaluate, although we know that Tracy held the work of Jean-Sylvain Bailly, the late astronomer who wrote a series of texts on Atlantis, in great esteem:[53] "the unfortunate and virtuous Bailly [. . .] is equally a historian of thought as of astronomy, seeing that he so wisely unravels the progress of the human spirit and the causes of its advancement" (Mémoire, 67). There can be no doubt, however, about the profound and lasting impression that the Institute made on the European cultural milieu, where its mythical promise did not pass unnoticed. Referring to its new epistemology, for instance, Friedrich von Schelling proclaimed that, "the peace of the golden age will make itself known for the first time in the harmonious union of all sciences."[54] Schelling's comment reveals the extent to which the cultural representation of the golden age had changed since the mid-eighteenth century: the fabled time of origins was now identified with absolute knowledge, not with the absence of the arts and sciences. The Institute's symbolic value was still most evident when it was abolished under the Restoration: at that time, Honoré de Balzac lamented how, "the Institute could have been the great government of the moral and intellectual world, but it was recently shattered by its constitution into separate academies"; Victor Hugo noted this same event in his chapter on "The Year 1817," in Les Misérables; and Pierre Leroux later called for its revival under the July Monarchy.[55]

Both as an epistemology and an institution, idéologie promoted a myth of scientific utopianism that would permeate nineteenth-century political culture and cement the foundational link between myths and revolutionary ideologies. Its influence on later political thinkers, however, arguably passes through one of Tracy's contemporaries, Henri de Saint-Simon. At the time the Institute was founded in 1795, Saint-Simon was residing in Paris, enjoying the life of nouveau riche that his land speculations had afforded him. Living opposite the newly founded Ecole Polytechnique, he began cultivating "scientific" acquaintances, both among the polytechniciens and the members of the Institute.[56] Saint-Simon had no formal, and little autodidactic, training in science, but became enthralled with the representation of a new scientific order, as it trickled down to him from the proceedings and structure of the Institute. He also accentuated its mythical undertones, portraying a larger-than-life Institute in his first political treatise, the 1803 *Lettres d'un habitant de Genève*. This pamphlet urged the creation of a "Council of Newton," which would unite "three mathematicians, three physicists, three chemists, three physiologists, three writers [*littérateurs*], three painters, three musicians."[57] The combination of arts and sciences in this Council mirrors the interdisciplinary structure of the Institute, but Saint-Simon also drew inspiration from Condorcet's commentary on Bacon's *New Atlantis*.[58] Moreover, in his ideal recasting of the Institute—all the more ideal that Napoleon had abolished the second class on "moral and political sciences" that very same year—the council of scientists adopted a messianic quality: these "twenty-one elect humans" (76) had been ordained by a divine revelation.[59] Saint-Simon would later underscore the mythical dimension of his scientific utopia in a phrase that was to ring throughout the nineteenth century: "the golden age of the human race is not behind us, it lies before us, in the perfection of the social order."[60] On this rock, the church of revolutionary socialism was built.[61]

As the testimony of Saint-Simon, Schelling, and others indicates, the Institut National encapsulated a millenarian alternative to the pastoral utopianism of revolutionary groups such as the Babouvists, an alternative in which science would transform the world into an Atlantean golden age. Invariably, it was believed that this transformation would occur thanks to the new ideological epistemology propounded by Tracy and his colleagues ("Revolution, yes, but first civilization," Victor Hugo's revolutionary ideologue declared in *Les Misérables*, 664). Saint-Simon placed his revolutionary hopes not in canals (like Plato's Atlanteans), but in a new *Encyclopédie*. In accordance with Tracy's genealogical order, Saint-Simon presented his own project as "organizational," as opposed to the "critical" approach of the *philosophes*.[62] Though he would not achieve his encyclopedic dream, it would be perpetuated by his disciple, Pierre Leroux, who published a highly influential *Revue encyclopédique* between 1831 and 1835 (in association with Jean Reynaud and Hippolyte Carnot, son of Lazare Carnot, the Jacobin deputy), followed by an *Encyclopédie nouvelle* (1834–40).[63] By this time, however, the ideological concept of a great chain of knowledge had become commonplace: Pierre-Simon Ballanche, in his 1833 *Palingénésie sociale*, similarly spoke of an "empire of invariable laws eternally governing the physical, moral, and even civil and political worlds."[64] Perhaps the most evocative example of this faith in an epistemological chain comes from Auguste Dupin, Poe's amateur detective, who could "retrace the course of [his companion's] meditations" along the unseen footpaths of his brain.[65] *Idéologie*, Frank Manuel observed, had sparked a veritable epidemic: "In the late-eighteenth and early-nineteenth centuries literally scores of thinkers were hawking about similar catch-alls to explain the social universe and the physical universe and their overwhelming complexities with a word or a concept or a law or a principle."[66] This myth of an original *logos*, vessel of all other knowledge, with the capacity of transforming the world, conveyed an enchanted sense of order and direction, but it was an order and direction that came at the expense of rational inquiry and doubt. *Idéologie* had ushered in the age of ideology, where myths could increasingly deform history and representations of the natural world. This type of reenchantment was certainly seductive, even intoxicating; to borrow Raymond Aron's phrase, it was "the opium of the intellectuals." Unfortunately, it led to delirium and violence as well.

Sorel's Critique of Ideology

Idéologie was obviously not the only epistemology of the eighteenth century—as we saw, the editors of the *Encyclopédie* opted for a more limited and human-scaled order of knowledge—but it was not a marginal theory, either. It derived, after all, from a mainstream intellectual current, the doctrine of sensationalism, championed in France by Condillac, a close friend of Rousseau's and Diderot's.[67] The surprising role that this *philosophe* ended up playing in the development of twentieth-century ideologies may ultimately force us to reconsider the relationship between Enlightenment and totalitarianism along very different lines than Max Horkheimer and Theodor Adorno.[68] The place of certain *philosophes* in this complex history is undoubtedly very vexed, although their demonization began early on. Even before the French Revolution was over, the abbé Barruel (among other counterrevolutionaries) was asserting that an unholy alliance of Jacobins, Masons, and *philosophes* had been conspiring to overthrow throne and altar since the last decades of the eighteenth century.[69] By the midnineteenth century, however, the Enlightenment progressives were not only being attacked on the Right. Karl Marx and Friedrich Engels derided Babouvism as communism "in its crudest form" in their *Communist Manifesto*,[70] and Engels, in *Socialism: Scientific and Utopian*, praised the contributions of his eighteenth-century predecessors, only to contrast their naïve theories with "scientific" Marxism. Yet another socialist writer took this critique one step further, accusing Marx himself of perpetuating the utopian naiveté of the *philosophes*. This writer was Georges Sorel.[71]

Sorel remains something of a mystery. His own political views evolved considerably over time: he is often depicted as a proto-fascist, but this portrayal unfairly rests on the convictions of some of his followers.[72] He was himself aware of the fluidity of his opinions, and even sought to represent this fluidity by not overly polishing his writing.[73] This studied neglect, however, has often come across as disorganization and confusion and has led to many misunderstandings—most critically, as we shall see, with regard to his role in the genealogy of Fascism.

While Sorel's thought was undeniably meandrous (not to say inconsistent), it was nonetheless marked by two interrelated and fundamental beliefs: a commitment to the revolutionary transformation of society, and a deep wariness of overly intricate political theories—in other words, of ideology. The excessive reliance on ideology, Sorel warned, was a great danger to revolutionary movements: "Ideological constructions may be necessary, but they are also the most common causes of our errors."[74] The problem with most political theorists, according to Sorel, was that they formulated ideological constructions in advance, whereas these could only become clear *after* the revolution.[75] In his most famous work, *Reflections on Violence*, he dismissed any pre-revolutionary social engineering as a "utopia," which he defined as:

an intellectual product; it is the work of theorists who, after observing and discussing the facts, seek to establish a model to which they can compare existing societies in order to estimate the amount of good and evil they contain; it is a combination of imaginary institutions having sufficient analogies to real institutions for the jurist to be able to reason about them; it is a construction which can be broken into parts and of which certain pieces have been shaped in such a way that they can (with a few alterations) be fitted into future legislation.[76]

On first glance, this definition of utopia does not sound very utopian: if a social theory can be more or less slotted into future legislation, then it would seem to exhibit the very pragmatic qualities that an admirer of William James would appreciate.[77] In fact, Sorel's opposition to "utopias" did not stem from their being too practical, but rather from their not being practical at all, when considered as driving forces for revolutionary change. Social theories could too easily be "refuted" through comparison and analysis, and more damningly, "the effect of utopias has always been to direct men's minds towards *reforms* which can be brought about by patching up the system" (*Reflections*, 29, my emphasis). Again, such "direction towards reforms" may appear to be a good movement, but the good, in Sorel's eyes, was the enemy of the best. In political terms, reform was the enemy of revolution. This hostility toward reform was commonplace in late nineteenth-century politics, and more particularly, among socialist theoreticians. To reform society meant to work within the political system, and parliamentary democracy was not always a pretty sight: during the Third Republic, ministries mostly held together (when they did at all) through opportunistic backroom deals.[78] Along with many of his contemporaries, Sorel frowned upon these *ballets russes* in the Council, and became increasingly disappointed with the socialists after they joined the government, but failed to deliver.[79] The preference given to revolution over reform thus stemmed from a deep disillusionment in democratic politics, a disillusionment shared by numerous anti-democratic groups across the political spectrum, from anarchists to Boulangistes.

But Sorel's rejection of reform in the *Reflections on Violence* was in fact another instance of his variable opinions, as he had been an early supporter of Eduard Bernstein. Remarking that none of Marx's prophecies about an inevitable revolution had been fulfilled, Bernstein argued that parliamentary reforms were a surer, if slower, way to achieve socialist goals.[80] His reformist message bitterly divided European socialists, but gained him the admiration of Sorel, with whom he began corresponding regularly. This admiration was counterbalanced, however, by Sorel's great dislike for the French Socialist leader Jean Jaurès, who also favored parliamentary over revolutionary action. At the time Sorel wrote the *Reflections*, he was thus firmly in the camp of revolutionary syndicalism, which was opposed to all forms of parliamentary engagement.

The criticism of "utopian" thinkers in the *Reflections* might be read as anti-intellectualism, which would in turn be contrary to a rational political project. Sorel's opposition to purely "reasonable" political proposals, however, was not unreasonable: following Henri Bergson, who had emphasized the creative powers of the human mind, Sorel's argument was simply that reason alone could not achieve revolutionary change. Poetry and imagination were equally (if not more) important for stirring men and women to action. Sorel apparently found this idea in Giambattista Vico's *New Science*, which taught him that "there was first in history, as the great Neapolitan said, a vulgar wisdom that feels things and expresses them poetically."[81] It was this poetic and emotional wisdom that Sorel called *myths*.

While Sorel's ideas about myths were partially shaped by Vico's theories, as well as by Platonic examples, he nonetheless came to formulate his own idiosyncratic definition.[82] Curiously, it was with respect to Marx that Sorel first theorized political myths, in a few pages of his 1902 *Introduction à l'économie moderne* (394–97). Here he argued that, although Marxist dogma had indeed been disproved by historical processes (as Bernstein claimed), it may still possess a pragmatic value. Marx's "catastrophic conception" (396) in particular struck Sorel as a powerful and practical "myth" for advancing the revolutionary cause. He expanded on this idea in *La Décomposition du Marxisme*, where he claimed that Marx "always conceived of the revolution in a mythical form," that is, as "an ideal upheaval [*bouleversement*], which he expresses in images."[83] Foreseeing the objection that such a myth, like Plato's myth of metals, was intentionally misleading, and that his entire theory was mere "intellectual sophistry" (*Reflections*, 21), he reversed the charge, asserting that it was the socialist theoreticians who were delusional: "*Contested theories* are made necessary by modern revolutionary action; and one could probably demonstrate, by the same token, that *informed, judicial, and practical* proposals, presently put forward by more or less socialist sociologists, are nothing but falsehoods and incorrect science" (*Introduction*, 396).

Unlike what some recent commentators have suggested, myths for Sorel were thus only valuable insofar as they were completely detached from ideological models.[84] Here again, Sorel credited Marx with having introduced this distinction: "Marx had the good merit of ridding his revolutionary myth of all the fantasies that too often promise a land of milk and plenty [*un pays de Cocagne*]" (*Décomposition*, 55). The absence of a description of a socialist future, a longtime puzzle to historians, distinguished Marxism from other utopian doctrines, which maintained that the future order could be determined in advance.[85] The myth of the catastrophic revolution or of the general strike could not, in Sorel's reading, provide what Roger Griffin calls the "mythic core" of political ideologies, since the specificity of Marx (and Sorel after him) was precisely that he broke with ideology—and with the *idéologues*.

This understanding of the relation between myth and ideology is clearly opposed to the epistemological conception that preceded it. The myth of the general strike did not entail any specific corollaries: there was no "murderous alphabet" (Arendt) at work in Sorel's political thought. None of his myths are "originary," in either a chronological or epistemological sense, nor do they even seem to bear much relation to what usually goes by the name of mythology: "As remarkable examples of myths I have given those which were constructed by primitive Christianity, by the Reformation, by the Revolution, and by the followers of Mazzini" (*Reflections*, 20). All of these myths are intrinsically modern: they do not look "three thousand years back" to a primitive golden age, or exhibit what Griffin calls a "palingenetic form" (*Nature of Fascism*, 26). These myths are entirely forward looking, and have been unlocked from the wisdom of the ancients.[86]

What is perhaps most interesting about Sorel's examples of myths is that they do not all relate to revolutionary endeavors. Myths were not simply a post-1789 phenomenon meant to lead humanity into a brave new world: they formed an intrinsic part of a long series of historical phenomena and could be used for a wide variety of political (and religious) purposes. "Intellectualist" interpretations of the past might miss this ubiquity of mythical thinking, but such interpretations were "entirely unable to explain great historical movements" (*Reflections*, 24). Every great historical movement, including the French Revolution, was propelled by myths, but myths were not uniquely revolutionary.

Sorel illustrates this point indirectly when he criticizes the historian Ernest Renan for overlooking the driving force of history: the human search for meaning. Renan is dismayed by much of the past, Sorel claims, because he cannot explain,

The sacrifice of his life made by the soldier of Napoleon in order to have had the honour of taking part in "eternal" deeds and of living in the glory of France knowing that "he would always remain a poor man"; the extraordinary virtues shown by the Romans who resigned themselves to an appalling inequality and yet who suffered so much to conquer the world; "the belief in glory [which was] a value without equal", created by Greece and as a result of which "a selection was made from the swarming masses of humanity, *life had a motive*, and there was a recompense for those who had pursued the good and the beautiful" (22, emphasis added).

Failing to comprehend why individuals across time have acted in such apparently incomprehensible manners, Renan can only conclude, with the Old Testament prophet Jeremiah, that they "labor[ed] for nothing." But for Sorel, their actions are perfectly clear: the Napoleonic soldier, Roman citizen, and Greek artist lived according to myths, myths that both spurred them into action and gave their lives meaning ("life had a motive"). Without such myths, Sorel suggests, we are all left purposeless; the variegated facets of our lives do not combine into a coherent image. Pragmatically, this absence of meaning translates into inaction: without myths, we are fated to be complacent. Enthusing the workers was thus the requisite first step for revolutionary action, just as drumming up the soldiers' thirst for glory was the key to military success.[87] But underpinning this pragmatic concern was a penetrating insight into how political animals conduct their lives. Rational calculation alone rarely provides human actions, especially extraordinary ones, with the sense of purpose needed to undertake them. For this motivation to occur, an individual needs to "see the bigger picture"—quite literally, for Sorel, since he conceived of myths in mainly visual terms.[88] This imperative was particularly pressing in the disenchanted world of Third Republic parliamentary intrigue, yet as Sorel's examples demonstrate, every historical epoch was determined by the hidden force of myths. These myths did not fulfill an epistemological purpose, as in revolutionary ideologies, but simply represented reality in such a manner that made human action (in Hannah Arendt's sense) appear within grasp and worthwhile.

It thus seems appropriate to speak in these cases of an alternative type of re-enchantment, one that differs completely from the type produced by mythical ideologies. Sorel's myths enchant human actions by bestowing aesthetic or moral value onto activities that could otherwise seem pointless, and might not be attempted. By some standards, these actions may appear unreasonable, but they are not necessarily irrational. Sorelian myths can coexist perfectly well with rational deliberation. Where reason often leaves us indecisive or complacent, however, myths can motivate us to undertake projects that may seem daunting or useless. They provide idealizations of events that enhance them, endow them with meaning, and make them more desirable. Unlike Versilov's dream, which portrayed a seductive *telos*, Sorel's myths embellish a *process*, one which is worthwhile in itself, independently from any end result. We can never know what the future world will resemble, but we must believe in our power to transform the present.

After the End of Ideology: Myths and Republicanism

In the explosive context of revolutionary stirrings and antidemocratic movements, Sorel's political theory easily lent itself to being misconstrued. As noted above, he is not the clearest of writers, and his work, beginning with the title *Reflections on Violence*, often implies a different subject. Sorel's theory of violence in fact constituted one of the most confusing aspects of his work: while he certainly would not have condoned the *squadri*, which propelled the Fascists to power in Italy,[89] he was nonetheless prone to glorifying violence, at least in aesthetic terms. A violent strike had a "sublime" quality to it, he claimed, to the extent that it was "cataclysmic"; quoting Emile Durkheim, Sorel even compared this violent beauty to the "sacred."[90] But these were common themes at the turn of the century: members of the *Collège de sociologie*, for instance, would soon be exploring and repeating these same concepts. They would also be the first to recognize certain parallels between such theories and fascist practices.[91] In neither their case nor Sorel's, however, does one find a generalized cult of violence. Only within the framework of the strike and of its specific purpose (overthrowing the capitalist regime), would Sorel insist on the need for violence; he considered it an inevitable part of any political insurrection. He adamantly opposed it, however, as an institutionalized form: "I have a horror of any measure which strikes the vanquished under a judicial disguise," he wrote, referring to the French revolutionary Terror.[92] Of course, this distinction between insurrectionary and institutional violence was easily lost in the rhetoric of his *apologie*.[93]

Perhaps the greatest problem with Sorel's theory was that the crucial separation operated between myth and utopia could be undone. Already for Mussolini, the myth of fascism was not a catalytic image, but the basic blueprint of a future society—"this greatness, *which we want to translate into a total reality*."[94] Sorel's theory of myth was ultimately reabsorbed by the ideological systems that he had so strongly criticized. Paradoxically, his emphasis on political myths ended up reinforcing their epistemological role in ideologies: by highlighting their central importance for revolutionary action, Sorel revitalized the political ideologies that already rested on a "palingenetic" myth. The result was a toxic merger of emotionally and aesthetically refined myths with utopian and totalitarian ideologies. Sorel's deconstruction of ideology became instead its user's manual.

When we assess Sorel from above the fray of twentieth-century totalitarianism, however, it may be possible to re-evaluate the role of social myths from a nonrevolutionary perspective. Has not disillusionment in traditional party politics remained a constant in democratic nations?[95] This disillusionment becomes particularly dangerous when it breeds anti-institutional movements, but can be a disruptive force even when expressed at the ballot box (as Ralph Nader taught Al Gore in 2000). Numerous commentators have blamed recent Democratic electoral losses on a deficiency of what George H. W. Bush infamously called "the vision thing";[96] others have pointed to the Democrats' inability to successfully "frame" the political debate.[97] What Sorel can add to these assessments is the fundamental insight that we require motivation to be propelled into action. Visionary politics and rhetorical skills must be buttressed by emotional and imaginary involvement for political choices to appear more enticing. More importantly, "vision," like Sorel's myths, may be less about where we arrive than about how to arrive there, that is, about the process of arriving. It is not the future that needs enchanting, but rather the actions through which change can be accomplished.

These acts need not be "revolutionary," but can be as simple as casting a ballot in an election or volunteering for a nongovernmental organization. While civism may be the perennial—and by extension, somewhat hopeless—hobbyhorse of ninth-grade teachers and uninspired politicians, its relative absence in contemporary democracies is nonetheless worrisome. It is all the more worrisome that it arguably results from a "systemic" problem with our modern understanding of democratic government. As Michael Sandel suggested in *Democracy's Discontent*, democracy has become identified over the past two hundred years (particularly in the United States) with liberalism. For liberals, government is expected primarily to defend the negative liberties of citizens, regardless of the implications for the whole of society.[98] Opposed to this model is republicanism, in which the common good is valued higher than individual rights, and which Sandel, following historians such as Bernard Bailyn and Gordon Wood, sees at the origin of the American Republic.[99] Critics have retorted that subjugating individual liberties to any other ideal leaves minorities at the mercy of a majority.[100] Others have suggested that republicanism and liberalism need not be viewed as oppositional:[101] even under a government that guarantees fundamental rights, one can hope that representations of the common good will guide both legislators and citizens. But who *acts* upon such representations? The problem with republicanism in a liberal democracy—and more generally, with republican concepts of citizenry and "civic virtue"—is structurally quite similar to the problem faced by revolutionary activists: what makes individuals translate ideas into actions? How are political and moral desires channeled into social transformation? Though designed for more radical measures, Sorel's myths may provide a means for overcoming the discontent and disenchantment liberal democracy can instill. The first step for achieving the common good is undoubtedly to *imagine* it, as Sorel claimed was necessary for revolutionary action. If a political process—be it institutional or civic in the larger sense—can be "re-enchanted," there is a far greater chance it will be pursued by many and that it may succeed.

An interesting example of a contemporary movement that seeks to enchant political action in this way is the "Apollo Alliance," an umbrella group of environmentalists and labor unions dedicated to the twin goals of energy independence and job creation. Its name is borrowed from the "Apollo project," John F. Kennedy's challenge to put a man on the moon within a decade. By setting a similarly short deadline, the alliance hopes to muster the enthusiasm and energy of volunteers and legislators.[102] It is clearly aware that achieving considerable feats is less a matter of envisioning a rosy future, than of motivating individuals to act at all. Though few today have much knowledge of classical mythology, it is hard to resist noting in conclusion the mythical overtones of the project's tutelary deity—Apollo, god of the sun, or in this case, the god of solar power. We are clearly very far away here from Charles Dupuis's sun god, who inspired such a fervor in Destutt de Tracy. Even in this modernized form, however, Apollo and the sun may have retained some of their powers to enchant.

CHAPTER 12

Nietzsche on Redemption and Transfiguration

R. LANIER ANDERSON

NIETZSCHE IS FAMOUS FOR incendiary attacks against Christianity and the Christian morality. The theme is central throughout his writings from early to late. He often complains that religious concepts are mere inventions, but their falsity is far from the worst thing about them. Christianity is not only supposed to be spurious, like other superstitions, but also catastrophically bad for us, working deeply destructive effects within the lives of believers. Targets of this critical program include core ideas and dogmas of the Christian myth—Incarnation, Resurrection, Life Everlasting, Miracles, Prevenient Grace, and of course the concept of God itself. But Nietzsche's critique is not limited to the myth. He also rejects more far-reaching moral psychological notions central to Christian life: sin, guilt, free will, asceticism, resignation, redemption, and the like.

The broad range of ideas Nietzsche takes the trouble to denounce hints at an important but underappreciated[1] aspect of the overall critical program. Despite the overwhelmingly negative tone of his discussion, Nietzsche was keenly aware of Christianity's supporting role in the practical lives of his contemporaries. Identifiably Christian ideas organized the fundamental frameworks that provided people's lives with meaning and purpose, and thereby with much of their value. It is this appreciation of Christianity's practical importance that motivates the rhetoric of doom and disaster in which Nietzsche couched his hyperbolic pronouncements against it—most famously in the proclamation of the "death of God" he put in the mouth of the "madman" of *The Gay Science* 125:

Whither is God? . . . I will tell you. *We have killed him*—you and I . . . What were we doing when we unchained this earth from its sun? . . . Are we not continually plunging? And backwards, sideways, forwards, in all directions?. . . Aren't we straying as through an infinite nothing? Doesn't empty space breathe on us? Hasn't it got colder? Isn't night continually closing in on us? Don't we need to light lanterns in the morning? . . . God is dead. God remains dead. And we have killed him. How shall we comfort ourselves, the murderers of all murderers? . . . What water is there for us to clean ourselves? What festivals of atonement, what sacred games shall we have to invent? (*GS* 125)[2]

God's death is devastating because the disenchanted world it leaves behind threatens us with *disorientation* ("plunging . . . in all directions," "straying through an infinite nothing").[3] Without God, Nietzsche worries, the values and ideals that have given life meaning hitherto can no longer serve us. The sunlike consolation they provided, the warmth and light they brought to our practical lives, is gone. We will have to provide our own comforts now, with uncertain and quite possibly insufficient resources.

But in spite of such disenchantment, Nietzsche remains surprisingly dependent on characteristically *religious*, and even quasi-*Christian*, materials in forging new comforts for life. The quoted passage fairly cries out for *absolution*, the washing away of sins, rites of atonement. Similar redeployments of concepts drawn from a sacred home context are common in Nietzsche. His search for replacements to fill the former practical role of religious commitment repeatedly returns to desacralized versions of religious notions like atonement, salvation, transfiguration, redemption.[4]

This essay explores the suggestion that the positive redeployment of religious concepts is every bit as central to Nietzsche's critique of Christianity as his more celebrated direct attacks against the notion of sin, the mendacity of ascetic priests, or the destructive effects of the moralized guilt concept. Precisely because his appreciation for the practical centrality of Christian moral ideas was so deep, Nietzsche embarked on a systematic effort to recast some such notions so that they could function within a *post*-Christian practical self-conception.

Any such program to reinvent or *re-enchant* these notions following systematic disillusionment with the Christian worldview should have two main components. First, it must identify and characterize both the practical roles and the harmful moral psychological effects of its targeted "moralized" (*GM* II, 21) Christian concepts. Then, second, it must reconfigure those notions so that they can still play some version of their role in life, while avoiding the negative moral psychological consequences prominent in the distinctively Christian deployment. I will try to give this abstract program more concrete shape by investigating Nietzsche's procedure in a particular case: the proposed reinterpretation of two interrelated concepts—redemption and transfiguration. Once we see the traditional shape of the two concepts and some of Nietzsche's complaints against them, we will be able to explain the difference between genuine redemption as he understands it, and (what he takes to be) the false redemption offered by Christianity.

1. The Target: Redemption as Compensation

Redemption is a fundamental concept within Christian life, practice, and self-understanding. The idea was already prominent within Jewish thought. It is central to the special relation with Yahweh, who redeemed the people of Israel by bringing them out of Egyptian captivity, and then again from Babylon (Exod. 6:6, Isa. 47:4). From that core sense of redemption as liberation from bondage, the idea was *generalized* to cover deliverance from tribulation more broadly,[5] and also *spiritualized* to cover liberation from sin or vindication from suspicion (e.g., Job 19:25, Ps. 130:8). To capture the notion, Hebrew writers deployed words (especially the verbs *padah, ga'al,* and derivatives) standardly used to describe the ransoming of persons from slavery, the repurchase of taken property, avenging or restitution for victims, and related notions of restoration. In later uses, these Hebrew terms seem to have undergone a semantic development in which the theme of liberation came to dominate over any specific connotations of ransom price or restitution,[6] but in the Christian appropriation, ideas of ransom and repayment return forcefully into the picture. Ransom and consequent release (e.g., from slavery) are emphasized in the Greek words used to translate Hebrew redemption concepts (especially *luo, lutron, antilutron,* and derivatives), just as in the Latinate "redemption." More important, the thought cuts to the core of the basic religious idea that Christ paid the price for our redemption by his blood: "the Son of man came not to be ministered unto, but to minster, and to give his life a ransom for many."[7] The redemption by Christ is the source of the new covenant with God.[8]

In the Christian context, the temporal logic of the redemption concept also receives emphasis. One can be a candidate for *redemption* only if one has somehow fallen from an idyllic, or at least better, past condition. The redemptive act can then enter the scene in the form of some sacrifice (or other ransom payment) that restores well-being or points toward its future restoration. Important New Testament texts (e.g., Lk. 21:28, Rom. 8:23) lend a strongly eschatological cast to the future-oriented side of redemption. Not only is restitution a future event (following some redemptive intervention), but more, the intervention itself assumes the character of a future-directed *promise*. Christ's sacrifice guarantees our salvation, but its consummation is deferred until the End Times, when Judgment will be passed, the faithful fully redeemed, and the damned punished. The Christian version of redemption thus sharpens two disruptions of temporal continuity built into the redemption concept: our loss of past welfare is deepened and spiritualized through the doctrine of the Fall and our inheritance of Adam's original sin (first break, separating us from the past paradise), and while the sacrifice of Christ promises redemption, its full realization is deferred until Judgment Day (second break, separating us from the future state).[9]

In its central Christian meaning, then, redemption is tied to the notion of a *ransom price*, which is called upon to play two distinct roles: recompense and liberation. Our place in the cosmos, Christianly understood, is fixed by original sin, which radically separates us from the past and future spiritual destinies of humanity. Not only are we born into a state of sin, but sinful tendencies are built into our most unavoidable natural drives and desires, which lead us ineluctably to compound original sin by additional special sins of our own. From a Christian point of view, our basic moral position is one of offense against the very God to whom we owe our existence. What is worse, we lack any resource through which this offense might be redressed, and so we are trapped in a kind of slavery within sin—held hostage by our own nature. This moral position gives rise to the need for redemption, understood as a process through which (1) God can be repaid for our sin and its affront against His honor, and (2) we can be ransomed, and so freed from our bondage in sin. The ransom price for our redemption is paid through the passion of Christ. The solution is elegant, because the distinctive standing of Christ as the God-Man simultaneously makes the repayment appropriate, and allows it to be sufficient. Since He is a Man, Christ participates in our humiliated condition, and his sacrifice is appropriate in the face of the particular wrong to be redressed (viz., human sin—or perhaps, humanity itself). Since He is also God, His actions have an infinite worth, and His sacrifice can thus be adequate to balance the astounding malice involved in sin against God (under the logic that the value accorded the sacrificial acts constituting repayment ought to be proportional to the merit of the redeeming agent).[10]

So redemption can be viewed from two points of view. From the point of view of God, redemption is a form of *repayment* that restores His offended honor and balances the evil of the sin. On this side, God (or the moral world order more generally) is made whole. But from the point of view of humankind, redemption is a form of *salvation*; it saves us, liberates us, delivers us from our sinful condition. On that side, we human beings are made whole by being delivered from our troubles— not only from sin, but also from its consequences, the evils of this mortal life.

What ties the two sides together—and this is now the crucial point— is that the sacrifice of Christ provides a kind of cosmic and spiritual *compensation*. It is simultaneously the repayment that satisfies Divine Justice, and the saving remedy that delivers us from evil and suffering, compensating us for the evils of this world through a promise of heavenly reward. *Compensation* is thus the fundamental idea unifying the two sides of the notion of redemption, Christianly understood.

Nietzsche was acutely attuned to the first side of this dynamic, in which God's honor is restored and His justice satisfied through the sacrifice of the Redeemer. He took particular umbrage at the so-called spiritual comfort offered to the poor sinners by this solution to the repayment problem. In his view (developed at *GM* II, 21–2), its real psychological logic is to *preclude* the possibility of any meaningful repayment, and thus of any genuine restoration of innocence and moral solvency. For under the Christian solution, *we* have not been allowed to pay our debts at all: on the contrary, "God himself makes payment to himself, God, as the only being who can redeem man from what has become unredeemable for man himself—the creditor sacrifices himself for his debtor, out of *love* (can one credit that?), out of love for his debtor!—" (*GM* II, 21). Nietzsche's indignation arises from the insight that we humans now owe God *not only* for our sins, but *also* for the "generous" payments He has advanced on our behalf. Through a move worthy of Don Corleone himself, we have been sunk further into debt than ever—indeed, truly *impossibly* into moral debt. And for Nietzsche, creating that impossible fix was in fact the aim of the entire mechanism: our guilt is now fully "moralized," precisely by being made unpayable. On his view, guilt emerges as a kind of exaptation within our moral psychology. It exploits a pre-existing tendency to self-directed cruelty by making that self-torturing arrangement of our drives seem *warranted* in any and all circumstances, thereby elevating it to a central place within moral psychological life as a principle around which we organize our *conscience*.[11] Self-defeating, self-punishing psychological structures like this are exactly the features of Christian moral life that Nietzsche is most concerned to reject, and on this side of the coin, we can expect that he will resist the logic of Christian redemption all along the line.

But there is the other side of the coin to consider, as well. On that side, the promise of redemption is meant to be, and actually does seem to be, *liberating*. It is supposed to deliver us from evil and from the sufferings of this world, compensating us for the bad things that have happened to us. It is this promise, of course, that gives the notion of redemption its intense inspirational power and attraction. The hope that the evils of life might somehow be redeemed is intoxicating, and given the inevitable portion of frustration and suffering proper to human life, if the sustaining role of this hope cannot be somehow replaced, then the Christian concepts of guilt, sin, and redemption will retain their seductiveness, notwithstanding their self-defeating consequences. What I want to emphasize is that the second, "positive" side of redemption is still animated by the basic idea of compensation. On the first side, it was God's justice that was compensated. Now, by contrast, suffering or frustrated agents are being promised compensation for their failings and setbacks. Nietzsche's efforts to transform the practical role of redemption aim to remove the basic compensation structure from the second, "liberatory" side of the notion.[12]

2. Nietzsche "On Redemption"

The Nietzschean treatment of the problem begins in earnest in a famous chapter of *Thus Spoke Zarathustra* ("On Redemption"), which occupies a prominent place near the end of Part II, just before Zarathustra's enunciation of his distinctive doctrine of Eternal Recurrence. Here I make five points toward a reading of that famous chapter.

The scene opens on an encounter between Zarathustra and a band of cripples and beggars. Their spokesman, a hunchback, offers to deliver the belief of the masses to Zarathustra's doctrines, if only he will first persuade the cripples, where the preferred method of persuasion would be miraculous cures: for example, to "heal the blind and make the lame walk" (Z II, "On Redemption," 249). Zarathustra demurs, quoting back to the hunchback some cynical wisdom from the people themselves, to the effect that curing the afflicted would only make matters worse—depriving hunchbacks of their special spirit, for instance, or allowing the blind to see the world's wickedness. Zarathustra's refusal is ironic: he does not endorse these reasons for refusing to help, but simply quotes the teachings of "the people." The irony prevents our seeing far into Zarathustra's stance on redemption, but as a first point, we can notice that Nietzsche raises the problem of redemption within a broadly Christian frame of reference. Redemption appears to be a matter of making whole those who are broken. The setup clearly evokes a Biblical (and especially New Testament) model, where "redemption" can be used in reference to healing (or releasing, *apoluo*) the sick, poor, blind, mad, or infirm.[13] Unlike Christ the Redeemer, however, Zarathustra refuses to make these people whole, and his ironic tone raises a question about why.

On a different point, however, Zarathustra is quite like the Christian Redeemer. Note, the Evangel's repeated examples of Christ's healing the blind, making the lame whole, and even raising the dead must have a *symbolic* function. As Kierkegaard points out,[14] there would hardly be any point in raising Lazarus from the dead if he must simply die later anyway. (All that heavy lifting—the maximum miracle, in fact— merely to change the date!) No, the deep point *has* to be symbolic: Christ's physical healings, however welcome, are but visible stand-ins for the true underlying redemption, namely, spiritual salvation, the deliverance from sin and evil, the healing of the soul. Here Zarathustra and Christ seem to agree on the general shape of the problem. For Zarathustra goes on to argue to the hunchback that the bodily impairments of visible cripples are not at all the most disturbing thing. He is much more worried about what he calls "inverse cripples"—people "who lack everything, except one thing of which they have too much— human beings who are nothing but a big eye or a big mouth or a big belly." He reports his horror at seeing "'An ear! An ear as big as a man!'. . . [but] underneath something was moving, something pitifully small and wretched . . . And no doubt, the tremendous ear was attached to a small, thin stalk—. . . a human being! . . . [with] a tiny envious face . . . [and] a bloated little soul" (Z II, "On Redemption," 250). Inverse cripples are worse off than their visibly crippled fellows because what is corrupted, degenerate, or smashed in their case is the very soul. The hypertrophy of one drive or another has pushed their

psyches completely out of balance into vice (voyeurism, gossip, glut-
tony, envy—whatever). These people, even more than the hunchback,
need redemption. They need it *more*, Nietzsche thinks, because with
the resource of a strong and harmonious soul a human being can make
something of external setbacks like being hunchbacked, whereas without such a spirit she is truly, hopelessly, lost. She *will* have external setbacks sooner or later in any case, and without the strength of soul to
do something with them, she will simply succumb, or react in ways
that make her worse off. (That is the grain of wisdom behind the cynical popular morality with which Zarathustra dismissed the demand
for miracles.) Our second point, then, is this: What is at stake in redemption is some form of spiritual wholeness, or harmony of the soul.

With this idea in place, Zarathustra turns from the hunchback to his
disciples and makes a speech. He begins with a lament for the human
condition: "I find man in ruins . . . : fragments and limbs and dreadful
accidents—but no human beings" (ibid.) But he immediately holds out
hope of a brighter future—the hope, that is, of redemption:

I should not know how to live if I were not also a seer of that which must come.
A seer, a willer, a creator, a future himself as well as a bridge to the future . . .

I walk among men as among the fragments of the future—that future which I
envisage.

And this is all my creating and striving, that I create and carry together into
one what is fragment and riddle and dreadful accident.

And how could I bear to be a man if man were not also a creator and guesser
of riddles and redeemer of accidents!

To redeem those who lived in the past and to recreate all "It was" into a "Thus
I willed it!"—that alone should I call redemption! (Z II, "On Redemption," 251)

Zarathustra, like Christ, promises a brighter future in which our shattered state will be redeemed and made whole. But the specific notion
of redemption on offer is curious, at least from the point of view of the
temporal logic of Christian redemption. Our restoration is to be effected not by deliverance into a radically different future, in which we
are compensated for past ills, but instead by something new about the
past. According to Zarathustra, and this is my third point, the only
thing *worthy* to count as redemption would be a certain kind of return
to the past, in which the "It was" is transformed into a "Thus I willed
it." The proposal is surprising in that it does not look forward to any
removal of the injuries that engender our need for redemption. On the

contrary, every piece of the "It was" looks set to remain in place. Only our *attitude* toward them is to change. In that new future, we are meant to *will* the "It was."

From this point, Zarathustra explores the notion of will involved in the changed attitude toward the past, through which the will "recreates the 'It was.'" Willing, he professes, ought to be the primary "liberator and joy-bringer" effecting our redemption (Z II, "On Redemption," 251). Instead, though, willing becomes fixated on its inability to *do* anything about the past, letting itself be oppressed by a past it can no longer even affect, much less control. Out of wrath at its "inability to go backwards," it gives birth to the spirit of revenge (Z II, "On Redemption," 252). In that spirit, it generates the compensation-based conception of redemption, in the two forms we saw. First, the will connects suffering to punishment and treats it as "payback," as the price it must pay for being hostage to an existence in which it cannot will backward. Then, in a further development, vengeful willing turns Schopenhauerian, indulging in skepticism that any ultimate repayment or final redemption is even possible:

"Alas, the stone *It was* is unmovable: all punishments must be eternal too." Thus preached madness.

"No deed can be negated: how can it be undone by punishment? This, this is the eternal in the punishment 'Existence,' that Existence must eternally again become deed and guilt! Unless the will should at last redeem itself, and willing should become not-willing." But my brothers, you know this fable of madness. (Z II, "On Redemption," 252–53)

In frustration at the immovability of the past, fixated on its regrets, the will indulges in the fantasy that everything would be better if there were no willing at all. Nothingness itself becomes the goal. Just here, the second, liberatory form of compensatory redemption also becomes visible. If willing could only become not-willing, training itself through Schopenhauerian asceticism for the ultimate, self-annihilating denial of the will, then perhaps it could escape the eternal punishment of existence, and be *compensated* for its suffering with a *reward*—total peace, Nirvana. The only drawback, of course, is that it thereby loses itself; it becomes nothing.[15]

But (Nietzsche insists) *it* is therefore hardly redeemed. The problem here is more general than the allusion to Schopenhauer's ethics of the denial of the will might suggest. As we will see, *any* proposed redemption that works by promising compensation in the form of some new life, utterly different from my actual life, confronts a structurally similar worry: the one who lives that new life has no colorable claim to be *me*, so *her* good fortune is no recompense for *my* misery. Just as in the Schopenhauerian case, *I* am no longer there to be redeemed.

The way out of the Schopenhauerian impasse (where self-annihilating "denial of the will" appears as the only possible redemption) is supposed to come through Zarathustra's conception of the will as *creative*: "I led you away from these fables when I taught you, 'The will is a creator.' All 'It was' is a fragment, a riddle, a dreadful accident—until the creative will says to it, 'But thus I willed it!'... 'But thus I will it! Thus I shall will it!'" (Z II, "On Redemption," 253). This suggestive conclusion seems intended to indicate a new conception of redemption, in which the past is redeemed not by some *different future* that compensates us, but by a new attitude (creative willing, affirmation), directed toward the *same past* that gave rise to the call for redemption in the first place. Just how this works, and just how such an attitude counts as "creative," need some explaining, which will involve Nietzsche's idea of eternal recurrence. But we can already make a fourth point: Nietzsche's reconceived notion of redemption relies crucially on a special attitude of affirmation, and on a special creative (or re-creative) relation to the past.

There is a final fifth point. At the end of "On Redemption," after the speech to his disciples, Zarathustra stops cold in horror. But then he decides to say nothing further, and relaxes. Clearly, he has just refused to articulate the Doctrine of Recurrence, contenting himself with the hints we saw. The hunchback challenges him, demanding to know why he speaks differently to the cripples than to his disciples. When Zarathustra fobs him off with a condescending explanation that the audiences are different, the cripple retorts with a demand to know why Zarathustra speaks otherwise to his disciples than to *himself*. And there the chapter ends—again ironically, leaving us uncomfortably aware that we have not been let into Zarathustra's full doctrine. There is a significant puzzle about why the chapter should close on that note.

Here then are our five points. First, Zarathustra refuses to heal the crippled, and we need to know why. Second, he does insist that being *spiritually* crippled, not mere physical malady, is the real problem facing human beings, but that does not explain his refusal to heal, since there he agrees with Christ the Redeemer. Where Zarathustra does not agree, third, is in the strange character of the promised redemptive future—it will not be a radically new world or life that compensates us

for present ills, but merely a new attitude toward the fragmentary, crippled *past itself.* That attitude, fourth, is connected to the doctrine of
eternal recurrence and a distinctive, "creative" attitude it calls for. Fifth
and finally, we need to know why Zarathustra holds back on explaining this doctrine and its redemptive power. To answer these questions,
we need a working understanding of the doctrine itself, and its connection to ideas about redemption.

3. Eternal Recurrence and the Temporal Structure of Redemption

Nietzsche saw the doctrine of eternal recurrence as his most important
thought (*EH* P, 4; also *EH* III, "Z," 1, 6, 8). It has often been read as a
cosmological theory that time runs in a circle, but recent commentators
have persuasively contended that it should rather be taken as a way to
assess the value of a life—not a theoretical doctrine but a practical
thought experiment.[16] Nietzsche asks us to imagine that our lives will
return, and our reaction is supposed to show something about how
good they are. It is not important that you believe your life *will* or even
could actually recur; you simply imagine its return so as to elicit a response, much as you might when pressed by your spouse to know
whether you would want to marry again, "if you had it to do all
over."[17] A reaction of joy is supposed to indicate that the life was good,
whereas sorrow, regret, and the like show it to have been wanting.
Evaluating life by such a thought experiment thereby posits the *affirmation of life* as an ideal.[18] The "Redemption" chapter indicated a similar idea, when it treated a kind of affirmation (willing the "It was")as
a criterion of genuine redemption.

Such a practical interpretation is strongly suggested by Nietzsche's
first introduction of the idea:[19]

The greatest weight.—What if some day or night a demon were to steal after you
into your loneliest loneliness and say to you: "This life as you now live it and
have lived it, you will have to live once more and innumerable times more;
and there will be nothing new in it, but every pain and every pleasure and
every thought and sigh and everything unutterably small or great in your life
will have to return to you, all in the same succession and sequence . . ." Would
you not throw yourself down and gnash your teeth and curse the demon . . .?
Or have you once experienced a tremendous moment when you could have
answered him: "You are a god, and I have never heard anything more divine!"?
If this thought gained dominion over you it would change you, as you are, or

perhaps crush you. The question in each and every thing, "Do you desire this once more and innumerable times more?" would lie upon your actions as the greatest weight. Or how well disposed would you have to become to yourself and to life *to wish for nothing more* than for this eternal confirmation and seal? (*GS* 341)

The demon's challenge clearly fixes us within a *practical* point of view from which we assess an individual life: you are to imagine that "'This life as you now lived it and have lived it, you will have to live once more and innumerable times more,'" and then evaluate your life by the reaction. In this setup, the standards used in the assessment are not specified independently; they are just the ones endorsed by the person herself, and thus implicated in her own reaction to her life's imagined return. The thought experiment thereby takes on a "formal" function: it is a kind of coherence or consistency measure that reveals how consonant a person's life is with her values.

There are a number of difficult questions about the plausibility (and proper interpretation) of Nietzsche's proposal. Here I limit myself to some points relevant to redemption. I focus first on its contrast to the *temporal logic* built into the Christian conception of redemption, before addressing questions about how *affirmation* contributes to redemption. With those ideas on the table, it will be easier to see (in section 4) how such affirmation is supposed to be "*creative*," and could, in the demon's words, "change you as you are."

Three ideas with temporal implications are built into the thought experiment. One is enjoined to imagine a *recurrence* that is *eternal*, and applies to the *very same* life one has lived. Consider first the notions of recurrence and eternity, where the temporal structure is explicit. In imagining my life to *recur*, I project it in its entirety into my future. This is crucial to the thought, because our natural practical attitudes toward our past and our future show a marked asymmetry. We normally take the past to be beyond our control, and for just that reason, not to be a primary object of our practical cares. While we do adopt some practical attitudes to the past (e.g., regret, taking the past for a lesson or model, etc.), these past-directed attitudes have decidedly secondary status in practical life (compared to future-directed hopes and anxieties), and even such practical import as past-oriented thinking does have tends to be parasitic on potential future application.[20] Nietzsche is keenly aware of this natural asymmetry,[21] and the idea of recurrence is meant to counter it in the service of sharpening and rationalizing the assessment of our life. Under the influence of the asymmetry, we are often tempted to "abandon" our past, as if it did not really concern us anymore.[22] That might be practically useful on occasion, but if what is wanted is a cold, clear-eyed assessment of whether a life has been good, the past can be so abandoned only at the cost of self-deception. Its being *past* in no way removes it from the life itself, and that fact is made manifest by the thought of life's *recurrence*. In projecting my entire life imaginatively into the future, the thought experiment induces me to consider it—*all* of it—with the same motivated (e.g., anxious, hopeful) care I normally reserve for my future self, thereby genuinely engaging my practical values in the assessment of my life.

The fact that the imagined recurrence is to be *eternal* enhances the same effect. If recurrence is eternal, then I can never look forward to a time when I could pretend to be thoroughly "finished" with an event, and the salience of its belonging to my life is thereby set squarely before me. Already here, Nietzsche's ideal contests Christian redemption both in its characteristic temporal structure and also in its animating values. What is imagined to be eternal is not the permanent, unchanging blessedness valorized in the Christian promise, but the *recurrence* of a life with its own pattern of fluctuating developments.[23] Even more important, though, is an extension of the previous point about imagining the futurity, and thereby preserving the practical salience, of one's whole life. No acceptance of life events under the restricting condition that they are *merely* past would count as life-affirmation in the Nietzschean sense. But the Christian promise has just such a structure. Perhaps the prospect of redemption might make our present life in sin seem acceptable from a Christian point of view, but that is so *only* because this life is compensated by a later redemption in which we are delivered from sin and moral order is restored (i.e., the sin is "paid for"). If we had to descend into sin all over again, as envisioned by recurrence, the practical priority of future over past orientation would be activated, and would deprive the redemption of its compensatory value. For what compensated us for our tribulations was never simply that the measure of bliss in heaven *outweighed* the measure of our suffering, but that suffering was to undergo some *final defeat*, so that we were saved from this life absolutely. To feel the force of the point, imagine you are an unhappy gambler, and the casino offers to pay back your losses up to now, but only on the condition that you continue at the table indefinitely, staking the payment in a game in which the odds are all against you. Such repayment would not be compensation, but added torment. In this sense, the final defeat of sin and suffering turns out to be essential to Christian redemption.

For the Christian, then, we are redeemed only if sin and suffering can be placed "once and for all" in the past, in precisely the sense in which, practically speaking, we tend to treat the past as something that has nothing to do with *us* anymore. Thus, the full function of *eternity* in the Christian redemption is not the bare permanence of paradise, but a *consequence* of that permanence, namely, that our future-oriented practical concern is relieved from all worry.[24] Real work here is done by the radical rupture of temporal continuity built into the redemption myth, which removes our salvation to a new, temporally discontinuous order. The thought of eternal recurrence contests the Christian conception by smoothing over that rupture, putting my past back into my future and thereby exploiting the temporal asymmetry of my practical concerns to enforce the idea that my past really matters to the question whether my life is good.

The same salience of the past is *re*-inforced by a third feature of the thought: the demand that what returns is *my very same life*. We have just seen a substantial worry about Christian redemption: it tries to *reduce*, or even eliminate, the practical importance of our pasts. It aims to render the past moot, to make it something that has as little as possible to do with *me*, and my cares. The resulting concern is that Christianity promises not the redemption *of* my life, but a redemption *from* my life. After all, the whole problem of redemption, Christianly understood, arises because our present condition is radically divorced from our true spiritual destiny. The idyllic past and future states are not merely separated from us by time, but exist in different histories—removed from ours by ruptures of continuity (the Fall, the Parousia) that suspend the basic moral framework proper to *our* history. The moral beings of those worlds are of a fundamentally different order. To attain redemption in this version, we must become different people in a real sense.

By contrast, Nietzsche insists that my past *is* just the life I have, the one that needs redeeming. The recurrence idea emphasizes the continuity of that past life with any redeemed self that counts as me; it makes the past a constraint on my efforts to make a life for myself that can be affirmed. The sameness demand thereby smoothes over the rupture between myself and my past, just as the demands for recurrence and eternality tend to smooth over the rupture between us and the future.

The resulting temporal continuity has substantial implications both for the content of what we are being asked to affirm, and for the type of affirmation at issue. If the life whose recurrence I imagine were simply to *omit* some events that really happened to me, then my managing to affirm it would hardly show a real harmony between my life and values. Affirmation of recurrence could easily be made compatible with quite serious disharmony between my values and my *actual* life, as long as I took care to exclude from the recurring events exactly those that are troubling (according to my values). Thus, if affirmation is to count as a genuine test of harmony, "sameness" is essential: I must include every event of my life in the sequence imagined to recur. In that case, affirmation will take the form of wholehearted endorsement of the life I have actually had.[25]

But of course, *no one* has a life free of any regrettable feature, so how could anyone will the recurrence of her life, *the same in every last detail*? Put another way, given the constraints of the Nietzschean assessment, how can we *redeem* the regrettable aspects of life—especially if we are being asked to renounce any hope of compensation in the Christian mode? The problem of affirmation thus turns out to be the very problem of redemption raised by Zarathustra. His original discussion offered a proposal: to redeem oneself, recall, one must:

create and carry into One what is fragment and riddle and dreadful accident . . . To redeem those who lived in the past, and to recreate all "It was" into a "Thus I willed it"—that alone should I call redemption . . . All "it was" is a fragment, a riddle, a dreadful accident—until the creative will says to it, "But thus I willed it'. Until the will says to it, "But thus I will it; thus I shall will it.' (Z II, "On Redemption," 251, 3)

The suggestion is that fragmentary, accidental, puzzling, or regrettable aspects of a person's life can be redeemed by being "carried into One," and "willed"—that is, brought into a *whole* that the person can *endorse*. Nietzsche's key strategy for unification focuses on building narrative continuity for my life. If I could tell my life story in such a way that I *will* the whole, then I could likewise affirm each event within it, in virtue of its essential contribution to the meaning of the whole story.[26] Thus, events that were, considered by themselves, regrettable ("fragment, riddle, dreadful accident") may be affirmed nonetheless. The new story of my life affords me a new attitude toward such fragments, which itself *changes their import*, and so redeems them. I thereby bring my life into greater harmony with my values, and thus improve it in the dimension of Nietzsche's concern.

Elsewhere,[27] I have tried to capture this idea by considering the career of Jimmy Carter, whose crushing 1980 defeat at the hands of Ronald Reagan sharply poses the problem of redemption. Carter's loss of the presidency was a sweeping repudiation of his core values and accomplishments, and ended his ongoing projects. Perhaps most troubling of all, it threatened to mark the end of his career and define the whole thing as a failure. Carter therefore needed to redeem the defeat, to turn it from a debilitating setback into something that could be accepted—even willed. His response to the challenge is well known. He transformed his presidential library into the Carter Center, thereby mounting a new project that allowed him to do work (in dispute resolution, disease eradication, poverty alleviation, etc.) that was rewarding for him and important for the world. In the event, Carter attained a kind of credibility as a moral leader that no other twentieth-century ex-president has even approached—leadership ultimately recognized quite broadly, culminating in the 2002 Nobel Peace Prize. It is by now a commonplace observation that Carter built the greatest U.S. ex-presidency ever.[28]

The crucial point to note is this: it is not at all likely that the Carter ex-presidency would have been as accomplished had he won re-election in 1980. The range of his activities has gone so far beyond the normal course of "elder statesman" politics that it is hard to imagine his even conceiving the project, let alone implementing it so energetically, without the *need* for redemption posed by that stinging defeat. In that sense, to wish for such an ex-presidency is also to wish for the defeat, and precisely that fact allows the later successes to redeem the earlier failure. To wish away the defeat would also be to wish away Carter's genuine achievement—namely, the invention of a whole new kind of public life (along with the many concrete accomplishments that make it up).

We can now see in more detail what the affirmation of a life amounts to, and how it involves redemption. One affirms one's life if one can wholeheartedly endorse it, complete with its setbacks as well as triumphs. Such endorsement is convincingly genuine if the person herself is happy at the prospect that the selfsame life would return to her. Affirmation of this sort will clearly require the redemption of some aspects of the life, since every life includes its "dreadful accidents." Arguably, though, Carter could well affirm his life in this sense, if only once he had implemented his redemptive program with some success. Notice, Carter is not redeemed by having his real life, which includes his catastrophic setback, *removed* from him, as in Christian redemption, nor by rejecting it and thereby removing himself from it (cf., repentance). On the contrary, if we think of his achievement in the light of the recurrence idea, the place of the 1980 defeat within his life is dramatically *reinforced*. From our new point of view, that defeat is the hinge around which his whole public life turns.

Even after his new life narrative is conceived, however, the *affirmability* of such a setback does not just emerge automatically, or as a simple matter of Carter himself coming to look at it a different way. To get redeemed, Carter had to *do* something that positively changed the meaning of his life itself—from the story of a failed political career into a narrative of moral leadership. He had to make the new life story into a *true* story.[29] That provides the practical upshot of Nietzsche's thought experiment, thereby highlighting our previous question about how affirming one's life has the creative power to "change you as you are."

4. Redemption and Transfiguration

In describing redemptive affirmation as "creative," Nietzsche is not only expressing his own valorization of creativity, but also acknowledging a basic demand built into the idea of redemption. Supposing that a person needs redemption in the first place, then if nothing effects real change in her life, nothing is yet redeemed. This observation might be thought to sit uncomfortably with the recurrence idea, which required that the life I affirm be the very same one I have lived, *without the least change*: Nietzsche's view seems to demand that we change ourselves, and yet remain the same. But the aura of paradox is merely apparent. The thought of recurrence was always supposed to provoke a *change in attitude* in the one who undergoes it. Nietzsche even presents that change as especially dramatic: "if this thought gained possession of you it would change" you as you are, or perhaps crush you" (*GS* 341). That said, there is a real puzzle about whether (and how) a *mere* change in attitude can make the dramatic difference Nietzsche suggests. Is changing your *attitude* really sufficient to change your *life*, and thereby count as "creative"? Even more serious, as Reginster observes,[30] is the worry that such an attitudinal shift amounts to no more than *counter-adaptation*. In the face of a world that frustrates my (real) desires, counter-adaptation counsels that I simply change desires and come to want what I actually have. That would be no redemption at all, but rather *capitulation* to a hostile world. Nietzsche's fervent insistence on the creative power of affirmation seems designed to block such an interpretation of the relevant attitudinal shift, but is he justified? Does affirmation really "change us as we are," in some more serious way than mere counter-adaptation?

To address this range of issues, Nietzsche often falls back on another concept taken over from a sacred context, and redeployed to his own ends—transfiguration.[31] In a Christian context, transfiguration signifies a specific incident in the life of Jesus (see Mk. 9:2–10, Matt. 17:1–13, Lk. 9:28–36). At a crucial moment in the ministry, just after Peter has recognized Jesus as the Christ and Jesus has begun trying to explain to his uncomprehending disciples about the coming passion, he retreated to a high mountain apart with Peter, James, and John, and "he was transfigured before them" (Mk. 9:2)—his face and clothing shining with the intense glory of a pure spirit. Moses and Elijah also appear, terrifying the disciples, and eventually the voice of God speaks from a cloud, to let them know that "This is my beloved Son: hear him" (Mk. 9:7). The Transfiguration seems to be intended as a revelation to the disciples of Christ's special status as the divine Son, so as to buttress their faith in the face of the severe trials soon to come.[32]

But what *is* transfiguration? The Greek term here is *metamorphosis*, which indicates a thing's change into another form. It is therefore tempting to understand transfiguration through ancient Greek hylomorphism, as a process in which the *form* of the object is altered, but the matter remains constant. In paradigm uses (e.g., Ovid), though, it is not at all clear that what is conserved through transformation is *matter* per se, in any strict philosophical sense of the term.[33] Still, however the details are handled, *something* preserves the object's identity,[34] and in that respect, the notion is well suited to Nietzsche's needs. In metamorphosis something changes radically (it gains a whole new form), but nevertheless remains the same thing, just as affirmation is meant to transform my life while leaving me the same person.

The metamorphosis concept received sustained exploration in Hellenistic thought and spirituality, culminating in Ovid's *Metamorphoses*, which takes such transformation as the organizing theme unifying a vast domain, including metaphysics, Mediterranean pagan mythology, and even heroic history down to its contemporary present. In Ovid, the metamorphosis concept has enormous flexibility. It is the poet's general theme from the very outset: "My mind leads me to something new, to tell of forms changed to other bodies."[35] It explains the creation of the world out of chaos, the transformations of the elements, the ages of history, and the variability of the moral world. But these general powers of metamorphosis are only the beginning; the notion is also deployed to conceptualize individual events. It covers apotheoses from mortal to divine (Hercules, Aeneas, Romulus, Caesar) and other spiritualizing transformations, but also changes that move in the reverse direction—gods assuming material form to act in the world, humans transformed into animals, animals into stone, and so forth. It subserves a bewildering variety of purposes and symbolic meanings.[36] Precisely this flexibility of the Hellenistic concept generated disquiet in the Christian appropriation, as evidenced by Luke's pointed avoidance of the word *metamorphosis* in his account of the Transfiguration. For Christian purposes, it was not only important to mark a strict separation between the Transfiguration of Christ and Hellenistic apotheoses (Julius Caesar, and Augustus even more so), but also to insist on the *spiritualizing significance* of the change. Christianly understood, transfiguration is an identity-preserving transformation that raises the person (Christ) onto a purely spiritual, divine plane.

Nietzsche's appropriation of the concept connects to both Christian and Hellenistic sources. In Nietzsche as in the Christian case, transfiguration is always a spiritualizing change,[37] even though it loses all mystical or otherworldly connotations. Transfiguration takes something mundane and ordinary, and bestows upon it some wider significance, deeper meaning, or new beauty. That meaning or beauty is what gives the transfigured thing new form. Nietzsche also preserves the Biblical association with radiance, though he does not take light as a mystical symbol of the divine glory. Instead, the physical light of the sun is a first-pass, all-purpose analogy for transfiguration more generally: just as the rays of the sinking sun can remove ordinary things into a new glory, gilding them with a beautiful covering and imbuing them with emotional resonance (*BGE* 255, 224, cf. *GS* 299), so all kinds of transfiguration "put things in a new light," and thereby glorify them.

This is especially true of *artistic* transfiguration, and in that context Nietzsche clearly intends to recover some of the flexibility of the Hellenistic metamorphosis concept. The most important type of metamorphosis he wants to make room for, in fact, is the sort Ovid means to perform on himself at the end of *Metamorphoses,* by a transmuting identification with the immortal greatness of his own poem:

I have now completed a work that neither Jupiter's wrath, nor fire, nor sword, nor time's corruption can ever destroy. Let that day that has dominion over nothing but this body end my life on earth whenever it may choose. The better part of me will be carried up and fixed beyond the stars forever, and my name will never die. Wherever Roman might extends, in all the lands beneath its rule, I shall be the one whom people hear and read. And if poets truly can foretell, in all centuries to come, I shall live. (Ovid XV, 871–79)

Now *that* is a case of "forms changed to other bodies" (Ovid I, 1)—or perhaps better, of a mere body changed to other form—that Nietzsche could believe in, and for him, artistic glorification along such lines was always the paradigm example of transfiguration.[38]

With this move, the full salience of transfiguration for Nietzschean redemption comes into focus:

> Only artists . . . have given men eyes . . . to see . . . with some pleasure what each man *is* himself, experiences himself, desires himself; only they have taught us to esteem the hero that is concealed in everyday characters; only they have taught us the art of viewing ourselves as heroes—from a distance and, as it were, simplified and transfigured . . . Only in this way can we deal with some base details in ourselves. Without this art we would . . . live entirely under the spell of that perspective which makes what is closest at hand and most vulgar appear as if it were vast, and reality itself. (*GS* 78)

So understood, transfiguration applies directly to the problem of redemption: it helps us "deal with some base details in ourselves." Moreover, the redemption of "vulgar" details by transfiguration *claims* to have just the properties we sought in trying to explain redemptive affirmation. First, it is genuinely creative, in the sense of being *effective*; vulgarities transfigured are no longer vulgar. Second, it is a special, imaginative "art," which is creative in the further sense of devising inventive, nonobvious ways to overcome vulgarity. And finally, we are to be saved, "transfigured," by a change in *attitude*. Transformation arrives through a new "artistic" way of looking at ourselves that broadens our perspective on our lives. Such are Nietzsche's claims, but are they justified? Can such a new way of looking actually effect real change in our lives themselves—change that is more than mere counter-adaptation?

To answer, we should consider Nietzsche's aesthetic model in greater detail. From his earliest work, Nietzsche understood transfiguration by appeal to artistic achievement and aesthetic experience, and he understood redemption though such transfiguration. The idea is prominent already in *Birth of Tragedy*, 4, where Nietzsche explores Raphael's portrayal of the *Transfiguration* (Fig. 12.1).[39] Raphael's altarpiece depicts not only the Transfiguration of Christ, in the upper part

FIG. 12.1. Raphael, *The Transfiguration* (1520), Vatican Palace. Courtesy of Art Resource, NY.

of the painting, but also (below) the immediately following story from the Gospels, about the failure of Christ's disciples to cast evil spirits out of a possessed boy. Nietzsche insists on the fundamental unity—indeed, the "necessary interdependence"—of the two scenes in Raphael's composition.[40] To explain it, he claims that the painting represents the transfiguring art impulse itself: its official content is merely a symbol for the real message—namely, the redemption of life through *art*. The possessed boy, confused disciples, and general chaos in the lower half of the painting stand for the troubling aspects of existence which need redeeming, while the glowing vision of Christ's Transfiguration symbolizes the promise of redemption. Nietzsche's redemptive understanding of the *Transfiguration* is highly suggestive, and has won followers,[41] but he goes further than most in claiming that the real redemption symbolized in the painting is not the Christian promise of another life but Raphael's artistic promise to redeem or beautify this one. We can assess the plausibility (and the philosophical import) of this last step only on the basis of a more developed understanding of the redemption-focused interpretation.

The key interpretive puzzle about the *Transfiguration* is raised by its bisected composition. We may set aside the standard eighteenth-century complaint that Raphael's use of two separate scenes is a fatal flaw (compromising the "unities" of space and time in the work),[42] but nevertheless, Nietzsche's mentor Jacob Burckhardt[43] —and many others since[44]—have surely been right to note the powerful contrast between them. Raphael's inclusion of the second scene marks an innovative (even unique?) departure from other treatments of the Transfiguration.[45] It fairly demands detailed explanation, since the choice dominates the composition problem, and various claims to trace it to Raphael's patron[46] have been persuasively challenged by Meyer zur Capellen's argument that Raphael's own artistic motives, rooted in painterly competition with Sebastiano del Pombo, were decisive.[47] So the painting is a unified whole, composed of two starkly contrasting parts. Explaining the unification of the disjoint parts is the basic interpretive challenge posed by the work.

The contrasts in question are formal and coloristic, as well as thematic. A dark horizontal shadow separates the top and bottom parts of the painting, and marks a dramatic rift in space between them.[48] Moreover, the two scenes deploy different perspectives orienting them toward different ideal viewing points, and a hieratic scale that makes the larger figure of Christ appear to stand out from the surface and hover closer to the beholder than the other figures on the mountain. Even more striking, Marcia Hall[49] shows in compelling detail that Raphael used contrasting coloristic modes in the painting's two zones: below, bold chiaroscuro emphasizes the drama of the scene (and effectively competes with Sebastiano on his own terms), while above, delicate high-valued colors express both the rarified spirituality of the subject, and Raphael's own distinctive mastery of *unione* coloristic mode.[50] Finally, from a visual thematic point of view, the two scenes are not merely separated but genuinely *opposed*, just as Nietzsche suggests. The bottom part of the painting creates a powerful feeling of chaos, disorder, darkness—even evil. The top, by contrast, is all goodness, glory, light.

A further point concerns the painting's relation to the source text. In the Gospels, the two episodes happen sequentially, and the reader's attention remains always with the person of Christ: we hear first about His Transfiguration, and then afterwards we follow His return to find the disciples confounded by the spirit-possessed boy. Raphael, by contrast, presents the two themes one over the other, creating an impression of simultaneity: *while* Christ is up on the mountain with Peter, James, and John, His remaining disciples appear below, confronting the possessed boy, his distraught parents, and the surrounding crowd. If the painting departs from the Gospels in its temporal plan, however, it is closely responsive to another aspect of the text: Raphael's image vividly captures the disciples' confusion and embarrassment, marked in the Gospels by the substantial frustration Christ expresses toward them. Before releasing the boy by a miracle, He rebukes His followers for their lack of faith (which, He says, prevented their healing the boy), finally exclaiming in evident exasperation, "O faithless and perverse generation, how long shall I be with you? How long shall I suffer you?" (Matt. 17:17). Some scholars have interpreted the painting, too, as a commentary on faith, noting that two of the disciples below are pointing up toward Christ, as if to indicate that only faith in Him can bring redemption.[51] But the reading is unconvincing. Raphael's simultaneous presentation of the two stories has the result that we see Christ's followers at the moment of their consternation, while Christ is away and they are in need of, and (according to Christ himself) in *doubt* of, His Aid. The lower figures point in all directions, and while this may refer vaguely to the absent Master, they do not know about the Transfiguration event.[52] It therefore stretches credibility to see them as literally pointing toward Christ's revealed divinity. Their pointing is more plausibly just what it appears to be—an expression not of faith, but of its *absence*; it is really just so much *finger pointing*.[53]

What is the significance, then, of Raphael's altered presentation of the Gospel story? The key factor, for me, is the central figure of the painting's lower part, the female figure in the immediate foreground, who has no plausible point of reference in the Biblical text. To my eye, she shares Christ's accusing attitude toward the disciples (Matt. 17:17, Mark 9:19), and by introducing her into the scene, Raphael effectively endorses Christ's accusation. In their effort to divert attention from their own failure, the pointing Apostles refer *us* visually (though without realizing this themselves) to the soon arriving Christ, but the central female figure will have none of it. She looks right at the most prominent pointer, and points back to the boy. It has been suggested that she is the boy's mother, which would explain her determination.[54] But the suggestion is otherwise implausible. She stands out too dramatically from the other figures in his entourage, by her distinctively classical dress,[55] by her elaborate hair, and by the very luminosity of her presence. The more recent consensus is that she is a symbolic figure,[56] and I want to propose that she, too, is a spiritual presence, balancing Christ in the top half of the painting. Not only is her costume classical, but her bared shoulder, twisted posture, and elaborate braided hairstyle suggest to me that Raphael meant to quote the Libyan Sibyl from Michelangelo's Sistine ceiling (see Fig. 12.2), thereby extending the competitive significance which, we have already noted, the painting had for Raphael himself.[57] (If this speculation is correct, then as a classical figure "reborn" into this Biblical scene at the behest of her Renaissance painter, she also indicates the dependence of the Transfiguration theme on the metamorphosis concept, with its broad Hellenistic, and even pagan, resonances.)

But whether or not the central female figure carries this last meaning, her presence reinforces the salience of redemption as a central theme for understanding the painting. In returning our attention so forcefully to the plight of the possessed child, she forces the beholder to recognize that the stakes of the event are not at all what we might first have thought. What is important, we are made to feel, is *the redemption of this child*—not so much the Transfiguration of the Christ into a pure spirit, denizen of some other world. The direction of purpose, the "for the sake of which," imposed by the picture moves from the top down, not from the bottom up. That is, it is not the case that we

FIG. 12.2. Michelangelo Buonarroti, *The Libyan Sibyl*, c. 1512 (detail from the Sistine ceiling, Vatican Palace). Courtesy of Art Resource, NY.

are here *in order* to glorify Christ or his Church. On the contrary, the transfigured Christ is here for the sake of redeeming the world: "the Son of man came not to be ministered unto, but to minister, and to give his life a ransom for many" (Mk. 10:45). The glory of Christ is important only insofar as it "points down"—insofar as it holds out the possibility for the redemption of this world here below, with all its darkness and tragedy. So Nietzsche is a hundred times right that the painting is centrally about the redemption of the boy, not the Transfiguration of the Christ.

But of course, Nietzsche himself takes a further step—and we are now in a position to grasp the philosophical import of his claim (though from this point on I do not assert that Raphael would follow him).[58] For Nietzsche, merely *compensating* the boy for his suffering by some otherworldly reward would be no redemption at all. To be redeemed in truth, he would have to be helped right here in this world, in a way that would transform his suffering itself, turning an "It was" into a "Thus I willed it." The disciples obviously fail to help him (so far Raphael emphatically agrees), but for Nietzsche, even Christ himself does not offer *actual* redemption. As we have seen, Christianity provides only the future-directed *promise* of a life without suffering; it does nothing to transfigure the suffering itself. The painting reflects this reality in important respects: within the frame, the boy remains in the grip of possession, notwithstanding Christ's presence above, which merely promises future compensation. Even when Christ heals the child in the Gospel, we saw that such healing can only be symbolic— the visible stand-in for genuine salvation from sin, whose consummation is deferred until the End Time. From whatever point of view, then, the force of the Transfiguration can only be symbolic. And as long as we view it as a symbol for Christian compensation, it seems strangely powerless in the face of the pressing demand made by the classical figure Raphael has placed in the foreground—the demand that what needs redeeming is this very suffering itself. By now you will have gathered what I am driving at. If, instead, we take the vision of Transfiguration as a symbol for the artistic achievement of the painting itself, then we can see suffering as redeemed by *Raphael*, within the very frame, by the beauty in which the boy is ensconced. For Nietzsche, the beauteous vision of Christ's Transfiguration symbolizes the experience of the painting itself, whose actual splendor does the *real* work of transfiguring the possessed boy, bewildered disciples, and the rest into something unquestionably beautiful.

Two philosophical points about artistic transfiguration are important for Nietzsche's reconfigured, desacralized use of the concept. First, transfiguration is creative, in both senses suggested above. It has a *real effect* on the transfigured subject. Despite whatever illusion may be involved in mimetic art, it does beautify its subject—and that is a real, not an illusory or pretend, change.[59] Even supposing a pretense theory of mimesis, when we view the painting, what we pretend is that certain patches of color are a possessed boy in the grip of a seizure. We do not *pretend* that he and his companions have been beautified. If we have to pretend that the painting is beautiful, then the artwork has failed, and nothing is redeemed. So the real lesson of art for Nietzsche is to show us a way that things might be redeemed by being *really made beautiful*. Artistic transfiguration is creative in the *psychological/imaginative* sense, as well: it must transform its subject in an inventive way, since it will rarely be clear in advance what new field of connections might be able to transform the meaning and value of some fragment that needs redeeming. Some contribution from the individual genius of the artist is thereby crucial. If we consider this individualizing thought together with Raphael's surprising choice to introduce the problematic of redemption so forcefully into his *Transfiguration*, perhaps it is not far-fetched after all to see the painting as an effort to address the artist's own spiritual dilemma through the means his special talents afforded—and thus to read it, with Nietzsche, as an exercise in the redemption of life through artistic glorification.[60]

As a second philosophical lesson, we can see that Nietzschean redemption requires a process with the structure of metamorphosis. The subject of change must remain the same in an important respect, so that *she* remains to be redeemed, though of course, something about her life must also change, if its "dreadful accidents" are genuinely to be *redeemed*. For this magic of transfiguration to happen, the process must draw a basic distinction between something constant in the life or subject, and something new that emerges in it. Artistic representation offers the needed resources, since it can always mark a basic distinction between *what* is represented and the *manner* of its depiction—that is, between a certain kind of matter and its form. The crucial alteration wrought by transfiguration operates not on the represented thing directly, but at the level of the meaning and value that give it a certain form. As Nietzsche was especially keen to emphasize, these interconnected features are especially apt to receive distinctive artistic treatment in the manner of their representation. For him, artists are the culture's special experts at manipulating the "coloring" of things along these lines (*GS*, 301, 84; *BGE*, 255; *TI*, IX, 9).

With a fuller account of transfiguration in hand, we can return to the problem of redemption. The thought of recurrence, recall, provided a practical recommendation for taking arms against our troubles—the construction of a unifying, redemptive story that renders one's life meaningful and affirmable, a story that "carr[ies] into One what is fragment and riddle and dreadful accident" and thereby "recreates all 'it was' into a 'thus I willed it'" (*Z* II, "Redemption"). Such a narrative works by *transfiguring* the life. It leaves the plain events of the life the same, but a new overall life story can nevertheless change the significance of particular events within the life in the way Carter's career exemplified. Note, the new narrative can alter not only the *relative importance* of events, but also their concrete *meaning* for the agent, and thereby whether (and in what degree and respect) they were good or bad for him or her. What was (in 1980) the obvious end of Carter's public life has by now become the very opportunity that made his second career—one is tempted to say, his *real* career—in public life possible at all. The new overarching narrative of the career therefore changed the meaning of his electoral defeat from "final failure" to "opportunity," and reversed its value in consequence. If successful, such a narrative works its way seamlessly into the life itself. It becomes crucial to the agent's self-understanding, and in that form becomes one causal factor fashioning the course of new life events, which serve, in turn, as the mechanism through which the narrative shapes the meaning of the past. In the end, the story and the life may interpenetrate so fully that they can no longer be cleanly distinguished. Endorsing the story can then make a person well-disposed to her life, thus promoting the consistency between her life and values which the affirmation of recurrence demands.[61]

Redemption in Nietzsche's sense thus does effect real change in the life of the redeemed, but without lapsing into mere counter-adaptation on the one side, or alienating the agent from the details of her actual life, on the other. On the first side, notice that while redemption does work through a change in the subject's attitude, it counts as successful only if it also eventually generates sufficient change in her life and in the world to alter what the redeemed events actually mean, and how they stand in light of the agent's real (not counter-adapted) desires and values. Such changes are just what is problematically lacking in counter-adaptation.

The second point marks the key contrast between *genuine redemption* in Nietzsche's sense, and mere *compensation* as it functions in Christian redemption (even in the more optimistic liberatory sense). Later goods can certainly be balanced against earlier evils, and can compensate me in part for bad things that have happened to me, but such compensation alone, Nietzsche insists, by no means redeems the bad things themselves. The recurrence test makes the point vivid, since imagined *return* of past evils inevitably invites comparison of my life—with its share of evils and compensating goods—to an alternative life that would contain the goods without the evils. The latter life will surely seem preferable to me unless the *evils themselves* are redeemed by some narrative that actually alters their meaning and value within my life. In this sense, the fundamentally compensatory Christian redemption is inadequate. *It redeems the wrong thing*. It ransoms me from my very own life, and then promises to compensate me for the evils of that life. But what really needed redeeming were the evils and setbacks of my life themselves.

The compensatory character of Christian redemption is therefore a fatal flaw: it leaves the actual afflictions of life unredeemed, even *condemned*, along with everything that is merely "world." Otherworldly redemption fails to make a person's actual life (here and now) better by one whit. And in fact, the case is worse. It is a precondition on admission to redemption in its Christian form that we *reject* many events of our lives, in our considered view. We are all sinners, and redemption requires repentance for sin.[62] In sharp contrast to all such demands for confession and repentance, Nietzsche's counter-ideal is rather "To commit no cowardice against one's actions! Not to leave them in the lurch afterwards!" (*TI* I, 10). For Nietzsche, it is the particular troubling events that really need redeeming, and so a story can *count* as redemptive only insofar as it incorporates each of the very same events in the life and gives it a significance that can be affirmed, rather than leaving it mired in regret.

5. Conclusion: The Nature of Redemption: Zarathustra versus the Crucified

We are now in a position to appreciate the distinctive character of redemption under its Nietzschean reconceptualization. Of course, he would insist, we should step back from the notion of the ransom price, and in particular, from the idea that God somehow needs to be repaid for the affront of our existence—as if He were really some kind of hostage taker. This set of ideas succumbs to the considerations from *GM* II 21–2, which I painted above in terms of the rejection of mafiosi tactics. But even the notion of redemption that still demands our attention—the saving, liberatory idea of redemption applied to humankind—cannot be accepted, since it redeems us *from* our life, rather than redeeming our life itself.

Moreover, we now have a working characterization of the new conception of redemption Nietzsche opposes to Christian redemption qua compensation. For Nietzsche, redemption operates crucially through transfiguration: it effects a metamorphosis of particular features and events of a life, giving them a new form, in the sense of a new significance and evaluative salience.

The notion of transfiguration adds philosophically significant structure to the redemption concept. Three characteristics are worth recalling explicitly. First, transfiguration introduces new form by bringing the various "fragments" of our life into a *whole*, and it therefore does its work through effects on contextual, holistically interdefined features of the life (e.g., the meaning or value of events within the life's overall context). Second, Nietzsche's account implicitly relies on a contrast between a description of the target life-event in terms of such contextual features, on one hand, and some "lower level" description that is invariant through the change, on the other. The contrast allows transfiguration to effect a real, but nevertheless identity preserving, change. At the level of what the life event means (the level of "form"), it may be radically changed—even into its opposite, as in the Carter case— while the lower level description of the event ("sweeping defeat in the 1980 election") remains the same as ever. Metamorphosis thus transforms the salience and/or value of life events, but does not renounce those events themselves or try to separate them from the life, as in compensatory redemption. Finally, third, we saw that transfiguration as Nietzsche conceives it is an *active* and *creative* process carried out in substantial measure by the agent herself, a feature emphasized by Nietzsche's artistic paradigm.

We can see the philosophical work these three points do in Nietzsche's alternative account of redemption by returning to our outstanding questions (from section 2) about the "Redemption" chapter in *Zarathustra*. First, recall that Zarathustra explicitly framed the problem of redemption as a matter of making us *whole*, unifying the "fragments" and "dreadful accidents" of our life. The first structural feature of transfiguring redemption is thus closely tuned to the problem as developed there. Our remaining open question, though, was why Zarathustra refuses to heal the band of cripples. As it seems to me, the refusal is meant to indicate that the redemption they seek—the traditional compensatory redemption of the Christian promise—is not the true redemption. What people need at bottom, Nietzsche suggests, is not some new life that removes them from the trials they face or somehow pays them back for their suffering, but the transfiguration of those very trials themselves, so that they assume new value for the person while remaining part of her life.

Next, we saw that Zarathustra focuses on *psychological, or spiritual, wholeness* (i.e., the case of the "inverse cripples"). There were pragmatic reasons for such a stance, since a strong-willed, unified person is better positioned to make something of her setbacks than someone basically at odds with herself, and as Nietzsche rightly insists, external setbacks are always on their way to us sooner or later. But with a fuller account of redemption in place, we can see a deeper, principled reason for this theme. The prospect for our genuine redemption rests on a changed attitude toward ourselves (self-affirmation) which is characterized by the harmony or unification it brings about within the self. Affirmation is the mark of a deep-going coherence between our values and our life, and therefore also *among* our values, drives, and other attitudes themselves. It is itself a form, as well as a source, of spiritual wholeness. Just such unification of the soul—what Nietzsche calls "strength"—is what is lacked by those standing in need of redemption, and it is what Nietzschean redemption brings to a life when it is successfully transfigured.[63] Here again, we see the fundamental contrast between Nietzschean redemption and Christian compensation. In the Christian case, redemption takes me away from myself; it demands that I separate from my actual life by repenting of being who I have been. But if the goal is my spiritual wholeness, Nietzsche reasonably suggests, then such a path is not even headed in the right direction.

Another puzzle from "On Redemption" concerned the curious character of Zarathustra's redeeming promise: rather than pointing toward a radically new future, it returned us sternly to our past, to the very "It was" that needs redeeming. The second (and most distinctive) structural feature of transfiguring redemption explains why this should be so. The dreadful accidents of my life are to be changed (in their meaning and value), but in such a way that their identity is preserved, and they remain just as much parts of my life as before. As Nietzsche insists, it is *only* in that way that the accidents themselves are redeemed by the transfigured form of my life. Otherwise, any new life I received could at best be compensation for those losses, which remain losses on the debit side of the ledger. Such compensation could in no way reconcile me to my past itself (to the contrary!), and so it fails to provide the promised harmony among my self-directed attitudes. What I need instead is an attitude of affirmation toward the fragmentary, crippled past itself, toward which Nietzsche thinks I can be guided by the thought of recurrence.

No redemption is yet effected, however, by a *mere* change in attitude. Unless the attitudinal shift has real effects in my life, it is so far still mere wishing, or at best counter-adaptation. Genuine redemption thus requires creation, or, as Zarathustra put it, re-creation of the past. As we have seen, my redemption depends on the invention of a new life story which becomes sufficiently central to my self-conception to produce ongoing effects on my actions and my world, changing the meaning of what I do, plan, and become. The *meanings* of these aspects of my life are holistic: they are what they are (in part) due to their relations to others. When we focus on their meanings, past events come to count, for example, as mistakes corrected or vices contracted, as spiritual callings foreshadowed or mere adolescent crises, as turning points or just bumps in the road—all depending on which ongoing future they have led to. Therefore, insofar as the narrative really guides my future life, the new life story it provides can also shape the past. Its creation can be a *re*creation, effecting a metamorphosis of my life through which my past really becomes something affirmable (turning the "It was" into a "Thus I willed it").

At this point, the third structural feature of transfiguration is also clearly in play, since in these respects Nietzschean redemption must be a creative, active process. But the present point (viz., that redemption must show real effects in my life) does not yet encompass the full importance of the appeal to creativity. Nietzschean redemption requires not merely that my life really be affected (passive voice) in some metamorphosis, but further, that I myself transfigure it (active voice). The effective agent of transformation is my own changed attitudes and self-conception. Why should this be so?

The answer takes us back to Nietzsche's basic criticism of the compensation model. So far from reconciling me to myself, the promise of compensation tends to reinforce in me an attitude of self-condemnation: I demand compensation precisely insofar as my life is *bad*, by my own lights. In the extreme, the compensation picture encourages me to get rid of myself entirely (as in Schopenhauerian denial of the will), or to assume a wholly new identity that is radically discontinuous with my current actual life (as enforced by the temporal discontinuities proper to Christian redemption). In either case, there is a real sense in which *I* am not redeemed. What I need is to heal my broken life—not to acquire some *other* life, radically distinct or discontinuous from my own. Indeed, on reflection, the postulated identity between the recipient of such "payments" and *me* is hard to accept: the complete difference between her life and mine militates against any such identity, and without identity, her bounty can hardly count even as recompense for my losses, much less as the actual redemption of my life.[64]

For Nietzsche, by contrast, genuine redemption must keep me, the one to be redeemed, firmly in view, even while my life undergoes more or less fundamental transformation. In part, we saw, what preserves my identity is the persistence of the particular events of that life, under some description. But these events do not do all the work. The same events construed as belonging to someone else would not establish my cross-temporal identity, nor would thinking of them in another person's life count as affirming my recurrence. It is *my attitude of identification* with my past life that matters here. That identification is grounded on my own responsibility for the life story I tell myself, in which the events figure only as constituents. In the end, therefore, I preserve my identity through transfiguring redemption only because I *myself* effected the changes in my life, and that is the deepest reason I must be creative if I am to be redeemed.

And this answers our final outstanding question from section 2. We saw that at the end of "On Redemption" Zarathustra recoils from the implications of his doctrine and refuses to articulate it to his followers. Ensuing sections reinforce his dissatisfaction with his companions. He is afraid they are not up to the task of redeeming themselves, and is reluctant even to lay the demand upon them. That very conclusion, however, sharpens the problem of why Zarathustra is not more like Christ: if the future he paints really promises redemption, and if we are so inept, then why doesn't he heal us himself, or at least help us by sharing what he knows?

The reason turns out to be built into the reconfigured notion of Nietzschean redemption. So understood, redemption is necessarily a species of *self*-transformation. It is something a person does for herself. The restriction is fundamental, because redemption requires thoroughgoing change in the agent's life, but without loss of identity. The point is to give myself a new life, proper to a new basic self-conception. But if my new, redemptive self-conception is to remain *mine*, so that the life it allows me to affirm remains the very same one that stood so sorely in need of redeeming, then the transfiguring narrative and its self-conception must be the product of my own action, creation, invention. It is the *continuity of my act* in developing it that ensures the identity of my new and former selves, and allows the new narrative to redeem *my* life.

For just that reason, Zarathustra cannot redeem or heal anyone else. Redemption, one last time, is not a kind of compensation that could be paid to me from abroad. The challenge, but also the promise, of Nietzsche's new conception is that each one's redemption can only be her own.

Epilogue:
What Hearing Knows

MICHEL SERRES

EMITTED BY INEXHAUSTIBLE CHATTERBOXES, the cries of politics—noises of conflicts, carnage, jealousies—keep us from hearing the world's song. A keen ear and silence give us over to its enchantment. Listen.

What Syntax Sings

On my first trip to Rome, nearly half a century ago, I found myself, one evening, in a tearoom.[1] Women of all ages savored sweets there while chittering trippingly, deafeningly, overwhelmingly. As I conversed with a friend, *sotto voce*, in French, I heard their voices, in Italian, around the edges—thus the sound more than the meaning. Then I heard Scarlatti; these feminine vocal exercises sounded like his sonatas.

Since almost as long ago, this musician has appeared to me to compose differently from many others, because he minimizes melody, often to the extent of canceling it out, in order to remain in grammar—repeated notes, arpeggios, scales, trills, triplets—as if he were reducing his score to morphology and syntax. Less melody, less meaning, more pure framework. In the Roman café where I understood little Italian, I thought that I heard, beneath its meaning, the scaffolding of that language, its sonorous skeleton, its scarlet or Scarlattine music.

When, commonly, we speak in order to say something, our intentional meaning is supported by a frame that uses lexicon and syntax blindly. Another technique, an artistic one, consists of making meaning surge forth from pure form. Take the grammar book and the dictionary, alone: what do they say, together and without any other intention? Either you speak through language or you let it speak for itself. The ordinary user chooses the first solution, the easy one: he talks. Devoted to the second, the artisan works with these two literally senseless treasures, dictionary and grammar, like an architect or a mason. A writer has no need for any book other than these two on his shelf; that's why my own works lack bibliographies. Meaning, which emanates from form, is all the more profound when the latter obeys these two books alone. Certainly, this is easier to hear in music; the will to mean crushes language so much that it turns the best writers into victims of their art. Everyone reads or hears meaning without hearing or reading pure language. Blind and deaf to artistic work, readers barely see words and their arrangement; listeners barely hear vowels and rhythms.

Now, we repeat the same things, indefinitely, without suspecting that we invent very little. Media and conversations return indefinitely to the hierarchical and violent circumstances that have glued our relations together since before prehistory. Like apes, we communicate with gestures accompanied by sounds. Like clothes on a clothesline, history hangs proper names on the long, monotonous strand of those who have died for power and glory. Meaning rarely matters: a little for philosophers; almost never for novelists, whose pages always flow from some failed love; or in the theater, whose scenes mime some murder; not at all for poets; never in daily life, where all that is announced or exchanged has already been known for millenia. Naïve, we stop at this meaning, although it is iterated, imitated, repeated, thrust forward, hammered out, rehearsed like a litany, dreary, hardly different from that of the beasts, comparable to the background noise that drifts up from anthills or the alternating calls of cetaceans invading the oceans. And, just as advertising blocks the landscape, just as speaking hinders seeing, this noise of meaning without meaning anesthetizes language.

Whereas everything is happening underneath. Whereas writing begins with its framework. Whereas style underlies surface meaning and expresses how, for thousands of years, the pillars, beams, and flying buttresses of this immense scaffolding, which no speaker commands entirely, have been vibrating. In scales and arpeggios, what does Scarlatti communicate? The acoustics of Italian grammar. Would you like to learn this language? Listen to its sonatas. Which single composer, among the Couperins, Rameaus, Berlioz, Bizets, Debussys and Ravels, the Duparcs, Chaussons, and Jean Français . . . , sounds my own language in the same way? *All* of them, in fact, vibrate in French syntax. The best writer, then, lets us hear the largest part of his language's scaffolding: he sings closest to its syntax.

Exclusively melodic, Gregorian plainsong retains only meaning. Does it express the Psalms in this way? Conversely, as if it had conserved the appogiaturas and the virtuosic passages of French baroque music—a source that historians propose for it—jazz gives an even more precise example of composition by syntax. Does it express Negritude in this way?

What Latin Sonorities Say

In Mexico City; San José, Costa Rica; Montevideo, Uruguay; Lima, Peru; in Urbino, Italy, not far from the Adriatic; in São Paulo and Belo Horizonte, Brazil, I have experimented with "inter-languages," on the model of the "intercom." Italian-, Portuguese-, or Spanish-speaking audiences can understand a talk given in French, if the orator dives into the sea that bathes these Latin language-islands, whose wild breath all around sings a music common to these sisters—tempo, rhythm, melodic line—producing, with the same vibration, a similar meaning. Montaigne and La Fontaine, Cervantes, Camões and Dante Alighieri go back in unison, through Quintilian, toward Cicero.

Changing Languages: What Murmurs in the Shadow[2]

The more Slavic notes of the Song to the Moon, in Dvořák's *Rusalka,* half-open a dark door before a deep well, a gulf of shadow in the world. Ordinary musics and pages, even beautiful ones, do not come from this place, but spread out like coverings that please, but conceal— vertical, iridescent, like curtains and veils stirred by a breeze; yet another page that spreads out, that speaks, that designates, explains, recounts, occupies space and passes time. But these true notes flow toward us and we perceive, at bottom, whence they originate, the sovereign fountain from which they come; in fact, they flow toward us and downhill, to make us understand where they spring from, upstream; they run toward the mouth to make their source heard in the most discreet way imaginable; they gush forth like a geyser to drive us into the cave where lava boils. They go in this direction so that we will retrace their path. Not toward the author, but toward the origin; not to the subject, but to the world.

Then, the notes as such yield and disappear as if melted, letting the hubbub that precedes them be heard, and we hear tumult, chaos, moaning and groaning leaving the box: not the meaning of words but the roar from which they are formed, stony and bleeding. That which gapes behind this door. The gulf of shadow, the black box; hell, heaven, purgatory; the desert, the high mountain, the high seas; the crevasses of the glacier, the bottom of the pit, the belly of the volcano; Danae's lap from which, in a torrent, stream the gold pieces whose value attests to hers.

As objective as the images of these thousand denominations may appear, the fact remains that I carry this black hole behind the bars of my thorax; when a writer or composer throws these words or these notes in my face, I recognize them as true, familiar, daily, mine, cenesthetic, in accordance with time and blood, the background noise of the world and the supplication of the body. They alone make me shed real tears, secreted by the well from which, like gasps for breath, the exceedingly rare true notes that I write when I can reproduce, body to body and under my tongue, the background noise of the world, also emanate.

Ur-Musik: What Birds Chirp

We will never speak all the languages of men and angels. That quantity exceeds the effort of an individual. But each of us can remember. When our ancestors left the cradle of Africa, before they diverged, before their separation was deepened by the ensuing mosaic of climatic constraints, cultures, and dialects, how did they communicate among themselves? Did they use an archaic Nostratic from which this explosive mass of languages descends? How might we rediscover this, our first channel of communication? We have retained not a single trace of it.

But what do we have in common even today? Music. We know of no culture without dance, rhythm or song, without ululation or threnody. *Homo musicus.* Alas, the traces we have retained are only recent ones. We date from only sixty thousand years ago the first flutes discovered in central Europe. In Mezin, Ukraine, archaeologists found a complete orchestra pit full of wind instruments, strings, and percussion; had the glacial Paleolithic already invented opera? Of course, all instruments vary by culture, as do all compositions, but it seems to me that I hear the cry, the tone, the low vocalization that unites them and from which they will emerge. Blocked, buried, hidden between the hubbub of the world, the crowd, and the body itself on the one hand and, on the other, the compact multiplicity of heard languages, that which cultures, ever since, have played under the name of music cries out: source of languages, born from the background noise of the world and of supplications, slipped in between the commotion of Genesis, Psalms, and Prophets, in existence before the Word was born in John, long before all tongues received it together on Pentecost morning. In the double well of my throat and my ears, in the double fold of storms and my desire, the *Ur-Musik* of humanity roars. We have never had anything but this with which to express time: the tempo—*allegro,* lively or dragging—and the melody, so that it runs or is broken with silences, meter to give it a rhythm, rhythm to give it a meter, the double bars and *da capo,* so that it will turn back on itself . . . in the first two Études, *allegro* and *presto,* of his Opus 25, Frédéric Chopin even gives voice to its whirlwinds . . .

I am waiting to hear this elemental panting that rises, in its half-muteness, above the cool wind, the deep-sea swell, the crackling fires, the earthquakes, the glaciers breaking up, and that touches down behind Couperin and my nostalgia, Rameau and the grace of your gestures, Ravel and the grain of your voice, under the trench of my solitude. I do not want to die before discovering the source from which the first murmur—grail of all inspiration—emerges. Music raises all the arts, codes all the sciences, breathes beneath languages, inspires all thoughts, better yet, gives rhythm to all numbers; under it, behind it, between it and the booming call of things and bodies, lies the mute mystery, coffer of all secrets. He who discovers it speaks, virtually, every language.

The robin has an enormous repertoire at its disposal: more than a thousand different songs. Between the marsh warbler and its neighbors, one hears organized polyphonies that exist even among different species of birds. Groups of chimpanzees screech at night in choirs that form and disband. Never in contact, the Peulhs of Niger, the Nagas of Assam, the Albanians sing in identical pentatonic modes with a drone. Universal in man, like numbers, music thus includes at least apes and birds as well. Equipped with such small brains, how do certain birds, who change melodies with each mating season, attain such pure masterpieces? Thanks to music, we fly like birds, dance in the three dimensions of water, gambol in trees, discover or construct place and space and time. But we have contrived to do this in the intimacy of our souls as well, or in that of our confessions to others.

If very few of us write, and if we have only begun to do so recently, there is no doubt that we have all spoken for thousands of years. But before this speech, music, millions of years old, dates from a colossal antiquity. Perhaps we came down from the trees like our cousins the apes, but in the same branches where we leapt, certain winged species fluttered. Even today, our plaintive modulations of desire or of mourning reach the profound neurons that we share, in our reptilian brain, with chaffinches, titmice, and hummingbirds. We must have communicated first with threnodies, melodic inflections and curves, with intricate dances and vocalizations mimicking gestures and situations. The aborigines of Australia still do this, with exquisite art, to describe the geography of a desert unchanged for millions of years. In these prethrenodies, where certain inflections must have served as prepositions—artisans of meaning—the modulations modulated space and time. Societies held together by means of these orchestras, occupied the expanse all around them, acted, predicted, remembered through these scores that, without leaving the body, sufficed for survival. Before the contingent, unnecessary, and, when all is said and done, recent adoption of articulate language, these proto-musics lasted millions of years, during which, immersed in the winged polyphony of certain expressive cousins, we continually perfected their excellence.

Like many peasants, the troubadour St. Francis, who spoke to birds, knew this; Ronsard, whose *Amours* invoke the nightingale chirping amid the willows for his beloved, who reciprocates his love, suspected it as well; the melancholy of the poet, a rejected lover, comes from the fact that when *he* tries to seduce, he uses only words fraught with meaning, "although we both have the same music."[3] Does the Holy Spirit descend upon us in the form of a dove so that a gusting wind and the roaring fire will come, inert vibrating waves, and the musical inspiration that lives, lies, burns under every tongue, and so that its murmuring can make itself understood by all the peoples present? In certain branches the bird of Pentecost still sings.

We all know it: why be scandalized by the fact that our conversations exchange meaning so rarely, since, for millions of years, only tones (rough or smooth), pitches, held notes and modulations, crescendos, andantes have brought us together? Exceptional and precious, meaning is set within a mounting of murmurs that, alone, animates our bitter or coalescent relations. Certain piano pieces stir with the left hand the dark masses of this clamor of wind, river, or volcano, of gatherings or secrets, while the right hand, high and clear, pins a few rare gems of meaning on this velvet cushion. This *Ur-Musik*, stemming from the background noise of the world and of bodies but barely detached from it, drives the world and bodies, collectivities and history. It places us together in space, where mass migration depends on the modulation of signals.

At the moment of the new catastrophe in which meaning was invented, we lost in appropriateness what we gained in precision. This is why the mountain of philosophy rises up, unique and rare like an atoll, among the archipelagos of recited evocations, which themselves emerged from an ocean of gasps for breath. We all know it: a text that only states—whose sonority and rhythm do not descend to this depth, toward these millions of years, toward these avian neurons in us—sounds garrulous and worthless, bores and wearies. Writing or speaking only have value if they suddenly capture, by dint of listening, that whole layer of language whose thickness is measured from the improbable meaning deposited, on top, over the acoustic flesh—vowels, rhythms, number and movement—down to the low base where this clamor touches the musical bole from which all languages bifurcate in branches.

See, in the same way, on the surface, mountains and lakes, river banks, churches and paths; dig in the earth, underneath, as a peasant labors, then as a miner excavates the coal beds, finally as geophysicists descend to the plates whose minuscule movements give rise to eruptive flares and the collapse of cities in the earthquakes of the historical superficies. Arrival at this dense and archaic magma, beneath recent signification and the subtle song that sculpts it, magnifies all singularities—the Frenchness of French, the Lusitanity of Portuguese, the mass of Latin in the Romance languages—but also opens onto the shadow-mouth from which *Ur-Musik* emerges. From every great work, as from this somber pocket, a sort of sonorous melancholy emanates, a calm breeze skimming a lake of tears, the immense space of meaning. Whoever makes this murmuring audible not only writes or speaks, but begins, like an angel, to articulate the density of languages.

I arrive, finally, at the summit of the dune from which I will see the ocean. As I ascend, the chaos of the waves, invisible behind the crest, increases. When life and time begin, far from the final slope and under the protection of this high barrier, we do not hear this surf. Its irregular noise fills our ears as we move forward, until it subdues distinct voices, reasonable words, rare confessions, subtle melodies; at some point, this formidable disorder will replace all discrete signals, drown out all the waves.

Even so, I believe I once heard—long before I arrived at the foot of the dune—the dispersion of numerous things gasping for breath; but familiar calls, beautiful demonstrations, rare musics, and even rarer amorous confessions distracted my ears from this murmuring. Now, with age, the eardrums break down, we say, in order to explain its rise; not so, for even the deaf keenly perceive this natural tinnitus whose wave looms before the temporal advancement of the body like a high swell, a wall of unfurling jagged spines, facing the prow of a boat.

Having arrived one morning at the top of the dune, open toward the horizon, I will see that vertical swell arrive, high in the sky and straight upon me; I will hear only its wave. Then the minute will have come when the crackling of God's fire drowns out the last of my laments, the one that has been traveling toward you for so long.

Physical Culture

For a long time, I have been trying to construct a physical culture, in which philosophy and art would discreetly step back from the black hole toward which collective relationships draw them and, through a literally superhuman effort, rejoin the very formation of things—global time, the chaos of the climate, the trembling of the living, our global habitat—in order eventually to connect again, once and for all, with the calls of individual humans. We live first of all in the world: nights, oceans, seasons, freezes and thaws . . . We do not see it, but could we sometimes hear it?

Drugged with cultures and languages, we do not see this physical culture coming; I invite you, then, to listen to it.

Poetry

Handle and head, the hammer goes along with the forearm and the elbow; the wheel with the rotation of ankles, hips and knees; writing with memory: technical objects stem from the body. Once they are present in external space in this exo-Darwinian way, we work with and on them: our external gestures act on these externalized things. The Greeks named this second technical action *praxis* (πρᾶξις).

I remember the moment when, conversely, writing became incarnate in me; the practice, the artisanal labor that used these objective things as external tools suddenly entered into my metabolism. Like a parasite turned symbiont, the work transformed into an organic function. This is my body; this is my blood. Since that internalization, a day without a line is torture, like a minute without breathing. From the paper or the screen toward the body, then, this incarnation revives, in reverse, the aforementioned origin of culture and of externalized tools. Because he secretes, gives birth, bleeds every day, the writer relives this initial connection, without ceasing to reproduce it. Following the Greek distinction, I call this corporeal and vital act of first externalization *poetry* (ποίησις).

Hence the distinction between external books and works that come in this way from the internal, matched up with it. Who hears the intimate voice of Chopin or the avian harmonies of Messaien with the same ear as they do the high-flown bluster of so-called Romanticism or the dull notes of Tchaikovsky? Two kinds of music, two kinds of poetry: one, attached to its culture, descends toward the sound of its language; the other, great, exceedingly rare, vibrates in order to express the tension of bodies, the sea breeze, the feminine trembling of the ice in the snowmelt season, the interlacing of universal relations, and the background noise of the world.

Return Path: The Universal Poetic Ear

Would I dare to say that I dream of a universal acoustics? I have just evoked the road to the bottom, a dark drop: leaving meaning behind, it descends toward nocturnal sonorities; next, under the sounds of Italian or French, it digs to reach tonalities common to Latinate languages; then to the originary noises that may be heard under all languages; from there, a blind footpath runs deeper still: birdsongs, whale calls, ant noises, storms at sea, the thunder of earthquakes—background noise of the world.

From the linguistic, do we descend in this way toward the acoustic, from the soft to the hard? Do we reach the song of enchantment of the things themselves? Yes.

Take heart, now, as we follow the path again, from low to high, from the hard to the soft, from the body to the mind, from the physical to the abstract, from understanding [*entente*] toward knowing. In going back up this path, I summon up the still poetic dream of another epistemology. Can I reconstruct knowledge starting from hearing?

We follow only a parallel road that, starting from vision, blossoms into intuitions, theories and ideas, all words that repeat the act of seeing in forgotten languages, Greek or Latin. We take this dazzling, luminous path from the eye to abstraction every day, in our transparent knowledges and the inventions that shine forth in minds. Leading from Plato and the age of the Enlightenment to science's clarities and distinctions, it left ποίησις to reach πρᾶξις more than two thousand years ago.

By contrast, the poetic path that begins with background noise, with sounds, with acoustics, with the ear does not lead us to knowledge in the recognized, methodical, operative, usual way. A mythical voyage barely, haltingly describes it. Through musical compositions, it leads, in fact, from Hades toward the surface; in Avernus' shadow, Eurydice comes back to life by following Orpheus' lyre—step by step, note by note, scales and chords—on this difficult, dangerous upward path. And suddenly, the climb is interrupted; Eurydice falls and slides toward the abyss. Later, Orpheus' life will be interrupted as well, under the dysharmonic cries of the crazy crowd of Thracian women carving his body into pieces. The acoustic or musical path to knowledge is missing.

Certainly, equations for vibrating strings and rules for fugues and counterpoint exist, but from hearing to general abstraction, we cannot follow a road as royal as the one that leads from vision to theories and ideas. In the case of sounds, we have only an interrupted myth, an unfinished dream, a blind poem. Will this slippery path, which descends to Hades and cannot come back up, one day become a road marked out for a pragmatic voyage? Will this poetry of epistemology (ποίησις) be changed into praxis (πρᾶξις)?

Of this broken chain, we no longer have more than a few links; on the fragments of the path, we now find only three or four traces of footsteps. I am attempting to mark Eurydice's.

From Rufus of Ephesus to Galen, the doctors of Antiquity believed that the muscle tone (*tonus*) of a living individual gave him life and characterized him. By their tension, the muscles of the back, stomach, and limbs balance the organism in such a way that, through his gestures and his bearing, he becomes aware of his body, therefore of himself. Here is a piece of advice, taken from the Greeks: lie down gently on your bed or fall abruptly to the ground; you will experience the difference between this *tonus* and its absence. Falls in the mountains, rest, sleep and death: every collapse follows from its interruption, from this disappearance. Did Orpheus lose his companion by misplaying her muscle tone? Did you dismiss me because, lacking in finesse, I jammed some keys together?

If you heard the music of my vital intensity and of my pulse, whose formula is given by this tone, you would understand me. If I heard the music of every species, would I know all living things? If, in the silence of my body and soul, I listened to the things of the world, would I have a new understanding of the physics of the universe? Did Orpheus try to reproduce on his lyre the *tonus* of cedar trees, of tigers, of rivers, of the sea, and of his absent lover?

Why does mathematics apply to the things of the world? Einstein takes up Kant's question without resolving it. Let's follow the blind path of those who hear well. What we know of the Pythagoreans encourages us to register a musical origin for geometry and arithmetic; Euclid's algorithm appears to be a derivate of measurements of vibrating strings, from which stemmed the proto-algebra of relationships and proportions. Later, modern physics was born with Euler's and Fourier's partial differential equations for heat and these same vibrating strings; before this discovery, optics, for example, dealt only with mechanics, or even simply with geometry. Thus, both the abstract and the applied sciences emerge from a forgotten acoustic and sonorous context. Here, then, is the solution: maybe mathematics sings all the noise of the world. If we could hear mathematics, maybe we would better understand the real.

In his *Harmonices mundi,* Kepler established the scales whose Pythagorean relationships separate and unite the celestial bodies and

make their movements heard.[4] For him, the universe hums symphoni-
cally. In an inspired confirmation of this intuition, the French mathe-
matician Souriau has just demonstrated that the exact intervals
between our solar system's planets are necessary and sufficient to keep
one of the planets from beginning to resonate and thus disorganizing
the system. In more or less visible spectra, we now depict all sorts of
waves that we receive from the universe; we no longer hear them. If I
knew how to hear them, and wavelets as well, would I better understand cosmology?

DNA has the form of a vibrating string; if I heard it, would I be better
equipped to answer the question: what is life? Schrödinger, for his part,
replied: life is an aperiodic crystal.[5] I dream of adding: life is the noise,
the sound, the music emitted by this crystal. How shall we hear it? If I
heard the *tonus* of your DNA, would I finally understand you better?

If we knew how to listen, in the same way, to the vibration of super-
strings, of the branes or membranes whose theory unifies general rela-
tivity (which explains the world) and quantum mechanics (whose
equations open the way to the microcosm), would we know the universe better?

My language can understand space and time (the latter of which
may derive from the Greek verb τείνειν) as two types of tension. By
means of elongations whose excess sometimes allows access to otherwise inaccessible targets, does our body-tensor construct volume and
duration around it?[6] Beyond space and time, as physics and philosophy teach us about them, is there a unified vibration or tension, as yet
undiscovered, that produces both of them? Does the poem of the
sonorous path, weak in science, lead to a strong invention?

Did Orpheus, poet, musician, and thinker, translate noises, desires,
furies, calls, and sounds into musical science in this way? Did he construct, did he know this mounting path? Did he spread peace among
wild animals by sounding the harmonic sum of the tigers' claws, of the
barking jackals and their trembling prey, but also of earthquakes, spiny
bushes, oaks with prickly leaves, winds tying the tall grasses into
bunches, since they say that flora, like fauna, bent toward him when
he passed? Had he deciphered their *tonus*? Did he successfully begin
Eurydice's resurrection by composing, in the dark, a score whose key
sang his companion's singular vital tension and the vertiginous scale

of her genes? Mutilated by the furious Thracian women, did he die of this torture because he could not at that moment find the Fourier sum that harmonized the tones according to which each woman trembled? Chaos and commotion made him—the conqueror, until then, of a thousand different noises—explode into pieces.

Breakdown of tension: no more space or time. Yes, Orphism leaves the genesis of a rational knowledge that we do not cultivate buried in the infernal limbo of myth. Poorly delivered from the shadows, Eurydice falls back into Hades. From the noises of the earth, the subterranean fires, the murmur of the forests, and the roaring of animals to music, language, and knowledge, an epistemological chain takes shape, begins, and breaks off, aborted. We will no longer hear the world, the crowd, or bodies.

Our limited ear, on the stiff nape of our neck, cannot hear these abstract vibrations: mathematical, astronomical, muscular, genetic, subatomic, spatiotemporal . . . But do we have an eye that perceives geometry's perfect triangles or multiple dimensions? Starting from sight, our knowledge forms theories and ideas; intuitions perpetuate the gaze in formal domains. We attribute to ourselves this universal eye.

Can I conceive of an equally general abstraction starting from hearing? Why not? Did not Lucretius, with his simulacra, try his hand at a new science, a science based on touch? If vibrations exist in every domain, a sort of universal acoustics, then music and language, both universal in some way, should be able to construct an epistemology founded on hearing at least as easily as the one that, beginning with Plato, we have founded on sight. This universal acoustics would allow us, finally, to hear the world's song and its enchantment.

I'm dreaming again: do music and language already know in this way? Do they constitute understanding and expression of the universe, of life, and of others in an inchoate, rudimentary, chaotic way? By descending to the foundations of hearing, could we then reappropriate this knowledge buried under common sense, refound it, redevelop it? Does sonorous language vibrate in order to resound in the universe, in life and in others? Does it hear them already, does it express them, in part? When a crowd hurries to a concert, does it repeat the gestures of fascinated ancestors who suddenly congregated around the ululation of larynxes imitating the background noise of the world and the agonizing desire of bodies? Most of our languages, of our musical scores, of our scholarly discoveries have forgotten the appeal of this far-away beginning. And some, never hearing the song of the world with their hardened ears, devoted to the human sciences and thus deafened by the noises of the collectivity, even believe that the universe is disenchanted.

Backtracking all the way up the universal Grand Narrative, this acoustic sequence would perhaps thaw out a theory of knowledge whose glaciation began with Plato, and which Einstein and cognitive science continue to harden. Our idea-idols converge into statue-systems whose distinction and clarity underline their crystalline profiles and their frosty diaphaneity, but make it difficult to think about movement, metamorphoses, and turbulences. Like hearing and burning, however, seeing vibrates. Color, sound, and heat are tremulous. Everything flows, granted, but it *trembles* as it flows.

I hear this shudder, therefore I understand. I understand what and when I hear.

Vox Dei

Does this other epistemological chain break because it makes way for the sound-mysteries that the ear sometimes hears? I know, I see representations, ideas, theories. I am going deaf with age—what does it matter for knowledge?—but behind the murmur of the waves or the background noise of the world, I am beginning to hear a voice.

The Hebrew language names the beginning of this third chain—the spirit's breath over the chaos of the sparse waters, in the morning of the world—*ruah*. This indecipherable noise behind Planck's wall, beneath which the sciences do not know how to go, defines, at a minimum and in physical terms, the metaphysical. Saint John's Greek calls *logos* the holy station of the road that begins with this breath—and, lower down, with this chaos—then runs through Psalms, the Song of Songs and the Prophetic furies, finally descending in tongues of fire, on Pentecost morning, on the heads of the Apostles, allowing them to speak in tongues. Obscure and deaf to knowledge, the path becomes divinely effable.

This breath over the first waters, this voice that cries out in the desert, did they begin and did they grow when men became men, passing from nature to cultures, a transition that they doubtless could not have made without decisive divine help? Stemming from the well of this caesura and filling its abyss, this audible wave throws the hominid beast into a new adventure and cascades back on all of nature, from its very beginning. I do not know whether the wave created the beast, but in any case, by knowing it, it *re*creates it.

We see nature and attempt to illuminate its obscurities, without hearing the voice that fills the universe, sky and earth, climate and storms, springs and wind, the tumult of the tides, the trembling of the poplars, the genesiac heat of the beasts, the murderous or fervent noise of men gathered together, the imploring prayer of love.

Hear, O Israel. *"Ephphatha"*: be opened.[7]

Has human knowledge, consciously or out of respect, left this path of listening exclusively to religion?

My friend, hear the silence, now. Smothered or thundering, noise, chaos, music and speech always rise from a source—faraway, near, accessible, vague—that closes space by polarizing it; there or here, this shrill origin point secures our prisons.

Sourceless, silence opens space, to infinity.

Is God silent?

MICHEL SERRES
translated by Trina Marmarelli

REFERENCE MATTER

Notes

INTRODUCTION

1. Max Weber, "Science as a Vocation," in *From Max Weber: Essays in Sociology*, ed. and trans. H. H. Gerth and C. Wright Mills (Oxford: Oxford University Press, 1946), 129–56, 155. See also Ronald M. Glassman and Vatro Muvar, eds., *Max Weber's Political Sociology: A Pessimistic Vision of a Rationalized World* (Westport, CT: Greenwood Press, 1984); Stephen Kalberg, "Max Weber's Types of Rationality," *American Journal of Sociology* 85, no. 5 (1980): 1145–79; Edward Shils, "Max Weber and the World Since 1920," in *Max Weber and His Contemporaries*, ed. Wolfgang Mommsen and Jurgen Osterhammel (London: Allen & Unwin, 1987), 547–80; Lawrence A. Scaff, *Fleeing the Iron Cage: Culture, Politics, and Modernity in the Thought of Max Weber* (Berkeley: University of California Press, 1989).

2. Weber may have drawn his phrase from Schiller, whose poem "Die Götter Griechenlands" refers to "die entgötterte Natur." In the late nineteenth century, *disenchantment* was often used synonymously with *pessimism*, the latter term given currency by the vogue for the philosophy of Arthur Schopenhauer; see Edgar Evertson Saltus, *The Philosophy of Disenchantment* (New York: Houghton, Mifflin & Co., 1885). The phrase *cultural pessimist* has been applied to a range of nineteenth- and twentieth-century thinkers who criticized aspects of the modern West, among them Friedrich Nietzsche, Matthew Arnold, Oswald Spengler, T. S. Eliot, Arnold Toynbee, and Martin Heidegger. See Arthur Herman, *The Idea of Decline in Western History* (New York: Free Press, 1997); for a more recent trajectory, see Oliver Bennett, *Cultural Pessimism: Narratives of Decline in the Postmodern World* (Edinburgh: Edinburgh University Press, 2001).

3. Albert Camus, *Le mythe de Sisyphe: Essai sur l'absurde* (Paris: Gallimard, 1942), 73.

4. See, e.g., J. M. Bernstein, *Adorno: Disenchantment and Ethics* (Cambridge: Cambridge University Press, 2001).

5. One fascinating, and counterintuitive, way in which modernity has re-enchanted the world is by means of the detective story. The adventures of Sherlock Holmes, to cite the most important example, transformed an undifferentiated mass of unruly material in the visible world (typewriter anomalies, street noises, stray dirt) into a set of potential or actual *clues*, thus restoring to them something of the relative significance they might have possessed within a religious hierarchical framework. For a discussion of enchantment in Holmes, see Michael Saler, "'Clap If You Believe in Sherlock Holmes': Mass Culture and the Re-Enchantment of Modernity, c. 1890–c. 1940," *The Historical Journal* 46 (2003): 599–622. Sir Arthur Conan Doyle's fictional world arguably depends as much on the figure of Moriarty as it does on that of Holmes, and it could be said that this is a re-enchantment via a secularized version of the Devil: only the Devil (or a master criminal) is capable of drawing the quasi-totality of matter into the force field of significance. Credit for this interpretation may belong to Elif Batuman and/or to the editors, but no one concerned is entirely certain of its provenance.

6. For a more detailed account on which this section is based, see Michael Saler, "Modernity and Enchantment: A Historiographic Review," *American Historical Review* 111.3 (June, 2006): 692–716.

7. See Lorraine Daston and Katherine Park, *Wonders and the Order of Nature* (New York: Zone Books, 1998). This marked a departure from the way the term had been used discursively from at least the Middle Ages, when it signified both delight in wonders and the possibility of being deluded by them. The *Oxford English Dictionary*, for example, lists as meanings of *enchant*: "to hold spellbound; in a bad sense, to delude, befool" as well as to "delight, enrapture." See *"enchant, v.*²" *The Compact Oxford English Dictionary*, 2nd ed. (New York: Oxford University Press, 1989), 511.

8. The literature on "folk," "popular," and "mass" cultures is extensive. For overviews of selected facets, see Peter Bailey, *Popular Culture and Performance in the Victorian City* (Cambridge: Cambridge University Press, 1998); Peter Burke, *Popular Culture in Early Modern Europe* (New York: Harper & Row, 1978); Herbert J. Gans, *Popular Culture and High Culture: An Analysis and Evaluation of Taste* (New York: Basic Books, 1975); Michael Kammen, *American Culture, American Tastes: Social Change in the Twentieth Century* (New York: Knopf, 1999); Lawrence Levine, *Highbrow/Lowbrow: The Emergence of Cultural Hierarchy in America* (Cambridge, MA: Harvard University Press, 1988); Barbara Maria Stafford, *Artful Science: Enlightenment Entertainment and the Eclipse of Visual Education* (Cambridge, MA: Harvard University Press, 1994); Dominic Strinati, *An Introduction to Theories of Popular Culture* (New York: Routledge, 1995).

9. Johann P. Arnason, "Reason, Imagination, Interpretation," in *Rethinking Imagination: Culture and Creativity*, ed. Gillian Robinson and John Rundell (London: Routledge, 1994), 156–69; Patrick Brantlinger, *The Reading Lesson: The Threat of Mass Literacy in Nineteenth-Century British Fiction* (Bloomington: Indiana University Press, 1998); John Tinnon Taylor, *Early Opposition to the English Novel: The Popular Reaction from 1760 to 1830* (New York: King's Crown Press,

1943). The anthropologist Arjun Appadurai describes the dramatic shift in attitudes toward fantasy and the imagination over the course of the past two centuries: "Until recently . . . a case could be made that fantasy and imagination were residual practices, confined to special moments or places . . . [but] this weight has imperceptibly shifted. More persons throughout the world see their lives through the prisms of possible lives offered by the mass media in all their forms. That is, fantasy is now a social practice; it enters, in a host of ways, into the fabrication of social lives for many people in many societies." Arjun Appadurai, *Modernity at Large: Cultural Dimensions of Globalization* (Minneapolis: University of Minnesota Press, 1997), 53–54.

10. Christopher Herbert, *Culture and Anomie: Ethnographic Imagination in the Nineteenth Century* (Chicago: University of Chicago Press, 1991), 35.

11. Peter Laslett, *The World We Have Lost* (1965; repr. ed., New York: Routledge, 2004). For other explorations of "modernity and nostalgia," see Sylviane Agacinski, *Time Passing: Modernity and Nostalgia* (New York: Columbia University Press, 2004); Svetlana Boym, *The Future of Nostalgia* (New York: Basic Books, 2002); Peter Fritzsche, *Stranded in the Present: Modern Time and the Melancholy of History* (Cambridge, MA: Harvard University Press, 2004); Romy Golan, *Modernity and Nostalgia: Art and Politics in France Between the Wars* (New Haven, CT: Yale University Press, 1995).

12. H. Stuart Hughes, *Consciousness and Society: The Reorientation of Social Thought, 1890–1930* (New York: Vintage Books, 1961). In addition to identifying thinkers who tended to express a binary view of modernity, Hughes does acknowledge the attempts by certain writers, such as Sigmund Freud and Max Weber, to hold opposing forces—especially reason and the irrational—in the tense harmony represented by the antinomial paradigm. A body of thought known as "Traditionalism" also developed in the late-nineteenth and twentieth centuries, an attitude that was avowedly "anti-modernist" and that in its more trenchant forms does fit this oppositional, "binary" model: see Mark J. Sedgwick, *Against the Modern World: Traditionalism and the Secret Intellectual History of the Twentieth Century* (New York: Oxford University Press, 2004).

13. Thus in an influential work Morris Berman captured an outlook shared by many progressive movements in Europe and America during the 1960s and 1970s, when he recounted the by now familiar argument: "The view of nature which predominated in the West down to the eve of the Scientific Revolution was that of an enchanted world. Rocks, trees, rivers, and clouds were all seen as wondrous, alive, and human beings felt at home in this environment . . . The story of the modern epoch, at least on the level of the mind, is one of progressive disenchantment. From the sixteenth century on, mind has been progressively expunged from the phenomenal world." Morris Berman, *The Reenchantment of the World* (1981; repr. ed., Ithaca, NY: Cornell University Press, 1988), 2.

14. Bataille was an important precursor to many of the poststructuralists and shared many intellectual affinities with them. Michel Surya, *George Bataille: An Intellectual Biography* (New York: Verso, 2002), 515, n.23.

15. Max Weber, for example, acknowledged the benefits entailed by rational procedures and bureaucratic organizations, while also recognizing the impoverishments of human experience that accompanied them, and feared that any alternative would almost certainly involve subservience to charismatic authority.

16. Jacques Derrida discusses Marx's recourse to ghost imagery in *Specters of Marx: The State of the Debt, The Work of Mourning, and the New International* (New York: Routledge, 1994).

17. Friedrich Nietzsche, *The Gay Science*, trans. Walter Kaufmann (New York: Vintage, 1974 [1882, 1887]), sec. 344.

18. Sigmund Freud, *Civilization and its Discontents*, trans. James Strachey (1930; repr. ed., New York: Norton, 1961), 104.

19. Max Horkheimer and Theodor Adorno, *Dialectic of Enlightenment: Philosophical Fragments*, trans. Gunzelin Schmid Noerr and Edmund Jephcott (Stanford: Stanford University Press, 2002), 19.

20. Ibid., 20.

21. Michel Foucault, *Madness and Civilization: A History of Madness in the Age of Reason* (New York: Vintage Books, 1988) and *Discipline and Punish: The Birth of the Prison* (New York: Vintage Books, 1979). Late in life Foucault expressed his admiration for the views of Horkheimer and Adorno; see James Miller, *The Passion of Michel Foucault* (New York: Simon and Schuster, 1993).

22. Terry Castle, *The Female Thermometer: Eighteenth Century Culture and the Invention of the Uncanny* (New York: Oxford University Press, 1995), 15.

23. Victoria Nelson, *The Secret Life of Puppets* (Cambridge, MA: Harvard University Press, 2002), viii.

24. Among an expanding literature, see Dipesh Chakrabarty, *Provincializing Europe: Postcolonial Thought and Historical Difference* (Princeton, NJ: Princeton University Press, 2000); Jean Comaroff and John Comaroff, eds., *Modernity and Its Malcontents: Ritual and Power in Postcolonial Africa* (Chicago: University of Chicago Press, 1993); Fernando Coronil, *The Magical State: Nature, Money, and Modernity in Venezuela* (Chicago: University of Chicago Press, 1997); Saurabh Dube, ed., "Enduring Enchantments" in special issue of *The South Atlantic Quarterly* 101, no. 4 (October 2002); Saurabh Dube, "Introduction: Colonialism, Modernity, Colonial Modernities," *Nepantla: Views from South* 3, no. 2 (2002): 197–219; James Ferguson, *Expectations of Modernity: Myths and Meanings of Urban Life in the Zambian Copperbelt* (Berkeley: University of California Press, 1999); Peter Geschiere, *The Modernity of Witchcraft: Politics and the Occult in Postcolonial Africa*, trans. Janet Roitman (Charlottesville: University of Virginia Press, 1997); Sanjay Joshi, *Fractured Modernity: The Making of a Middle Class in Colonial North India* (New York: Oxford University Press, 2001); Henrietta L. Moore and Todd Sanders, eds., *Magical Interpretations, Material Realities: Modernity, Witchcraft, and the Occult in Postcolonial Africa* (London: Routledge, 2001); Gyan Prakash, *Another Reason: Science and the Imagination of Modern India* (Princeton, NJ: Princeton University Press, 1999); Sumathi Ramaswamy, *The Lost Land of Lemuria: Fabulous Geographies, Catastrophic Histories* (Berkeley: Uni-

versity of California Press, 2004); Michael Taussig, *The Magic of the State* (New York: Routledge, 1997).

25. As Lorraine Daston and Katherine Park observed, "the last twenty years have seen a deep questioning of ideals of order, rationality, and good taste— 'traditional hierarchies of the important and the essential'—that had seemed self-evident to intellectuals since the origins of the modern Republic of Letters in the late seventeenth century." *Wonders and the Order of Nature*, 10.

26. Kevin Repp, *Reformers, Critics, and the Paths of German Modernity: Anti-Politics and the Search for Alternatives, 1890–1914* (Cambridge, MA: Harvard University Press, 2000).

27. Lynda Nead, for example, suggests that "modernity . . . can be imagined as pleated or crumpled time, drawing together past, present, and future into constant and unexpected relations," and Dipesh Chakrabarty characterizes modernity's "problem of entangled times" with the equally evocative image of a "timeknot." See Lynda Nead, *Victorian Babylon: People, Streets and Images in Nineteenth-Century London* (2000; repr. ed., New Haven, CT: Yale University Press, 2005), 8; Dipesh Chakrabarty, *Provincializing Europe*, 243.

28. James Cook, *The Arts of Deception* (Cambridge, MA: Harvard University Press, 2001); Simon During, *Modern Enchantments: The Cultural Power of Secular Magic* (Cambridge, MA: Harvard University Press, 2002); see also Jane Bennett, *The Enchantment of Modern Life: Crossings, Attachments, and Ethics* (Princeton, NJ: Princeton University Press, 2002) and Alex Owen, *The Place of Enchantment: British Occultism and the Culture of the Modern* (Chicago: University of Chicago Press, 2004).

1. NIGHTINGALE: "BROKEN KNOWLEDGE"

1. Bacon discusses this idea in "Advancement of Learning," in *The Works of Francis Bacon* vol. 6, ed. J. Spedding et al. (Boston: Taggard and Thompson, 1860–4), 96; and in "Valerius Terminus of the Interpretation of Nature" (ibid., 29).

2. Lorraine Daston discusses the notion of "economies of attention" to nature in an essay on the disciplines of attention developed by naturalists in the Enlightenment ["Attention and the Values of Nature in the Enlightenment," in *The Moral Authority of Nature*, ed. L. Daston and F. Vidal (Chicago: University of Chicago Press, 2004), 100–126]. Daston uses the word *economy* in its eighteenth-century sense of "an intricate system of interrelated, functional parts" (120). I use the term in the modern (and more limited) sense of "economizing" one's attention (which is one strand of Daston's conception of "economies of attention"). Of course there were different economies of attention and approaches to nature in modern science—in this essay, I will be focusing on several different economies of attention to nature in the modern period.

3. See Alexander Nehamas, *Nietzsche: Life as Literature* (Cambridge, MA: Harvard University Press, 1985), 107, for an excellent discussion of Nietzsche's conception of "blind-spots."

4. "The present is so made that it passes into the past, [so] how can we say that this present also 'is'? The cause of its being is that it will cease to be. So we cannot truly say that time exists except in the sense that it tends towards nonexistence." *Saint Augustine, The Confessions,* trans. Henry Chadwick (Oxford: Oxford University Press, 1991), 11.11. I am using Chadwick's translation of Augustine's *Confessions* in this essay, though I occasionally change some of his wording to achieve a more literal translation. I refer to the *Confessions* using the books and chapters of the Latin original.

5. Ibid., 11.29.

6. On the "sorrows of time" in Augustine, see Paul Ricoeur, *Time and Narrative* vol. 1, trans. K. McLaughlin and D. Pellauer (Chicago: University of Chicago Press, 1984), 5–29.

7. Augustine, *Confessions,* 11.29.

8. Ibid., 10.40.

9. Ibid., 11.38.

10. Ibid., 10.35.

11. Ibid., 10.35.

12. René Descartes, *Philosophical Essays,* trans. L. Lafleur (New York: Macmillan, 1989), 10.

13. Ibid., 11.

14. Ibid., 7.

15. Ibid., 12.

16. Ibid., 18.

17. Ibid., 20.

18. For a discussion of the collapse of the Classical and Christian ideal of self-mastery and its replacement by scientific control of human needs/desires in the early modern period, see Robert Pippin, "Technology as Ideology," in *Idealism as Modernism: Hegelian Variations* (Cambridge: Cambridge University Press, 1997), 202.

19. Descartes, (1989), 25.

20. Descartes was but one voice in a very lively debate over human and animal nature in modernity (his claim that animals are machines that do not feel pain was in fact a minority position). For a detailed study of the various conceptions of the distinction between humans and animals in the eighteenth century, see A. Garrett, "Human Nature," in *The Cambridge History of Eighteenth-Century Philosophy,* ed. K. Haakonssen (Cambridge 2006).

21. Descartes, *Philosophical Essays* (1989), 43.

22. Ibid., 41.

23. Ibid., 35.

24. René Descartes, "The Passions of the Soul" part 2, LXX–LVIII, in *The Philosophical Work of Descartes* vol. I, ed. E. Haldane and G. R. T. Ross (Cambridge: Cambridge University Press, 1978), 362–66. For a useful investigation of different activities and conceptions of curiosity in the early modern period, see Barbara Benedict, *Curiosity: A Cultural History of Early Modern Inquiry* (Chicago: University of Chicago Press, 2001).

25. Cf. the claim in Part IV : "As for my ideas about many other things outside of me, such as the sky, earth, light, heat and thousands of other things, I was not so much troubled to discover where they came from, because I found nothing in them superior to my own nature. If they really existed, I could believe that whatever perfection that they possessed might be derived from my own nature." Descartes, *Philosophical Essays* (1989), 25.

26. Robert Harrison, *Forests: The Shadow of Civilization* (Chicago: University of Chicago Press, 1992), 113.

27. *Homo Faber* is not, of course, Descartes's term. Note that Descartes himself elevates the scientific "discoveries" that he sets forth in parts V–VI over the ontological discussions in parts I–IV: as he says in part V, he has come to find "truths more useful and more important than anything I had previously learned." *Philosophical Essays* (1989), 31.

28. As Descartes claims, if the body is completely destroyed, the mind will remain "all that it now is," *Philosophical Essays* (1989), 25.

29. Ibid., 45–46.

30. This may have been deliberate: certainly Emerson responds quite explicitly to Descartes. For an analysis of Emerson's use of Descartes, see Stanley Cavell, *Emerson's Transcendental Études*, ed. D. Hodge (Stanford: Stanford University Press, 2003), 84–99.

31. Henry David Thoreau, *Walden and Civil Disobedience* (New York: Penguin, 1983), 365–66. All quotes from *Walden* come from this edition.

32. Ibid., 380.

33. Henry David Thoreau, "Walking," in *The Portable Thoreau*, ed. C. Bode (New York: Penguin, 1982), 623.

34. Ibid., 622.

35. Thoreau, *Walden*, 158.

36. Martin Heidegger, "The Origin of the Work of Art," in *Basic Writings*, ed. D. Krell (San Francisco: Harper & Row, 1977), 169, 171. As Heidegger suggests, a work of art brings the earth into the open region of the human world, brings earth out of its "self-seclusion." It creates, in the viewer, "an eye for how differently everything faces us." The artwork alters habitual modes of attention, allowing us to see earth "jutting through the world" even as the "world grounds itself on the earth" (177).

37. Thoreau, *Walden*, 372.

38. Emerson, Ralph Waldo, "Nature," in "First Essays," *Emerson. Essays and Lectures* (New York: The Library of America, 1983), 48–49.

39. Thoreau, *Walden*, 355–56.

40. Ibid., 277.

41. Ibid., 380.

42. Ibid., 381.

43. Ibid., 177.

44. Ibid., 174.

45. Ibid., 180.

46. Thoreau, "Walking," (1982), 592–93.

47. Thoreau, *Walden*, 206.

48. Ibid., 200.

49. Martin Heidegger, *Being and Time*, trans. J. Stambaugh (Albany: State University of New York Press, 1996), 63.

50. Thoreau, "Walking," (1982), 628.

51. Thoreau, *Walden*, 142–43.

52. Harrison, *Forests*, 229–30.

53. Thoreau, *Walden*, 362.

54. Ibid., 59.

55. Stanley Cavell, *The Senses of Walden* (San Francisco: North Point Press, 1981) 9–10.

56. Note that Thoreau goes on to say, directly after this passage, that he "long ago lost a hound, a bay horse and a turtle-dove and am still on their trail." Here, he moves from present to past, and acknowledges the basic fact of loss and longing. He then follows this up with his claim to "anticipate, not the sunrise and the dawn merely but, if possible, Nature herself." Here, he moves from *memoria* to *expectatio* (to use Augustine's terms).

57. Thoreau, *Walden*, 156.

58. Ibid., 355.

59. Ibid., 366.

60. Ibid., 352–53.

61. Ibid., 356.

62. Martin Heidegger, *Basic Questions of Philosophy*, trans. R. Rojcewicz and A. Shuwer (Bloomington: Indiana University Press, 1994), 143.

63. Ibid., 144.

64. Henry David Thoreau, "Maine Woods," in *Henry David Thoreau: A Week on the Concord and Merrimack Rivers; Walden; or, Life in the Woods; The Maine Woods, Cape Cod* (New York: The Library of America, 1985), 646.

65. On "poor in world" and "without world," see Martin Heidegger, *The Fundamental Concepts of Metaphysics: World, Finitude, Solitude*, trans. William McNeil and Nicholas Walker (Bloomington: Indiana University Press, 1995), sections 49–50.

66. Ibid., 255–56.

67. Alasdair MacIntyre, *Dependent Rational Animals* (Chicago: University of Chicago Press, 1999), 46. MacIntyre argues that many higher mammals possess beliefs, and are not driven solely by instincts (or captive to their environment).

68. See, e.g., the following passages [Thoreau, *Walden*]: "The earth is not a mere fragment of dead history, to be studied by geologists and antiquaries chiefly, but living poetry . . . not a fossil earth but a living earth; compared with whose great central life all animal and vegetable life is merely parasitic" (357); "The gentle rain which waters my beans and keeps me in the house today is not drear and melancholy, but good for me too. Though it prevents my hoeing them, it is of far more worth than my hoeing. If it should continue so long as to cause my seeds to rot in the ground and destroy the potatoes in the low lands, it would still be good for the grass on the uplands, and, being good for the

grass, it would be good for me." (176); "These beans have results which are not harvested by me. Do they not grow for woodchucks partly? . . . How, then, can our harvest fail? Shall I not rejoice also at the abundance of weeds whose seeds are the granary of birds?" (212).

69. Ibid., 217. Cf. Descartes, who advises anyone who gets lost in a forest to get out as fast as he can by choosing one direction and walking in a straight line until he escapes. *Philosophical Essays* (1989), 19.

2. SIMON: BEWITCHED, BOTHERED, AND BEWILDERED

1. David Hollinger, *In the American Province* (Bloomington: Indiana University Press, 1985), 4.

2. William James, "Is Life Worth Living?" in *The Will to Believe and Other Essays in Popular Philosophy* (New York: Dover, 1956 [1897]), 42, 40.

3. James, "What Psychical Research Has Accomplished," *Will to Believe*, 302.

4. William James, *A Pluralistic Universe* (Lincoln: University of Nebraska, 1996 [1909]), 283. Among scholars who consider chaos in James's philosophy are Charlene Siegfried, *Chaos and Context: A Study in William James* (Athens: Ohio University Press, 1978) and Frederick J. Ruf, *The Creation of Chaos: William James and the Stylistic Making of a Disorderly World* (Albany: State University of New York Press, 1991).

5. Paul Croce, *Science and Religion in the Era of William James,* vol. I. (Chapel Hill: University of North Carolina Press, 1995), 229.

6. William James, *Principles of Psychology,* vol. I (New York: Holt, 1910), 245–46; this passage appears also in "On Some Omissions in Introspective Psychology," *Mind* 9 (January 1884): 146.

7. James, "The Dilemma of Determinism," *Will to Believe*, 168.

8. Henry David Thoreau, *Walden and Civil Disobedience* (New York: Penguin, 1983), 257.

9. William James, *Pragmatism* (Cambridge, MA: Harvard University Press, 1978 [1907]), 56.

10. James, "What Psychical Research Has Accomplished," *Will to Believe*, 299, 300.

11. George Santayana, *Persons and Places* (London: Constable, 1944), 249.

12. George Santayana, "William James," in *William James Remembered*, ed. Linda Simon. (Lincoln: University of Nebraska, 1996), 103.

13. James, *A Pluralistic Universe*, 45.

14. William James, "Confidences of a Psychical Researcher," in *Essays in Psychical Research* (Cambridge, MA: Harvard University Press, 1986), 364.

15. James, "What Psychical Research Has Accomplished," *Will to Believe,* 324.

16. James, "Is Life Worth Living?" *Will to Believe,* 52–53.

17. William James, *Some Problems of Philosophy* (Cambridge, MA: Harvard University Press, 1979), 39.

18. James, *A Pluralistic Universe,* 246.

19. Ibid., 244.

20. James, *Some Problems of Philosophy*, 42–43.

21. Ibid., 48–49, 50 (italics in original).

22. Ibid., 54.

23. For a discussion of introspection and its implications for understanding the unconscious, see Gerald E. Myers, "Introspection and the Unconscious," in *Theories of the Unconscious and Theories of the Self* (Hillsdale, NJ: The Analytic Press, 1987), 91–108.

24. James, "Human Immortality," *Will to Believe*, 21.

25. William James, "A World of Pure Experience," in *Essays in Radical Empiricism* (Cambridge, MA: Harvard University Press, 1976), 25 (italics in original).

26. Ibid., 31.

27. Ibid., 24.

28. James, *Principles of Psychology*, vol. I, 256, 259, 260.

29. James, "A World of Pure Experience," *Essays in Radical Empiricism*, 26.

30. Ibid., 42.

31. James, *Principles of Psychology*, vol. I, 237–39.

32. Ibid., 243.

33. Ibid., 240–41.

34. James, "Does Consciousness Exist?" *Essays in Radical Empiricism*, 4.

35. James, *Principles of Psychology*, vol. I, 199–200.

36. Hugo Munsterberg, et al., *Subconscious Phenomena* (Boston: Richard G. Badger, 1910).

37. Ibid., 10–15. See also Frederic W. H. Myers, *Human Personality and its Survival of Bodily Death*, ed. Susy Smith (New Hyde Park, NY: University Books, 1961 [1903]).

38. James, "Frederic Myers's Service to Psychology," *Essays in Psychical Research*, 193.

39. Ibid., 199.

40. James, *Principles of Psychology*, vol. I, 296–298.

41. William James, *Manuscript Lectures* (Cambridge, MA: Harvard University Press, 1988), 426.

42. James, *Principles of Psychology*, vol. I, 299.

43. James, "Is Life Worth Living?" *Will to Believe*, 61.

44. James, "Frederic Myers's Service to Psychology," *Essays in Psychical Research*, 201.

45. See William James, "The Energies of Men," in *The Writings of William James*, ed. John J. McDermott (Chicago: University of Chicago Press, 1977 [1967]), 681; and James, *The Varieties of Religious Experience* (Cambridge, MA: Harvard University Press, 1985 [1902]), 412.

46. James, *Varieties of Religious Experience*, 410, 411, 413, 414.

47. James, *Manuscript Lectures*, 426.

48. William James to Thomas Davidson, 30 March 1884, *The Correspondence of William James*, vol. v., ed. Ignas K. Skrupskelis and Elizabeth M. Berkeley (Charlottesville: University of Virginia Press, 1997), 499.

49. James, "What Psychical Research Has Accomplished," *Will to Believe,* 319, 320.

50. Ibid., 325, 327.

51. Hollinger, *American Province,* 34.

52. William James to Alice Howe Gibbens, 7 June 1877, *The Correspondence of William James,* vol. iv. ed. Ignas K. Skrupskelis and Elizabeth M. Berkeley (Charlottesville: University of Virginia Press, 1995), 570–71.

53. James, *A Pluralistic Universe,* 324.

54. William James to Oliver Wendell Holmes, Jr., 15 May 1868, *Correspondence,* vol. iv, 301–4.

55. William James to Henry Pickering Bowditch, 29 December 1870, *Correspondence,* vol. iv, 411.

56. William James to Henry James, Sr. [24 August 1860], *Correspondence of William James,* vol. iv, 40.

57. See Ralph Waldo Emerson, journal entry, 13 July 1833, in *Emerson in His Journals,* 110–11.

58. James, "Is Life Worth Living?" *Will to Believe,* 47.

59. James, "The Dilemma of Determinism," *Will to Believe,* 123.

60. James, *Manuscript Lectures,* 425.

61. Ibid., 411; James, "squeeze of this world's life": *Some Problems in Philosophy,* 60.

62. Ibid., 78.

63. James, *Manuscript Lectures,* 271.

64. See James, *A Pluralistic Universe,* 283, 320–21.

65. James, "Is Life Worth Living?" *Will to Believe,* 62.

3. SALER: WASTE LANDS AND SILLY VALLEYS

1. Ludwig Wittgenstein, *Culture and Value,* ed. G. H. von Wright, trans. Peter Winch (Chicago: University of Chicago Press, 1980), 76.

2. James C. Klagge, ed., *Wittgenstein: Biography and Philosophy* (Cambridge: Cambridge University Press, 2001), 119.

3. Norman Malcolm, *Ludwig Wittgenstein: A Memoir* (Oxford: Oxford University Press, 1984 [1958]), 101. On October 30, 1945, Wittgenstein wrote to Malcolm, "If I read your mags I often wonder how anyone can read 'Mind' with all its impotence & bankruptcy when they could read Street & Smith mags." Ibid., 100.

4. Ibid., 107.

5. Ray Monk, *Ludwig Wittgenstein: The Duty of Genius* (New York: Penguin, 1990), 423.

6. Jean-Paul Sartre, *The Words,* trans. Bernard Frechtman (New York: Vintage, 1981 [1964]), 76.

7. Monk, *Ludwig Wittgenstein,* 153, 520.

8. When a co-worker at Guy's Hospital visited Wittgenstein's rooms during the Second World War, he "was surprised to see no philosophy books at all, but only neat piles of detective magazines." Ibid., 443.

9. This was the recollection of Wolfe Mays in K. T. Fann, ed., *Ludwig Wittgenstein: The Man and His Philosophy* (New York: Dell Publishing Co., 1967), 82.

10. Ludwig Wittgenstein, "The Language of Sense Data and Private Experience-I (Notes taken by Rush Rhees of Wittgenstein's Lectures, 1936)," cited in Monk, *Ludwig Wittgenstein*, 355.

11. James C. Klagge and Alfred Nordmann, *Ludwig Wittgenstein: Public and Private Occasions*, (Lanham, MD: Roman & Littlefield Publishers, Inc., 2003), 29, 97.

12. Ludwig Wittgenstein, *Philosophical Investigations*, trans. G. E. M. Anscombe (New York: Macmillan, 1968 [1953]), §309, 103.

13. Malcolm, *Memoir*, 109.

14. Klagge, *Biography*, 187.

15. Wittgenstein, *Culture and Value*, 6.

16. H. Stuart Hughes, *Consciousness and Society: The Reorientation of European Social Thought, 1890–1930* (New York: Vintage Books, 1961).

17. Wittgenstein, *Culture and Value*, 73.

18. Ibid., 59.

19. In addition to many of the French surrealists, Walter Benjamin, Sigfried Kracauer, and Humphrey Jennings were among the early twentieth-century intellectuals in Europe who tried to reconcile the processes of modernity with the idea of enchantment, although until recently their project tended to be overshadowed by the greater attention given to the "cultural pessimists" (Horkheimer and Adorno, Ortega y Gasset et al.) who saw mass culture as evidence for the decline of the West. See Michael Saler, "Whigs and Surrealists: The 'Subtle Links' of Humphrey Jennings' *Pandaemonium*," in *Singular Continuities: Tradition, Nostalgia, and Identity in Modern British Culture*, ed. George Behlmer and Fred Leventhal (Stanford: Stanford University Press, 2000), 123–42.

20. Nietzsche, *The Gay Science*, sec. 374.

21. He argues that Wittgenstein attempted to resurrect in himself and others a sense of wonder by delimiting that which could be known by philosophy into a "limited whole," thereby drawing attention to the mysteries that existed beyond these boundaries. Peter C. John, "Wittgenstein's 'Wonderful Life,'" *Journal of the History of Ideas* 49.3 (July–September, 1988): 495–510.

22. Wittgenstein, "Lecture on Ethics." *Philosophical Review* 74 (1965): 3–12.

23. Monk, *Ludwig Wittgenstein*, 480; Fann, *Man*, 61.

24. Malcolm, *Memoir*, 60.

25. Wittgenstein, *Philosophical Investigations*, §109, 47.

26. Ludwig Wittgenstein, *The Blue and Brown Books: Preliminary Studies for the 'Philosophical Investigations'* (New York: Harper Colophon, 1965 [1958]), 6.

27. Wittgenstein, *Culture and Value*, 11.

28. Malcolm, *Memoir*, 43. Wittgenstein also discussed "Hamlet" in his "Lecture on Ethics" (1929).

29. Ludwig Wittgenstein, *Remarks on Frazer's Golden Bough*, ed. Rush Rhees, trans. A. C. Miles (Atlantic Highlands, NJ: Humanities Press, 1979), 5–6. R. G.

Collingwood engaged in a similar critique of Frazer, and a sustained defense of "modern enchantment," in a manuscript that was left unfinished at his death: see R. G. Collingwood, *The Philosophy of Enchantment*, ed. David Boucher, Wendy James, and Philip Smallwood (Oxford: Oxford University Press, 2005).

30. Wittgenstein, *Philosophical Investigations*, part II.

31. Wittgenstein, *Culture and Value*, 5. Science itself had erected an iron cage, limiting the ways one viewed the world: "Science lays down railway tracks. And for scientists it is important that their work should move along those tracks." Quoted in Monk, *Ludwig Wittgenstein*, 486. It's important to note that Wittgenstein, a trained engineer and logician, was criticizing the modern spirit in which science was conducted, rather than science per se or its findings. Anticipating Thomas Kuhn's concept of scientific paradigms emerging within the social network of science, Wittgenstein disliked the way science as a communal effort directed its participants in particular directions: "Science: enrichment and impoverishment. One particular method elbows all the others aside. They all seem paltry by comparison, preliminary stages at best. You must go right down to the original sources so as to see them all side by side, both the neglected and the preferred." *Culture and Value*, 60–61.

32. Ibid., 16.

33. Malcolm, *Memoir*, 84.

34. Ludwig Wittgenstein, *Zettel*, ed. G. E. M. Anscombe and G. H. Wright, trans. G. E. M. Anscombe (Berkeley: University of California Press, 1970), §168, 30. The editors of Wittgenstein's miscellaneous remarks collected in this volume believe they were most likely made between 1929 and 1948.

35. Wittgenstein, *Philosophical Investigations*, §6.43, 72.

36. Wittgenstein, *Zettel*, 91–92.

37. Klagge and Nordmann, *Public and Private Occasions*, 123.

38. Monk, *Ludwig Wittgenstein*, 53.

39. Wittgenstein, *Culture and Value*, 59.

40. Ibid., 3.

41. Ibid., 50.

42. Wittgenstein, *Philosophical Investigations*, §129, 50.

43. Wittgenstein, *Culture and Value*, 57.

44. Wittgenstein, *Philosophical Investigations*, §19, 8.

45. For Wittgenstein's fondness for "nonsense," see George Pitcher, "Wittgenstein, Nonsense, and Lewis Carroll" in K. T. Fann, *Man*. Wittgenstein loved "Blödeln," silly jokes, and once characterized his philosophical remarks as "wisecracks." See Klagge, *Biography*, 181.

46. Klagge, *Biography*, 175.

47. Ibid., 143, 404.

48. Wittgenstein, *Culture and Value*, 79.

49. Ibid., 78.

50. Ibid., 50.

51. Ibid., 56.

52. Ibid., 39.

53. Ibid., 58.
54. Ibid., 65.
55. Ibid., 18.
56. Ibid., 38.
57. Ibid., 39.
58. Ibid., 74, 76.
59. Ibid., 82.
60. Monk, *Ludwig Wittgenstein*, 423.
61. Norbert Davis, *The Mouse in the Mountain* (Colorado: Rue Morgue Press, 2001 [1943]). The book was retitled *Rendezvous with Fear* for its English publication, which is the title used by Wittgenstein.
62. Malcolm, *Memoir*, 109.
63. Monk, *Ludwig Wittgenstein*, 528–30.
64. Wittgenstein, *Philosophical Investigations*, §49, 122.
65. Ibid., §224.
66. Davis, *Mouse*, 44.
67. Wittgenstein, *Philosophical Investigations*, §49, 122.
68. Davis, *Mouse*, 66.
69. Ibid., 120.
70. Ibid., 143.
71. Wittgenstein, *Philosophical Investigations*, §49, 122.
72. T. S. Eliot, "The Waste Land."
73. John, 'Wonderful Life,' 510.
74. Malcolm, *Ludwig Wittgenstein*, 28.

4. HARRISON: HOMELESS GARDENS

1. Margaret Morton and Diana Balmori, *Transitory Gardens, Uprooted Lives* (New Haven, CT: Yale University Press, 1995), 7.
2. Ibid., 4.
3. Dylan Thomas, "The Force That Through the Green Fuse Drives the Flower," *Selected Poems 1934–1952* (New York: New Directions, 2003), 9.
4. Patricia Yollin, "Bayview block in bloom: Two neighbors create public garden that's pride of the area," *San Francisco Chronicle* (2 September 2003): A-1.
5. Heidegger, *Being and Time*, trans. J. Stambaugh (Albany: State University of New York Press, 1996), 225.

5. UMBACH: THE MODERNISTIC IMAGINATION OF PLACE

1. Heidegger, "Creative Landscape: Why Do We Stay in the Provinces?" in *The Weimar Republic Sourcebook*, ed. Anton Kayes and Martin Jay (Berkeley: University of California Press, 1994, 427).
2. Frederick C. Beiser, *Enlightenment, Revolution, and Romanticism: The Genesis of Modern German Political Thought, 1790–1800* (Cambridge, MA: Harvard

University Press, 1992); Theodore Ziolkowski, *German Romanticism and its In-stitutions* (Princeton, NJ: Princeton University Press, 1990); Kai Buchholz et al., *Die Lebensreform: Entwürfe zur Neugestaltung von Leben und Kunst um 1900*, 2 vols (Darmstadt: Hausser, 2001); T. J. Jackson Lears, *No Place of Grace: Anti-modernism and the Transformation of American Culture, 1880–1920* (New York: Pantheon Books, 1981); Eva Barlösius, *Naturgemässe Lebensführung: zur Geschichte der Lebensreform um die Jahrhundertwende* (New York: Campus, 1997); Diethart Kerbs and Jürgen Reulecke, *Handbuch der deutschen Reformbewegungen 1880 bis 1933* (Wuppertal: Hammer, 1998).

3. Jürgen Habermas, *The Structural Transformation of the Public Sphere*, trans. Thomas Burger (Cambridge, MA: MIT Press, 1992); Craig Calhoun, ed., *Haber-mas and the Public Sphere* (Cambridge, MA: MIT Press, 1992); Stephen Kern, *The Culture of Time and Space, 1880–1918* (Cambridge, MA: Harvard University Press, 1983); Michel Foucault, "Space, Knowledge and Power," in *Rethinking Architecture: A Reader in Cultural Theory*, ed. Neal Leach (London: Routledge, 1997), 367–79; Paul Glennie and Nigel Thrift, "The Spaces of Clock Time," in *The Social in Question: New Bearings in History and the Social Sciences*, ed. Patrick Joyce (London: Routledge, 2002), 151–74.

4. James C. Scott, *Seeing Like a State: How Certain Schemes to Improve the Human Condition Have Failed* (New Haven, CT: Yale University Press, 1998).

5. This is evident in a resurgence of subnational language groups challeng-ing the cultural hegemony of nation-states. Ian Buruma, "The Road to Babel" in *The New York Review of Books* 48.9 (2001): 23–26; Andreas Gardt and Bernd Hüppauf, eds., *Globalization and the Future of German* (New York: Mouton de Gruyter, 2004).

6. Bruno Latour, *We Have Never Been Modern*, trans. Catherine Porter (Cam-bridge, MA: Harvard University Press, 1993). See also Jean-Francois Lyotard, *The Postmodern Condition: A Report on Knowledge*, trans. Geoff Bennington and Brian Massumi (Minneapolis: University of Minneapolis Press, 1984); Susan Stanford Friedman, "Definition Excursions: The Meanings of Modern, Moder-nity, Modernism," in *Modernism/Modernity* 8.3 (2001): 493–513.

7. Max Horkheimer and Theodor Adorno, *Dialektik der Aufklärung: Philoso-phische Fragmente* (Frankfurt am Main: S. Fischer, 1969).

8. Scott Lash and Jonathan Friedman, eds., *Modernity and Identity* (Oxford: Blackwell Publishing, 1992), 1.

9. Eric Rothstein, "Broaching a Cultural Logic of Modernity," in *Modern Languages Quarterly* 61.2 (2000): 359–94; Bernard Yack, *The Fetishism of Moderni-ties: Epochal Self-Consciousness in Contemporary Social and Political Thought* (Notre Dame, IN: University of Notre Dame Press, 1997).

10. Celia Applegate, *A Nation of Provincials: The German Idea of Heimat* (Berkeley: University of California Press, 1990); Alon Confino, *The Nation as a Local Metaphor: Württemberg, Imperial Germany and National Memory 1871–1918* (Chapel Hill: University of North Carolina Press, 1997); Maiken Umbach and Bernd Hüppauf, eds., *Vernacular Modernism: Heimat, Globilization, and the Built Environment* (Stanford: Stanford University Press, 2006); Christopher Reed, ed.,

Not At Home: The Suppression of Domesticity in Modern Art And Architecture (London: Thames and Hudson, 1996).

11. This is why some scholars refer to it as "ironic." Saler, "At Home in the Ironic Imagination: The Rational Vernacular and Spectacular Texts," *Vernacular Modernism* (Stanford: Stanford University Press, 2005), 53–83.

12. Horst Hina, *Kastilien und Katalonien in der Kulturdiskussion, 1714–1939* (Tübingen: Niemeyer, 1978), 5.

13. Judith Rohrer et al., *Josep Puig i Cadafalch: L'arquitectura entre la casa i la ciutat* (Barcelona: Centre Cultural de la Fundació Caixa de Pensions, 1989); Jordi Romeu Costa, *Josep Puig i Cadafalch. Obres i projectes des del 1911* (Barcelona: Escola Técnica Superior d'Arquitectura de Barcelona, 1989); Lluís Permanyer and Lluís Casals, *Josep Puig i Cadafalch* (Barcelona: Ediciones Polígraphia, 2001).

14. The year 1888 marked the start of a series of industrial expositions, in which Barcelona's bourgeoisie celebrated its own role in the process of economic progress and expansion. J. M. Garrut, *L'Exposició Universal de Barcelona de 1888* (Barcelona: Ajuntament. Delegació de Cultura, 1976); M. C. Grandas, *L'Exposició Internacional de Barcelona de 1929* (Barcelona: Els Llibres de la Frontera, 1988); Ignasi Solà-Morales, "L'Exposició Internacional de Barcelona (1914–1929) com a instrument de política urbana," *Recerques* 6 (1976): 137–45 and idem., *L'Exposició Internacional de Barcelona, 1914–1929: Arquitectura i ciutat* (Barcelona: Fira de Barcelona, 1985).

15. Christopher Ealham, *Class, Culture and Conflict in Barcelona, 1898–1937* (London: Routledge, 2005).

16. In nineteenth-century Europe, protectionism is typically associated with conservatism, e.g., Anna Gambles, *Protection and Politics: Conservative Economic Discourse, 1815–1852* (London: Boydell Press, 1999).

17. On the linkage between political Catalanism and economic protectionism, see Siobhan Harty, "Lawyers, Codifications, and the Origins of Catalan Nationalism, 1881–1901," *Law and History Review* 20.2 (2002): 349–84, especially 372–74.

18. Santiago Sobrequés i Vidal, *Història de la producció del dret català fins al decret Nova Planta* (Girona: Collegi Universitari de Girona, 1978). See also James S. Amelang, "Barristers and Judges in Early Modern Barcelona: The Rise of a Legal Elite," *American Historical Review* 89.5 (1984): 1264–84.

19. Stephen Jacobson, "Law and Nationalism in Nineteenth-Century Europe: The Case of Catalonia in Comparative Perspective," *Law and History Review* 20.2 (2002): 307–47, esp. 326–28.

20. Enric Prat de la Riba, *La nacionalitat catalana* 4th edition (Barcelona: Edicions 62, 1998 [1906]).

21. Bartolomé Clavero, "Formación doctrinal contemporánea del derecho catalán de sucesiónes: La primogénitura de la libertad," in *La reforma de la Compilación: El sistema successor* (Barcelona: Universitat de Barcelona, 1984), 10–37.

22. Jacobson, "Law and Nationalism," 337–38.

23. M. Tuñón de Lara, et. al., *Revolución burguesa, oligarquía y constitucional-ismo, 1834–1923* (Barcelona: Labor, 1981); Joan-Lluís Marfany *La cultura del cata-lanisme: El nacionalisme català en els seus inicis* (Barcelona: Empuréis, 1995); Josep M. Fradera, *Cultura nacional en una societat dividida: Patriotisme i cultura a Catalunya, 1838–68* (Barcelona: Curial, 1992); Albert Balcells, *Catalan National-ism: Past and Present* (New York: Macmillan, 1996).

24. Jordi Llorenz i Vil, *La Unió Catalanista i els orígens del catalanisme polític* (Barcelona: Barcelona Publicacions de l'Abadia de Montserrat, 1992); J. A. González Casanova, *Federalisme i autonomia a Catalunya, 1868–1936: Documents* (Barcelona: Curial, 1974); Isidro Molas, *Lliga Catalana: Un estudi d'estasiologia* 2 vols. (Barcelona: Edicions 62, 1972), I: 27; Harty, "Lawyers, Codifications, and the Origins of Catalan Nationalism, 1881–1901," 349–84.

25. Charles Ehrlich, "The Lliga Regionalista and the Catalan Industrial Bourgeoisie," *Journal of Contemporary History* 33 (1998): 399–417.

26. Joseph Harrison, "An Espanya Catalana: Catalanist Plans to Transform Spain into a Modern Capitalist Economy, 1898–1923," *Journal of Iberian and Latin American Studies* 7.2 (2001): 143–56. Similarly in Ealham, *Class, Culture and Conflict*.

27. Antoni Rovira i Virgili, *Els Corrents ideològics de la Renaixença catalana* (Barcelona: Barcino, 1966); *La Renaixença: Cicle de conferèncias fet a la Institu-ció cultural del CIC de Terrassa, curs 1982/83* (Montserrat: Publicacions de l'Abadia de Montserrat, 1986); Joan R. Varela, *La Renaixença: la represa cultural i política, 1833–1886* (Barcelona: Graó, 1991); Emili Giralt et al., *Romanticisme i Re-naixença, 1800–1860* (Barcelona: Edicions 62, 1995); Antoni Comas, Martí de Ri-quer, and Joaquim Molas, *Història de la literatura catalana* 11 vols (Barcelona: Ariel, 1984–88); Johannes Hösle, *Die katalanische Literatur von der Renaixença bis zur Gegenwart* (Tübingen: Max Niemeyer Verlag 1982); Mireia Freixa, *El mo-dernisme a Catalunya* (Barcelona: Barcanova, 1991): Joan-Lluís Marfany, "El Modernisme," in *Història de la literatura catalana* 11 vols, eds., Marti de Riquer, Antoni Comas, and Joaquim Molas (Barcelona: Ariel, 1987), IIX: 76–142.

28. Joan-Lluís Marfany, *La llengua maltractada. El castellà i el català a Catalunya del segle XVI al segle XIX* (Barcelona: Editorial Empúries, 2001).

29. Stéphane Michonneau, "Barcelone 1900–1910: la construction d'un es-pace symbolique," *Rives nord-méditerranéennes, Patrimoine et politiques urbaines en Méditerranée* 16 November 2005, http://rives.revues.org/document438 .html; Idem., *Barcelona, memòria i identitat. Monuments, commemoracions i mites* (Barcelona: Eumo, 2002).

30. Stanley G. Payne, "Nationalism, Regionalism and Micronationalism in Spain," *Journal of Contemporary History* 26.3/4 (1991): 179–91; Daniel Conversi, *The Basques, the Catalans, and Spain* (London: C. Hurst, 1997); Balcells, *Catalan Nationalism: Past and Present*.

31. Chris Brooks, *The Gothic Revival* (London: Phaidon, 1999); Georg Ger-mann, *Gothic Revival in Europe and Britain: Sources, Influences and Ideas* (London: Lund Humphries, 1972).

32. M. H. Port, ed., *Houses of Parliament* (New Haven, CT: Yale University Press, 1976); Sir Robert Cooke, *The Palace of Westminster* (London: Burton Skira,

1987); Martin Damus, *Das Rathaus: Architektur und Sozialgeschichte von der Gründerzeit zur Postmoderne* (Berlin: Mann, 1988); G. Ulrich Großmann and Petra Krutisch, eds., *Renaissance der Renaissance: Ein bürgerlicher Kunststil im 19. Jahrhundert. I: Aufsätze* (München: Deutscher Kunstverlag, 1992).

33. Steven Adams, *The Art of the Pre-Raphaelites* (London: Apple, 1988); Elizabeth Prettejohn, *The Art of the Pre-Raphaelites* (London: Tate Publishing, 2000); Jan Marsh, *The Pre-Raphaelites* (London: National Portrait Gallery, 1998).

34. John M. Ganim, *Medievalism and Orientalism: Three Essays on Literature, Architecture and Cultural Identity* (Basingstoke: Palgrave Macmillan, 2005).

35. Ibid.

36. Iain Boyd-Whyte, *Bruno Taut and the Architecture of Activism* (Cambridge: Cambridge University Press, 1982); Kristiana Hartmann, "Bruno Taut—the Architect, the Painter, the Colour," *Daidalus* 42.15 (1991): 24–39. See also Michael Saler, *The Avant-Garde in Interwar England: Medieval Modernism and the London Underground* (New York: Oxford University Press, 1999).

37. Josep Puig i Cadafalch, *La géographie et les origines du premier art roman,* trans. Jeanne Vielliard (Paris: H. Laurens, 1935).

38. Josep Puig i Cadafalch, *L'architectura romànica a Catalunya* 3 vols (Barcelona: Institut d'Estudis Catalans, 1909–1918).

39. Between 1906 and 1918, Puig restored Sant Martí Sarroca, Sant Joan de les Abadesses, Santa Maria de la Seu d'Urgell, Egara in Terrassa, and Saint-Michel-de-Cuxa.

40. The Ciutadella Museum opened its Romanesque fresco collection officially in June 1924, after wooden and plaster frameworks had been constructed for all apses. This later became the core of the MNAC's collection. Jordi Camps i Sòria, Montserrat Pagès i Paretas, and Gemma Ylla-Català, *Puig i Cadafalch i la col.lecció de pintura romànica del MNAC* (Barcelona: Museu Nacional d'Art de Catalunya, 2001); Joan Sureda, *La Pintura románica en Cataluña* (Madrid: Alanza Editorial, 1981); *Arte Románcia de Cataluña: colecciones del museu nacional d'art de Catalunya* (Barcelona: Museu Nacional d'Art de Catalunya Palau Nacional, 2001).

41. This was the reason cited by the director of the Catalan National Museum in Barcelona, Joachim Folch i Torres, in his essay "La peinture murale," in *La Catalogue à l'Epoque Romane: Conférences fuites à la Sorbonne en 1930 par MM Angles, Folch i Torres, Ph. Lauer, Nicolau D'Olwer, Puig i Cadafalch* (Paris: Librairie Ernest Lekoux, 1932), 111–28, reference 118.

42. The international art world's interest was aroused by a series of reproductions of the frescoes, which had been published by the Catalan Board of Museums in four parts, in 1907, 1910, 1911 and 1921. Relevant primary source extracts documenting this process are reproduced in Camps i Sòria et al., *Puig i Cadafalch i la col.lecció de pintura romànica,* 53–55.

43. As documented in Camps i Sòria et al., 53–59, quote 55.

44. Ibid., 56–57.

45. Friedrich Wilhelm Deichmann, *Frühchristliche Kirchen in Rom* (Basel: Amerbach-Verlag, 1948), 9.

46. Ibid., 14–15.

47. An interesting comparative case is the 1977 Bagsvaerd church in Denmark. Architect Jørn Utzon, the creator of the Sydney Opera House used the same ancient hall church shape, which critics described as reminiscent of an "agricultural building . . . that recalls the holy barn [in Bethlehem] . . . the prototype of early Christian communities . . . and the authenticity of a preindustrial past." Kenneth Frampton, *Grundlagen der Architektur. Studien zur Kultur des Tektonischen* (München: Oktagon, 1993), 330.

48. In Puig's own words, published in *La Renaixença* on 1 January 1889, Catalan Romanesque architecture embodied a "conjunction of ideas" that arose from the combination of "Christian spirituality and the spirit of the soil." Quoted from Enric Jardí, *Puig i Cadafalch : arquitecte, politic i historiador de l'art* (Barcelona: Editorial Ariel, 1975), 14–15, my translation.

49. Andrea Mesecke, *Josep Puig i Cadafalch, 1867–1956: Katalanisches Selbstverständnis und Internationalität in der Architektur* (Frankfurt: Lang, 1995), 49.

50. Puig refers to Kingsley-Porter's letter in his *La Géographie et les origines du premier art roman*, 8, in which Kingsley-Porter pointed out that in his work on *Lombard Architecture* 4 vols (New Haven, CT: Yale University Press, 1915–17), 16, 17, he had reached "similar conclusions" to Puig in *L'architectura romànica*, while he had used completely "different methods" (my translation).

51. Quoted from Peter Betthausen, et al., *Metzler Kunsthistoriker-Lexikon* (Stuttgart: Metzler, 1999), 56, my translation. The quote is from Georg Dehio (1850–1932), who began his career with a general work on ecclesiastical architecture in the West [*Die kirchliche Baukunst des Abendlandes* (Stuttgart: Cotta, 1887–1901)], moved on to a handbook of German art history, [*Handbuch der Deutschen Kunstgeschichte* 5 vols (Munich: Dt. Kunstvert, 1905–12)], and finally published his *Geschichte der deutschen Kunst* 3 vols (Berlin: De Gruyer, 1919–26), from which the above citation is taken.

52. Quoted in Andreas Hartmann-Virnich, *Was ist Romanik? Geschichte, Formen und Technik des romanischen Kirchenbaus* (Darmstadt: Wissenschaftliche Buchgesellschaft, 2004), 43.

53. Entry on Arthur Kingsley-Porter by Bernd Nicolai in Heinrich Dilly, ed., *Altmeister moderner Kunstgeschichte* (Berlin: Reimer, 1990), 220–32, quote 222–23, my translation.

54. Quoted in Dilly, 224.

55. Puig introduced this notion at an archaeological congress in 1906 (cited in Mesecke, *Josep Puig I Cadafalch,* 52), and developed it in *L'arquitectura romànica a Catalunya.*

56. Puig i Cadafalch, *La géographie et les origines du premier art roman,* 400.

57. Fernand Braudel, *La Méditerranée et le monde méditerranéen à l'époque de Philippe II* 2 vols, 2nd edition (Paris: Colin, 1966).

58. Puig, *La géographie,* 400–401.

59. Ibid., 57.

60. Ibid., 401.

61. Ibid., 138. The only exception to this geographical pattern was Rome, which was "abnormal" in maintaining flat wooden ceilings on the grounds of a particular "religious conservatism." Ibid., 136–37.

62. Ibid., respectively 141, 145–47, 146–48.

63. Ibid., 176.

64. Liana Castelfranchi Vegas, "Die ottonische Lombardei und Aribert," in *Europas Kunst um 1000*, ed. Liana Castelfranchi Vegas (Regensburg: Verlag Schnell & Steiner, 2001), 88–107, esp. 88.

65. Puig, 191–92.

66. Erich Kubach, "Die Architektur zur Zeit der Karolinger und Ottonen," in *Das frühmittelalterliche Imperium*, eds. Erich Kubach and Victor H. Elberm (Baden-Baden: Holle, 1968), 5–106; Günter Bandmann, *Die Bauformen des Mittelalters* (Bonn: Athenäum-Verl. von Reutern, 1949), esp. 129–33.

67. Puig, 13.

68. Arturo Soria y Puig, ed., *Cerdà: The Five Bases of the General Theory of Urbanization*, trans. Bernard Miller and Mary Fons I. Fleming (Madrid: Electa, 1999), 66.

69. Ibid., 57.

70. Ibid., 128, 132.

71. Ibid., 63.

72. "Discurs del president del Centre Escolar Catalanista de Barcelona," Barcelona, 1891, quoted from Mesecke, *Josep Puig i Cadafalch*, 69.

73. Puig i Cadafalch, "La Barcelona d'anys a venir," Il *La Veu* (8 January 1901), quoted from Jardí, *Josep Puig I Cadafalch: arquitecte*, 62, my translation.

74. Camillo Sitte, *Der Städtebau nach seinen künstlerischen Grundsätzen* (Basel: Birkhäuser, 2002 [1889]).

75. "Discurs" 1891, quoted from Mesecke, *Josep Puig i Cadafalch*, 69. There is little evidence to support the claim that such ideas stemmed specifically from Puig's readings of Wagner and Nietzsche, who, beyond a general rejection of rationalism and functionalism, had little to say on such topics (Mesecke, *Josep Puig I Cadafalch*, 72).

76. Ignasi Sola-Morales, *Gaudí* (Barcelona: Edicions Poligrafa 1982); Rainer Zerbst, *Antoni Gaudí* (Taschen: Benedikt Taschen Verlag, 1985); J. M. Carandell, and P. Vivas, *Park Guell—Gaudi's utopia* (Sant Lluís, Menorca: Triangle Postals, 1998); Nonell J. Bassegoda, *Modernisme a Catalunya* (Barcelona: Edicions de Nou Art Thor, 1989).

77. For literature on the 1888 Exposition, see note 18.

78. Sagnier collaborated with Domènech i Estapa, but was the driving force behind the building's overall design. Juan Miró y Murtó, *El Palacio de Justícia y la Ciudad de Barcelona* (Barcelona: Imp. L. Tasso Serra, 1883); Josep Emili Hernàndez-Cros, Gabriel Mora, and Xavier Pouplana, *Arquitectura de Barcelona* (Barcelona: Demarcació de Barcelona del Collegi d'Arquitectes de Catalunya, 1989), 290–91; Francesc Fontbona and Francesco Miralles, *Història de l'Art Català* (Barcelona: Edicions 62, 1996–2001), 34.

79. Maiken Umbach, "A Tale of Second Cities: Autonomy, Culture and the Law in Hamburg and Barcelona in the Long Nineteenth Century," *American Historical Review*, 110.3 (June 2005): 659–92.

80. Oriol Bohigas, *Lluis Domènech i Montaner* (Barcelona: Lluis Carulla i Canals, 1973).

81. This echoed the only other surviving exhibition structure, the *Arc de Triumf*, where the classical form was almost literally subverted by the humble material.

82. The idea of a natural affinity of Catalan and German ideas was later, and famously, articulated by Enric Prat de la Riba in his *La nacionalitat catalana*, a work deeply influenced by German thinkers such as Friedrich Herder and Friedrich Carl von Savigny. Enric Prat de la Riba, *La nacionalitat catalana*. In 1914, Prat de la Riba was elected president of the *Mancomunitat de Catalunya*, and thus Puig i Cadafalch's immediate political predecessor. On the German sources of Catalan nationalism, see also E. Bou, *La llum que ve del nord: Joan Maragall i la cultura alemanya* (Barcelona: Editorial Claret, 1997).

83. Michael Bright, *Cities Built to Music: Aesthetic Theories of the Victorian Gothic Revival* (Columbus: Ohio State University Press, 1984); Basil Fulford Lowther Clarke, *Church Builders of the Nineteenth Century: A Study of the Gothic Revival in England* (Newton Abbot: David & Charles, 1969); Keith Hartley et al., eds., *The Romantic Spirit in German Art 1790–1990* (London: Thames & Hudson, 1994); Werner Busch, *Caspar David Friedrich: Ästhetik und Religion* (München: C. H. Beck, 2003).

84. M. F. Hearn, ed., *The Architectural Theory of Viollet-le-Duc: Readings and Commentary* (Cambridge, MA: MIT Press, 1995); Kevin D. Murphy, *Memory and Modernity: Viollet-le-Duc at Vézelay* (University Park: Pennsylvania State University Press, 2000).

85. Frampton, *Studies in Tectonic Culture: The Poetics of Construction in Nineteenth and Twentieth Century Architecture* (Cambridge, MA: MIT Press, 1995).

86. This approach could be likened to that of German architectural theorist Gottfried Semper (1803–79). Semper had challenged prevailing "tectonic" theories of architecture, and argued that textile patterns should be seen as the origins of building art. Wolfgang Herrmann, *Gottfried Semper: In Search of Architecture* (Cambridge, MA: MIT Press, 1984); John Ziesemer, *Studien zu Gottfried Sempers dekorativen Arbeiten am Aussenbau und im Interieur: ein Beitrag zur Kunst des Historismus* (Weimar: VDG, 1999); Mari Hvattum, *Gottfried Semper and the Problem of Historicism* (Cambridge: Cambridge University Press, 2004); Hermann Sturm, *Alltag und Kult: Gottfried Semper, Richard Wagner, Friedrich Theodor Vischer, Gottfried Keller* (Basel: Birkhäuser, 2003).

87. The convention opposition between tectonics as "serious architecture" and ornament as "mere fashion" led scholars to either reduce modernism to a "fashion," or to deny the significance of ornamentation for the meaning of Puig's buildings altogether. The latter view is expounded by Mesecke, *Josep Puig i Cadafalch*, 123.

88. Josep Puig i Cadafalch, *La géographie*, 400.

89. In 1880, Valentí Almirall wrote in *Articles:* 58 that "the distance between Madrid and Barcelona increases every day even as the distance between our city [Barcelona] and the civilized cities of Europe continually decreases." Quoted from Brad Epps, "Modern and Moderno: Modernist Studies, 1898, and Spain," *Catalan Review* XIV (2000): 75–116, quote 102.

90. Puig had commented on the exemplary beauty of Nuremberg, Bruges, and Florence in "La Barcelona d'anys a venir," III i última, *La Veu* (22 January 1901), quoted from Jardí, *Puig i Cadafalch*, 62.

91. Permanyer and Casals, *Josep Puig i Cadafalch*, 54, lists the craftsmen involved: Eusebi Arnau, sculpture; Alfons Juyol, ornamental sculpture; Franzi Hermanos, marble; Joan Paradís, sgrafitti; Esteve Andorrà and Manual Ballarin, wrought-iron; Masriera i Campins, bronze; son of J. Pujol and Torres Mauri, ceramics; Casas i Bardés, carpentry; Joan Coll, plaster; Escofet, paving; Mario Maragliano, mosaic; Gaspar Homar, furniture; Miret i Ascens and Antoni Tàpies, lights.

92. Henri Bergson, *Essai sur les données immédiates de la conscience* (Paris: PUF, 1889).

93. Evelyne Ender, *Architexts of Memory: Literature, Science, and Autobiography* (Ann Arbor: University of Michigan Press, 2005); Christie McDonald, *The Proustian Fabric: Associations of Memory* (Lincoln; London: University of Nebraska Press, 1991); Adam Piette, *Remembering and the Sound of Words: Mallarmé, Proust, Joyce, Beckett* (Oxford: Clarendon Press, 1996); Richard Terdiman, *Present Past: Modernity and the Memory Crisis* (Ithaca, NY; London: Cornell University Press, 1993).

94. Roland Kany, *Mnemosyne als Programm. Geschichte, Erinnerung und die Andacht zum Unbedeutenden im Werk von Usener, Warburg und Benjamin* (Tübingen: Max Niemeyer, 1987); Horst Bredekamp, Michael Diers, and Charlotte Schoell-Glass, eds., *Aby Warburg: Akten des internationalen Symposions, Hamburg, 1990* (Weinheim: VCH, 1991).

95. Eugen Weber, *Peasants into Frenchmen: The Modernization of Rural France, 1870–1914* (London: Chatto and Windus, 1977). See also Walt Whitman Rostow, *The Stages of Economic Growth: A Non-Communist Manifesto* (Cambridge: Cambridge University Press, 1960).

6. LANDY: MODERN MAGIC

1. Friedrich Nietzsche, *The Gay Science*, trans. Walter Kaufmann (New York: Vintage 1974 [1882, 1887]), sec. 7 (1882). The German word *Wissenschaft* can of course also denote scholarship more generally, but the narrower definition seems appropriate here. The two epigraphs are from Weber, "Science as a Vocation," *Max Weber: Essays in Sociology*, ed. H. H. Gerth and C. Wright Mills (Oxford: Oxford University Press, 1946), 129–56, 139 and Arthur C. Clarke, *Report on Planet Three and Other Speculations* (New York: Harper and Row, 1972), 139.

2. For the Cartesian disenchantment of the rainbow, see Philip Fisher, *Wonder, the Rainbow, and the Aesthetics of Rare Experiences* (Cambridge, MA: Harvard University Press, 1998), 118–19. Fisher points out (10) that in Plato's *Theaetetus*, Socrates casts Iris (the rainbow) as the daughter of Thaumas (wonder). The rainbow begets wonder, wonder begets philosophy, and philosophy begets science—which then goes on to kill the rainbow. Cf. Andrea Nightingale in this volume.

3. Some key dates in nineteenth-century disenchantment: D. F. Strauss's *Life of Jesus*, 1846; Ludwig Feuerbach's *The Essence of Christianity*, 1854; Charles Darwin's *The Origin of Species*, 1859; Ernest Renan's *La vie de Jésus*, 1863.

4. On Nietzsche's account, what brought about the demise of Christianity as belief system is—paradoxically enough—Christianity's own morality (of ruthlessly honest self-examination): "it is the awe-inspiring *catastrophe* of two thousand years of training in truthfulness that finally forbids itself the *lie involved in belief in God*" (*Genealogy of Morals*, III:27; cf. *Gay Science*, sec. 357). In his own way, Marcel Gauchet also traces the disenchantment of the world to Christianity. Gauchet, *The Disenchantment of the World: A Political History of Religion*, trans. Oscar Burge (Princeton: Princeton University Press, 1999), 4 et passim.

5. "Have you not heard of that madman who lit a lantern in the bright morning hours, ran to the market place and cried incessantly: "I seek God! I seek God!"—As many of *those who did not believe in God* were standing around just then, he provoked much laughter" (*Gay Science*, sec. 125, my emphasis).

6. Bill Severn, *Magic and Magicians* (New York: Van Rees Press, 1958), 32–35.

7. Jean-Eugène Robert-Houdin, *Memoirs of Robert-Houdin*, trans. Lascelles Wraxall (New York: Dover, 1964), 159.

8. James Cook, *The Arts of Deception* (Cambridge, MA: Harvard University Press, 2001), 200. Thus, for example, Alexander Herrmann and Harry Kellar exposed the tricks of the spiritualists (ibid., 199; Bill Severn, *Magic and Magicians*, 50). Robert-Houdin was of course not the first magician to downplay his own powers (Cook, 185). Some seventeenth-century magicians were already speaking in terms of *légerdemain* (ibid., 171), a tradition which continued in the eighteenth century with Comus and the soberly dressed Isaac Fawkes (Simon During, *Modern Enchantments: The Cultural Power of Secular Magic*, Cambridge, MA: Harvard University Press, 2002, 81–89). In the early nineteenth century, Robertson and Rubens Peale were presenting their *phantasmagorias* as the very antidote to belief (Cook, *Arts of Deception*, 172–73, 177), and Antonio Blitz, one of Robert-Houdin's immediate precursors, claimed the same thing for his conjuring (ibid., 180). Still, Robert-Houdin consolidated the practice, making it henceforth nonoptional.

9. Thus Robert-Houdin: "These fanatics took him for a real sorcerer, and attacked him with sticks; and they were even going to throw him into a lime-kiln, had not Comte escaped by causing a terrible voice to issue from the kiln, which routed them" (*Memoirs of Robert-Houdin*, 98). Jules Garinet reports other events from this period, such as the 1818 murder by one Julien Desbourdes of a man who, he thought, had cursed him (Jules Garinet, *Histoire de la Magie en*

France, depuis le Commencement de la Monarchie jusqu'à nos Jours, Paris: Foulon, 1818, 289–90). For Oehler and Giovanni Pinetti, see During, *Modern Enchantments*, 93–94, and Cook, *Arts of Deception*, 179.

10. Antonio Blitz, *Fifty Years in the Magic Circle* (Hartford, CT: Belknap & Bliss, 1871), 36.

11. Blitz, *Fifty Years*, 37. Even during the American Civil War, when Blitz was performing in Philadelphia hospitals, "many declared I was the devil in disguise; others exclaimed, 'That man is Satan's agent;' others affirmed I would be dangerous in a crowd . . . ; while others thought I was the person to go to the front, and extract the bullets from the enemy's guns. Not a few considered me anti-religious, because I performed, apparently, such wicked things," (420).

12. Charles Mackay, *Memoirs of Extraordinary Popular Delusions* (London: Routledge, 1869), II:176. See Julia de Fontenelle for Christian arguments against magic in seventeenth-century France (Jean Sébastien Eugène Julia de Fontenelle, *Nouveau Manuel complet des Sorciers*, Paris: Roret, 1837, esp. 3, 13). In England, by contrast, witchcraft as crime was alive and well, thanks to the *Demonology* of King James, a work which established criteria for determining the guilt of an accused party.

13. Mackay, *Memoirs*, I:220; Pierre Mariel, *Cagliostro: Imposteur o Martyr?* (Paris: Culture, Art, Loisirs, 1973), 164. Even Cagliostro's death notice presented him as having possessed special powers (ibid., 168). For Boissier and company, see the entry "Sorcellerie" in the *Dictionnaire européen des lumières*, ed. Michel Delon (Paris: PUF, 1997), 1009; Jean Baptiste Fiard, *De la France trompée par les magiciens et les démonolâtres du dix-huitième siècle, fait démontré par des faits* (Paris: Grégoire, 1803) passim; and Garinet, *Histoire*, 279–81, 345.

14. ". . . des pratiques que le maintien, à la cour papale, d'une charge en vue de les confondre, désigne comme vivaces" (Stéphane Mallarmé, "Magie," *Oeuvres Complètes*, Paris: Gallimard, 1998 & 2003, II:307). For the Code of Pasquelone, see Mariel, *Cagliostro* (1973), 153.

15. ". . . finit par prendre position dans le *pudendum* de la demoiselle" (Garinet, *Histoire*, 289).

16. Around 1770, after all, a certain Father Apollinaire had been "caught in bed, chasing the Devil from the lower parts of the maidservant of Henriet, vicar of Saint–Humiers" ("surpris au lit, chassant le diable des parties inférieures de la servante d'Henriet, curé de Saint-Humiers") (Garinet, *Histoire*, 344).

17. Blitz, *Fifty Years*, 34, 85.

18. "There shall not be found among you any one that maketh his son or his daughter to pass through the fire, or that useth divination, or an observer of times, or an enchanter, or a witch. Or a charmer, or a consulter with familiar spirits, or a wizard, or a necromancer. For all that do these things are an abomination unto the Lord: and because of these abominations the Lord thy God doth drive them out from before thee." (*Deut* 18:10–12). The New Testament tale of porcine possession is also told in Matthew 8:28–34 and Luke 8:26–39.

19. The spiritualist movement, of course, claimed many high-born victims. In 1857, Napoléon III himself was taken in by the performance of medium

Daniel Dunglas Home. And Robert-Houdin himself claimed to have thought his first street magician a "superhuman being" (*Memoirs of Robert-Houdin*, 11).
20. Ibid., 38.
21. Mackay, *Memoirs*, II.188–9.
22. In general, Robert-Houdin attracted a more well-heeled audience—and charged more for admission—than contemporaries such as John Henry Anderson (see During, *Modern Enchantments*, 117, 119, 128). Magic's move into the theatre only solidified its new status as middle-class (and upper-class) entertainment (James Cook, *Arts of Deception*, 167).

23. Messieurs, disais–je avec le sérieux d'un professeur de la Sorbonne, je viens de découvrir dans l'éther une nouvelle propriété vraiment merveilleuse. «Lorsque cette liqueur est à son plus haut degré de concentration, si on la fait respirer à un être vivant, le corps du patient devient en peu d'instants aussi léger qu'un ballon.» Cette exposition terminée, je procédais à l'expérience. Je plaçais trois tabourets sur un banc de bois. Mon fils montait sur celui du milieu, et je lui faisais étendre les bras, que je soutenais en l'air au moyen de deux cannes qui reposaient chacune sur un tabouret. Je mettais alors simplement sous le nez de l'enfant un flacon vide que je débouchais avec soin, mais dans la coulisse on jetait de l'éther sur une pelle de fer très-chaude, afin que la vapeur s'en répandît dans la salle. Mon fils s'endormait aussitôt, et ses pieds devenus plus légers commençaient à quitter le tabouret. Jugeant alors l'opération réussie, je retirais le tabouret de manière que l'enfant ne se trouvait plus soutenu que par les deux cannes. Cet étrange équilibre excitait déjà dans le public une grande surprise. Elle augmentait encore lorsqu'on me voyait retirer l'une des deux cannes et le tabouret qui la soutenait; et enfin elle arrivait à son comble, lorsqu'après avoir élevé avec le petit doigt mon fils jusqu'à la position horizontale, je le laissais ainsi endormi dans l'espace, et que pour narguer les lois de la gravitation, j'ôtais encore les pieds du banc qui se trouvait sous cet édifice impossible.

Jean-Eugène Robert-Houdin, *Confidences de Robert-Houdin: Une Vie d'artiste*. Paris: Librairie Nouvelle, 1861, vol. 2, 303–4. The English translation (312) is not faithful here, and gives only a fragment of the text I have cited.
24. Robert-Houdin, *Memoirs of Robert-Houdin*, 214; cf. Geoffrey Lamb, *Victorian Magic* (London: Routledge, 1976), 34.
25. Cf. Grete de Francesco: "the mythology they drove out and expelled was not gone from the world; it hid itself and became entrenched where the Enlightened least expected it and where it therefore remained most invisibly concealed: behind modern science itself, behind technology. Science and technology became magical." *The Power of the Charlatan*, trans. Miriam Beard (New Haven, CT: Yale University Press, 1939), 235.
26. Robert-Houdin, *Memoirs of Robert-Houdin*, 215.
27. Cf. Philip Fisher: "Every stage of explanation . . . has consistently dispelled the extraordinary only to produce, in the very act of explanation, newer

forms of wonder" (*Wonder*, 89). And see James Cook, *Arts of Deception*, 173; During, *Modern Enchantments*, 20–21, 83–89; and especially Andrea Nightingale, in this volume.

28. Blitz, *Fifty Years*, 86. This rather militates against During's claim (*Modern Enchantments*, 62–64)—perhaps the only one from which I would depart—that magic shows are not a replacement for faith. Cf. to some extent James Cook, *Arts of Deception*, 179–80.

29. Ernst Renan, *L'Avenir de la science: Pensées de 1848* (Paris: Calmann-Lévy, 1890), 74. My translation.

30. Auguste Comte, *The Catechism of Positive Religion*, trans. Richard Congreve (London: Kegan Paul, 1891 [1852]), 100. For Comte's new faith, see 51; God (now in the form of Humanity), 45; Providence, 1; explanation of the world, 41; immortality, 55; morality, 51; rituals, 90. In Littré's opinion, Comte was not *compos mentis* when he wrote all this; Lévy-Bruhl, however, felt that the "religion" followed logically from the other doctrines. And Comte and Renan were not alone in considering positivism a new religion. Thus, for example, Charles Jeannolle concurred that "Le positivisme est une Eglise, une religion. Si nous ne sommes pas religieux, nous n'avons pas de raison d'être." For Littré, Lévy-Bruhl, and Jeannolle, see Alice Gérard, "Auguste Comte Au Purgatoire," in *Auguste Comte, Qui Êtes-Vous?* ed. Edgar Faure (Paris: La Manufacture, 1988), 160.

31. Homais: "What fanaticism promised in times past to the elect, science is now achieving for all men!" Renan: "Science is thus a religion; science alone will make symbols henceforth; science alone can resolve for man the eternal problems whose solution his nature imperiously demands." Gustave Flaubert, *Madame Bovary*, trans. Francis Steegmuller (New York: Random House, 1992), 209; Renan, *L'avenir de la Science* 108, my translation.

32. Robert-Houdin, *Memoirs of Robert–Houdin*, 92–3. P. T. Barnum felt similarly: "The public appears to be disposed to be amused even when they are conscious of being deceived." Barnum, *The Life of P. T. Barnum, Written By Himself* (London: Sampson Low, 1855), 171; qtd. James Cook, *Arts of Deception*, 16).

33. Qtd. H. J. Burlingame, *History of Magic and Magicians* (Chicago: Burlingame, 1895), 42. The writer is an anonymous theatre critic of the 1860s.

34. This idea has something in common with Freud's suggestion, in "The Uncanny," that certain forms of literature provide their readers or spectators with an opportunity for re-immersion in atavistic beliefs, beliefs which have ostensibly (rationally) long been superseded. There are, however, two differences: in terms of the content, Robert-Houdin shows science itself (counterintuitively enough) to be joining the ranks of superseded beliefs; in terms of the process, Robert-Houdin's audience, unlike the readership of E. T. A. Hoffmann (say), is being invited to indulge *consciously* in the fantasy—perhaps even to spin lucid fantasies of their own, on return to everyday life. Sigmund Freud, "The Uncanny," trans. Joan Riviere, *Collected Papers*, ed. Ernest Jones (New York: Basic Books, 1959), Vol. 4, 368–407, 394–96, 401–2.

35. Robert Irwin, Introduction to Joris-Karl Huysmans, *Là-Bas: A Journey into the Self*, trans. Brendan King (London: Dedalus, 1986), vi.

36. The Church of Carmel was founded by self-proclaimed prophet Eugène Vintras in 1839 and deemed sacrilegious by Pope Pius IX in 1848. On the death of Vintras in 1875, Boullan—an excommunicated priest—took over, and moved to Lyon with some of Vintras's adherents. By all accounts, these Carmelites celebrated black masses (or at the very least scandalously sexualized ceremonies), under the guise of conventional religious observance. See Irwin, Introduction, iv, and Pierre Mariel, *Dictionnaire des Sociétés Secrètes en Occident* (Paris: Culture, Art, Loisirs, 1971), 84–85.

37. See James Webb, *The Flight from Reason* (London: Macdonald, 1971), 97, 258n8; Joanny Bricaud, *J.-K. Huysmans et le Satanisme* (Paris: Chacornac, 1912), 40; and Irwin, Introduction, iv.

De Guaïta had learned of the Church of Carmel's practices from Oswald Wirth, who had posed as a prospective convert in order to extract information from Boullan, in 1887 (Webb, *Flight*, 97; Oswald Wirth, *Stanislas de Guaïta: souvenirs de son secrétaire* (Paris: Editions du symbolisme, 1935), 101–2). The following year, de Guaïta founded the French Rosicrucian order, in conjunction with Joséphin Péladan. The two parted company in 1890, in what came to be known as the "War of the Two Roses." Péladan founded the *Ordre de la Rose-Croix du Temple et du Graal* (Order of the Rose Cross of the Temple and the Grail), and the two orders immediately excommunicated each other. See Mariel, *Dictionnaire*, 374; Webb, *Flight*, 108–14.

38. Bois: "C'est maintenant un fait incontestable . . . l'abbé Boullan, qui vient de mourir subitement à Lyon, a été frappé par des colères invisibles et par des mains criminelles armées de foudres occultes, de forces redoutables et inconnues" (*Gil Blas*, January 9, 1893). Huysmans (speaking to Horace Bianchon): "A moi qui vous parle, ils ont tout fait pour me nuire! Chaque soir, à la minute précise où je vais m'endormir, je reçois sur le crâne et sur la face . . . comment dirais-je? . . . des coups de poing fluidiques. Je voudrais croire que je suis tout bonnement en proie à de fausses sensations purement objectives, dues à l'extrême sensibilité de mon système nerveux; mais j'incline à penser que c'est bel et bien affaire de magie. La preuve, c'est que mon chat, qui ne risque pas, lui, d'être un halluciné, a des secousses à la même heure et de la même sorte que moi" (*Le Figaro*, January 10, 1893). For Huysmans' exorcism paste, see Irwin, *Introduction*, vi.

39. Jules Bois also fought a duel with occultist Gérard Encausse, a.k.a. "Papus," whom he had classed along with de Guaïta as a sorcerer. No real damage was done in either duel. See Irwin, *Introduction*, vi; Webb, *Flight*, 98–99; and Lucien Descaves, "Note," in Joris-Karl Huysmans, *Oeuvres Complètes XII* (Geneva: Slatkine Reprints, 1972), 256.

40. Joris-Karl Huysmans, *Oeuvres Complètes XII* (Genève: Slatkine Reprints, 1972), 219–23.

41. Je dis qu'existe entre les vieux procédés et le Sortilège, que demeure la poésie, une parité secrète . . . Evoquer, dans une ombre exprès, l'objet tu,

par des mots allusifs, jamais directs, se réduisant à du silence égal, présente la tentative proche de créer: qui tire sa vraisemblance de ceci, que l'opération tient entière dans la limite de l'idée. Or l'idée d'un objet uniquement est mise en jeu par l'Enchanteur de Lettres, avec une justesse telle que, certes, cela scintille, à l'illusion du regard. Le vers, trait incantatoire! et, qui suivant me déniera au cercle que perpétuellement ferme, ouvre la rime une similitude avec les ronds, parmi l'herbe, de la fée ou du magicien.

(*The National Observer*, 28 January 1893): 263–64; reprinted in full in Stéphane Mallarmé, *Oeuvres Complètes* (Paris: Gallimard, 1998 & 2003; henceforth *OC*), II: 307–9. Mallarmé is here echoing (among others) Charles Baudelaire, who felt that "manier savamment une langue, c'est pratiquer une espèce de sorcellerie évocatoire" ("Théophile Gautier," *Oeuvres Complètes*, Paris: Robert Laffont, 1980, 501) and saw speech and writing as "opérations magiques, sorcellerie évocatoire" ("Fusées," idem, 395). When translating Mallarmé's impenetrable prose, throughout this article, I have aimed for relative clarity and simplicity of expression, and can only apologize for the many oversimplifications this has required.

42. ". . . une fenêtre nocturne ouverte, . . . sans meubles, sinon l'ébauche plausible de vagues consoles, un cadre, belliqueux et agonisant, de miroir appendu au fond, avec sa réflexion, stellaire et incompréhensible, de la Grande Ourse, qui relie au ciel seul ce logis abandonné du monde" (Letter to Cazalis, 18/7/1868, Stéphane Mallarmé, *Correspondance*, ed. Henri Mondor (Paris: Gallimard, 1959–1985), I:278–79). Mallarmé appended this note on sending the original version of this sonnet ("Sonnet allégorique de lui-même") for publication in a collection of poems. Oddly, Mallarmé's piece ended up not being included in the collection.

43. For the identity of the two apparitions, cf. Jean-Pierre Richard, *L'univers imaginaire de Mallarmé* (Paris: Seuil, 1961), 221. On this reading, the stars which appear in the window are reflected in the mirror—just as they are in the sonnet's 1868 precursor, "Sonnet allégorique de lui-même": "sur la glace encor / De scintillations le septuor se fixe" (ll. 13–14). Yet in the 1887 version, the mirror is said to be near to ("proche") the window. If the mirror is next to the window, how can the stars be reflected in it? At the risk of pedantry, let me suggest a resolution. The window is at the right edge of the north wall, and the mirror is on the left edge of the eastern wall; starlight, traversing the window at an angle, is reflected in the mirror which stands "close to" it.

44. It might be objected that the poem's two parts cannot be analogous, since they are separated, at the *volta*, by the word "*mais.*" It might further be objected, more specifically, that the sestet is more optimistic than the octave (see, e.g., Roger Pearson, *Unfolding Mallarmé: The Development of a Poetic Art*, Oxford: Oxford University Press, 1996, 158–59). While this would, to be sure, bring *Ses purs ongles* into line with sonnets like "Une dentelle," I am not quite convinced that it is an accurate assessment. Mallarmé was content, in the earlier version, to join the two halves with an "et," and with good reason. For an equal quantity of suffering and transcendence is surely to be found on both

sides of the said conjunction. In the octave, there is not only anguish but also the resplendent elevation that emerges from it; in the sestet, there is not only a septet of scintillations but also a nymph in her death throes. Indeed, the nymph's "agony" neatly reproduces the "anguish" of the opening: just as "L'Angoisse" opens the second line of the quatrains, "Agonise," its near-anagram, kicks off the second line of the tercets. Thus the conjunction "mais" does not, in fact, lead us from darkness to light. Instead, it leads directly into suffering ("But near the vacant window to the north, something gold / Twists in agony"), and only indirectly into transcendence. What, then, *is* the force of the "mais"? I would tentatively suggest that the contrast is a *spatial* one: on the tables, no ptyx (a happy absence), but by the window, a mirror (an agonized presence).

45. Of the four sonnets collected together under the rubric "plusieurs sonnets," no fewer than three contain allusions to constellations: not just "le septuor" in *Ses purs ongles* (l.14) but also the "guirlandes célèbres" in *Quand l'ombre* (l.6) and "le Cygne" (presumably Cycnus) which emerges at the end of *Le vierge* (l.14). The constellation also plays a prominent, and famous, role in *Un Coup de Dés*, where some capital letters loudly proclaim "RIEN . . . N'AURA EU LIEU . . . QUE LE LIEU . . . EXCEPTÉ PEUT–ÊTRE UNE CONSTELLATION."

46. Ovid tells the Callisto story in *Metamorphoses*, trans. Michael Simpson. (Amherst: University of Massachusetts Press, 1986), at 2:401–507, and Mallarmé mentions it in *Les dieux antiques* (*OC*, II:1528–9). The allusion is perhaps clearer in Mallarmé's earlier version, which speaks of "un dieu que croit emporter une nixe" ("a god whom a nixie thinks she is carrying off") rather than of unicorns. According to Gardner Davies (*Mallarmé et le drame solaire* (Paris: Corti, 1959, 136n19), the first critic to spot the Callisto allusion was Christopher Brennan.

47. Ursa Major rotates around the North Star (Polaris). If Mallarmé does indeed have Callisto in mind, then presumably the "septuor" is the Ursa Minor part of the constellation, sometimes known as the "Plough," "Big Dipper," or, as in *Un Coup de Dés*, "Septentrion."

48. In French, the word *croisée* is also used to mean "transept crossing," i.e. the place in a cathedral at which the nave intersects with the transept. The religious connotations of the term are perhaps clearest in Mallarmé's poem "Les Fenêtres": "Je fuis et je m'accroche à toutes les croisées / D'où l'on tourne l'é-paule à la vie, et, béni, / Dans leur verre, lavé d'éternelles rosées, / Que dore le matin chaste de l'Infini / Je me mire et me vois ange!" (ll.25–99). For *crédence*, one should bear in mind that the term also means "credence table" (again found in gothic cathedrals). See Betrand Marchal, *Lecture de Mallarmé: Poésies, Igitur, Le coup de dés* (Paris: Corti, 1985), 172n4.

49. ". . . ce vieux et méchant plumage, terrassé, heureusement, Dieu"—Mallarmé to Cazalis, *Correspondance* I:241–2, 1867. Cf. Mallarmé's wonderful and untranslatable injunction in "La Musique et les Lettres" (*OC* II:73): "Là-bas, où que ce soit, nier l'indicible, qui ment." ("Over there, wherever it is, deny the unsayable, which lies.")

50. Cf. Robert J. Nelson, "Mallarmé's Mirror of Art: An Explication of *Ses Purs Ongles*," *Modern Language Quarterly* 20 (1959): 55.

51. The three-part drama is reflected in the structure of the verbs. Each panel of the diptych opens with a pair of active verbs (*dédiant, soutient; agonise, ruant*), briefly surrenders to passives (*brûlé, aboli; défunte, fermé*), and finally resolves in reflexives (*s'honore, se fixe*). This is a double repetition of *Le vierge*, in which we see a frozen swan attempting, actively, to shake himself loose from the ice ("tout son col *secouera* cette blanche agonie," l.9), then the fact that this "agony" is inflicted—the swan now passive—by the universe ("par l'espace *infligé*," l.10), and finally the swan accepting his fate, choosing it, making active what was passive, in a culminating moment of middle-voice *amor fati*: "Il *s'immobilise* au songe froid de mépris / Que vêt parmi l'exil inutile le Cygne" (ll.13–14).

52. To some extent, Mallarmé is using what Gardner Davies would call the "solar drama"—the daily death of the sun—as the armature on which to prop the rest of his poem. See Davies, *Mallarmé*, esp. 108–14 and 137.

53. Without too much argument, Charles Chadwick suggests ("Mallarme's 'Sonnet allégorique de lui-même'—Allegorical of Itself or of Himself?" *Nineteenth-Century French Studies* 31.1, 2002, 104–10) that the idea of something being allegorical of itself is a patent absurdity. Chadwick concludes that the sonnet must be allegorical of *him*self (Mallarmé) rather than *it*self (the poem). (This, incidentally, was already a common view in the 1950s: see, e.g., Guy Michaud, *Mallarmé* (Paris: Hatier, 1958), 75.) Chadwick also dismisses the "sensation . . . cabalistique" Mallarmé attributes to his poem (108). The present essay hopes to show that these Mallarméan claims of incantation and self-allegoresis are at least not trivially false.

54. Judging by Mallarmé's 1868 letter to Cazalis (cited earlier), "vacante" may mean "ouverte" (open)—vacant, then, in the sense of having no glass, no bars, nothing to form a barrier between inside and outside worlds.

55. Thus E. S. Burt: "This representation of the scene depends on a spectator (the poet), and insofar as there is a point of view, this eye must be located. But, as the poem tells us, there is no I: 'Car le Maître est allé puiser des pleurs au Styx.'" E. S. Burt, "Mallarmé's 'Sonnet En *Yx*': The Ambiguities of Speculation," *Modern Critical Views: Stéphane Mallarmé*, ed. Harold Bloom (New York: Chelsea House, 1987), 101.

56. "L'oeuvre pure implique la disparition élocutoire du poëte, qui cède l'initiative aux mots" (*Crise de vers*, in *OC* II:211).

57. So too in *Un coup de dés*, the "Maître" is shipwrecked, but a consciousness remains to imagine that "RIEN . . . N'AURA EU LIEU . . . QUE LE LIEU . . . EXCEPTÉ PEUT-ÊTRE UNE CONSTELLATION" (my emphasis).

58. Needless to say, those critics are legion who have wished to present Mallarmé as a poet ceding all control to the entirely random play of language. Roger Pearson, for example, claims in *Unfolding Mallarmé* that after the existential crisis of 1867, "a Post-structuralist Mallarmé is conceived: the willing, passive instrument of words which have more to say than he can ever foresee or adequately control" (41); "he no longer sought to express himself through language but now sought to let language express itself through him" (142);

"his own writing had shown him how little the poet writes the poem; how it is rather the poem . . . which 'writes' the poet" (297); and of course "the signifier is allowed free play" (172). "Du fait que l'homme parle," Maurice Blanchot agrees, "l'homme est déjà mort . . . ce langage ne suppose personne qui l'exprime, personne qui l'entende: il *se* parle et il s'écrit." *La Part du Feu* (Paris: Gallimard, 1949), 48. "Lire reviendrait alors," Vincent Kaufmann adds, "à ne pas imposer au poème un sens qui lui serait comme extérieur, relevant de l'imaginaire du seul lecteur, mais à entendre . . . toutes les virtualités d'une langue" (*Le Livre et ses adresses: Mallarmé, Ponge, Valéry, Blanchot* (Paris: Méridiens Klincksieck, 1986), 51. Leo Bersani, too, speaks of "Mallarmé's extraordinary surrender to the contingent," *The Death of Stéphane Mallarmé* (Cambridge: Cambridge University Press, 1981), 57. Yet Mallarmé expressly states, in more than one place, that his work is *not* aleatory in the slightest. In good literature, he writes, there is only room for the *illusion* of chance: "tout hasard doit être banni de l'oeuvre moderne et n'y peut être que feint" (*Le Corbeau, OC* II:772); "[le] hasard . . . ne doit jamais qu'être simulé" (*Planches et feuillets, OC* II:195).

59. Some scholars—like Barbara Johnson ("Les Fleurs du Mal Armé: Some Reflections on Intertextuality," in *Lyric Poetry: Beyond New Criticism*, eds. Chavia Parker, Patricia Hosek and Jonathan Arac (Ithaca: Cornell University Press, 1985), 264–80, 265—have pushed the idea of a Mallarmé driven to write, paradoxically, by a fear of not being able to. There is some support for this approach in Mallarmé's "Symphonie Littéraire," where he refers to the "muse moderne de l'Impuissance" (*OC* II:281); still, it is far from clear that this early essay should be taken as providing the key to the entirety of his poetic production.

60. "Il a ployé son aile indubitable en *moi*" (*Quand l'ombre*, l. 4); "*mon* absent tombeau" (*Victorieusement fui*, l. 4); and, in admittedly more muted fashion, "Va-t-il *nous* déchirer avec un coup d'aile ivre" (*Le vierge*, l. 2). My emphasis throughout.

61. ". . . je suis maintenant impersonnel, et non plus Stéphane que tu as connu,—mais une aptitude qu'a l'univers Spirituel à se voir et à se développer, à travers ce qui fut moi" (Mallarmé to Cazalis, *Correspondance* I:241–2, 1867). Cf. "j'aime à me refugier dans l'impersonnalité—qui me semble une consécration" (*Correspondance* I:246, 1867), and also the mention of a "type permanent impersonnel" in "Sur Verlaine" (*OC* II:661).

62. In the 1868 letter to Cazalis, Mallarmé explicitly states that the poem's content—an empty room, with stars reflected in a mirror—is supposed to stand for its action: "une fenêtre nocturne ouverte, . . . sans meubles, sinon l'ébauche plausible de vagues consoles, un cadre, belliqueux et agonisant, de miroir appendu au fond, avec sa réflexion, stellaire et incompréhensible, de la Grande Ourse, qui relie au ciel seul ce logis abandonné du monde. *J'ai pris ce sujet d'un sonnet nul et se réfléchissant de toutes les façons*" (*Correspondance*, I:279, my emphasis; translation for the first part of this statement is given in an earlier footnote). For emptiness and mirroring, cf. Mallarmé's remark to François Coppée in 1866: "ce à quoi nous devons viser surtout est que, dans le poème, les

mots . . . se reflètent les uns sur les autres jusqu'à paraître ne plus avoir leur couleur propre, mais n'être que les transitions d'une gamme" (ibid., 234).

63. It is extremely unusual for a sonnet to use only two rhymes. Further, "Ses purs ongles" is unique among Mallarmé's mature sonnets in having three sets of *rimes croisées* (abab) as well as the couplet (cc). The rhyme scheme here is abab abab bb abab; Mallarmé's other mature sonnets either begin with two sets of *rimes embrassées* (abba abba cc dede: this is the case for all of the other three "plusieurs sonnets," and all three in the triptych) or leave the couplet till last (abab cdcd efef gg: "Toute l'âme résumée," the "Petits airs," "La chevelure vol," etc.). The unpublished "Sonnet allégorique de lui-même," with its abab abab baa bba rhyme scheme, is again unique in Mallarmé's *oeuvre*.

For the reversal of masculine and feminine rhymes, cf. Pearson, 146; Éric Garnier, *Commentaire: Le Sonnet En X De Stéphane Mallarmé* (Pau: Editions de Vallongues, 2003), 28; Emilie Noulet, *Vingt Poèmes De Stéphane Mallarmé* (Geneva: Droz, 1967), 177. A "feminine" rhyme-word is one which ends in a mute *e* ("amphore," for example).

64. The earlier version, "Sonnet allégorique de lui-même," has seven rhymes in [ix] and seven rhymes in [oR]: a perfect counterpart, at the level of form, to the reflected constellation. (For the general idea of fourteen lines and seven reflected stars, see Noulet, *Vingt Poèmes*, 191; Noulet claims here that this is what makes the sonnet "allegorical of itself.")

65. Roger Dragonetti: "l'oreille qui entend *-or, -ix* se souvient de l'*oryx*. On raconte que la corne de la licorne était en réalité la corne d'une antilope appelée *oryx*." *Etudes sur Mallarmé* (Gent: Romanica Gandensia, 1992), 69. Graham Robb concurs: "The unicorn of the *sonnet en yx* may have been conjured up by the unused rhyme, 'oryx.'" *Unlocking Mallarmé* (New Haven, CT: Yale University Press, 1996), 12. Cf. also Pierre Citron, "Ses purs ongles très haut," *Stéphane Mallarmé: Poésies* (Paris: Imprimerie Nationale, 1986), 306.

66. For Mallarmé, it would not be enough merely to rhyme on [ix]. Following Banville and others (Banville: "Sans consonne d'appui, pas de Rime et, par conséquent, pas de poésie"), Mallarmé insists on including the preceding consonant in the rhyme. See Danièle Wieckowski, *La Poétique de Mallarmé: la fabrique des iridées* (Paris: SEDES, 1998), 139. The "pyx" idea is Chisholm's (from "Mallarmé and the Riddle of the Ptyx," qtd. Davies, *Mallarmé*, 117).

67. Cf. Lucien Dällenbach, *The Mirror in the Text*, trans. Jeremy Whitely (Chicago: University of Chicago Press, 1989), 180.

68. Robert G. Cohn, *Toward the Poems of Mallarme* (Berkeley: University of California Press, 1979), 244. Could there perhaps be an analogous effect at the alphabetic level, with **ab**oli (6), **c**ar (7), and **déf**unte (11)? Such a reading would be impermissibly far-fetched were it not for Mallarmé's "Une dentelle s'abolit," whose first stanza includes the words "s'**ab**olit" and "**ab**sence," and whose second stanza spells out C-D-E-F in acrostic ("**C**et unanime blanc conflit / **D**'une guirlande avec la même, / **E**nfui contre la vitre blême / **F**lotte plus qu'il n'ensevelit"). It may *still* be impermissibly far-fetched.

69. For the connection between "Ses purs" and "septuor," see Jean Ricardou, *Mallarmé ou l'obscurité lumineuse* (Paris: Editions Hermann, 1999), 209–13. There are, in fact, exactly seven seven-letter words in the poem: *bibelot* (6), *inanité* (6), *croisée* (9), *vacante* (9), *agonise* (10), *défunte* (12), *septuor* (14). *Septuor*, of course, sends us back to "ses purs" (1), itself a seven-letter unit. As Ricardou points out (211–3), "ses purs" is a group of 3+4 letters, "sept-uor" a group of 4+3: the "handle" and "bowl" of Ursa Minor, he suggests, reflected in a mirror.

70. In a "straight" crossword, each clue is a synonym for the target word (thus, for example, "cease" could be a straight clue for "stop"). In a "cryptic" crossword, by contrast, each clue still contains a synonym, but adds a second way of arriving at the target word. This second path no longer deals exclusively in meanings, but has to do instead with the letters or sounds contained in the target word. Thus, for example, "cease upending pots" could be a cryptic clue for "stop": "cease" is still the synonym, while the remainder of the clue invites us to reverse the order of letters P, O, T, S. Or again "conceal Jekyll's double, by the sound of it" might yield "hide" (a pun on "Hyde"); and so too might "conceal in the March ides" (here, the letters H-I-D-E are literally *in* the letters M-A-R-C-H-I-D-E-S).

Is it too much of a stretch to read certain Mallarméan devices in a similar way? In *A la nue*, for example, a siren (*sirène*) is *heard*, and not just seen, "*dans le* **si** *blanc cheveu qui* **traine**" (my emphasis). Or again, in *Le pitre châtié*, "nacre" (at the end of one line) morphs anagrammatically into "rance" (at the start of the next) just as the clown's makeup starts to run. And so here at the heart of *Ses purs ongles*, it is as though we were set the challenge of finding a word that accurately characterizes line 6 while also punning on "s'honore"; "sonore" becomes the only possible solution.

71. In the manner of T. S. Eliot's "objective correlative." See T. S. Eliot, "Hamlet," *Selected Prose of T. S. Eliot*, ed. Frank Kermode (New York: Harcourt Brace, 1975), 48.

72. Proust's narrator speaks, in *The Guermantes Way*, of "those finished works of art . . . in which every part in turn receives from the rest a justification which it confers on them in turn" ("ces oeuvres d'art achevées . . . où chaque partie . . . reçoit des autres sa raison d'être"). Marcel Proust, *The Guermantes Way*, trans. C. K. Scott Moncrieff, Terence Kilmartin, and D. J. Enright (London: Chatto & Windus, 1992), 737; Proust, *Le Côté de Guermantes* (Paris: Gallimard, 1988), 520. For this idea, cf. Alexander Nehamas, *Nietzsche: Life as Literature* (Cambridge, MA: Harvard University Press, 1985), 229.

73. Mallarmé to Lefébure in 1868: "concertez-vous pour m'envoyer le sens réel du mot ptyx, on m'assure qu'il n'existe dans aucune langue, ce que je préférerais de beaucoup afin de me donner le charme de le créer par la magie de la rime" ("put your heads together to send me the real meaning of the word ptyx, they tell me it does not exist in any language, which I would greatly prefer, so that I might charm myself with the thought of creating it by the magic of rhyme") (*Correspondance*, I:274). As Noulet points out, the word had already been used by Victor Hugo in his poem "Satyre"; whether or not Mallarmé had

"Satyre" in mind, it is most unlikely he believed the word *ptyx* to be entirely nonexistent. Noulet, *Vingt Poèmes*, 184.

74. "A côté d'*ombre*, opaque, *ténèbres* se fonce peu; quelle déception, devant la perversité conférant à *jour* comme à *nuit*, contradictoirement, des timbres obscur ici, là clair." ("Crise de vers," *OC* II:208.) Astonishingly perhaps, Mallarmé seems to go out of his way to use these precise terms, and in prominent positions at that. In *Toast funèbre*, for example, "nuit" and "jour" are both placed at the end of a line, "nuit" in fact twice, since it is used both as noun ("night") and as verb ("harms"). In *Hérodiade*, "ténèbres" also finds itself at the rhyme twice (once in the *Ouverture ancienne*, once in the *Cantique de Saint Jean*). And *Quand l'ombre*, as if wishing to make palpable the claim that "à côté d'*ombre*... *ténèbres* se fonce peu," actually places the two words "next to" one another (they are separated only by six lines). It is, presumably, the recalcitrant terms which stand most in need of relegitimation. Perhaps this is also why Mallarmé so often places proper nouns at the rhyme: "tutélaire / Baudelaire," "haleine / Verlaine," "altier / Gautier," "tu vis / Puvis," "jusqu'au / Vasco," and the rather daring "que puisse l'air / Whistler," to cite a few examples. (See *Le Tombeau de Charles Baudelaire, Tombeau, Toast funèbre, Toute aurore..., Au seul souci de voyager,* and *Billet à Whistler,* respectively). It is as though Mallarméan poetry gradually extends the perimeter of its magic circle in order to draw more and more of the recalcitrantly unruly world within its scope.

75. "... un mot total, neuf, étranger à la langue et comme incantatoire ... niant, d'un trait souverain, le hasard demeuré aux termes" ("Crise de vers," *OC* II:213).

76. "... le hasard vaincu mot par mot, indéfectiblement le blanc revient, tout à l'heure gratuit, certain maintenant, pour conclure que rien au delà et authentiquer le silence" ("Le Mystère dans les lettres," Mallarmé, *OC* II:234). (I take "rien au delà" to mean "nothing further remains to be said.") Compare also *Crise de vers* (Mallarmé, *OC* II:208): "Qu'une moyenne étendue de mots, sous la compréhension du regard, se range en traits définitifs, avec quoi le silence." ("Let an average expanse of words, under the comprehension of the gaze, organize themselves into definitive lines, with which—silence.") "Mimique," similarly, begins "Le silence, seul luxe après les rimes ..." (Mallarmé, *OC* II:178).

77. Cf. Paul Bénichou: "Il faut du réel ... pour figurer le néant." *Selon Mallarmé* (Paris: Gallimard, 1995), 146.

78. "Les choses existent, nous n'avons pas à les créer; nous n'avons qu'à en saisir les rapports; et ce sont les fils de ces rapports qui forment les vers et les orchestres" ("Sur l'évolution littéraire," Mallarmé, *OC* II: 702). In *Crise de vers,* Mallarmé similarly defines the ideal poetic "Music" as "the set of connections existing in everything" ("l'ensemble des rapports existant dans tout," Mallarmé, *OC* II:212). And Mallarmé instructs Edmund Gosse to "use 'Music' in the Greek sense, at bottom signifying Idea, or rhythm among the connections" ("Employez Musique dans le sens grec, au fond signifiant l'Idée ou rythme entre les rapports": Mallarmé, *Correspondance,* VI:26). For *rapports,* cf. Dan Edel-

stein, "Moving through the Looking-Glass: Deleuzian Reflections on the Series in Mallarmé," *L'esprit créateur* 40 (2000): 55–57.

79. In his eulogy for Villiers, Mallarmé defines the act of writing, rather paradoxically, as a "duty to recreate everything . . . in order to affirm that one is indeed where one should be" ("quelque devoir de tout recréer, . . . pour avérer qu'on est bien là où l'on doit être," Mallarmé, *OC* II:23). We do not need to be transported to another world; we just need to "recreate" this one, by imagining connections between everything and everything else. In a sense, perhaps, this is akin to Nietzsche's *amor fati*.

80. "En se laissant aller à le murmurer plusieurs fois on éprouve une sensation assez cabalistique." (The 1868 letter to Cazalis, Mallarmé, *Correspondance*, I:278.)

81. For the literary reading experience as itself sublime, cf. Kirk Pillow, *Sublime Understanding* (Cambridge, MA: MIT Press, 2001), esp. ch. 3.

82. Compare also the famous line from *Crise de vers* (Mallarmé, *OC* II:213): "Je dis: une fleur! et, hors de l'oubli où ma voix relègue aucun contour, en tant que quelque chose d'autre que les calices sus, musicalement se lève, idée même et suave, l'absente de tous bouquets." ("I say: a flower! and, from the oblivion to which my voice banishes all contours, as something other than the known calyces, there musically arises—the idea itself, delicate—the one [flower] missing from all bouquets.")

83. Further remarks on lucid self-delusion in Mallarmé may be found in my "Music, Letters, Truth and Lies: 'L'après-Midi d'un Faune' as an Ars Poetica" (*Yearbook of Comparative and General Literature* (1994): 57–69).

84. Some, like Noulet, have wanted to see the ptyx as a seashell, perhaps on the questionable assumption that its "inanité sonore" means "emptiness that produces noise." Many, like Nelson (52), now prefer the idea that *ptyx* means "fold." The "fold" reading seems to me to be vitiated by the fact that the 1868 version characterizes the ptyx as a "vessel" (*vaisseau*, l. 6).

85. "Quel pivot . . . à l'intelligibilité? Il faut une garantie—La Syntaxe." (Mallarmé, *OC* II:232–33)

86. Robb, *Unlocking Mallarmé*, 63 (citing Ross G. Arthur). Davies, *Mallarmé* (117) already rules out this reading, on the same grounds.

87. Cf. Davies, *Mallarmé*, 118. It might be objected that "nul ptyx" explains "salon vide," rather than "pas de cinéraire amphore." My reading is, however, given some support by the 1868 version, which speaks of a "*noir* salon," not a "salon *vide*." Here in the 1868 version, the absence of a ptyx cannot possibly explain why the room would be dark; it must, therefore, explain the absence of funereal urns mentioned slightly earlier.

88. Reportedly, Mallarmé explained to Leconte de Lisle that "le ptyx est insolite, puisqu'il n'y en a pas; il résonne bien, puisqu'il rime; et ce n'en est pas moins un vaisseau d'inanité, puisqu'il n'a jamais existé!" ("the ptyx is unusual, since there aren't any; it is resonant, since it rhymes; and it is nevertheless a vessel of inanity, since it never existed!") (Adolphe Racot, "Les Panassiens," *Le Gaulois*, 26 March 1875; qtd. in Robb, *Unlocking Mallarmé*, 63). If true, this would

suggest that Mallarmé understood the sonority as attaching to the *word,* not to the *object.* No need, then, for seashells.

89. In *L'Azur,* the poet seeks to escape from the lure of transcendence (figured as the blue of the sky) only to conclude, famously, "Où fuir dans la révolte inutile et perverse? / *Je suis hanté.* L'Azur! l'Azur! l'Azur! l'Azur!" The "certes, n'est que ce qui est" line comes from "La Musique et les Lettres," Mallarmé, *OC* II:67.

90. "Oui, *je le sais,* nous ne sommes que de vaines formes de la matière, mais bien sublimes pour avoir inventé Dieu et notre âme. Si sublimes, mon ami! que je veux me donner ce spectacle de la matière, ayant conscience d'être et, cependant, s'élançant forcenément dans le Rêve qu'elle sait n'être pas, chantant l'Ame et toutes ces divines impressions pareilles qui se sont amassées en nous depuis les premiers âges et proclamant, devant le Rien qui est la vérité, ces glorieux mensonges!" (Letter to Cazalis, 1866, Mallarmé, *Correspondance,* I:207–8; my emphasis in the English.) On glorious lies, cf. Marshall C. Olds, "Mallarmé's 'Glorieux Mensonge,'" *West Virginia University Philological Papers* 30 (1984): 1–9, passim.

91. For this, one should compare Mallarmé's *L'après-midi d'un faune.* On waking up in the heat of the afternoon, Mallarmé's faun finds that the nymphs he has apparently embraced were in fact mere figments of his imagination. Yet the faun is as much thrilled as disappointed at the idea that he is responsible for their existence. "Réfléchissons . . . / ou si les femmes dont tu gloses / Figurent un souhait de tes sens fabuleux!" (ll.8–9; note the excited exclamation mark). The faun takes a fierce and defensive pride (ll. 14–22) in the purely internal nature of his creation, in the fact that the scene is generated not by inspiration from above but by the exhalation of an artificial breath, "Le visible et serein souffle artificiel / De l'inspiration" (ll. 21–22). For a more extensive treatment, see my "Music, Letters, Truth and Lies."

92. This restriction of the definition is important, since it is entirely possible for a work to point to itself *without* undermining the referential illusion. Indeed in some cases, self-conscious interludes are positively supposed to *strengthen* the audience's suspension of disbelief (consider, for example, the prologue to Shakespeare's *Henry V*). Mentions of fictional characters from works by other authors can have a similar effect. See Robert Alter, *Partial Magic* (Berkeley: University of California Press, 1975) 109; Dällenbach, *Mirror,* 115.

93. James Joyce, *Ulysses* (New York: Vintage, 1990), 769; Marcel Proust, *Time Regained,* trans. Andreas Mayor, Terence Kilmartin, and D. J. Enright (New York: Modern Library, 1993), 225; André Gide, *Paludes* (Paris: NRF, 1920 [1895]), 12; Samuel Beckett, *Endgame* (New York: Grove, 1958), 78; Eugène Ionesco, *Le roi se meurt* (Paris: Gallimard, 1963), 22 ("tu vas mourir à la fin du spectacle"); Bertolt Brecht, *Brecht on Theatre,* trans. John Willett (New York: Hill and Wang, 1964), 136–40; Italo Calvino, *If on a winter's night a traveler* (New York: Harvest, 1982), 3.

94. See Alter, ch. 4 and D. C. Muecke, *The Compass of Irony* (London: Methuen, 1967), 183–85 (esp. 185, where Muecke points out that even Friedrich

Schlegel's own *Lucinde* does not really fit the bill, and neither, in spite of Schlegel's claims, does Goethe's *Wilhelm Meister*). There are of course some legitimately reflexive premodernist fictions, such as Henry Fielding's *Tom Jones* (1749), Lawrence Sterne's *Tristram Shandy* (1760–67), and Denis Diderot's *Jacques le fataliste* (1765–83); other examples could no doubt be adduced too. But the definition of genuine reflexivity (or "Romantic irony") should not be overstretched. I do not think it should be applied, for example, to pure parodies, since here the oscillation between credulity and skepticism is lacking (cf. Alastair Fowler, *Kinds of Literature: An Introduction to the Theory of Genres and Modes*, Cambridge, MA: Harvard University Press, 1982, 126). The criterion of fundamental seriousness (cf. Lloyd Bishop, *Romantic Irony in French Literature from Diderot to Beckett*, Nashville: Vanderbilt University Press, 1989, 1) might pose problems for works like Byron's *Don Juan* (1821), and for some of the works cited by Nicholas Paige in this volume. Further, it is not clear that Stendhal and Thackeray, with their gentle mockery, poke major holes in the referential fabric (see Alter, *Partial Magic*, 116, 126; René Bourgeois, "Modes of Romantic Irony in Nineteenth-Century France," trans. Cecilia Grenier, in *Romantic Irony*, ed. Frederick Garber, Budapest: Akadémiai Kiadó, 1988, 106). Finally, one should I think rule out (*contra* Bourgeois, "Modes of Romantic Irony," 102–4) those texts that merely start or end with a bursting of the fictional bubble. As Alter argues, a properly reflexive text is one which "*systematically* flaunts its own condition of artifice" (x, my emphasis); it must be, in Friedrich Schlegel's terms, a "permanente Parekbase" ("permanent parabasis"), an "incessant self-parody," filled with irony "durchgängig im Ganzen und überall" ("thoroughly, entirely, and ubiquitously"), "a wonderfully perennial alternation of enthusiasm and irony, which lives even in the smallest part of the whole." See Friedrich Schlegel, "Philosophische Lehrjahre," *Philosophische Fragmente: Kritische F. Schlegels Ausgabe*, vol. 18, ed. E. Behler (Paderborn: Schöningh, 1958), 85, and *Lucinde and the Fragments*, trans. Peter Firchow (Minneapolis: University of Minnesota Press, 1971), 42, 108, and Bishop, *Romantic Irony*, 8. On these grounds, Aristophanes himself is to be excluded from the reflexive canon, and so perhaps is Cervantes, given that the oft-mentioned *Don Quixote* (1605–15) is only briefly self-undermining.

95. For the idea of the "shifting dominant" in literary history, see Roman Jakobson, "The Dominant," trans. Herbert Eagle, *Readings in Russian Poetics*, ed. Ladislav Matejka and Krystyna Pomorska (Cambridge, MA: MIT Press, 1971), 85. By 1925, it was possible for Ortega y Gasset to "doubt that any young person of our time can be impressed by a poem, a painting, or a piece of music that is not flavored with a dash of irony." Fredric Jameson, in 1984, went even further. For him, it is "a commonplace that the very thrust of literary modernism . . . has had as one significant structuralist consequence the transformation of the cultural text into an *auto-referential* discourse, whose content is a perpetual interrogation of its own conditions of possibility." José Ortega y Gasset, "The Dehumanization of Art," *The Dehumanization of Art and Other Essays on Art, Culture, and Literature*, trans. Helene Weyl (Princeton, NJ: Princeton

University Press, 1968 [1925]), 48. Fredric Jameson, "Progress Versus Utopia: Or, Can We Imagine the Future?" *Art after Modernism: Rethinking Representation*, ed. Brian Wallis (New York: New Museum of Contemporary Art, 1984), 250.

According to Michael Saler ("Clap if You Believe," 2003: 621), reflexivity became a staple of *mass* cultural productions too, starting at the turn of the twentieth century. Saler (2005) is also invaluable on the subject of what he calls the "ironic imagination." His position and mine differ only, it seems to me, on the role of literary reflexivity. See Michael Saler, "At Home in the Ironic Imagination: The Rational Vernacular and Spectacular Texts," in *Vernacular Modernism*, ed. Maiken Umbach and Bernard Huppauff (Stanford: Stanford University Press, 2005), 65.

96. For this position, see e.g. Muecke, *Compass*, 189 and Hans Ulrich Gumbrecht, "Stendhals nervöser Ernst," *Sprachen der Ironie/ Sprachen des Ernstes*, ed. Karl Heinz Bohrer (Frankfurt: Suhrkamp, 2000), 209–10. Gumbrecht draws on Niklas Luhmann's concept of a "second-order observer."

97. Cf. Roland Barthes, "Longtemps, je me suis couché de bonne heure . . .," *The Rustle of Language*, trans. Richard Howard (New York: Hill & Wang, 1986 [1978]), 287. And Robert Penn Warren: "the poet wishes to indicate that his vision has been earned, that it can survive reference to the complexities and contradictions of experience." ("Pure and Impure Poetry," *New and Selected Essays*, New York: Random House, 1989, 26, qtd. in Bishop, *Romantic Irony*, 14). See also Umberto Eco's delightful postscript to *The Name of the Rose*: "I think of the postmodern attitude as that of a man who loves a very cultivated woman and knows he cannot say to her, 'I love you madly,' because he knows that she knows (and that she knows that he knows) that these words have already been written by Barbara Cartland. Still, there is a solution. He can say, 'As Barbara Cartland would put it, I love you madly.' At this point, having avoided false innocence, having said clearly that it is no longer possible to speak innocently, he will nevertheless have said what he wanted to say to the woman: that he loves her." Umberto Eco, *The Name of the Rose*, trans. William Weaver (San Diego, CA: Harcourt Brace, 1994), 530–31.

98. "J'enrage d'être empêtré d'une diable de philosophie que mon esprit ne peut s'empêcher d'approuver et mon coeur de démentir." (Letter to Sophie Volland, qtd. Bishop, *Romantic Irony*, 35).

99. For the general point about Romantic irony, cf. Bishop, *Romantic Irony*, 2; for Diderot's distance from his characters in *Jacques*, see Robert J. Loy, *Diderot's Determined Fatalist: A Critical Appreciation of Jacques le Fataliste* (New York: King's Crown Press, 1950), 151.

100. The first quotation is from "Über Goethes Meister" (KA 2:131), qtd. in Bishop, *Romantic Irony*, 4 (cf. Muecke, *Compass*, 200); the second is from "Philosophische Lehrjahre" (KA 18:628), qtd. in Lilian R. Furst, *Fictions of Romantic Irony* (Cambridge, MA: Harvard University Press, 1984), 28. Elsewhere, Schlegel extols "the mood that surveys everything and rises infinitely above all limitations, even above its own art, virtue, or genius" (*Lyceum*, 42). For Romantic irony as a route to freedom, see Bishop, *Romantic Irony*, 1; Lilian R.

Furst, "Romantic Irony and Narrative Stance," *Romantic Irony,* ed. Frederick Garber (Budapest: Akadémini Kindó, 1988), 293–309; Muecke, *Compass,* 198; Georg Lukács, *The Theory of the Novel,* trans. Anna Bostock, Cambridge, MA: MIT Press, 1971), 93.

101. Malcolm Bradbury and James McFarlane, "The Name and Nature of Modernism," *Modernism,* Ed. Malcolm Bradbury & James McFarlane, London: Penguin, 1976, 19–55, 25 (my emphasis).

102. Astradur Eysteinsson, *The Concept of Modernism* (Ithaca, NY: Cornell University Press, 1990) 113–14. "Self–consciousness," according to Eysteinsson, "relates to the very possibility of becoming aware of the social process of operating communication and generating meaning" (113), which is to say "becoming aware that conventionalized relations between reality and received modes of communication are by no means 'natural' and inevitable" (115).

103. Patricia Waugh, *Metafiction: The Theory and Practice of Self-Conscious Fiction.* London: Methuen, 1984, 2, 18–19. Eugene Lunn is more nuanced: "The modernist work often willfully reveals its own reality as a construction or artifice, which may take the form of an hermetic and aristocratic mystique of creativity (as in much early symbolism); visual or linguistic distortion to convey intense states of mind (strongest in expressionism); or suggestions that the wider social world is built and rebuilt by human beings and not 'given' and unalterable (as in Bauhaus architecture or constructivist theatre)." Eugene Lunn, *Marxism and Modernism* (Berkeley: University of California Press, 1982), 35. The addition of the adjective "social" is particularly important.

Compare also Charles Russell, in whose view the postmodernist text or artwork "points to itself as a particular expression of a specific meaning system, as a construct that explicitly *says something* about the process of creating meaning" (my emphasis); Michael Bell, who writes that "the pervasive concern with the construction of meaning helps explain the emphasis in all the modernist arts on the nature of their own medium"; and Christian Quendler, who suggests that in postmodernist metafiction, "the critical self-exposure of fiction correlates on to a critique of established conception of reality." Charles Russell, The Context of the Concept," in *Romanticism, Modernism, Postmodernism,* ed. Harry R. Garvin (Lewisburg, PA: Bucknell University Press, 1980), 183; Michael Bell, "The Metaphysics of Modernism," *The Cambridge Companion to Modernism,* ed. Michael Levenson (Cambridge: Cambridge University Press, 1999), 16; Christian Quendler, *From Romantic Irony to Postmodernist Metafiction,* Frankfurt: Peter Lang, 2001, 160.

104. This is Jorge Luis Borges's explanation of the *mise en abyme* effects in Shakespeare and Cervantes. "Why does it disturb us that Don Quixote be a reader of the *Quixote* and Hamlet a spectator of *Hamlet*? I believe I have found the reason: these inversions suggest that if the characters of a fictional work can be readers or spectators, we, its readers or spectators, can be fictitious." See Jorge Luis Borges, *Labyrinths: Selected Stories and Other Writings,* ed & trans. Donald A. Yates and James E. Irby (New York: New Directions, 1962), 196. Yet it should be remembered that the same Borges elsewhere admits that

skepticism is just a convenient fantasy: denying the world and denying the self are, he writes, "apparent desperations and secret consolations." Our destiny "is not frightful by being unreal; it is frightful because it is irreversible and iron-clad . . . The world, unfortunately, is real; I, unfortunately, am Borges." Ibid., 233–34.

105. I am grateful to Dan Edelstein, Michael Saler, and Angela Sebastiana for their suggestions and inspiration.

7. WALZ: THE ROCAMBOLESQUE

1. Max Weber, "Science as a Vocation," in *From Max Weber: Essays in Sociology*, ed. and trans. H. H. Gerth and C. Wright Mills (Oxford: Oxford University Press, 1946), 155.

2. Susan Buck-Morss, *The Dialectics of Seeing: Walter Benjamin and the Arcades Project* (Cambridge, MA: The MIT Press, 1989), 253.

3. Ibid., 254.

4. "Rocambolesque," *Larousse du XXe siècle* (Paris: Librairie Larousse, 1930). All translations from French throughout the article are those of the author.

5. Jean-Luc Buard, "Pourquoi il faillait appeler notre bulletin *Le Rocambole*," *Le Rocambole* 1 (Spring 1997), 9.

6. Charles Grivel, "Le retournement parodique des discours à leurres constants," in *Dire la parodie: colloque de Cerisy*, eds. Clive Thomson and Alain Pagès (New York: P. Lang, 1989), 12–14.

7. Gabriel Thoveron, *Deux Siècles de Paralittératures: Lecture, Sociologie, Histoire* (Liège: Editions du CÉFAL, 1996), 168.

8. François Caradec, *Trésors du pastiche* (1971), quoted in Grivel, "Le retournement," 29.

9. Quoted in Jean-Luc Buard, "Les Infortunes critiques d'un Romancier, ou Charges, parodies et caricatures littéraires du Ponson du Terrail (1858–1863)," *Le Rocambole* 2 (Fall 1997): 23.

10. It is difficult to determine Ponson's actual written output, as the author recombined and republished his work in various formats. Even the *Rocambole* feuilleton is subject to divisions and recombination. *Les Drames de Paris* originally appeared under four titles: *L'Héritage mystérieux*, *Le Club des Valets de Cœur*, *Les Chevaliers du claire de lune*, and *Les Exploits de Rocambole*, with this final novel further subdivided into *Une Fille d'Espagne*, *La Mort du sauvage*, and *La Revanche de Baccarat*. *La Résurrection de Rocambole* comprises seven novels: *Le Bagne de Toulon*, *Antoinette* (a.k.a. *Les Orphelines*), *Saint-Lazare*, *L'Auberge maudite*, *La Maison de fous*, *Rédemption*, and *La Vengeance de Vasilika*. *Le Dernier mot de Rocambole* constitutes: *Les Ravageurs*, *Les Millions de la bohémienne*, *La Belle jardinière*, *La Retour de Rocambole*, and *La Vérité sur Rocambole*. The status of *Les Mystères de Londres* and *Les Démolitions de Paris* within the Rocambole series is contested. The Rocambole editions consulted for this article include: *Les Drames de Paris: Rocambole*, reissue feuilleton in 157 weekly installments (Paris:

Jules Rouff, 1883–1886); Rocambole in 3 vols, *L'Héritage mystérieux* and *Le Club des valets de cœur* (Brussels: Éditions Complexe, 1991); and *Rocambole* in 2 vols, *Les Exploits de Rocambole* and *La Résurrection de Rocambole,* Preface by Laurent Bazin (Paris: Robert Laffont, 1992).

11. The biographical details of Ponson's life are primarily drawn from Klaus-Peter Walter, "La carrière de Ponson du Terrail," *Le Rocambole* 9 (Winter 1999), 13–48.

12. See Henri-Jean Martin and Roger Chartier, eds., *L'Histoire de l'édition française,* vol. III *Les temps des éditeurs: Du Romantisme à la Belle Époque* (Paris: Promodis, 1985).

13. Facsimile of *La Vérité sur Rocambole* (1867) reproduced in René Guise, ed., *Ponson du Terrail: Éléments pour un histoire des texts* (Nancy: Centre de Recherches sur le Roman populaire, 1986), 515–87.

14. Pierre Alexis Ponson du Terrail, *L'Héritage mystérieux,* vol. 1 *Rocambole* (Brussels: Éditions Complexe, 1991), 2, 9.

15. Ibid., 66.

16. Buard, "Pourquoi," 11.

17. Régis Messac, *Le "Detective Novel" et l'influence de la pensée scientifique* (Paris: Honré Champion, 1929), 388.

18. Ponson du Terrail, *L'Héritage Mysterieux* vol. 1, 256.

19. Grivel, "Le retournement," 17.

20. Messac, *Le "Detective Novel,"* 391.

21. Increased newspaper figures for both *Le Petit Journal* and *La Petite Presse,* which carried Ponson's subsequent Rocambole feuilletons, are provided in M. L. Chabot, *Rocambole: Un roman feuilleton sous le Second Empire* (Paris: Société des Gens de Lettres, 1995), 12.

22. Ponson du Terrail, *La Résurrection de Rocambole* (Paris: Laffont, 1992), 748.

23. A complete listing of the aliases of Rocambole is presented in Didier Blonde, *Les Voleurs de visages: Sur quelques cas troublants de changements d'identité : Rocambole, Arsène Lupin, Fantômas, & Cie* (Paris: Métailié, 1992), 136–38.

24. Facsimile reproductions of both entries in Guise, *Ponson du Terrail,* D4.

25. Cited in Ponson du Terrail, "Annexes," *La Résurrection de Rocambole* (Paris: Robert Laffont, 1992), 787.

26. Ibid., 778.

27. Ibid. Italics and capitalization in the original.

28. See Elisabeth Ripoll, "La fin de Rocambole?" in *Du Côté du populaire* (Saint-Etienne: Centre interdisciplinaire d'études et de recherches sur l'expression contemporaine, 1994).

29. See Jean-Marc Lofficier and Randy Lofficier, *Shadowmen: Heroes and Villains of French Pulp Fiction* (Encino, CA: Black Coat Press, 2003).

30. Pierre Mabille, *The Mirror of the Marvelous: The Classic Surrealist Work on Myth,* preface by André Breton, trans. Jody Gladding (Rochester, VT: Inner Traditions, 1998), 14.

8. GUMBRECHT: "LOST IN FOCUSED INTENSITY"

1. Quoted from my book *In Praise of Athletic Beauty* (Boston: Harvard University Press, 2006), 50ff. This text is the source for several historical facts and, above all, the point of departure for some concepts and motifs that I try to develop on the following pages.

2. For more evidence regarding this thesis, and a list of Heidegger references, see Hans Ulrich Gumbrecht, *Production of Presence: What Meaning Cannot Convey* (Stanford: Stanford University Press, 2004), 64–78.

3. Martin Heidegger, *An Introduction to Metaphysics*, trans. Ralph Manheim (New Haven, CT: Yale University Press, 1986), 1.

4. The second chapter of *In Praise of Athletic Beauty* presents more evidence for this view.

9. PAIGE: PERMANENT RE-ENCHANTMENTS

1. Sigmund Freud, "The Uncanny," trans. Joan Riviere, *Collected Papers*, ed. Ernest Jones, vol. 4 (New York: Basic Books, 1959), 389. Coincidentally, Freud's essay on the uncanny, which I take to be a subspecies of re-enchantment, appeared in 1919, the same year Weber coined his famous phrase in "Science as a Vocation."

2. Barbara M. Benedict, *Curiosity: A Cultural History of Early Modern Inquiry* (Chicago: University of Chicago Press, 2001), 175.

3. See Jacques Rancière, *The Politics of Aesthetics: The Distribution of the Sensible*, trans. Gabriel Rockhill (London: Continuum, 2004). I will return briefly in my conclusion to Rancière's critique of the common view that maintains the aesthetic's oppositional stance (i.e., its "autonomy") with respect to historical and material reality.

4. For notable recent disenchantment narratives pointing respectively to the figures of Spinoza and Hobbes, see Jonathan Israel, *Radical Enlightenment: Philosophy and the Making of Modernity, 1650–1750* (Oxford: Oxford University Press, 2001), and Bruno Latour, *We Have Never Been Modern*, trans. Catherine Porter (Cambridge, MA: Harvard University Press, 1993). Latour, who argues that the idea of disenchantment is in fact a result of an error of perspective, is able to avoid both of the modes characterizing most discussions of the subject—modern triumphalism and wistful eulogy.

5. A mere fifteen years earlier a comet had apparently been taken a good deal more seriously as a possible sign of future upheaval, as had been the solar eclipse of 1654. For a sample assessment of the period's astrological beliefs and the inroads of the scientific spirit, see Elisabeth Labrousse, *L'Entrée de Saturne au lion (l'éclipse de soleil du 12 août 1654)* (The Hague: M. Nijhoff, 1974); a more recent look at comets as an early modern cultural phenomenon is provided in Sara Schechner Genuth, *Comets, Popular Culture, and the Birth of Modern Cosmology* (Princeton, NJ: Princeton University Press, 1997). Mary Terrall contextualizes the type of vulgarization practiced by Bayle and Fontenelle in "Natural Philosophy for Fashionable Readers," *Books and the Sciences in History*, ed. Ma-

rina Frasca-Spada and Nick Jardine (Cambridge: Cambridge University Press, 2000), 239–54.

6. Important erudite works that continue to parse the considerable religious ramifications of disenchantment include Meric Casaubon, *Of Credulity and Incredulity in Things Natural, Civil, and Divine* (1668); Jean-Baptiste Thiers, *Traité des superstitions selon l'écriture sainte* (1679); Balthasar Bekker, *De Betoverde wereld* (*The World Bewitched*, 1691); Pierre LeBrun, *Histoire critique des pratiques superstitieuses* (1702); and John Trenchard, *The Natural History of Superstition* (1709). For an overview of the religious literature on superstition, see Bernard Dompnier, "Les Hommes d'Eglise et la superstition entre XVIIe et XVIIIe siècles," *La Superstition à l'âge des lumières*, ed. Bernard Dompnier (Paris: Champion, 1998), 13–47.

7. The term *literature of roguery*—referring to narratives that take the trickster or criminal's exploits as the center of their narrative—is taken from an early study, Frank Wadleigh Chandler, *The Literature of Roguery* (Boston: Houghton Mifflin and Company, 1907). Whatever their pedigree, and whatever the skepticism they display—I am thinking of the exorcism scene of *King Lear*, as analyzed by Stephen Greenblatt (*Shakespearean Negotiations: The Circulation of Social Energy in Renaissance England* [Berkeley: University of California Press, 1988], 94–128)—impostor or trickster plots did not actually create a subject position for the skeptic or view the uncovering of error as narratively productive; they are about the power to fool, not the power of truth. For more on the subject position created by *La Devineresse*, see Nicholas Paige, "L'Affaire des poisons et l'imaginaire de l'enquête: De Molière à Thomas Corneille," *Littératures Classiques* 40 (2000): 195–208.

8. Anthony J. Cascardi, "The Critique of Subjectivity and the Re-Enchantment of the World," *Revue internationale de philosophie* 196 (1996): 252. Cascardi's main argument is that this vision has always been incomplete, that the desire for a re-enchantment of the world is embedded within Enlightenment subjectivity itself (as opposed to a reaction against it).

9. Adrien-Thomas Perdoux de Subligny, *La Fausse Clélie, histoire française, galante et comique* (Nijmegen: Regnier Smetius, 1680), 257–58; future references will be given parenthetically in the text. (All translations are my own unless otherwise indicated.) Subligny's text is little read and commented; for a quick appraisal, see Jean Serroy, *Roman et réalité: Les Histoires comiques au XVIIe siècle* (Paris: Minard, 1981), 670–79; for an argument that places the novel against the development of referential language in fiction, see Nicholas Paige, "Relearning to Read: Truth and Reference in Subligny's *La Fausse Clélie*" in *Forms of Instruction: Education, Pedagogy, and Literature in Seventeenth-Century France*, ed. Anne Birberick (Amsterdam: Rodopi, 2008), 15–51.

10. One cannot "easily change the habit, contracted in earliest childhood, of shivering at the mention of ghosts, and this in spite of all our reason" (Subligny, *La Fausse Clélie*, 260–61); Subligny might be said to scoop Malebranche (1674) and Locke (1690), who both remarked that adult fears and superstitions could be traced to maids telling children about goblins and sprites (*La Recherche de la vérité*, II, viii; *An Essay Concerning Human Understanding* II, xxxiii)—but

the explanation is fairly commonplace in these years, as its early appearance in Subligny suggests. That such fear is actually pleasurable, a notion not yet explicit in Subligny's text, will be a staple theme of early aesthetic theory, from Du Bos's *Réflexions critiques sur la poésie et sur la peinture* (1719), through Burke's *A Philosophical Enquiry into the Origin of Our Ideas of the Sublime and the Beautiful* (1757), all the way to Anna and John Aikin's popularizing essay, "On the Pleasure derived from objects of Terror" (1773). On the relation of aesthetic speculation on fear to the early gothic, see E. J. Clery, *The Rise of Supernatural Fiction, 1762–1800* (Cambridge: Cambridge University Press, 1995), 80–83.

11. Bayle, for instance, maintained for this reason that one could not deny the *possible* existence of demons (cf. *Dictionnaire historique et critique* [1697], art. "Ruggeri"). Joseph Addison, though mainly dismissive of ghosts and witchcraft, stops short of declaring them impossible, calling instead for a certain "hovering faith," "absolutely necessary in a Mind that is careful to avoid Errors and Prepossessions" (*The Spectator*, ed. Donald F. Bond, 3 vols. Oxford: Clarendon Press, 1965, 479 [July 14, 1711]; see also his issue on ghosts of July 6). For an account of "hovering faith" in English polemics about ghosts, see Clery, *Rise of the Supernatural*, 18–24. Bayle and Addison's position, perhaps necessitated by religious questions, was also typical of an empiricism that had no firm means of separating, say, the inquiry into ghosts from interest in meteorites (Mark A. Schneider, *Culture and Enchantment* [Chicago: University of Chicago Press, 1993], chap. 5), or the amazing flight of hot-air balloons from the equally amazing possibility of animal magnetism (Robert Darnton, *Mesmerism and the End of the Enlightenment in France* [Cambridge, MA: Harvard University Press, 1968]). For a later example still, see Alex Owen, *The Place of Enchantment: British Occultism and the Culture of the Modern* (Chicago: University of Chicago Press, 2004), 239: "[late nineteenth-century] occultists themselves epitomized an unbending faith in rationality worthy of any Victorian proponent of scientific rationalism." Such reasoning, by which scientific doubt is invoked to bolster the possibility of the paranormal, continues to this day; see Bruno Latour, "Why Has Critique Run Out of Steam? From Matters of Fact to Matters of Concern," *Critical Inquiry* 30 (2004): 225–48.

12. *Gabalis*, brought out by Claude Barbin, the publisher of the most sought-after authors of the period, appears to have gone through three editions in several months; it was enough in view to be mentioned in the correspondence of Madame de Sévigné and Christiaan Huygens. On *Gabalis*, see Philippe Sellier, "L'Invention d'un merveilleux: *Le Comte de Gabalis* (1670)," in *Amicitia Scriptor: Littérature, histoire des idées, philosophie. Mélanges offerts à Robert Mauzi*, ed. Annie Becq, Charles Porset, and Alain Mothu (Paris: Champion, 1998), 53–62; and Jean-Paul Sermain, *Métafictions: La Réflexivité dans la littérature d'imagination* (1670–1730) (Paris: Champion, 2002), 137–59. (My remarks in this section on Subligny, Villars, and fairy tales are largely inspired by Sermain's book, which provides a brilliant account how early French novels are united by the common function of converting purportedly true utterances into "mere fables.")

13. Terry Castle, *The Female Thermometer*, 162.

14. Clery, *Rise of the Supernatural*, esp. 13–32. For a timetable that sees full-blown skepticism only in place at the end of the nineteenth century, in the work of Wilde or James, see Theodore Ziolkowski, *Disenchanted Images: A Literary Iconology* (Princeton, NJ: Princeton University Press, 1977), 230. Critical propensity for inventing moments in which aesthetic maturity takes over from a credulous infancy is dissected in Tom Gunning's classic re-examination of what the first cinematic spectators did or did not believe about the Lumière brothers' projected train bearing down on them; see Tom Gunning, "An Aesthetic of Astonishment: Early Film and the (In)Credulous Spectator," in *Film Theory and Criticism: Introductory Readings*, ed. Leo Braudy and Marshall Cohen (New York: Oxford University Press, 1999), 818–32.

15. Voltaire, "Superstition." *Dictionnaire philosophique*, ed. Julien Benda and Raymond Naves (Paris: Garnier, 1954), 396.

16. Joseph Addison, "The Pleasures of the Imagination" (1712), *The Spectator*, ed. Donald F. Bond, vol. 3 (Oxford: Clarendon Press, 1965). On the rupture between classical poetics and modern aesthetics, see, e.g., Ernst Cassirer, *The Philosophy of the Enlightenment* (Princeton, NJ: Princeton University Press, 1951); M. H. Abrams, *The Mirror and the Lamp: Romantic Theory and the Critical Tradition* (New York: Oxford University Press, 1953); and Annie Becq, *Genèse de l'esthétique française moderne: De la raison classique à l'imagination créatrice, 1680–1814*, 2 vols. (Pisa: Pacini, 1984).

17. Timothy Reiss has called this "analytico-referential" discourse—one that "provides in its very syntax a correct *analysis* of both the rational and material orders, using elements that *refer* adequately through concepts to the true, objective nature of the world" (Timothy J. Reiss, *The Discourse of Modernism*, Ithaca, NY: Cornell University Press, 1982, 31, his emphasis). Reiss builds his account of the analytico-referential on Foucault's theory of classical representation; see Michel Foucault, *The Order of Things: An Archeology of the Human Sciences* (New York: Pantheon, 1971). For another influential account of the turn toward language as a transparent means of representing the empirical world, see Louis Marin, *La Critique du discours: Sur la "Logique de Port-Royal" et les "Pensées" de Pascal* (Paris: Minuit, 1975).

18. Raymonde Robert, *Le Conte de fées littéraire en France de la fin du XVIIe à la fin du XVIIIe siècle* (Nancy: Presses Universitaires de Nancy, 1981), 171. Robert's thesis provides a very thorough overview of French fairy-tale production. Recent work on the subject, particularly from the perspective of gender studies, has been extensive; see Lewis Carl Seifert, *Fairy Tales, Sexuality, and Gender in France, 1690–1715: Nostalgic Utopias* (Cambridge: Cambridge University Press, 1996) and Patricia Hannon, *Fabulous Identities: Women's Fairy Tales in Seventeenth-Century France* (Amsterdam: Rodopi, 1998).

19. Susan Stewart, "Notes on Distressed Genres," *Crimes of Writing: Problems in the Containment of Representation* (New York: Oxford University Press, 1991), 74. Stewart's account is valuable, but insists too heavily, I believe, on the "mournful" and ideologically retrograde character of the distressed

genre; many of her remarks on the specifically French context are also factually misleading.

20. Catherine Bernard, *Inès de Courdoue, nouvelle espagnole* (Paris: Jouvenel, 1696), 80; Catherine Durand, *Les Petits soupers de l'été de l'année 1699, ou aventures galantes, avec l'origine des fées* (Paris: Jean Musier, 1702), 158.

21. Sermain, *Métafictions*, 358; the link between fairy tales and the Modern camp is well known, but Sermain's account of the genre as metafictional reflection is particularly informative. See also Marc Fumaroli, "Les *Contes* de Perrault, ou l'éducation de la douceur," *La Diplomatie de l'esprit: De Montaigne à La Fontaine* (Paris: Hermann, 1994), 441–78, on the genre's implicit self-positioning vis-à-vis classical rhetoric. Madame D'Aulnoy is credited with the first printed French tale, which appeared embedded within her historical novel *Histoire d'Hippolyte, comte de Duglas* (1690). On the significance of embedding fairy tales within larger narratives, see Sermain, *Métafictions*, 380–92.

22. See Aurélia Gaillard, *Le Corps des statues: Le Vivant et son simulacre à l'âge classique (de Descartes à Diderot)* (Paris: Champion, 2003), 169–84. The new art of lyric tragedy, or opera, was also seen as recuperating various forms of the marvelous (ancient myth and chivalric literature, primarily) excluded from the dramatic stage; it did not, however, press superstition into ironic use, as did the comic stage. See Catherine Kintzler, *Poétique de l'opéra français, de Corneille à Rousseau* (Paris: Minèrve, 1991).

23. By calling such genres "frivolous," I do not mean to suggest they are unimportant, but that frivolity was deliberately cultivated for reasons relating to the literary field as it was then contested and configured. Exotic and fairy tales may now appear "minor" only in the sense that the space allotted them in the modern literary field is much diminished. For a detailed look at why a work as foundational and successful as Galland's no longer fulfills our criteria of readability, see Georges May, *Les Mille et une nuits d'Antoine Galland, ou, le chef-d'oeuvre invisible* (Paris: PUF, 1986).

24. Jean-Paul Sermain, *Le Singe de don Quichotte: Marivaux, Cervantes et le roman postcritique* (Oxford: Voltaire Foundation, 1999), 242. The "meta" fairy tale was only one of the ways the genre renewed itself; it survived mostly by serving as a veil for political or erotic gossip, again with an openly ironic stance; see Robert, *Le Conte de fées littéraire*, 225–82. Later Romantic variants would stress other issues, such as the authentic recovery of popular wisdom.

25. This change—the loss of imagination's status as mere mechanical relay between perception and thought (as in Malebranche and Condillac), and its incorporation within the operation of reason and scientific invention—is at least implicit in Voltaire's article ("Imagination") in the *Encyclopédie*, or in a text such as Diderot's *Rêve de d'Alembert*. (Voltaire, significantly, evokes fairy tales as emblematic of a now devalued, frivolous conception of imaginative activity.) In addition to Becq, *Genèse de l'esthétique française moderne*, see Jacques Marx, "Le Concept d'imagination au XVIIIe siècle," *Thèmes et figures du siècle des Lumières: Mélanges offerts à Roland Mortier*, ed. Raymond Trousson (Geneva: Droz, 1980), 147–59; Jean Starobinski, "Jalons pour une histoire du concept d'imagination,"

L'Oeil vivant II (Paris: Gallimard, 1970), 173–95, provides a complementary look that stresses the Neoplatonic roots of the romantic conception of the faculty.

26. Michael McKeon, *The Origins of the English Novel, 1600–1740* (Baltimore: Johns Hopkins University Press, 1987). The dialectical opposition McKeon describes between naïve empiricism and extreme skepticism might be said to underwrite the polarity I have established between referential discourse and pure fancy.

27. Catherine Gallagher, *Nobody's Story: The Vanishing Acts of Women Writers in the Marketplace, 1670–1820* (Berkeley: University of California Press, 1994), xvi.

28. These tales, through their metaleptic switching of narrative levels and codes, overtly thematize the exhaustion of the genre and of the writer himself, whose inventive wit must, "without ever resting, perform incessant acrobatics" (Jacques Cazotte, *Les Mille et une fadaises: Contes à dormir debout* [Baillons (Paris?): Chez l'Endormi, 1742], 9). Cazotte's title is one of those "ironizings" of a discourse never meant to have been taken seriously in the first place— *A Thousand and One Nights*.

29. If the text ultimately allows the reader to decide in favor of either a natural or supernatural explanation, it ceases to be, according to Todorov, properly fantastic; see Tzvetan Todorov, *The Fantastic: A Structural Approach to a Literary Genre*, trans. Richard Howard (Ithaca, NY: Cornell University Press, 1975). Todorov's emphasis on readerly hesitation, however, is vulnerable from a number of points of view; see for instance the remarks of Nancy H. Traill, *Possible Worlds of the Fantastic: The Rise of the Paranormal in Fiction* (Toronto: University of Toronto Press, 1996), 4–5, 9, and 15.

30. Jacques Cazotte, *Le Diable amoureux*, ed. Georges Décote (Paris: Gallimard, 1981), 39, 37. Future references will be included parenthetically.

31. The dream or hallucination model, which subjectivizes the supernatural, although not new (Voltaire, for instance, used it as a framing device for his faux fairy tale *Le Crocheteur borgne* [c. 1715]), largely supplants earlier trickster or materialist explanations. (The latter explain phenomena by revealing them as sensory errors—a trick of the light, for example.) The novel's undecidability is explored by Roger Cardinal, "*Le Diable amoureux* and the Pure Fantastic," *Studies in French Fiction in Honour of Vivienne Milne*, ed. Robert Gilson (London: Grant and Cutler, 1988), 67–79.

32. "Fairy-tales quite frankly adopt the animistic standpoint of the omnipotence of thoughts and wishes, and yet I cannot think of any genuine fairy-story which has anything uncanny about it" (Freud, "The Uncanny," 400); Roger Caillois, "De la féerie à la science-fiction" (1962), in *Obliques* (Paris: Gallimard, 1987), 17–48.

33. "We—or our primitive forefathers—once believed in the possibility of these things and were convinced that they really happened. Nowadays we no longer believe in them, we have *surmounted* such ways of thought; but we do not feel quite sure of our new set of beliefs, and the old ones still exist within us ready to seize upon any confirmation" (Freud, "The Uncanny," 401–2, his emphasis).

34. For an overview of intellectual and religious attitudes towards the supernatural in the course of the century, see Max Milner, *Le Diable dans la littérature française de Cazotte à Baudelaire, 1772–1861*, 2 vols. (Paris: Corti, 1960), 1:19–68; unsurprisingly, Milner concludes that belief in the devil was on a clear downward trend.

35. Clery, *Rise of Supernatural Fiction*, 41. I would emphasize, however, that apart from this unnecessary recourse to real beliefs, Clery's main point regarding the gothic is in fact very close to mine here—to wit, that a newly serious treatment of the supernatural "is the sign of an autonomous sphere of art in the process of formation" (35).

36. Here, I follow Marshall Brown, who has recently argued for a more capacious understanding of the gothic, notably by insisting on its pan-European manifestations; see Marshall Brown, *The Gothic Text* (Stanford: Stanford University Press, 2005).

37. The distressed medievalism of the well-documented "Ossian" controversy is discussed in the context of *Otranto* by Clery, *Rise of Supernatural Fiction*, 53–59. See also Arthur Johnston, *Enchanted Ground: The Study of Medieval Romance in the Eighteenth Century* (London: Athlone Press, 1964) for a detailed account of the antiquarian interest in medieval romance.

38. Horace Walpole, *The Castle of Otranto: A Gothic Story*, ed. W. S. Lewis and E. J. Clery (Oxford: Oxford University Press, 1996), 9–10.

39. The importance of tears to Walpole's brand of the gothic, as well as the comparison to Rousseau, is suggested by Clery, *Rise of Supernatural Fiction*, 79.

40. For a reading of Cazotte that is complementary to the one I offer here, see Dorothea E. Von Mücke, *The Seduction of the Occult and the Rise of the Fantastic Tale* (Stanford: Stanford University Press, 2003), who argues that the fantastic stages the pleasures and dangers of a new, identificatory mode of reading. The patent erotics of the fantastic might also be put into parallel with the roughly contemporaneous discourse on masturbation, given that the genre is essentially about the imagination's propensity to exert physiological effects through reading. See Thomas W. Laqueur, *Solitary Sex: A Cultural History of Masturbation* (New York: Zone, 2004), esp. 302–58. Finally, it remains to understand if and how the serious, gothic use of the supernatural is related to the uses it had prior to the ironic re-enchantments of the late seventeenth-century—notably in Shakespeare, where ghosts are "a figure of theater," and their inclusion a manner of objecting to those "who view the imagination as the dialectical opposite of truth" (Stephen Greenblatt, *Hamlet in Purgatory* [Princeton, NJ: Princeton University Press, 2001], 157, 164). As much as I am in sympathy with Greenblatt's main point—"that [ghosts] are good for thinking about theater's capacity to fashion realities, to call realities into question, to tell compelling stories, to puncture the illusions that these stories generate, and to salvage something on the other side of disillusionment" (200)—I find his characterizations have less historical purchase than is initially apparent, and merit a broader contextualization.

41. Hans Blumenberg, "The Concept of Reality and the Possibility of the Novel," trans. David Henry Wilson. *New Perspectives in German Literary Criticism: A Collection of Essays,* ed. Richard E. Amacher and Victor Lange (Princeton, NJ: Princeton University Press, 1979), 29. Especially since the Renaissance, literary history can be viewed as one long "flight from fiction" (the expression is William Nelson's), an endlessly renewed attempt to deny that the inventions of poets are mere lies; see William Nelson, *Fact or Fiction: The Dilemma of the Renaissance Storyteller* (Cambridge, MA: Harvard University Press, 1973). On the theoretical importance of lies to modern fictional practice, with special attention to the cases of Defoe and Stendhal, see John Vignaux Smyth, *The Habit of Lying: Sacrificial Studies in Literature, Philosophy, and Fashion Theory* (Durham, NC: Duke University Press, 2002). Finally, for a typological approach to the problem of fictionality, see the cogent synthesis of Thomas Pavel, *Fictional Worlds* (Cambridge, MA: Harvard University Press, 1986); part of what I am attempting here is a historicization of an issue whose most searching explorations have tended to be philosophical.

42. Sir Philip Sidney, *An Apology for Poetry,* in *The Critical Tradition: Classic Texts and Contemporary Trends,* ed. David H. Richter (New York: St. Martin's Press, 1989), 149.

43. Cited in McKeon, *Origins of the English Novel,* 61. (Bayle had issued a straight-faced call for a law against letting novels masquerade as history, on the grounds that posterity would become confused.)

44. See Barbara Foley, *Telling the Truth: The Theory and Practice of Documentary Fiction* (Ithaca, NY: Cornell University Press, 1986), whose valuable account has unfortunately been overlooked by most specialists of the question. Other important efforts to explain how this transitional form of "naïve empiricism" functioned include Lennard J. Davis, *Factual Fictions: The Origins of the English Novel* (New York: Columbia University Press, 1983) and Gallagher, *Nobody's Story.* Of course, modern literature can stake out claims to truth other than that of realist fiction, just as Sidney did; see Charles Altieri, "Poetics as 'Untruth': Revising Modern Claims for Literary Truths," *New Literary History* 29.2 (1998), 305–28.

45. Or, in Foley's formulation, "[b]anished from the manner of representation, . . . history resurfaces in the referent" (Foley, *Telling the Truth,* 143). It bears pointing out that well into the nineteenth century, novelists worried about the historicity of their utterances in terms that differ little from those used by their predecessors; see Claude Duchet, "L'Illusion historique: L'Enseignement des préfaces (1815–1832)," *Revue d'histoire littéraire de la France* 75.2–3 (1975) 245–67.

46. See Todorov, *The Fantastic,* 126–39; Todorov's explanation for the death of the fantastic at the end of the nineteenth century appeals to Freud's discoveries, which in rendering explicit the work of the genre make it unnecessary (160–61). Of course, the more general idea that the fantastic demands to be read through the Freudian lens of desire and repression has become a critical commonplace.

47. Castle, *The Female Thermometer,* 143.

48. Brown, *The Gothic Text*, 12.

49. Todorov, *The Fantastic*, 168. For a recent example, witness Victoria Nelson's positioning of realism as the mystifying opposite of the supernatural tradition she valorizes: "With the preexisting bias toward the empirically verifiable fact creating a powerful backward pull into realism, the resulting plethora of socially emblematic novels were attempts to organize, explain, describe, and ultimately control the events of this confusing time" (Victoria Nelson, *The Secret Life of Puppets* [Cambridge, MA: Harvard University Press, 2001], 84).

50. See, e.g., Peter Brooks, *Realist Vision* (New Haven, CT: Yale University Press, 2005); Brooks remarks but does not actually explore the apparent contradiction between this observation and his overall aim of showing how realism's project is to show us the real.

51. Catherine Gallagher and Stephen Greenblatt, "The Novel and Other Discourses of Suspended Belief," *Practicing New Historicism* (Chicago: University of Chicago Press, 2000), 168; the quote by Marx is taken from *Capital*. Gallagher and Greenblatt suggest that Marx's disenchanting gesture has its earliest roots in Hamlet's doubt.

52. Gallagher and Greenblatt, "The Novel," 169. The presence of various ghosts in Dickens is thus seen as of a piece with the realist project, as opposed to an aberrant intrusion from another mode altogether.

53. Samuel Taylor Coleridge, "Biographia Literaria," *Collected Works of Samuel Taylor Coleridge*, ed. James Engell and Walter Jackson Bate, vol. 7 (Princeton, NJ: Princeton University Press, 1983), 6–7.

54. Deborah Elise White, *Romantic Returns: Superstition, Imagination, History* (Stanford: Stanford University Press, 2000), 12.

55. See Jacques Rancière, *La Parole muette: Essai sur les contradictions de la littérature* (Paris: Hachette, 1998), in which he stresses the new rapport between thought and matter that characterizes the aesthetic regime—which includes the realist novel as much as symbolist verse.

56. Jacques Rancière, "The Aesthetic Revolution and Its Outcomes: Emplotments of Autonomy and Heteronomy," *New Left Review* 14 (2002): 135.

57. "In other words," writes Latour, "no one, absolutely no one, ever believed in anything according to the manner imagined by science. To put it more polemically, the only believers are the ones, immersed in scientific networks, who believed that the others believed *in* something" (Bruno Latour, "How to Be Iconophilic in Art, Science, and Religion?" in *Picturing Science, Producing Art*, ed. Caroline A. Jones and Peter Galison, New York: Routledge, 1998, 433).

58. See Lorraine Daston and Katherine Park, *Wonders and the Order of Nature, 1150–1750* (New York: Zone Books, 1998), who take pains to uncouple early modern wonder from its modern association with fiction. For a presentation of Renaissance theories of the literary marvelous—which, like natural wonders, also sought to produce astonishment and wonder—that makes clear that the question of credibility had little of the empirical about it, see Baxter Hathaway, *Marvels and Commonplaces: Renaissance Literary Criticism* (New York:

Random House, 1968); the medieval ground is covered by Daniel Poirion, *Le Merveilleux dans la littérature française du moyen âge* (Paris: PUF, 1982). Paul Veyne's indispensable work on the problem of belief in the classical world, however, insists on a then-nascent alternative between truth and falsehood that conflicted with other regimes of knowledge production to which such considerations were alien; see Paul Veyne, *Did the Greeks Believe in Their Myths? An Essay on the Constitutive Imagination*, trans. Paula Wissing (Chicago: University of Chicago Press, 1988). For an account of the relation between wonder and early modern literature different from the one I have been offering here, see Mary Baine Campbell, *Wonder and Science: Imagining Worlds in Early Modern Europe* (Ithaca, NY: Cornell University Press, 1999).

59. Ziolkowski, *Disenchanted Images,* 230; modernist twists on the supernatural are well examined by Nelson, *Secret Life of Puppets.*

60. Franco Moretti, "Graphs, Maps, Trees: Abstract Models for Literary History—1," *New Left Review* 24 (2003): 89.

10. TANAKA: GNOSOPHILIA

1. Norbert Bolz, *Auszug aus der entzauberten Welt* (München, Wilhelm Fink Verlag, 1989).

2. Ernst Bloch, *Geist der Utopie,* Faksimile der Ausgabe von 1918 (Frankfurt am Main: Suhrkamp Verlag, 1985), 271. This passage is retained in the revised second edition of 1923. The translation here is mine.

3. I refer here to Karen King's powerful suggestion that "There was and is no such thing as Gnosticism, if we mean by that some kind of ancient religious entity with a single origin and a distinct set of characteristics. *Gnosticism* is, rather, a term invented in the early modern period to aid in defining the boundaries of normative Christianity." Karen L. King, *What is Gnosticism?* (Cambridge, MA: The Belknap Press of Harvard University Press, 2003), 1–2. I have relied on King's work in this section for information on the modern historiography of Gnostic studies.

4. The account is provided in detail in Elaine Pagels' now classic *The Gnostic Gospels* (New York: Vintage, 1979, 1989), xiii–xxxvi.

5. Hans Jonas, *The Gnostic Religion. The Message of the Alien God and the Beginnings of Christianity,* 2nd ed. (Boston: Beacon Press, 1958, 1963), 39, 49.

6. Walter Sokel, "Between Gnosticism and Jehovah: The Dilemma in Kafka's Religious Attitude," in *South Atlantic Review* 50.1 (1985): 5.

7. Michael Pauen, *Dithyrambiker des Untergangs. Gnostizismus in Ästhetik und Philosophie der Moderne* (Berlin: Akademie Verlag, 1994), 224. See also Jonas, *Gnostic Religion,* 44.

8. Jonas, *Gnostic Religion,* 34–35.

9. I am grateful to Stanley Corngold for pointing out this distinction. See Stanley Corngold, *Lambent Traces: Franz Kafka* (Princeton, NJ: Princeton University Press, 2004), especially pp. 8–12.

10. Jonas, *Gnostic Religion,* 320ff.

11. Richard Smith, "The Modern Relevance of Gnosticism," in *The Nag Hammadi Library: The Definitive Translation of the Gnostic Scriptures Complete in One Volume*, 3rd edition, ed. James M. Robinson et al. (San Francisco: Harper Collins, 1990), 532–549, 533.

12. Rainer Maria Rilke, *Duino Elegies*, trans. C. F. MacIntyre (Berkeley: University of California Press, 1961), 3.

13. Sokel, *Between Gnosticism and Jehovah*, 10.

14. Anson Rabinbach, *In the Shadow of Catastrophe: German Intellectuals between Apocalypse and Enlightenment* (Berkeley: University of California Press, 1997), 47.

15. Ernst Bloch, *Geist der Utopie*, Bearbeitete Neuauflage der zweiten Fassung von 1923 (Frankfurt am Main: Suhrkamp Verlag, 1985), 347. Citations refer to this second edition unless otherwise noted.

16. Pauen, *Dithyrambiker des Untergangs*, 199–254.

17. Bloch, *Geist der Utopie*, 19.

18. Ibid., 48.

19. Pauen, *Dithyrambiker des Untergangs*, 222–23; Jonas, *Gnostic Religion*, 44–45.

20. For a lucid presentation of Riegl's ideas, particularly with respect to his influence on Benjamin, see Michael W. Jennings, *Dialectical Images: Walter Benjamin's Theory of Literary Criticism* (Ithaca, NY: Cornell University Press, 1987) 152–63.

21. Bloch, *Geist der Utopie*, 42.

22. Ibid., 47.

23. Alois Riegl, *Problems of Style: Foundations for a History of Ornament*, trans. Evelyn Kain (Princeton, NJ: Princeton University Press, 1992), 235, 237.

24. Bloch, *Geist der Utopie*, 104.

25. Ibid., 123.

26. Ibid., 126.

27. Ernst Bloch, *Kritische Erörterungen über Rickert und das Problem der modernen Erkenntnistheorie*. Inaugural dissertation submitted to the University of Würzburg, 1908 (Ludwigshafen am Rhein, 1909), 65.

28. Pauen, *Dithyrambiker des Untergangs*, 249.

29. Jennings, *Dialectical Images*, 159.

30. Theodor Adorno, *Über Walter Benjamin* (Frankfurt am Main: Suhrkamp, 1970), 14.

31. Here I follow Anson Rabinbach's contention that the Messianism shared by Bloch and the young Benjamin is fundamentally anti-political.

32. Walter Benjamin, *Selected Writings, Volume 1: 1913–1926*, ed. Marcus Bullock and Michael Jennings (Cambridge, MA: Harvard University Press, 1996), 62–74.

33. Walter Benjamin, *Gesammelte Briefe*, vol. II 1919–1924, eds. Christoph Gödde and Henri Lonitz (Frankfurt am Main: Suhrkamp, 1996), 45.

34. Jennings, *Dialectical Images*, 132f., 166.

35. Astrid Deuber-Mankowsky, *Der frühe Walter Benjamin und Hermann Cohen: Jüdische Werke, Kritische Philosophie, vergängliche Erfahrung* (Berlin: Verlag Vorwerk 8, 2000), 325. I have drawn here on Deuber-Mankowsky's presentation of Monism. But whereas she shows its relevance for Benjamin's early text on religion, I see it as comprising the necessary background to his entire conception of myth, particularly in the Goethe essay.

36. Michael Burleigh and Wolfgang Wippermann, *The Racial State: Germany 1933–1945* (Cambridge: Cambridge University Press, 1991), 28–31; see also Daniel Gasman, *The Scientific Origins of National Socialism: Social Darwinism in Ernst Haeckel and the German Monist League* (London: Macdonald & Co., 1971).

37. Deuber-Mankowsky, *Der frühe Walter Benjamin und Hermann Cohen,* 327f., 328n. The article was entitled "Finde dich selbst!" and appeared in the June, 1913 issue of *Der Anfang.*

38. Ernst Haeckel, *Die Welträthsel. Gemeinverständliche Studien über Monistische Philosophie* (Bonn: Verlag von Emil Strauß, 1899), 258–59.

39. Benjamin, *Selected Writings,* 315.

40. Ibid., 317.

41. Ibid., 352.

11. EDELSTEIN: THE BIRTH OF IDEOLOGY FROM THE SPIRIT OF MYTH

An early version of this essay was presented at the Department of Romance Languages and Literatures at The Johns Hopkins University: special thanks to Elena Russo and Wilda Anderson. I would also like to thank Sepp Gumbrecht, Keith Baker, and the editors of this volume for their comments.

1. Fyodor Dostoevsky, *The Adolescent* (1875), trans. Richard Pevear and Larissa Volokhonsky (New York: Knopf, 2003), 466–67; on the author's repeated use of this myth (and dream sequence), see Richard Peace, "Dostoyevsky and 'The Golden Age,'" *Dostoyevsky Studies,* 3 (1982): 61–78.

2. For a historical example of an individual drawn to a political ideology through a mythical vision, see the British historian G. D. H. Cole, who converted to socialism immediately after reading William Morris's *News From Nowhere,* a dream narrative about an arts-and-crafts golden age: "I became a socialist more than fifty years ago when I read *News from Nowhere* as a schoolboy and realised quite suddenly that William Morris had shown me the vision of a society in which it would be a fine and fortunate experience to live," *William Morris as a Socialist* (London: William Morris Society, 1960), 1.

3. On the modern concept of revolution, see Reinhart Koselleck, "Historical Criteria of the Modern Concept of Revolution," in *Futures Past: On the Semantics of Historical Time,* trans. Keith Tribe (New York: Columbia University Press, 2004). A helpful introduction to ideology can be found in Raymond Williams's *Keywords: A Vocabulary of Culture and Society* (New York: Oxford University Press, 1983), s.v. "Ideology."

4. For Clifford Geertz, see "Ideology as a Cultural System," in *The Interpretation of Cultures* (New York: Basic Books, 1973); William H. Sewell, Jr., argued

against the Marxist usage of this term in historiography: see "Ideologies and Social Revolutions: Reflections on the French Case," *Journal of Modern History* 57.1 (1985): 57–85. For the use of Geertz's definition by historians, see Robert Darnton "History and Anthropology," in *The Kiss of Lamourette: Reflections in Cultural History* (New York: Norton, 1990); Joyce Appleby, *Liberalism and Republicanism in the Historical Imagination* (Cambridge, MA: Harvard University Press, 1992); and more recently, David A. Bell, *The Cult of the Nation in France: Inventing Nationalism, 1680–1800* (Cambridge, MA: Harvard University Press, 2001).

5. Throughout this essay, I use the French term *idéologie* when referring specifically to Tracy's theory, and the English equivalent, *ideology*, when referring to the common political sense.

6. Bruce Lincoln, in *Theorizing Myth: Narrative, Ideology, and Scholarship* (Chicago: University of Chicago Press, 2000), suggests that all myths, including those still ritually recounted in traditional tribal communities, express an "ideology"; but his understanding of ideology is essentially Geertzian.

7. See, for instance, Roger Griffin, *The Nature of Fascism* (London: Routledge, 1993), 27–29.

8. For an extensive survey of political theories about myth, see Christopher G. Flood, *Political Myth* (New York: Routledge, 2002).

9. See Karl Mannheim, *Ideology and Utopia: An Introduction to the Sociology of Knowledge*, trans. Louis Wirth and Edward Shils (London: Routledge, 1966 [1929]). For an excellent discussion of Mannheim's definitions, see Ben Halpern, "'Myth' and 'Ideology' in Modern Usage," *History and Theory*, 1.2 (1961): 141–49.

10. On Nazi uses of mythology, see Nicolas Goodrick-Clarke, *The Occult Roots of Nazism: Secret Aryan Cults and Their Influence on Nazi Ideology* (New York: New York University Press, 1985); on Robert Cecil Rosenberg, *The Myth of the Master Race: Alfred Rosenberg and Nazi Ideology* (New York: Dodd, Mead & Co., 1972); Jean-Luc Nancy and Philippe Lacoue-Labarthe, "The Nazi Myth," trans. Brian Holmes, *Critical Inquiry*, 16.2 (1990): 291–312; I discuss a central Nazi myth in "Hyperborean Atlantis: Jean-Sylvain Bailly, Madame Blavatsky, and the Nazi Myth," ed. Jeffrey S. Ravel and Linda Zionkowski, *Studies in Eighteenth-Century Culture*, 35 (2006): 267–91.

11. As Corinna Treitel argues in *A Science for the Soul: Occultism and the Genesis of the German Modern* (Baltimore: The Johns Hopkins University Press, 2004), the Nazi party grew increasingly hostile toward occultist movements, going so far as to ban them in 1937 (224). Still, as Hitler's taped table talk reveals, the Führer remained enthralled by mythical fantasies well into the 1940s: see *Hitler's Secret Conversations, 1941–44*, trans. Norman Cameron and R. H. Stevens (New York: Signet Books, 1953).

12. On the Thule society's ties to the Nazi party, see Reginald Phelps, "'Before Hitler Came:' Thule Society and Germanen Order," *Journal of Modern History* 35 (1963): 245–61.

13. "We have created our myth. The myth is a faith, a passion [. . .] Our myth is the nation, our myth is the greatness of the nation! And to this myth, this greatness, which we want to translate into a total reality, we subordinate everything else"; see Benito Mussolini, "The Naples Speech," October 24, 1922, in *Fascism*, ed. and trans. Roger Griffin (New York: Oxford University Press, 1995), 44.

14. See Georges Sorel, *Reflections on Violence*, ed. Jeremy Jennings (Cambridge: Cambridge University Press, 1999), 20 and passim. On Sorel's definition of myth, see Zeev Sternhell, *The Birth of Fascist Ideology: From Cultural Rebellion to Political Revolution*, trans. David Maisel (Princeton, NJ: Princeton University Press, 1984), 56–78.

15. Alice Yaeger Kaplan, *Reproductions of Banality: Fascism, Literature, and French Intellectual Life*, foreword by Russell Berman (Minneapolis: University of Minnesota Press, 1986), 59.

16. Karl Popper, *The Open Society and Its Enemies* 2 vols. (London: Routledge & Kegan Paul, 1966 [1945]), 2:128–34.

17. See Ernst Bloch, *The Spirit of Utopia*, trans. Anthony Nassar (Stanford: Stanford University Press, 2000 [1918]); on Bloch, see Josef Pieper, *Hope and History*, trans. Richard and Clara Winston (New York: Herder, 1969).

18. Alfred de Musset, *La Confession d'un enfant du siècle* (Paris: GF, 1993 [1836]), 37; on Mallarmé, see Joshua Landy's contribution to this volume.

19. See the Prologue to Paul Verlaine, *Poèmes saturniens* (Paris: Librairie Générale Française, 1996 [1866]).

20. Hannah Arendt, *The Origins of Totalitarianism* (New York: Meridian Press, 1958), 470, 472.

21. Emmet Kennedy, *A Philosophe in the Age of Revolution: Destutt de Tracy and the Origins of "Ideology"* (Philadelphia: American Philosophical Society, 1978), 47. This book remains the classic work on Tracy. Sergio Moravia, by contrast, argued that "The signification of ideology for the *idéologues* was profoundly diverse from its meaning in the nineteenth century," *Il tramonto dell'illuminismo* (Bari: Laterza, 1968), 16.

22. On theories of language during the Enlightenment, see Sophia Rosenfeld, *A Revolution in Language: The Problem of Signs in Late Eighteenth-Century France* (Stanford: Stanford University Press, 2001).

23. Destutt de Tracy, *Eléments d'idéologie, I. Idéologie proprement dite* (Paris: Vrin, 1970 [1801]), XVI.

24. Étienne Bonnot de Condillac, *Essai sur l'origine des connoissances humaines* (Amsterdam: P. Mortier, 1746), 56. On Condillac's epistemology, see Hans Aarsleff, *From Locke to Saussure: Essays on the Study of Language and Intellectual History* (Minneapolis: University of Minnesota Press, 1982); see also Isabel Knight, *The Geometric Spirit: The Abbé de Condillac and the French Enlightenment* (New Haven, CT: Yale University Press, 1968).

25. Destutt de Tracy, *Mémoire sur la faculté de penser, De la métaphysique de Kant, et d'autres textes*, ed. Anne and Henry Deneys (Paris: Fayard, 1992), 37.

26. Destutt de Tracy, *Quels sont les moyens de fonder la morale chez un peuple?* (Paris: Agasse, an VI [1798]), 16–17.

27. *Encyclopédie, ou, Dictionnaire raisonné des sciences, des arts et des métiers,* ed. Diderot and d'Alembert (Paris: Briasson, 1751–65), 17 vols., 1:xiv. On the tension between totalizing and fragmentary epistemological models, see Robert Darnton, "The Philosophes Trim the Tree of Knowledge," in *The Great Cat Massacre and Other Episodes in French Cultural History* (New York: Basic, 1984), and Keith Baker, "Epistémologie et politique: pourquoi l'*Encyclopédie* est-elle un dictionnaire?" trans. Philippe Roger, in *'L'Encyclopédie:' du réseau au livre et du livre au réseau,* ed. Robert Morrissey and Philippe Roger (Paris: Honoré Champion, 2001). On the question of chronology and epistemology, see J. G. A. Pocock, *Barbarism and Religion, I. The Enlightenments of Edward Gibbon, 1737–1764* (Cambridge: Cambridge University Press, 1999), 169; Daniel Rosenberg, "An Eighteenth-Century Time Machine: The *Encyclopedia* of Denis Diderot," in *Postmodernism and the Enlightenment,* ed. Daniel Gordon (New York: Routledge, 2001).

28. Destutt de Tracy, *Analyse raisonnée de l'"Origine de tous les cultes ou religion universelle"* (Paris: Courcier, an XII [1804]; first edition 1799, WRITTEN IN 1795), 156, emphasis added.

29. Michel Foucault, *Les Mots et les choses* (Paris: Gallimard, 1966), 255, emphasis added.

30. In Rose Goetz's study of *idéologie, Destutt de Tracy: philosophie du langage et science de l'homme* (Geneva: Droz, 1993), she similarly argues that, "we must reject the myth according to which Tracy developed his entire theory of Ideology while in prison or soon thereafter" (58); Tracy studied Condillac while incarcerated during the Terror.

31. See Destutt de Tracy, *Eléments d'idéologie, II. Grammaire* (Paris: Vve Courcier, 1804), 18.

32. Although Tracy's first publication was a rebuttal of Burke's attack on the Revolution (*M. de Tracy à M. Burke,* 1790), in his own speeches to the assembly he often "spoke like a Burkean conservative" (Kennedy, *Philosophe in the Age of Revolution,* 21). His repressive vision is most clearly (and extremely) detailed in *Quels sont les moyens de fonder la morale chez un peuple?* which posits that to establish justice, "one must make the punishment of crimes as unavoidable as possible" (8).

33. On Maximilien Robespierre's obsessive references to his principles, see David P. Jordan, *The Revolutionary Career of Maximilien Robespierre* (New York: Free Press, 1985); Marisa Linton, "Robespierre's political principles," in *Robespierre,* ed. Colin Haydon and William Doyle (Cambridge: Cambridge University Press, 1999); and Lucien Jaume, *Le Discours jacobin et la démocratie* (Paris: Fayard, 1989), 183–87. To take a few examples, the first issue of Robespierre's *Le Défenseur de la Constitution* began with an "Exposition of my principles" (as had the first *Lettres à ses commettans*); his July 29, 1792, speech calling for the removal of the king discusses "details which will be the consequences of these principles"; and in his May 10, 1793 speech on the constitution, he claims: "from this incontestable principle, let us now draw practical consequences," *Œuvres de Maximilien Robespierre,* ed. Société des études robespierristes, 10 vols.

(1913; Ivry: Phénix éditions, 2000), 8:417, 9:498. A similar "ideological" epistemology can be detected in Louis de Saint-Just, who no doubt emulated his
senior colleague: see for instance, "We have laid down principles; we have neglected their most natural consequences," *Œuvres complètes*, ed. Michèle Duval
(Paris: Lebovici, 1984), 377.

34. See Tracy, *Analyse raisonnée de l'"Origine de tous les cultes ou religion universelle*," v–vii.

35. On Tracy and the *société de 1789*, see Kennedy, *Philosophe*, 23; on the society itself, see Keith Baker, "Politics and Social Science in Eighteenth-Century
France: The *Société de 1789*," in *French Government and Society, 1500–1850: Essays in Honor of Alfred Cobban*, ed. J. F. Bosher (London: Athlone Press, 1973)
and *Condorcet: From Natural Philosophy to Social Mathematics* (Chicago: University of Chicago Press, 1975), 156–59 and 163–66.

36. On Dupuis's life and works, see the entry in Michaud's *Biographie universelle ancienne et moderne* (Paris: Mme C. Desplaces, 1855), s.v. "Dupuis,
Charles-François" (12:51–55), and Frank Manuel, *The Eighteenth Century Confronts the Gods* (Cambridge, MA: Harvard University Press, 1959).

37. In his *Monde Primitif, analysé et comparé avec le monde moderne, considéré
dans son génie allégorique et dans les allégories auxquelles conduisit ce génie* (Paris,
1773), Antoine Court de Gébelin had argued that the original cult of humanity
was a mixture of sun and moon worshipping (1:68); see Anne-Marie Mercier-
Faivre, *Un Supplément à l'"Encyclopédie:" Le "Monde Primitif" d'Antoine Court de
Gébelin* (Paris: Champion, 1999).

38. Jean Terrasson, *Sethos, histoire, ou Vie tirée des monumens anecdotes de l'ancienne Egypte: traduite d'un manuscrit grec* (Paris: J. Guérin, 1731), 23, 270. On
this so-called "heliocentric" anthropological theory, also known as "diffusionism," see Marvin Harris, *The Rise of Anthropological Theory: A History of Theories
of Culture* (New York: Crowell, 1968), 373–92; on diffusionism in Enlightenment
anthropology, see my "Hyperborean Atlantis."

39. A similar theory had in fact already been expressed by Nicolas de
Bonneville, *De l'esprit des religions* (Paris: Cercle Social, 1790).

40. On the reception of Dupuis's mythographic opus, see Manuel, *Eighteenth Century Confronts the Gods*; on Napoleon and *idéologie*, see George
Lichtheim, *The Concept of Ideology and Other Essays* (New York: Random House,
1967), 3–46.

41. In large part thanks to Max Müller, who plundered Dupuis's work. For
a history of this mythographic school, see Richard M. Dorson, "The Eclipse of
Solar Mythology," *Journal of American Folklore*, 68 (1955): 393–416.

42. Charles-François Dupuis, *Lettre sur le Dieu Soleil, adressée à MM. Les Auteurs du Journal des Sçavans; par M. Dupuis, Professeur de Rhétorique, Avocat en
Parlement, de l'Académie de Rouen* (Paris, 1780), 2.

43. Dupuis refers to Plato's allegory of the cave as the source for these
"*sages*," but his wording is more Swedenborgian than Platonic; on Swedenbor-
gianism in the late eighteenth century, see Joscelyn Godwin, *The Theosophical
Enlightenment* (Albany: State University of New York Press, 1994).

44. To borrow Terry Castle's neologism: *The Female Thermometer: Eighteenth-Century Culture and the Invention of the Uncanny* (New York: Oxford University Press, 1995), 122.

45. See for instance Shelley's *Prometheus Unbound* (notably the last act; for the French Revolution, see act I, l. 567–70) and *Epipsychidion,* with its depiction of "a God throned on a winged planet" (L.226); for Keats, see in particular *Endymion,* a myth about the moon goddess. See Douglas Bush, *Mythology and the Romantic Tradition in English Poetry* (Cambridge, MA: Harvard University Press, 1937). Dupuis's theory had been popularized by Wordsworth in *The Excursion* (ll. 687–756). On politics and the occult in early Romanticism, see Auguste Viatte, *Les Sources occultes du romantisme* (Paris: Champion, 1979), 2 vols.; Frank Bowman, *Le Christ romantique* (Geneva: Droz, 1973) and *Le Christ des barricades, 1789–1848* (Paris: Cerf, 1987); and Brian Juden, *Traditions orphiques et tendances mystiques dans le romantisme français (1800–1855)* (1971; Geneva: Slatkine Reprints, 1984).

46. Charles Fourier, for instance, had a vivid theory about how planets lived, died, and even reproduced: see his posthumous "Cosmogonie. Du clavier polyversel," published in the first tome of *La Phalange* (1845). The famous "magician" Eliphas Lévi began his writing career by publishing a series of revolutionary tracts (under his given name of Alphonse-Louis Constant): see *Eliphas Lévi, visionnaire romantique,* ed. Frank Bowman (Paris: PUF, 1969). On the intricate relations between socialism and *spiritisme,* see Nicole Edelman, *Voyantes, guérisseuses et visionnaires en France, 1785–1914* (Paris: Albin Michel, 1995).

47. See Tracy, *Mémoire* (38). The other five sections were moral, social science and legislation, political economy, history, and geography. The first class was dedicated to the physical sciences, the second to the moral and political sciences, and the third to the fine arts. For an overview of this structure, see Laurent Clauzade, *L'idéologie ou la revolution de l'analyse* (Paris: Gallimard, 1998), 326–28.

48. Tracy, *Mémoire,* 89. Or at least the five sections (out of ten) dedicated to life sciences. The gap between "physiological" and "rational" ideology would be bridged by Cabanis, Tracy's close friend and colleague in the first section of the second class, in his *Rapports du physique et du moral de l'homme* (1802), early versions of which were read at the Institute between 1796–97; on Cabanis, see Sergio Moravia, *Il pensiero degli idéologues* (Florence: Nuova Italia, 1974).

49. Kennedy, *Philosophe,* 41.

50. "What surprised him [Candide] most, and what procured him the greatest pleasure, was the palace of sciences, in which he saw a two-thousand-foot-long gallery, filled with mathematical and scientific instruments," *Candide,* in Voltaire, *Romans et contes* (Paris: Garnier-Flammarion, 1966), 219. The "engineers" and "*physiciens*" from this institution build the machine that carries Candide and Cacambo up the mountains and out of El Dorado (221).

51. Marquis de Condorcet, *Fragment sur l'Atlantide, in Esquisse d'un tableau historique,* in *Esquisse d'un tableau historique des progrès de l'esprit humain; Frag-*

ments de l'histoire de la quatrième époque; Fragment sur l'Atlantide (Paris: Bureau de la bibliothèque choisie, 1829), 383. As Keith Baker notes in *Condorcet: From Natural Philosophy to Social Mathematics* (Chicago : University of Chicago Press, 1975), 54–55, Bacon's *Atlantis* had fascinated Condorcet ever since the 1770s, when the *philosophe* suggested reorganizing the *Académie des sciences* on this model; on the *Fragment* itself, see Baker, 340–41; Frank Manuel, *The Prophets of Paris* (New York: Harper, 1965), 81–92; and Charles Coutel, "Utopie et perfectibilité: significations de l'Atlantide chez Condorcet," *in Condorcet: Homme des Lumières et de la Révolution,* ed. Anne-Marie Chouillet and Pierre Crépel (Paris: ENS, 1997).

52. For the legislative details surrounding the Institute's foundation, see Roger Hahn, *The Anatomy of a Scientific Instiution: The Paris Academy of Sciences, 1666–1803* (Berkeley: University of California Press, 1971), 286–312; see also Martin Staum, *Minerva's Message: Stabilizing the French Revolution* (Montreal: McGill-Queen's University Press, 1996).

53. On Bailly and the Atlantis myth in late eighteenth-century France, see my "Hyperborean Atlantis." Bailly, who presided over the Tennis Court Oath and became the first mayor of Paris, had also been a member of the *Société de 1789.*

54. Friedrich von Schelling, *The Ages of the World,* trans. Frederick de Wolfe Bolman, Jr. (New York: Columbia University Press, 1942), 92. On the international reception of the Institute, see Charles Gillipsie, *The Edge of Objectivity: An Essay in the History of Scientific Ideas* (Princeton, NJ: Princeton University Press, 1960), 176ff.

55. For Honoré de Balzac, see *Louis Lambert* (Paris: Gallimard, 1980), 111–12; for Victor Hugo, *Les Misérables* (Paris: Pléiade, 1951), 125; for Pierre Leroux, *Encyclopédie nouvelle,* s.v. "Culte," in *A la source perdue du socialisme français: Pierre Leroux,* ed. Bruno Viard (Paris: Desclée de Brouwer, 1997), 226.

56. On Saint-Simon's emulating relation to the *idéologues,* see Frank Manuel: "Saint-Simon was afire with an ambition to outstrip the *idéologues,* to prove the actual unity of all material and spiritual existence in a world governed by one law, one irreducible principle," *The New World of Henri Saint-Simon* (Cambridge, MA: Harvard University Press, 1956), 119. The biographical details in this paragraph are from this source.

57. Saint-Simon, *Lettres d'un habitant de Genève à ses contemporains* (n.p., n.d. [1803]), 4.

58. As Manuel points out, "the ritual prescribed in *the Lettres d'un habitant de Genève* bore more than passing resemblance to the practices of the scientists in Salomon's House in Bacon's utopia" (*New World,* 124).

59. "God spoke to me" (Saint-Simon, *Lettres,* 98); for this divine message, see ibid., 71–97.

60. This expression was launched in Saint-Simon's pamphlet, *De la réorganisation de la société européenne* (Paris: Egron, 1814), 112. The Saint-Simonians later adopted it as the epigraph for their journal, *Le Producteur;* Maxime du Camp ended the preface to his 1855 *Chants modernes* with this same call; across the Atlantic, Ralph Waldo Emerson praised it in his *Notebooks;* and at the end

of the century, Paul Signac quoted it in the subtitle of his painting, *Au temps de l'harmonie (L'âge d'or n'est pas dans le passé, il est dans l'avenir)* (1893–95).

61. On Saint-Simon's importance for the revolutionary tradition, see Manuel, *New World*. The father of modern communism, Pierre-Joseph Proudhon, revealed his debt to Saint-Simon and the *idéologues* in his remarks on the governing power of the Institute: "The science of government belongs rightfully to one of the sections of the Academy of sciences, whose perpetual secretary becomes by necessity prime minister; and since every citizen can submit a memorandum to the Academy, every citizen is a legislator," qtd. in Louis de Carné, "Publications démocratiques et communistes," *Revue des Deux Mondes* (14 September 1841): 402. Friedrich Engels expressed his (mitigated) admiration for Saint-Simon in *Socialism: Utopian and Scientific* (1880), in *The Marx-Engels Reader*. ed. Robert C. Tucker (New York: Norton, 1978), 685–90.

62. "The philosophy of the eighteenth century was critical and revolutionary, that of the nineteenth will be inventive and organizational" (qtd. Manuel, *New World*, 87).

63. On the widespread European influence of Leroux, see Jacques Viard, *Pierre Leroux et les socialistes européens* (Le Paradou: Actes Sud, 1982). Saint-Simon's encyclopedic efforts would also be perpetuated by another of his disciples, Auguste Comte, notably in his *Cours de philosophie positive.*

64. Pierre-Simon Ballanche, *Œuvres complètes* (Genève: Slatkine, 1967), 304.

65. "[We] will first retrace the course of your meditations, from the moment in which I spoke to you until that of the *rencontre* with the fruiterer in question. The larger links of the chain run thus—Chantilly, Orion, Dr. Nichols, Epicurus, Stereotomy, the street stones, the fruiterer," Edgar Allan Poe, *The Murders in the Rue Morgue*, in *Selected Tales* (London: Penguin, 1994), 124.

66. Manuel, *New World*, 119.

67. On sensationalism, see Jessica Riskin, *Science in the Age of Sensibility: The Sentimental Empiricists of the French Enlightenment* (Chicago: University of Chicago Press, 2002). D'Alembert described Condillac as "un de nos meilleurs Philosophes" (*Encyclopédie*, 1:xxxi).

68. In his critique of *Dialectic of Enlightenment* (1947), Ronald Schechter justly points out that sensationalism, rather than rationalism, was the dominant epistemology of the Enlightenment: see "Rationalizing the Enlightenment: Postmodernism and Theories of Anti-Semitism," in Gordon, ed., *Postmodernism and the Enlightenment.*

69. Darrin McMahon, *Enemies of the Enlightenment: The French Counter-Enlightenment and the Making of Modernity* (Oxford: Oxford University Press, 2001).

70. In Robert C. Tucker, ed., *The Marx-Engels Reader*, 497. In *The Holy Family* (1844), Marx and Engels had pronounced a more favorable judgment on Babouvism, and in so doing, had retraced a more accurate intellectual history of socialism: "The French Revolution brought forth *ideas* of the entire old world system. The revolutionary movement which began in 1789 in the *Cercle social*, which in the middle of its course had as its chief representatives *Leclerc* and *Roux* and which finally was temporarily defeated with *Babeuf*'s conspiracy,

brought forth the *communist* idea which *Babeuf*'s friend *Buonarotti* reintroduced into France after the Revolution of 1830. This idea, consistently developed, is the *idea of the new world system.*" Karl Marx and Friedrich Engels, *The Holy Family* (Moscow: Foreign Language Publishing, 1956), 161.

71. Sorel began to criticize Marx as "utopian" in 1897, four years after announcing his own conversion to Marxism: see Jack J. Roth, *The Cult of Violence: Sorel and the Sorelians* (Berkeley: University of California Press, 1980), 10.

72. Kaplan, *Reproductions of Banality*, 60.

73. Roth, *The Cult of Violence*, 34.

74. Sorel, *Introduction à l'économie moderne* (1902; Paris: Rivière, 1922), 390.

75. Ibid., 391.

76. Sorel, *Reflections*, 28.

77. On Sorel's pragmatism, see John Stanley, *The Sociology of Virtue: The Political and Social Theories of George Sorel* (Berkeley: University of California Press, 1981).

78. See Jean-Marie Mayeur and Madeleine Rebirioux, *The Third Republic from Its Origins to the Great War, 1871–1914*, trans. J. R. Foster (Cambridge/Paris: Cambridge University Press/Maison des sciences de l'homme, 1984).

79. The socialist deputy Alexandre Millerand joined the Waldeck-Rousseau cabinet in 1899.

80. Eduard Bernstein outlined his argument in *Die Vorraussetzungen des Sozialismus und die Aufgaben der Sozialdemokratie* (1899), translated as *The Preconditions of Socialism*, ed. and trans. Henry Tudor (Cambridge: Cambridge University Press, 1993).

81. Sorel, *Introduction,* 390.

82. For Vico, see his "Étude sur Vico," in Georges Sorel, *Le Devenir social*, 2.9 (Oct. 1896): 785–817; 2.10 (Nov. 1896): 906–41; and 2.11 (Dec. 1896): 1013–46. Sorel points to Platonic myths as an example of "social myths," in his *Introduction à l'économie moderne* (394).

83. Sorel, *La Décomposition du marxisme* (Paris: M. Rivière, 1908), 54.

84. For instance, Roger Griffin cites Sorel to back up his assertion that myths "refer to the inspirational, revolutionary power which an ideology can exert whatever its apparent rationality or practicality," *Nature of Fascism*, 28.

85. On Marx and post-revolutionary society, see notably Robert C. Tucker, *Philosophy and Myth in Karl Marx* (Cambridge: Cambridge University Press, 1961) and Melvin J. Lasky, *Utopia and Revolution* (Chicago: University of Chicago Press, 1976).

86. I analyze these features more closely in "The Modernization of Myth, from Balzac to Sorel," *Yale French Studies* 2007 (111): 32–44.

87. "[T]he world of today is very inclined to return to the opinions of the ancients and to subordinate ethics to the *smooth working* of public affairs [. . .] but this transformation [back to the status quo of antiquity] is obviously impossible when the myth of the general strike is introduced," Sorel, *Reflections* (24, emphasis added).

88. "[M]en who are participating in great social movements always picture their coming action in the form of images of battle in which their cause is

certain to triumph. I proposed to give the name of 'myths' to these constructions," Sorel, *Reflections*, 20.

89. Roberta Suzzi Valli, "The Myth of *Squadrismo* in the Fascist Regime,"
Journal of Contemporary History 35.2 (2000): 131–50.

90. The strike "awakens in the depth of the soul a sentiment of the sublime
proportionate to the conditions of a gigantic struggle," Sorel, *Reflections*, 159;
see also 205–12. For Durkheim and the sacred, see Sorel, *Reflections*, 205.

91. See notably Georges Bataille, "La structure psychologique du fascisme,"
in *La Critique Sociale*, 10 (Nov. 1933), 11 (March 1934); reprinted in *La Critique
sociale* (Paris: Découverte, 1983).

92. "I have a horror of any measure which strikes the vanquished under a
judicial disguise," Sorel, *Reflections*, 280.

93. "Apology for violence," in Ibid., Appendix II.

94. In Mussolini, *Fascism*, ed. Griffin, 44.

95. Particularly evident in France, where protest votes for non-traditional
candidates cost Lionel Jospin his place in the second round of the 2002 presidential elections.

96. See for instance Adam Werbach's "November 3rd Theses," published
online at http://www.3nov.com/theses.html [June 13, 2006].

97. See George Lakoff, *Moral Politics: How Liberals and Conservatives Think*
(Chicago: University of Chicago Press, 2002) and *Don't Think of an Elephant:
Know Your Values and Frame the Debate—The Essential Guide for Progressives*
(White River Junction, VT: Chelsea Green Publishing Company, 2004).

98. Michael Sandel, *Democracy's Discontent: America in Search of a Public Philosophy* (Cambridge: Belknap Press of Harvard University Press, 1996). The
classic statement of political liberalism is John Rawls's *A Theory of Justice* (Cambridge: Belknap Press of Harvard University Press, 1971).

99. On the historiographical debate concerning political theory in the early
American Republic, see Joyce Appleby, *Liberalism and Republicanism in the Historical Imagination* (Cambridge, MA: Harvard University Press, 1992).

100. See in particular the essays collected in Anita L. Allen and Milton C.
Regan Jr., eds., *Debating Democracy's Discontent: Essays on American Politics,
Law, and Public Philosophy*, (Oxford: Oxford University Press, 1998).

101. See, e.g., Will Kymlicka, "Liberal Egalitarianism and Civic Republicanism: Friends or Enemies?" in Allen and Regan's *Debating Democracy's Discontent*. In fact, classical republicanism emphasized the importance of a social
behavior in general (in French, *les mœurs*) alongside direct political engagement. Civic virtue pertains to the whole of the *polis*, not just such activities as
voting or running for office. On classical republicanism, see J. G. A. Pocock,
*The Machiavellian Moment: Florentine Political Thought and the Atlantic Republican
Tradition* (Princeton, NJ: Princeton University Press, 1975).

102. "America needs to hope again, to dream again, to think big, and to be
called to the best of our potential by tapping the optimism and *can-do spirit*
that is embedded in our nation's history," emphasis added; see http://www
.apolloalliance.org/about_the_alliance/ [June 13, 2006].

12. ANDERSON: NIETZSCHE ON REDEMPTION AND TRANSFIGURATION

My work on the topics treated in this essay has benefited from sustained conversations over the years with Joshua Landy, Alexander Nehamas, Katherine Preston, and Bernard Reginster. For specific comments on earlier versions, my thanks are due to them and also to Sarah Darby, Gary Hatfield, Nadeem Hussain, Paul Katsafanas, Elijah Millgram, Kristin Primus, Don Rutherford, Alison Simmons, Allen Wood, and colloquium audiences at the University of Pennsylvania, University of California–San Diego, and the Harvard Humanities Center. I got research assistance from Kristin Primus and specialized scholarly advice from H. U. Gumbrecht and Thomas McGrath. Conversations with McGrath, in particular, were indispensable in working out my thoughts on Raphael. (He is naturally not responsible for any errors that remain in my interpretation.)

1. The underemphasis I have in mind is more pronounced in the English language reception. Nietzsche's abiding concern with Christian religious ideas has received somewhat greater attention in the German language secondary literature than in the English and French commentary. For classic treatments, see Karl Jaspers, *Nietzsche and Christianity*, trans. E. B. Ashton (Chicago: H. Regnery Co., 1961 [1938]) and Eugen Biser, *'Gott ist Tot': Nietzsches Destruktion des christlichen Bewusstseins* (München: Kösel Verlag, 1962). Manfred Kaempfert offers attention to Nietzsche's own positive use of religious concepts, as well as to the critique of religion [see *Säkularisation und neue Heiligkeit: Religiöse und religionsbezogene Sprache bei Friedrich Nietzsche* (Berlin: Erich Schmidt Verlag, 1971)]. In English, the trend has been to focus on Nietzsche's condemnations of Christianity and Christian morality, without much focus on his own use of religious ideas. This is beginning to change, however; see esp. Julian Young, *Nietzsche's Philosophy of Religion* (Cambridge: Cambridge University Press, 2006) and to some extent Tyler Roberts, *Contesting Spirit: Nietzsche, Affirmation, Religion* (Princeton, NJ: Princeton University Press, 1998), as well as work in progress by Sarah Darby and others. Thanks to Babette Babich for discussion and references.

2. For Nietzsche's German, I used Friedrich Nietzsche, *Werke: Kritische Studienausgabe*, ed. G. Colli and M. Montinari (Berlin: W. de Gruyter, 1980 ff.). Nietzsche's published works are cited in the text according to the abbreviations listed below, using Nietzsche's section numbers which are the same in all editions. I consulted (and largely follow) the translations listed among the references, though I occasionally depart from them without notice, in the interest of literalness.

BT *The Birth of Tragedy*, trans. Walter Kaufmann (1872; New York: Vintage, 1966).

GS *The Gay Science*, trans. Walter Kaufmann (1882, 1887; New York: Vintage, 1974).

Z   *Thus Spoke Zarathustra*, trans. Walter Kaufmann (1883–5; New York: Viking, 1954).

BGE *Beyond Good and Evil*, trans. Walter Kaufmann (1886; New York: Vintage, 1966).

GM *On the Genealogy of Morals*, trans. Walter Kaufmann (1887; New York: Vintage, 1968).

TI   *Twilight of the Idols*, trans. Walter Kaufmann (1888; New York: Vintage, 1954).

EH   *Ecce Homo*, trans. Walter Kaufmann (1888; New York: Vintage, 1968).

3. See Bernard Reginster, *The Affirmation of Life: Nietzsche on Overcoming of Nihilism* (Cambridge, MA: Harvard University Press, 2006) for a penetrating account of Nietzsche's conception of the nature of our normative disorientation, and its relation to the problem of nihilism.

4. Such moves constitute the central rhetorical strategy of *Thus Spoke Zarathustra*, which mimics not only the conceptual repertoire, but even the tone and voice of the Bible itself. (The matter is discussed in detail by Manfred Kaempfert, *Säkularisation und neue Heiligkeit: Religiöse und religionsbezogene Sprache bei Friedrich Nietzsche* (Berlin: Erich Schmidt Verlag, 1971), 102–4, et passim). For Nietzsche, moreover, the *Zarathustra* cut to the heart of his most important concerns as a thinker. While the book can be forbidding for present-day readers, Nietzsche counted it as his greatest literary achievement: "This work stands altogether apart" (*EH* III, "Z," 6); "Nothing like this has ever been written, felt, or *suffered*" (*EH* III, "Z," 8).

5. The broader idea not only encompasses various kinds of tribulation, but also extends beyond the case of God Himself as savior to include deliverance by a kinsman or saving messiah, who has a special right and/or responsibility to restore the dispossessed. See, e.g., Lev. 25:23–6, 51f.; Lev. 27:13 f.; Num. 35:18–27; Jos. 20:3–5; Ruth 3: 13, 4:6, and Ps. 31:5, 72:14, 103:4, 119:134. These examples are drawn from a great many other relevant texts cited by Colin Brown et al., *The New International Dictionary of New Testament Theology* (Grand Rapids, MI: Zondervan, 1978), 190–95.

6. This argument is made by David Hill, *Greek Words and Hebrew Meanings: Studies in the Semantics of Soteriological Terms* (Cambridge: Cambridge University Press, 1967), 55 ff., and is discussed by Brown, 193.

7. Mk. 10:45; Matt. 20:28; cf. 1 Tim. 2:5–6.

8. For many points in this paragraph, I am indebted to Colin Brown's article on "Redemption" (in Brown et al., *New International Dictionary*, 1978, 177–223), which offers interesting discussion and references.

9. The temporal dimensions of the redemption concept receive attention in the treatment of G. Bitter (in W. Kasper et al., *Lexikon für Theologie und Kirche* [Freiburg: Herder, 1995], 799–814). For further discussion, including suggestions about the broader and continuing relevance of similar temporal features of redemption myths within recent European culture, see Hans Ulrich Gumbrecht, "'I redentori della vittoria.' Über den Ort Fiumes in der Genealogie des Faschismus," in *Der Dichter als Kommandant. D'Annunzio erobert Fiume*, eds.

Hans Ulrich Gumbrecht, Friedrich Kittler, and Bernhard Siegert (Munich: Wilhelm Fink Verlag, 1996), 83–116. Special thanks to Gumbrecht for discussion and references on this topic.

10. This unique role for the God-Man in the structure of Christian redemption receives classic expression in St. Anselm (see *Cur Deus Homo*, Bk. II, ch. vi, et passim, in *Basic Writings*). (Thanks to Kristin Primus for calling my attention to this formulation of the idea.)

11. See Nietzsche, *GM* II, 21. Thus, the unpayability of our spiritual debts dovetails nicely with the moralization of guilt as Nietzsche understands it: since our debts can never be finally paid, they are always available as a principle of conscience around which we can orient our lives. In this sense, the criticism of redemption as repayment to God is central to Nietzsche's overall argument tracing the origins of the guilt concept in *GM* II. The argument begins from the notion of bad conscience, which arises upon the formation of society when people's drive to reshape the world in their own image (= will to power) is turned inward, constrained "within the walls of society and peace" (*GM* II, 16). Bad conscience is thus treated as mere self-directed cruelty, a relatively simple, almost merely animal, drive structure. Guilt, by contrast, is a more complicated, essentially psychological formation which arises when people's feelings of being indebted to ancestors and/or gods are "pushed back into the conscience" in a process Nietzsche calls "moralization" (*GM* II, 21). Now, according to the account of conscience in *GM* II, 1–3, conscience *simpliciter* is some structure of principles through which the agent herself assumes control over herself and her drives, allowing her to take responsibility for herself. So something is "pushed back into the conscience" if it is taken up as a basic principle around which the agent organizes her practical life. It follows that bad conscience is "moralized" into guilt when our self-disciplining will to power is, first, interpreted as a punishment that contributes to repaying our indebtedness, and then, second, elevated into a central principle of conscience. The crucially distinctive feature of "moralized" guilt, therefore, is precisely the way it orients us toward a project of repayment, while simultaneously rendering final repayment impossible. This structure is exemplified in paradigmatic form by the Christian doctrine of sin and compensatory redemption.

12. Commentators have not always appreciated Nietzsche's systematic rejection of the compensation idea as such—and therewith the anti-Christian critical force that attaches to his use of the redemption concept. Ted Sadler (*Nietzsche: Truth and Redemption. Critique of the Postmodernist Nietzsche* [London: Athlone Press, 1995]) is an especially clear case in point; his failure to appreciate Nietzsche's intended *reconfiguration* of the concept leads to an interpretation of Nietzsche as a kind of quasi-Christian thinker, with (in my view) fairly far-reaching distorting effects. The details of Nietzsche's transformation of the notion so as to remove the distinctively Christian compensation idea will emerge below.

13. See Mk. 7:35, Lk. 13:12, Matt. 18:27, Dan. 4:31–4, Acts 2:24, Jn. 11:44, and by extension perhaps Lk. 9:42, Mk. 10:45–52. For references to uses of *apoluo* with the sense of "release," see Brown et al., 1978, 189.

14. See the discussion of Lazarus in the introduction to Søren Kierkegaard, *The Sickness unto Death*, trans. H. V. Hong and E. H. Hong (Princeton, NJ: Princeton University Press, 1980 [1849]), 7–8.

15. Clearly, the position being expressed in Zarathustra's "fable of madness" is best captured (at least in Nietzsche's mind) by Schopenhauer's pessimistic doctrine that the will—the underlying essence of everything, whose inevitable frustration underwrites the conclusion that the world is fundamentally unacceptable—can only be saved through a form of ascetic self-denial. Such asceticism begins as a will to nothingness, and may eventually succeed in degrading the will itself to such an extent that it really does become nothing. See Arthur Schopenhauer, *The World as Will and Representation*, trans. E. F. J. Payne (New York: Dover, 1958), vol. 1, §§ 68–71, and esp. the final pages of § 71 (pp. 410–12 in this edition).

16. Among the more notable recent developments of such a "practical" interpretation are Ivan Soll, "Reflections on Recurrence," *Nietzsche: a Collection of Critical Essays*, ed. R. Solomon (Garden City, NY: Anchor Doubleday, 1973), 322–42; Alexander Nehamas, *Nietzsche: Life as Literature* (Cambridge, MA: Harvard University Press, 1985); Maudemarie Clark, *Nietzsche on Truth and Philosophy* (Cambridge: Cambridge University Press, 1990); and Bernard Reginster, *The Affirmation of Life: Nietzsche on Overcoming of Nihilism* (Cambridge, MA: Harvard University Press, 2006); Karl Löwith made early suggestions about the practical importance of the doctrine in *Nietzsche's Philosophy of the Eternal Recurrence*, trans. J. H. Lomax (Berkeley: University of California Press, 1997 [1935]). I favor a minimal version of this broadly practical interpretation, which I can only sketch here. I explore my interpretation in some additional detail in R. Lanier Anderson, "Nietzsche on Truth, Illusion, and Redemption," *The European Journal of Philosophy* 13 (2005): 196–203.

17. This general way of thinking about the thought experiment (and also the spouse example) are due to Maudemarie Clark. She fruitfully suggests that we are meant to construe the thought of recurrence "unrealistically"—reading for its practical salience, rather than focusing on just what the metaphysics of time would have to be if everything really recurred. For discussion see Clark, *Nietzsche*, 266–70, as well as the deservedly influential surrounding chapter.

18. The basic importance of "life affirmation" in Nietzsche's thought was recognized by Clark, 159–67 and 245–86, and receives fundamental emphasis in Reginster's *Affirmation of Life*.

19. This famous passage is the penultimate section of *The Gay Science* (1st ed.). As is well known, the following section is largely identical to the first section of *Thus Spoke Zarathustra* (Nietzsche's next book). Quite obviously, the two works are meant to be read together, and this particular presentation of the Recurrence Doctrine (later advanced as Zarathustra's main teaching) at the end of *GS* gains added weight from its placement.

20. This is most obviously so where thinking about the past plays its most direct role in guiding action—viz., where our understanding of the recent developments within an ongoing process guides our efforts to shape the process

in accord with our ends. In this case, the representation of the past plays a large practical role, but the relevance of that representation to our action derives from its subordination to future oriented attitudes. By contrast, the attitudes that establish the cross-temporal identity of my present self with my various past selves are largely *theoretical* in character (e.g., memories), or else they are simply the present continuations of (or else higher order states referring to) past practical attitudes (e.g., intentions, plans), which are themselves fundamentally *future*-directed. For detailed development of the idea that future-oriented plans and their persistence in the agent are crucial to action, and also to cross-temporal identity itself, see the planning theory of agency developed by Michael Bratman, *Intention, Plans, and Practical Reason* (Cambridge, MA: Harvard University Press, 1987) and *Faces of Intention* (Cambridge: Cambridge University Press, 1999).

21. Recall "the will's ill will against time" (Nietzsche, Z II, "On Redemption," 252), which expresses frustration about that same asymmetry.

22. Temptations to such thinking are strong enough to have worked their way into conventional expressions of consolation ("Well, at least that's behind you now"; "What a relief! I'll never have to live through that again!").

23. Great significance is attributed to this differentiating feature by Reginster (*Affirmation of Life*, 222–27). He concludes that Nietzsche's recurrence doctrine goes beyond the sort of formal ideal of consistency between the agent's life and values, which many scholars (including me, in the text above) emphasize. For Reginster, the doctrine incorporates a substantive evaluative commitment that privileges impermanence and becoming over permanence. Despite my preference for a more "formalistic" account, it does seem to me that Reginster's focus on the *evaluative* significance of "becoming" for Nietzsche marks a helpful advance over the deployment of theoretical/metaphysical notions of becoming and being in the commentary tradition descended from Heidegger (*Nietzsche* [Pfullingen: Neske, 1961]). For a good indication of how misleading the theoretical focus can become, see Sadler, *Nietzsche: Truth and Redemption*, 116–73, who seriously underappreciates the challenge Nietzsche's notion of an ever-changing recurrence poses to the *value* of permanence.

24. Bernard Reginster (*Affirmation of Life*, 201–27) deserves credit for identifying the importance of the *eternality* of the imagined recurrence, and he points out that many readings have difficulty explaining it. (Why should it matter, after all, that we imagine our return *eternally*—as opposed, say, to our being willing to accept its repetition *one more time*? A person might well be willing to marry her spouse again (or even several more times), without necessarily welcoming the prospect of *infinite* repetitions, or preferring that prospect over some variety in spousal arrangements over eternity.) Reginster insists that the only way to explain the importance of eternality is to incorporate a substantive valuation of "becoming" into life affirmation. I remain unconvinced that the recurrence idea entails any such substantive valuation (though I do not deny that Nietzsche himself held such values). For now, I note simply that Nietzsche's emphasis on *eternal* recurrence *can* be explained along the lines discussed in the text, consistent with a "merely formal" interpretation of the

import of the recurrence thought experiment. Versions of an afterlife that came to an end, or else advanced to some eternal stage very different from my actual life (as in the typical Christian conception) would lose the clarifying, rationalizing power the Nietzschean assessment derives from putting my actual life imaginatively into the future.

25. That is, the attitude of affirmation itself can be understood as a form of wholehearted endorsement, and the object of that attitude is the agent's actual life. The notion of wholehearted endorsement deployed here takes its inspiration from Harry Frankfurt (see "Identification and Wholeheartedness," in *The Importance of What We Care About: Philosophical Essays* [Cambridge: Cambridge University Press, 1988] and the large literature that followed it). There are well-known difficulties about the proper characterization of the notion of wholeheartedness, and space precludes any substantial discussion of them. I can note that the recurrence idea might usefully be taken as a rough and ready practical guide for self-assessments of wholeheartedness: plausibly, an agent is wholehearted in endorsing an aspect of her life if she would joyfully affirm its eternal recurrence. I do not contend, obviously, that this affords any kind of reductive analysis of the notion of wholeheartedness, since presumably the joyful affirmation would itself be an *instance* of wholeheartedness.

26. The *locus classicus* for the development of the broad approach to the recurrence doctrine defended here is Alexander Nehamas, *Nietzsche: Life as Literature* (Cambridge, MA: Harvard University Press, 1985), 141–99, but cf. also Alexander Nehamas, "The Eternal Recurrence," *Philosophical Review* 89 (1980): 331–56 and "How One Becomes What One Is," *Philosophical Review* 92 (1983): 385–417.

27. See Anderson, "Nietzsche on Truth, Illusion, and Redemption," 200–03, 208, 209–11.

28. The value of Carter's achievements is of course not *universally* acknowledged. See Joshua Muravchik, "Our Worst Ex-President" (*Commentary*, February 2007, 17–26) for a particularly strident critical assessment—one that, indeed, veers on occasion even into the gratuitously uncharitable. I myself find Muravchik's judgment thoroughly unconvincing. Still, it was perhaps to be expected that Carter would attract renewed unsympathetic criticism in the wake of his recent book (Jimmy Carter, *Palestine: Peace Not Apartheid* (New York: Simon & Schuster, 2006), since its argument injects him again into the Israel-Palestine conflict, where partisans have long been animated by such great passion (and such short patience for opposing views).

29. For further discussion, see Anderson, "Nietzsche on Truth, Illusion, and Redemption," 203–11 (esp., 207–11).

30. Reginster, *Affirmation of Life*, 229–30, et passim.

31. The importance of this idea in Nietzsche was recognized already by Tracy Strong, *Friedrich Nietzsche and the Politics of Transfiguration* (Urbana: University of Illinois Press, 2000 [1975]). My discussion here will focus on Nietzsche's distinctive deployment of the Christian-inflected notion of *Verklärung*, but Strong rightly notes that Nietzsche also sometimes makes related use of

similar concepts of transformation less explicitly tied to the Christian home context (e.g., *Verwandlung, Umgestaltung*).

32. John Anthony McGuckin argues convincingly (via redactive critical interpretation) that a (perhaps *the*) primary significance of this event is christological; it is meant to establish the unique status of Jesus as the Son (*The Transfiguration of Christ in Scripture and Tradition. Studies in the Bible and Early Christianity*, Vol. 9 [Lewiston: Edwin Mellin Press, 1986]). The most convincing point is that Mark seems to have introduced into the textual tradition a rebuke against Peter's suggestion that the disciples build three tabernacles, one dedicated to each of Moses, Elijah, and Jesus. Mark goes out of his way to *excuse* Peter for this suggestion—"For he knew not what to say, for they were sore afraid" (Mk. 9:6)—thereby intimating that Peter failed to understand the significance of the event (presumably because he has placed Christ on the same level as the other two prophets). Immediately thereafter, God's voice announces Jesus' unique sonship, indicating that the controlling theological agenda of the episode is to separate Christ from other prophets (especially from Moses, who had also been made radiant by the Lord on a mountain) as the promised royal Son (Ps. 2:7), or beloved only Son (Gen. 22:2) sent to be the saving Messiah. This is not incompatible with the event's *also* having some symbolic significance as a foreshadowing of the Parousia, as G. H. Boobyer would prefer (*St. Mark and the Transfiguration Story* [Edinburgh: T. & T. Clark, 1942]), but McGuckin presents a compelling close reading of the text of Mark to support the primary theological importance of the christological angle.

33. It seems unlikely, for example, that when Jove assumes the form of golden rain to make love to Danae shut up in her box (begetting Perseus), there is some definite matter of the god that is preserved through the change. Even when the metamorphosis involves a recognizable change of something like an Aristotelian substantial form, it can be hard to identify something we would want to call "matter" that is conserved. For example, Daedalion is transformed from a human into a bird, but who can say whether there is identifiable matter that makes it true that the hawk really is Daedalion, who has just jumped off Mt. Parnassus in grief for his lost daughter Chione—much less that *all* the matter of Daedalion is conserved in his being as a hawk. Ovid's own suggestion is rather that there are identifiable *passions and character traits* of Daedalion in the hawk, and they, it seems, underwrite the thought that the hawk really is Daedalion (see Ovid, *Metamorphoses*, trans. Michael Simpson [Amherst: University of Massachusetts Press, 1986], XI, 260–345). In other cases, other factors underwrite the identity judgment.

34. Ovid emphasizes this aspect of his conception of metamorphosis, and has the voice of Pythagoras explain it through an analogy to wax, which remains the same substance through the many different shapes it can take on. See Ovid, *Metamorphoses*, XV, 171–75, and more generally the surrounding speech.

35. Ovid, *Metamorphoses*, I, 1. I quote Ovid in the prose translation of Michael Simpson, *The Metamorphoses of Ovid* (Amherst: University of

Massachusetts Press, 2001). I have also consulted the Melville verse translation (Ovid, *Metamorphoses*, trans. A. D. Melville [Oxford: Oxford University Press, 1986]).

36. Gods, humans, and things are transformed, among other reasons, for sex (too many times to list); for revenge (Minerva makes Arachne into a spider [VI, 133 ff.], and Diana turns Acteon into a stag hunted by his own hounds [III, 195ff.]); out of pity (Alcyone and Ceyx turned into birds [XI, 725 ff.]); out of grief (Venus transforms Adonis [X, 732–39], and Hyrie cries herself into a lake [VII, 365 ff.]); or out of rage (Cycnus becomes a swan [VII, 365 ff.]); to punish mortals (Hippomenes and Atalanta [X, 638 ff.)] and Midas [XI, 100 ff.]); or to reward them (apotheosis of Aeneas [XIV, 580 ff.], Pygmalion [X, 265 ff.]); to escape a god (Daphne flees Apollo [I, 532 ff.]); or to embrace a god (Peleus captures Thetis and begets Achilles [XI, 221 ff.]); to bring mortals together (Iphis changed into a man so as to wed Ianthe [IX, 667–797], and Hippomenes and Atalanta again); or keep them apart (Bacchus gets Anius's daughters away from Agamemnon by turning them into doves [XIII, 645–74]); and so on, and on.

37. Kaempfert (*Säkularisation*, 1971, 486) also appreciates this point. For further characterization of the distinctively Christian conception of transfiguration (and the Christian appropriation of the metamorphosis concept), see W. L. Liefeld, "Transfigure," 1978 (in Brown et al. *New International Dictionary*, 1978, 861–64), Johannes Behm ("Metamorphose," in *Theological Dictionary of the New Testament*, eds. Gerhard Friedrich and Gerhard Kittel, trans. G. W. Bromley [Grand Rapids, MI: Eerdmans Publishing Co., 1968], 755–9), and Nützel et al., "Verklärung Jesu," in W. Kasper et al., *Lexikon für Theologie und Kirche* (Freiburg: Herder, 1995), 678–80, as well as the work of McGuckin (*Transfiguration*, 1986) and Boobyer (*St. Mark*, 1942), cited above.

38. This is quite clear from a quick survey of his published uses of "verklären" and derivatives: see Nietzsche, *GS* P, 3–4, and 78; *BGE* 28, 61, 187, 188, 207, 224, 229, 255, and 269; *GM* II, 19 and III, 8; *TI* IX, 10. In almost all these passages, Nietzsche seems to have artistic glorification in mind as at least one possible example of what he has in mind, and in some instances (*GS* 78, *GM* III, 8) it is the only salient, or else the controlling, case, in light of which any other kind of transfiguration must be understood.

39. Raphael's masterpiece was initially commissioned as an altarpiece for the cathedral at Narbonne by Cardinal Guilio de Medici, but it was never taken to France. It was given first to the church of San Pietro in Montorio—see John Shearman, *Raphael in Early Modern Sources (1483–1602)*. (New Haven, CT: Yale University Press, 2003), I, 764—and eventually went to the Vatican.

40. Nietzsche here follows the famous reaction of Goethe (in the *Italian Journey*), who rejected the eighteenth-century critical consensus against the painting as an objectionable violation of the unities of space and time. See Jürg Meyer zur Capellen, *Raphael: a Critical Catalogue of His Paintings*, trans. Stefan Polter (Landshut: Arcos, 2005), II.198. and Konrad Oberhuber, *Raphael: the Paintings* (Munich: Prestel, 1999 [1983]), 225.

41. For example, Nietzsche's suggestion about the relation between the parts of the image has clearly influenced the interpretation of Oberhuber, *Raphael: the Paintings*, 225–29, esp. 229.

42. For a helpful digest of the reception history, see Meyer zur Capellen, *Raphael: a Critical Catalogue*, II.198–200.

43. Jacob Burckhardt, *The Altarpiece in Renaissance Italy*, ed. and trans. P. Humfrey (Oxford: Phaidon, 1988 [1898]), 185.

44. Notably Marcia Hall, *Color and Meaning: Practice and Theory in Renaissance Painting* (Cambridge: Cambridge University Press, 1992), 131–36, and Oberhuber, *Raphael: the Paintings*, 225–29.

45. On this point, see Oberhuber, *Raphael: the Paintings*, 225, Leopold Ettlinger and Helen S. Ettlinger, *Raphael* (Oxford: Phaidon, 1987), 224, and Meyer zur Capellen, *Raphael: a Critical Catalogue*, II.198.

46. For example, by Ettlinger and Ettlinger, *Raphael*, 224, and by Kathleen Weil-Garris Posner, *Leonardo and Central Italian Art: 1515–1550* (New York: New York University Press, 1974), 45ff.

47. See Meyer zur Capellen, *Raphael: a Critical Catalogue*, 198–203. The competition was set up when Cardinal Guilio (perhaps through the influence of Michelangelo) issued a second commission for a large format altarpiece to Sebastiano, also for the cathedral at Narbonne, where he was preparing to take up the See (see Shearman, *Raphael in Early Modern Sources*, 280–81, 352–53; cf. also 847–48). That commission resulted in Sebastiano's *Raising of Lazarus*. Sebastiano's theme offered the chance for a scene comprising many figures, with substantial occasion for dramatic artistic and coloristic effects. Given the importance of the competition—which pitted Raphael not only against the up-and-coming Sebastiano, but also against his champion and collaborator Michelangelo, who provided ideas for the design of Sebastiano's *Lazarus*—Raphael would naturally have sought to handle the *Transfiguration* so as to afford similar dramatic opportunities. For additional details on the artistic significance of the competition, see Costanza Barbieri, "The Competition between Raphael and Michelangelo and Sebastiano's Role in It," in *The Cambridge Companion to Raphael*, ed. Marcia Hall (Cambridge: Cambridge University Press, 2005), 141–64, who shows persuasively how the competition came to embody not only the debate over the pre-eminence of Raphael or Michelangelo as master artists, but also the broader *paragone* about the relative importance of design versus color within painting, and by extension, about the relative standing of sculpture and painting within the hierarchy of arts.

48. It is possible to see a rift in time between the two as well, as the eighteenth-century reception seems to have done, but this is by no means necessary, and

as I argue below, the strong visual *suggestion* of the composition is an inference to the simultaneity of the two scenes. This departs in an interesting way from the presentation of the Gospels, contra Meyer zur Capellen, *Raphael: A critical Catalogue*, II.200.

49. Marcia Hall, *Color and Meaning: Practice and Theory in Renaissance Painting* (Cambridge: Cambridge University Press, 2005), 131–36.

50. For further discussion of these characteristic coloristic modes themselves, and their significance within Italian painting of the period, see the fascinating treatment in Hall, *Color and Meaning*, 92–148.

51. Ettlinger and Ettlinger, *Raphael*, 224–26.

52. This is obvious from the fact that on the way down from the mountain, Christ enjoins Peter, James, and John to share nothing of what they have seen with anyone else (Matt. 17:9). Such an injunction would make no sense if the other disciples (and maybe even the party with the boy) had already seen or knew about the Transfiguration.

53. This is not to deny that the pointing Apostles refer *us beholders* visually to the glorified Christ and his significance for redemption. That is surely true, and crucial to the unity of the composition. But it is another thing altogether to conclude that the painting depicts the disciples themselves as faithful.

A different aspect of the Ettlingers' interpretation (*Raphael*, 225–26) of the painting's religious import is better supported. As they note, Raphael was at work on the painting in 1518–20, when his patrons would have been maximally concerned to reinforce the authority of faith—especially faith in the Church, and in papal legitimacy inherited from Peter—in the aftermath of Luther's Ninety-five Theses (1517). Such concerns explain the central role of the figure of Peter in the grouping on the mountain, a feature that is even more pronounced in the early study for the work identified by Oberhuber (*Raphael: the Paintings*, 223, 228) which depicts only the Transfiguration event itself. The interpretation (anticipated in some respects by Oberhuber (*Raphael: the Paintings*, 226–28) is sealed by the inscription Cardinal Giulio placed on the frame when the painting was finally placed (not in Narbonne, but) in the San *Pietro in Montorio*: "Blessed Peter, Prince of the Apostles" (see Shearman, *Raphael in Early Modern Sources*, 764–65). Still, Raphael's responsiveness to his patron's interest in highlighting the importance of Peter does not show that the *other* Apostles confronting the boy are depicted in a moment of *faith* (even in Christ, much less in Peter's special authority)—to the contrary! (Thanks to Thomas McGrath for discussion.)

It is an irony worth noting, finally, that in the oldest Gospel version of the Transfiguration event, Mark goes out of his way to *rebuke* Peter for failing to understand the significance of the event. (See McGuckin *Transfiguration* and note 32, above.)

54. See A. P. Oppé, *Raphael*, ed. C. Mitchell (New York: Praeger, 1970 [1909]) and Carlo Pedretti, *Raphael: His Life and Work in the Splendors of the Italian Renaissance* (Florence: Giunti, 1989).

55. Also noted by Meyer zur Capellen, *Raphael: a Critical Catalogue*, II, 195.

56. See Ibid., II.198, for discussion.

57. The circumstances described in note 47, above, set up the competition, which quickly became heated, as the letters from Sebastiano to Michelangelo show (see Shearman, *Raphael in Early Modern Sources*, 352–54). The competitive atmosphere supports the suggestion that Raphael's return to the twisting female figure (deployed earlier in his *Expulsion of Heliodorus*) is now meant to be seen *also* as an effort to surpass Michelangelo's treatment, in the Libyan Sibyl. (The Ettlingers [*Raphael*, 226] also note the importance of the *paragone* here, and suggest a reference to the *Delphic* Sibyl, but I can see no visual connection in that case, so perhaps the Libyan Sibyl was what they intended. Meyer zur Capellen [*Raphael: a Critical Catalogue*, II.202–3] and Barbieri ["The Competition"] likewise make useful points about the influence of the Sebastiano competition on Raphael's conception of the painting's composition.)

58. Special thanks to Thomas McGrath for helping me to analyze, clarify, and sort out the different claims I mean to make in this part of the paper.

59. Recent art has taught us to see such beautifying effects as inessential, and indeed often absent. Even in non-beautifying cases, however, transfiguring art does still place its subject into a context of significance that establishes a frame of reference with powerful effects on the meaning and importance of the subject. The recent history of art has shown that these effects need not operate narrowly through the enhancement of *beauty per se,* but they remain dramatically effective nonetheless, and that is the essential point for present purposes. Nietzsche himself, of course, tended to view art as essentially glorifying and beautifying (see, e.g., *GS* P 4, 78, 85, 107; *TI* IX, 8–11, et passim). (For a developed account of a pretense theory of mimesis, of the sort alluded to in the text, see the field-shaping Kendall Walton, *Mimesis as Make-Believe* (Cambridge, MA: Harvard University Press, 1990).)

60. Nietzsche himself clearly continued to think of the matter in this way, as evidenced by his late reference to Raphael as an exemplar of the power of art to transform life:

> In this state one enriches everything out of one's own fullness: whatever one sees, whatever one wills, is seen swelled, taut, strong, overloaded with strength. A man in this state transforms things until they mirror his power— until they are reflections of his perfection. This *having* to transform into perfection is—art . . . It would be possible to imagine an opposite state, a specific anti-artistry by instinct—a mode of being which would impoverish all things . . . This is, for example, the case of the genuine Christian . . .: a Christian who would at the same time be an artist simply does not occur. One should not be childish and object by naming Raphael . . . : Raphael said Yes, Raphael *did* Yes; consequently, Raphael was no Christian. [*TI* IX, 9]

The key thought here is that, far from condemning this mortal life or his own life, Raphael was rather disposed to glorify it (and thereby, himself) by means of artistic transfiguration. As we will see below, such an attitude stands in tension with the compensatory conception of redemption, whether Raphael himself was aware of that or not. Thus, what Raphael *did* with his life and work—and in the case of *Transfiguration*, he did it more or less explicitly in response to the problem of redeeming the tragic parts of life—can be assimilated without forcing to Nietzsche's transfiguring conception of redemption. As a last point, I note that such an interpretation of Raphael's artistic activity claims it as a project of *self*-redemption, which connects it to a further dimension of Nietzsche's conception, discussed in section 5, below. Thanks to Don Rutherford for conversations which made me see the importance of these issues.

61. The discussion in this paragraph benefited from exchanges with Alexander Nehamas.

62. Notice, this is true even on Christian conceptions which emphasize some fortunate aspects of our sinful condition (e.g., that the sin of the human race is an opportunity for God's grace, which redeems us through Christ's sacrifice). Notions of a "Happy Fall" (as found in Milton, in Mormonism, etc.) still would not permit honest affirmation of the eternal recurrence of the *same* particular life. While it might be some *consolation* to view Adam's Fall as providential in a limited sense (within the context of God's overall plan to show grace), such thoughts are by no means genuinely *redemptive*, precisely because it remains crucial to the Christian doctrine that sin is an evil state, and the particulars of our condition are by no means to be willed as such. On the contrary, they must be renounced in full repentance if we are even to be worthy of God's grace. Thanks to an anonymous reviewer for penetrating comments that led to this note.

63. I defend this interpretation of Nietzschean "strength" as a matter of internal coherence or unity at greater length in R. Lanier Anderson, "Nietzsche on Strength and Achieving Individuality," *International Studies in Philosophy* (Forthcoming).

64. This idea is even sometimes appreciated within the Christian context: it forms the basis, for example, for one of Kierkegaard's famous jokes. Kierkegaard opines that people trapped in the superficial life he calls "immediacy" often worry to their pastors about whether they will know themselves in Heaven, and he insists that they are right to do so. Since they lack the "inwardness" of genuine personality, their transition out of this life and its immediate concerns threatens to leave *no remainder*. They are, he says, like that peasant who went into town with just enough money to buy new shoes and get rip roaring drunk. Having passed out on the road home, the peasant was awakened by a coach, whose driver shouted warnings, lest his legs be run over. Looking down, and not recognizing himself in the new shoes, he replies: "Go ahead, run them over; they're not my legs!" Comic, but also sad, at least in the intended analogy to someone who cannot recognize her own inward soul. The key point for us, again, is that too great a transformation of the self through redemption threatens to violate this recognition condition, with the result that the person herself is *eliminated*, not redeemed. Recurrence blocks such a result by redirecting redemptive attention onto the past (and also, we will see in a moment, onto the agent herself, and her efforts at self-transformation).

SERRES: EPILOGUE: WHAT HEARING KNOWS

1. Translator's note: I am grateful to Joshua Landy for his careful reading and inspired suggestions, which have improved this translation tremendously.

2. "Ce dont bruit le trou d'ombre": an allusion to Victor Hugo's poem "Ce que dit la bouche d'ombre," in *Les Contemplations* (Paris: Hachette, 1922 [1856]), book VI, poem 26. [Trans.]

3. From "Rossignol, mon mignon . . ." In Pierre Ronsard, *Oeuvres complètes*, ed. Gustave Cohen, 2 vols. (Paris: Gallimard, 1950), 2:817. Translation mine. [Trans.]

4. Johannes Kepler, *Harmonices mundi* (Bologna: Ferri, 1969 [1619]). [Trans.]

5. Erwin Schrödinger, *What Is Life? The Physical Aspect of the Living Cell* (New York: Macmillan, 1945). [Trans.]

6. Michel Serres, *Variations sur le corps*, 2nd ed. (Paris: Pommier, 2002) 125–31. [Trans.]

7. Deut. 6:4, Mark 7:34. [Trans.]

Works Cited

Aarsleff, Hans. *From Locke to Saussure: Essays on the Study of Language and Intellectual History.* Minneapolis: University of Minnesota Press, 1982.

Abrams, M. H. *The Mirror and the Lamp: Romantic Theory and the Critical Tradition.* New York: Oxford University Press, 1953.

Adams, Steven. *The Art of the Pre-Raphaelites.* London: Apple, 1988.

Addison, Joseph. "The Pleasures of the Imagination." *The Spectator.* 1712. Ed. Donald F. Bond. Vol. 3. Oxford: Clarendon Press, 1965. 535–82.

Adorno, Theodor. *Über Walter Benjamin.* Frankfurt am Main: Suhrkamp, 1970.

Agacinski, Sylviane. *Time Passing: Modernity and Nostalgia.* New York: Columbia University Press, 2004.

Allen, Anita L., and Milton C. Regan, Jr., eds. *Debating Democracy's Discontent: Essays on American Politics, Law, and Public Philosophy.* Oxford: Oxford University Press, 1998.

Alter, Robert. *Partial Magic.* Berkeley: University of California Press, 1975.

Altieri, Charles. "Poetics as 'Untruth': Revising Modern Claims for Literary Truths." *New Literary History* 29.2 (1998): 305–28.

Amelang, James S. "Barristers and Judges in Early Modern Barcelona: The Rise of a Legal Elite." *American Historical Review* 89.5 (1984): 1264–84.

Anderson, R. Lanier. "Nietzsche on Truth, Illusion, and Redemption," *The European Journal of Philosophy* 13 (2005): 185–225.

———. "Nietzsche on Strength and Achieving Individuality," *International Studies in Philosophy.* (forthcoming)

Anselm, Saint. *Basic Writings.* Translated by S. W. Deane. La Salle, IL, Open Court, 1962.

Apollo Alliance. 13 June 2006. <http://www.apolloalliance.org/about_the _alliance/>.

Appadurai, Arjun. *Modernity at Large: Cultural Dimensions of Globalization.* Minneapolis: University of Minnesota Press, 1997.

Appleby, Joyce. *Liberalism and Republicanism in the Historical Imagination.* Cambridge, MA: Harvard University Press, 1992.

Applegate, Celia. *A Nation of Provincials: The German Idea of Heimat.* Berkeley: University of California Press, 1990.

Arendt, Hannah. *The Origins of Totalitarianism.* New York: Meridian Press, 1958.

Arnason, Johann P. "Reason, Imagination, Interpretation." *Rethinking Imagination: Culture and Creativity.* Eds. Gillian Robinson and John Rundell. London: Routledge, 1994.

Arte Románcia de Cataluña: colecciones del museu nacional d'art de Catalunya. Barcelona: Museu Nacional d'Art de Catalunya Palau Nacional, 2001.

Bacon, Francis. *The Works of Francis Bacon: Volume 6.* Ed. J. Spedding et al. Boston: Taggard and Thompson, 1860–64.

Bailey, Peter. *Popular Culture and Performance in the Victorian City.* Cambridge: Cambridge University Press, 1998.

Baker, Keith. *Condorcet: From Natural Philosophy to Social Mathematics.* Chicago: University of Chicago Press, 1975.

———. "Epsitémologie et politique: pourquoi l'*Encyclopédie* est-elle un dictionnaire?" Trans. Philippe Roger. *'L'Encyclopédie:' du réseau au livre et du livre au réseau.* Ed. Robert Morrissey and Philippe Roger. Paris: Honoré Champion, 2001.

———. "Politics and Social Science in Eighteenth-Century France; The *Société de 1789.*" *French Government and Society, 1500–1850: Essays in Honor of Alfred Cobban.* Ed. J. F. Bosher. London: Athlone Press, 1973.

Balcells, Albert. *Catalan Nationalism: Past and Present.* New York: Macmillan, 1996.

Ballanche, Pierre-Simon. *Œuvres complètes.* Genève: Slatkine, 1967.

Balzac, Honoré de. *Louis Lambert.* Paris: Gallimard, 1980.

Bandmann, Günter. *Die Bauformen des Mittelalters.* Bonn: Athenäum-Verl. von Reutern, 1949.

Barbieri, Costanza. "The Competition between Raphael and Michelangelo and Sebastiano's Role in It." *The Cambridge Companion to Raphael.* Ed. Marcia Hall. Cambridge: Cambridge University Press, 2005, 141–64.

Barnum, P. T. *The Life of P. T. Barnum, Written By Himself.* London: Sampson Low, 1855.

Barlösius, Eva. *Naturgemässe Lebensführung: zur Geschichte der Lebensreform um die Jahrhundertwende.* New York: Campus, 1997.

Barthes, Roland. "Longtemps, je me suis couché de bonne heure . . ." Trans. Richard Howard. *The Rustle of Language.* New York: Hill & Wang, 1986, 277–90.

Bassegoda Nonell, J. *Modernisme a Catalunya.* Barcelona: Edicions de Nou Art Thor, 1989.

Bataille, Georges. "La structure psychologiue du fascisme." *La Critique sociale.* Paris: Découverte, 1983 [Nov. 1933, Mar. 1934].

Baudelaire, Charles. *Oeuvres Complètes.* Paris: Robert Laffont, 1980.

Beckett, Samuel. *Endgame.* New York: Grove, 1958.

Becq, Annie. *Genèse de l'esthétique française moderne: De la raison classique à l'imagination créatrice, 1680–1814.* 2 vols. Pisa: Pacini, 1984.

Behm, Johannes. "Metamorphose." *Theological Dictionary of the New Testament,* vol. 4. Gerhard Friedrich and Gerhard Kittel, eds., trans. G. W. Bromley. Grand Rapids, MI: Eerdmans Publishing Co., 1968, 755–59.

Beiser, Frederick C. *Enlightenment, Revolution, and Romanticism: The Genesis of Modern German Political Thought, 1790–1800.* Cambridge, MA: Harvard University Press, 1992.

Bell, David A. *The Cult of the Nation in France: Inventing Nationalism, 1680–1800.* Cambridge, MA: Harvard University Press, 2001.

Bell, Michael. "The Metaphysics of Modernism." *The Cambridge Companion to Modernism.* Ed. Michael Levenson. Cambridge, MA: Cambridge University Press, 1999, 9–32.

Benedict, Barbara M. *Curiosity: A Cultural History of Early Modern Inquiry.* Chicago: University of Chicago Press, 2001.

Bénichou, Paul. *Selon Mallarmé.* Paris: Gallimard, 1995.

Benjamin, Walter. *Gesammelte Briefe.* Vol. II 1919–1924. Eds. Christoph Gödde and Henri Lonitz. Frankfurt am Main: Suhrkamp, 1996.

———. *Selected Writings, Volume 1: 1913–1926.* Ed. Marcus Bullock and Michael Jennings. Cambridge, MA: Harvard University Press, 1996.

Bennett, Jane. *The Enchantment of Modern Life: Crossings, Attachments, and Ethics.* Princeton, NJ: Princeton University Press, 2002.

Bennett, Oliver. *Cultural Pessimism: Narratives of Decline in the Postmodern World.* Edinburgh: Edinburgh University Press, 2001.

Bergson, Henri. *Essai sur les données immédiates de la conscience.* Paris: PUF, 1889.

Berman, Morris. *The Reenchantment of the World.* Ithaca, NY: Cornell University Press, 1981 [repr. ed. 1988].

Bernard, Catherine. *Inès de Courdoue, nouvelle espagnole.* Paris: Jouvenel, 1696.

Bernstein, Eduard. *The Preconditions of Socialism.* Ed. and trans. Henry Tudor. Cambridge: Cambridge University Press, 1993.

Bernstein, J. M. *Adorno: Disenchantment and Ethics.* Cambridge: Cambridge University Press, 2001.

Bersani, Leo. *The Death of Stéphane Mallarmé.* Cambridge: Cambridge University Press, 1981.

Betthausen, Peter et al. *Metzler Kunsthistoriker-Lexikon.* Stuttgart: Metzler, 1999.

Bianchon, Horace. "L'envoûtement." *Le Figaro* 10 Jan. 1893.

Biser, Eugen. *'Gott ist Tot': Nietzsches Destruktion des christlichen Bewusstseins.* München: Kösel Verlag, 1962.

Bishop, Lloyd. *Romantic Irony in French Literature from Diderot to Beckett.* Nashville, TN: Vanderbilt University Press, 1989.

Bitter, Gottfried. "Erlösung." In W. Kasper et al. *Lexikon für Theologie und Kirche.* Freiburg: Herder, 1995.

Blanchot, Maurice. *La Part du Feu.* Paris: Gallimard, 1949.

Blitz, Antonio. *Fifty Years in the Magic Circle.* Hartford, CT: Belknap & Bliss, 1871.

Bloch, Ernst. *Geist der Utopie.* Faksimile der Ausgabe von 1918. Frankfurt am Main: Suhrkamp Verlag, 1985.

———. *Geist der Utopie.* Bearbeitete Neuauflage der zweiten Fassung von 1923. Frankfurt am Main: Suhrkamp Verlag, 1985.

———. *Kritische Erörterungen über Rickert und das Problem der modernen Erkenntnistheorie.* Inaugural dissertation submitted to the University of Würzburg, 1908 (Ludwigshafen am Rhein, 1909).

———. *The Spirit of Utopia.* Trans. Anthony Nassar. Stanford: Stanford University Press, 2000.

Blonde, Didier. *Les Voleurs de visages: Sur quelques cas troublants de changements d'identité : Rocambole, Arsène Lupin, Fantômas, & Cie.* Paris: Métailié, 1992.

Blumenberg, Hans. "The Concept of Reality and the Possibility of the Novel." Trans. David Henry Wilson. *New Persepctives in Germany Literary Criticism: A Collection of Essays.* Ed. Richard E. Amacher and Victor Lange. Princeton: Princeton University Press, 1979.

Bohigas, Oriol. *Lluis Domènech i Montaner.* Barcelona: Lluis Carulla i Canals, 1973.

Bois, Jules. "L'envoûtement et la mort du docteur Boullan." *Gil Blas* Jan. 9 1893.

Bolz, Norbert. *Auszug aus der entzauberten Welt.* München: Wilhelm Fink Verlag, 1989.

Bonneville, Nicolas de. *De l'esprit des religions.* Paris: Cercle Social, 1790.

Boobyer, G. H. *St. Mark and the Transfiguration Story.* Edinburgh: T.&T. Clark, 1942.

Borges, Jorge Luis. *Labyrinths: Selected Stories and Other Writings.* Ed & Trans. Donald A. Yates and James E. Irby. New York: New Directions, 1962.

Bou, Enric. *La llum que ve del nord: Joan Maragall i la cultura alemanya.* Barcelona: Editorial Claret, 1997.

Bourgeois, René. "Modes of Romantic Irony in Nineteenth-Century France." Trans. Cecilia Grenier. *Romantic Irony.* Ed. Frederick Garber. Budapest: Akadémiai Kiadó, 1988. 97–119.

Bowman, Frank. *Le Christ des barricades, 1789–1848.* Paris: Cerf, 1987.

———. *Le Christ romantique.* Geneva: Droz, 1973.

Boyd-Whyte, Iain. *Bruno Taut and the Architecture of Activism.* Cambridge: Cambridge University Press, 1982.

Boym, Svetlana. *The Future of Nostalgia.* New York: Basic Books, 2002.

Bradbury, Malcolm, and James McFarlane. "The Name and Nature of Modernism." *Modernism.* Ed. Malcolm Bradbury & James McFarlane. London: Penguin, 1976. 19–55.

Brantlinger, Patrick. *The Reading Lesson: The Threat of Mass Literacy in Nineteenth-Century British Fiction.* Bloomington: University of Indiana Press, 1998.

Bratman, Michael. *Intention, Plans, and Practical Reason.* Cambridge, MA: Harvard University Press, 1987.

———. *Faces of Intention.* Cambridge: Cambridge University Press, 1999.

Braudel, Fernand. *La Méditerranée et le monde méditerranéen à l'époque de Philippe II.* 2 vols. 2nd edition. Paris: Colin, 1966.

Brecht, Bertolt. *Brecht on Theatre.* Trans. John Willett. New York: Hill and Wang, 1964.

Bredekamp, Horst, Michael Diers, Charlotte Schoell-Glass, eds. *Aby Warburg: Akten des internationalen Symposions, Hamburg, 1990.* Weinheim: VCH, 1991.

Bricaud, Joanny. *J-K. Huysmans et le Satanisme.* Paris: Chacornac, 1912.

Bright, Michael. *Cities Built to Music: Aesthetic Theories of the Victorian Gothic Revival.* Columbus: Ohio State University Press, 1984.

Brooks, Chris. *The Gothic Revival.* London: Phaidon, 1999.

Brooks, Peter. *Realist Vision.* New Haven, CT: Yale University Press, 2005.

Brown, Colin, et al. *The New International Dictionary of New Testament Theology.* Grand Rapids, MI: Zondervan, 1978. This work is a translation, with additions and revisions, of Coenen et al. (1971).

Brown, Marshall. *The Gothic Text.* Stanford: Stanford University Press, 2005.

Buard, Jean-Luc. "Pourquoi il faillait appeler notre bulletin *Le Rocambole.*" *Le Rocambole* 1 (Spring 1997): 7–22.

———. "Les Infortunes critiques d'un Romancier, ou Charges, parodies et caricatures littéraires du Ponson du Terrail (1858–1863)." *Le Rocambole* 2 (Fall 1997): 23–70.

Buchholz, Kai et al. *Die Lebensreform: Entwürfe zur Neugestaltung von Leben und Kunst um 1900.* 2 vols. Darmstadt: Hausser, 2001.

Buck-Morss, Susan. *The Dialectics of Seeing: Walter Benjamin and the Arcades Project.* Cambridge, MA: The MIT Press, 1989.

Burckhardt, Jacob. *The Altarpiece in Renaissance Italy.* Ed. and trans. P. Humfrey. Oxford: Phaidon, 1988 [1898].

Burke, Peter. *Popular Culture in Early Modern Europe.* New York: Harper & Row, 1978.

Burleigh, Michael, and Wolfgang Wippermann. *The Racial State: Germany 1933–1945.* Cambridge: Cambridge University Press, 1993.

Burlingame, H. J. *History of Magic and Magicians.* Chicago: Burlingame, 1895.

Burt, E. S. "Mallarmé's 'Sonnet En Yx': The Ambiguities of Speculation." *Modern Critical Views: Stéphane Mallarmé.* Ed. Harold Bloom. New York: Chelsea House, 1987, 97–120.

Buruma, Ian. "The Road to Babel." *The New York Review of Books* 48.9 (2001): 23–26.

Busch, Werner. *Caspar David Friedrich: Ästehtik und Religion.* München: C. H. Beck, 2003.

Bush, Douglas. *Mythology and the Romantic Tradition in English Poetry.* Cambridge, MA: Harvard University Press, 1937.

Caillois, Roger. "De la féerie à la science-fiction" (1962). *Obliques.* Paris: Gallimard, 1987, 67–79.

Calhoun, Craig, ed. *Habermas and the Public Sphere.* Cambridge, MA: MIT Press, 1992.

Calvino, Italo. *If on a winter's night a traveler.* New York: Harvest, 1982.

Campbell, Mary Baine. *Wonder and Science: Imagining Worlds in Early Modern Europe*. Ithaca, NY: Cornell University Press, 1999.

Camus, Albert. *Le mythe de Sisyphe: Essai sur l'absurde*. Paris: Gallimard, 1942, 73.

Carandell, J. M., and P. Vivas. *Park Guell—Gaudi's Utopia*. Sant Lluís, Menorca: Triangle Postals, 1998.

Cardinal, Roger. "*Le Diable amoureux* and the Pure Fantastic." *Studies in French Fiction in Honour of Vivienne Milne*. Ed. Robert Gilson. London: Grant and Cutler, 1988, 67–79.

Carné, Louis de. "Publications démocratiques et communistes." *Revue des Deux Mondes*. 14 September 1841: 402.

Carter, Jimmy. *Palestine: Peace Not Apartheid*. New York: Simon & Schuster, 2006.

Cascardi, Anthony J. "The Critique of Subjectivity and the Re-Enchantment of the World." *Revue internationale de philosophie* 196 (1996): 243–63.

Cassirer, Ernst. *The Philosophy of the Enlightenment*. Princeton, NJ: Princeton University Press, 1951.

Castelfranchi Vegas, Liana. "Die ottonische Lombardei und Aribert." *Europas Kunst um 1000*. Ed. Liana Castelfranchi Vegas. Regensburg: Verlag Schnell & Steiner, 2001.

Castle, Terry. *The Female Thermometer: Eighteenth-Century Culture and the Invention of the Uncanny*. New York: Oxford University Press, 1995.

Cavell, Stanley. *Emerson's Transcendental Études*. Ed. D. Hodge. Stanford: Stanford University Press, 2003.

———. *The Senses of Walden*. San Francisco: North Point Press, 1981.

Cazotte, Jacques. *Le Diable amoureux*. 1772. Ed. Georges Décote. Paris: Gallimard, 1981.

———. *Les Mille et une fadaises: Contes à dormir debout*. Baillons [Paris?]: Chez l'Endormi, 1742.

Chabot, M. L. *Rocambole: Un roman feuilleton sous le Second Empire*. Paris: Société des Gens de Lettres, 1995.

Chadwick, Charles. "Mallarme's 'Sonnet Allegorique De Lui-Meme'—Allegorical of Itself or of Himself?" *Nineteenth-Century French Studies* 31.1 (2002): 104–10.

Chakrabarty, Dipesh. *Provincializing Europe: Postcolonial Thought and Historical Difference*. Princeton, NJ: Princeton University Press, 2000.

Chandler, Frank Wadleigh. *The Literature of Roguery*. Boston: Houghton Mifflin and Company, 1907.

Citron, Pierre. "Ses Purs Ongles Très Haut." *Stéphane Mallarmé: Poésies*. Paris: Imprimerie Nationale, 1986, 302–7.

Clark, Maudemarie. *Nietzsche on Truth and Philosophy*. Cambridge: Cambridge University Press, 1990.

Clarke, Arthur C. "Technology and the Future." *Report on Planet Three and Other Speculations*: 138–51. New York: Harper and Row, 1972.

Clarke, Basil Fulford Lowther. *Church Builders of the Nineteenth Century: A Study of the Gothic Revival in England*. Newton Abbot: David & Charles, 1969.

Clauzade, Laurent. *L'idéologie ou la revolution de l'analyse.* Paris: Gallimard, 1998.

Clavero, Bartolomé. "Formación doctrinal contemporánea del derecho catalán de sucesiónes: La primogénitura de la libertad." *La reforma de la Compilación: El sistema successor.* Barcelona: Unviersitat de Barcelona, 1984, 10–37.

Clery, E. J. *The Rise of the Supernatural Fiction, 1762–1800.* Cambridge: Cambridge University Press, 1995.

Coenen, L. et al. *Theologisches Begriffslexikon zum Neuen Testament.* Wuppertal: Rolf Brockhaus, 1971.

Cohn, Robert G. *Toward the Poems of Mallarmé.* Berkeley: University of California Press, 1979.

Cole, G. D. H. *William Morris as Socialist.* London: William Morris Society, 1960.

Coleridge, Samuel Taylor. "Biographia literaria." *Collected Works of Samuel Taylor Coleridge.* Eds. James Engell and Walter Jackson Bate. Vol. 7. Princeton, NJ: Princeton University Press, 1983.

Collingwood, R. G. *The Philosophy of Enchantment.* Eds. David Boucher, Wendy James, and Philip Smallwood. Oxford: Oxford University Press, 2005.

Comaroff, Jean, and John Comaroff, eds. *Modernity and Its Malcontents: Ritual and Power in Postcolonial Africa.* Chicago: Chicago University Press, 1993.

Comas, Antoni, Martí de Riquer, and Joaquim Molas. *Història de la literatura catalana.* 11 vols. Barcelona: Ariel, 1984–88.

Comte, Auguste. *The Catechism of Positive Religion.* Trans. Richard Congreve. London: Kegan Paul, 1891 [1852].

Condillac, Étienne Bonnot de. *Essai sur l'origine des connoissances humaines.* Amsterdam: P. Mortier, 1746.

Condorcet, Marquis de. *Esquisse d'un tableau historique des progrès de l'esprit humain; Fragments de l'histoire de la quatrième époque; Fragment sur l'Atlantide.* Paris: Bureau de la bibliothèque choisie, 1829.

Confino, Alon. *The Nation as a Local Metaphor: Württemberg, Imperial Germany and National Memory 1871–1918.* Chapel Hill: University of North Carolina Press, 1997.

Conversi, Daniel. *The Basques, the Catalans, and Spain.* London: C. Hurst, 1997.

Cook, James. *The Arts of Deception.* Cambridge, MA: Harvard University Press, 2001.

Cook, Sir Robert. *The Palace of Westminster.* London: Burton Skira, 1987.

Corngold, Stanley. *Lambent Traces: Franz Kafka.* Princeton, NJ: Princeton University Press, 2004.

Coronil, Fernando. *The Magical State: Nature, Money, and Modernity in Venezuela.* Chicago: University of Chicago Press, 1997.

Costa, Jordi Romeu. *Josep Puig i Cadafalch. Obres i projectes des del 1911.* Barcelona: Escola Técnica Superior d'Arquitectura de Barcelona, 1989.

Court de Gébelin, Antoine. *Monde Primitif, analysé et comparé avec le monde moderne, considéré dans son génie allégorique et dans les allégories auxquelles conduisit ce génie.* Paris, 1773.

Coutel, Charles. "Utopie et perfectibilité: significations de l'Atlantide chez Condorcet." *Condorcet: Homme des Lumières et de la Révolution.* Ed. Anne-Marie Chouillet and Pierre Crépel. Paris: ENS, 1997.

Croce, Paul. *Science and Religion in the Era of William James.* Vol. I. Chapel Hill: University of North Carolina Press, 1995.

Dällenbach, Lucien. *The Mirror in the Text.* Trans. Jeremy Whitely. Chicago: University of Chicago Press, 1989.

Damus, Martin. *Das Rathaus: Architektur- und Sozialgeschichte von der Gründerzeit zur Postmoderne.* Berlin: Mann, 1988.

Darnton, Robert. *The Kiss of Lamourette: Reflections in Cultural History.* New York: Norton, 1990.

———. *Mesmerism and the End of the Enlightenment in France.* Cambridge, MA: Harvard University Press, 1968.

———. "The Philosophes Trim the Tree of Knowledge." *The Great Cat Massacre and Other Episodes in French Cultural History.* New York: Basic Books, 1984.

Daston, Lorraine. "Attention and the Values of Nature in the Enlightenment." *The Moral Authority of Nature.* Eds. L. Daston and F. Vidal. Chicago: Chicago University Press, 2004.

Daston, Lorraine, and Katherine Park. *Wonders and the Order of Nature, 1150–1750.* New York: Zone Books, 1998.

Davies, Gardner. *Mallarmé et le drame solaire.* Paris: Corti, 1959.

Davis, Lennard J. *Factual Fictions: The Origins of the English Novel.* New York: Columbia University Press, 1983.

Davis, Norbert. *The Mouse in the Mountain.* Colorado: Rue Morgue Press, 2001 [1943].

Deichmann, Friedrich Wilhelm. *Frühchristliche Kirchen in Rom.* Basel: Amerbach-Verlag, 1948.

Derrida, Jacques. *Specters of Marx: The State of the Debt, The Work of Mourning, and the New International.* New York: Routledge, 1994.

Descartes, Rene. *Philosophical Essays.* Trans. L. Lafleur. New York: Macmillan, 1989.

———. *The Philosophical Work of Descartes.* Vol. 1. Ed. E. Haldane and G. R. T. Ross. Cambridge: Cambridge University Press, 1978.

Descaves, Lucien. "Note." In Joris-Karl Huysmans, *Oeuvres Complètes* vol. XII. Geneva: Slatkine Reprints, 1972: 238–60.

Deuber-Mankowsky, Astrid. *Der frühe Walter Benjamin und Hermann Cohen: Jüdische Werke, Kritische Philosophie, vergängliche Erfahrung.* Berlin: Verlag Vorwerk 8, 2000.

Dictionnaire européen des Lumières. ed. Michel Delon. Paris: PUF, 1997.

Dehio, Georg. *Geschichte der deutschen Kunst,* 3 vols. Berlin: De Gruyer, 1919–26.

———. *Handbuch der Deutschen Kunstgeschichte,* 5 vols. Munich: Dt. Kunstvert, 1905–12.

———. *Die kirchliche Baukunst des Abendlandes.* Stuttgart: Cotta, 1887–1901.

Dompnier, Bernard. "Les Hommes d'Eglise et la superstition entre XVIIe et XVIIIe siècles." *La Superstition à l'âge des lumières.* Ed. Bernard Dompnier. Paris: Champion, 1998, 13–47.

Dorson, Richard M. "The Eclipse of Solar Mythology." *Journal of American Folklore* 68 (1955): 393–416.

Dostoevsky, Fyodor. *The Adolescent.* Trans. Richard Pevear and Larissa Volokhonsky. New York: Knopf, 2003 [1875].

Dragonetti, Roger. *Etudes Sur Mallarmé.* Gent: Romanica Gandensia, 1992.

Dube, Saurabh. "Introduction: Colonialism, Modernity, Colonial Modernities." *Nepantla: Views from South* 3, no. 2 (2002): 197–219.

———, ed. "Enduring Enchantments" in special issue of *The South Atlantic Quarterly* 101, no. 4 (October 2002).

Duchet, Claude. "L'Illusion historique: L'Enseignement des préfaces (1815–1832)." *Revue d'histoire littéraire de la France* 75.2–3 (1975): 245–67.

Dupuis, Charles-François. *Lettre sur le Dieu Soleil, adressée à MM. Les Auteurs du Journal des Sçavans; par M. Dupuis, Professeur de Rhétorique, Avocat en Parlement, de l'Académie de Rouen.* Paris, 1780.

Durand, Catherine. *Les Petits soupers de l'été de l'année 1699, ou avantures galantes, avec l'origine des fées.* Paris: Jean Musier, 1702.During, Simon. *Modern Enchantments: The Cultural Power of Secular Magic.* Cambridge, MA: Harvard University Press, 2002.

Ealham, Christopher. *Class, Culture and Conflict in Barcelona, 1898–1937.* London: Routledge, 2005.

Eco, Umberto. *The Name of the Rose.* Trans. William Weaver. San Diego, CA: Harcourt Brace, 1994.

Edelman, Nicole. *Voyantes, guérisseuses et visionnaires en France, 1785–1914.* Paris: Albin Michel, 1995.

Edelstein, Dan. "Hyperborean Atlantis: Jean-Sylvain Bailly, Madame Blavatsky, and the Nazi Myth." Ed. Jeffry S. Ravel and Linda Zionkowski. *Studies in Eighteenth-Century Culture* 35 (2006): 267–291.

———. "The Modernization of Myth, from Balzac to Sorel." *Yale French Studies* 111 (2007): 32–44.

———. "Moving through the Looking-Glass: Deleuzian Reflections on the Series in Mallarmé." *L'esprit créateur* 40 (2000): 50–60.

Ehrlich, Charles. "The Lliga Regionalista and the Catalan Industrial Bourgeoisie." *Journal of Contemporary History* 33 (1998): 399–417.

Eliot, T. S. "Hamlet," *Selected Prose of T. S. Eliot.* Ed. Frank Kermode. New York: Harcourt Brace, 1975, 45–49.

Eliot, T. S. "The Waste Land." *The Waste Land and Other Poems.* Ed. Frank Kermode. New York: Penguin Books, 2003: 53–76.

Emerson, Ralph Waldo. *Emerson. Essays and Lectures.* New York: The Library of America, 1983.

———. *Emerson in His Journals.* Ed. Joel Porte. Cambridge, MA: Harvard University Press, 1984.

"Enchant." *The Compact Oxford English Dictionary.* 2nd ed. New York: Oxford University Press, 1989.

Encyclopédie, ou, Dictionnaire raisonné des sciences, des arts et des métiers. Vol. 1:XIV. Eds. Denis Diderot and Jean le Rond d'Alembert. Paris: Briasson, 1751–65.

Ender, Evelyne. *Architexts of Memory: Literature, Science, and Autobiography.* Ann Arbor: University of Michigan Press, 2005.

Engels, Friedrich. "Socialism: Utopean and Scientific" (1880). In *The Marx-Engels Reader*, ed. Robert C. Tucker. New York: Norton, 1978, 685–90.

Epps, Brad. "Modern and Moderno: Modernist Studies, 1898, and Spain." *Catalan Review* XIV (2000): 75–116.

Ettlinger, Leopold, and Helen S. Ettlinger. *Raphael.* Oxford: Phaidon, 1987.

Eysteinsson, Astradur. *The Concept of Modernism.* Ithaca, NY: Cornell University Press, 1990.

Fann, K. T., ed. *Ludwig Wittgenstein: The Man and His Philosophy.* New York: Dell Publishing Co., 1967.

Ferguson, James. *Expectations of Modernity: Myths and Meaning of Urban Life in the Zambian Copperbelt.* Berkeley: University of California Press, 1999.

Fiard, Jean Baptiste. *De la France trompée par les magiciens et les démonolâtres du dix-huitième siècle, fait démontré par des faits.* Paris: Grégoire, 1803.

Fisher, Philip. *Wonder, the Rainbow, and the Aesthetics of Rare Experiences.* Cambridge, MA: Harvard University Press, 1998.

Flaubert, Gustave. *Madame Bovary.* Trans. Francis Steegmuller. New York: Random House, 1992.

Flood, Christopher G. *Political Myth.* New York: Routledge, 2002.

Folch i Torres, Joachim. "La peinture murale." *La Catalogue à l'Epoque Romane: Conférences fuites à la Sorbonne en 1930 par MM Angles, Folch i Torres, Ph. Lauer, Nicolau D'Olwer, Puig i Cadafalch.* Paris: Librarie Ernest Lekoux, 1932, 111–28.

Foley, Barbara. *Telling the Truth: The Theory and Practice of Documentary Fiction.* Ithaca, NY: Cornell University Press, 1986.

Fontbona, Francesc, and Francesco Miralles. *Història de l'Art Català.* Barcelona: Edicions 62, 1996–2001.

Foucault, Michel. *Discipline and Punish: The Birth of the Prison.* New York: Vintage Books, 1979.

———. *Madness and Civilization: A History of Madness in the Age of Reason.* New York: Vintage Books, 1988.

———. *Les Mots et les choses: Une archéologie des sciences humaines.* Paris: Gallimard, 1966.

———. *The Order of Things: An Archeology of the Human Sciences.* New York: Pantheon, 1971.

———. "Space, Knowledge and Power." *Rethinking Architecture: A Reader in Cultural Theory.* Ed. Neal Leich. London: Routledge, 1997, 367–79.

Fowler, Alastair. *Kinds of Literature: An Introduction to the Theory of Genres and Modes.* Cambridge, MA: Harvard University Press, 1982.

Fradera, Josep M. *Cultura nacional en une societat dividida: Patriotisme i cultura a Catalunya, 1838–1868.* Barcelona: Curial, 1992.

Frampton, Kenneth. *Grundlagen der Architektur. Studien zur Kultur des Tektonischen.* München: Oktagon, 1993.

———. *Studies in Tectonic Culture: The Poetics of Construction in Nineteenth and Twentieth Century Architecture.* Cambridge, MA: MIT Press, 1995.

Francesco, Grete de. *The Power of the Charlatan.* Trans. Miriam Beard. New Haven, CT: Yale University Press, 1939.

Frankfurt, Harry. "Identification and Wholeheartedness." In *The Importance of What We Care About: Philosophical Essays*. Cambridge: Cambridge University Press, 1988.

Freixa, Mireia. *El modernisme a Catalunya*. Barcelona: Barcanova, 1991.

Freud, Sigmund. *Civilization and its Discontents*. Trans. James Strachey. New York: Norton, 1961 [1930].

———. "The Uncanny." Trans. Joan Riviere. *Collected Papers*. 1919. Ed. Ernest Jones. Vol. 4. New York: Basic Books, 1959, 368–407.

Friedman, Susan Stanford. "Definition Excursions: The Meanings of Modern, Modernity, Modernism." *Modernism/Modernity* 8/3 (2001): 493–513.

Friedrich, Gerhard, and Gerhard Kittel, eds. *Theological Dictionary of the New Testament*. Trans. G. W. Bromley. Grand Rapids, MI: Eerdmans Publishing Co., 1968.

Fritzsche, Peter. *Stranded in the Present: Modern Time and the Melancholy of History*. Cambridge, MA: Harvard University Press, 2004.

Fumaroli, Marc. "Les *Contes* de Perrault, ou l'éducation de la douceur." *La Diplomatie de l'esprit: De Montaigne à La Fontaine*. Paris: Hermann, 1994, 441–78.

Furst, Lilian R. *Fictions of Romantic Irony*. Cambridge, MA: Harvard University Press, 1984.

———. "Romantic Irony and Narrative Stance." *Romantic Irony*. Ed. Frederick Garber. Budapest: Akadémini Kindó, 1988, 293–309.

Gaillard, Aurélia. *Le Corps des statues: Le Vivant et son simulacre à l'âge clasique (de Descartes à Diderot)*. Paris: Champion, 2003.

Gallagher, Catherine. *Nobody's Story: The Vanishing Acts of Women Writers in the Marketplace, 1670–1820*. Berkeley: University of California Press, 1994.

Gallagher, Catherine, and Stephen Greenblatt. "The Novel and Other Discourses of Suspended Belief." *Practicing New Historicism*. Chicago: University of Chicago Press, 2000, 163–210.

Gambles, Anna. *Protection and Politics: Conservative Economic Discourse, 1815–1852*. London: Boydell Press, 1999.

Ganim, John M. *Medievalism and Orientalism: Three Essays on Literature, Architecture and Cultural Identity*. Basingstoke: Palgrave Macmillan, 2005.

Gans, Herbert J. *Popular Culture and High Culture: An Analysis and Evaluation of Taste*. New York: Basic Books, 1975.

Gardt, Andreas, and Bernd Huppauf, eds. *Globalization and the Future of German*. New York: Mouton de Gruyter, 2004.

Garinet, Jules. *Histoire De La Magie En France, Depuis Le Commencement De La Monarchie Jusqu'à Nos Jours*. Paris: Foulon, 1818.

Garnier, Éric. *Commentaire: Le Sonnet En X De Stéphane Mallarmé*. Pau: Editions de Vallongues, 2003.

Garrett, Aaron. "Human Nature." *The Cambridge History of Eighteenth-Century Philosophy*. Ed. K. Haakonssen. Cambridge: Cambridge University Press, 2006, 160–233.

Garrut, J. M. *L'Exposició Universal de Barcelona de 1888*. Barcelona: Ajuntament. Delegació de Cultura, 1976.

Gasman, Daniel. *The Scientific Origins of National Socialism: Social Darwinism in Ernst Haeckel and the German Monist League.* London: Macdonald & Co., 1971.

Gauchet, Marcel. *The Disenchantment of the World: A Political History of Religion.* Trans. Oscar Burge. Princeton, NJ: Princeton University Press, 1999.

Geertz, Clifford. *The Interpretation of Cultures.* New York: Basic Books, 1973.

Genuth, Sara Schechner. *Comets, Popular Culture, and the Birth of Modern Cosmology.* Princeton, NJ: Princeton University Press, 1997.

Gérard, Alice. "Auguste Comte Au Purgatoire." In *Auguste Comte, Qui Êtes-Vous?* Ed. Edgar Faure. Paris: La Manufacture, 1988, 143–79.

Germann, Georg. *Gothic Revival in Europe and Britain: Sources, Influences and Ideas.* London: Lund Humphries, 1972.

Geschiere, Peter. *The Modernity of Witchcraft: Politics and the Occult in Postcolonial Africa.* Trans. Janet Roitman. Charlottesville: University of Virginia Press, 1997.

Gide, André. *Paludes.* Paris: NRF, 1920 [1895].

Gillipsie, Charles. *The Edge of Objectivity: An Essay in the History of Scientific Ideas.* Princeton, NJ: Princeton University Press, 1960.

Giralt, Emili et al. *Romanticisme i Renaixença, 1800–1860.* Barcelona: Edicions 62, 1995.

Glassman, Ronald M., and Vatro Muvar, eds. *Max Weber's Political Sociology: A Pessimistic Vision of a Rationalized World.* Westport, CT: Greenwood Press, 1984.

Glennie, Paul, and Nigel Thrift. "The Spaces of Clock Time." *The Social in Question: New Bearings in History and the Social Sciences.* Ed. Patrick Joyce. London: Routledge, 2002, 151–174.

Godwin, Joscelyn. *The Theosophical Enlightenment.* Albany: State University of New York Press, 1994.

Goetz, Rose. *Destutt de Tracy: philosophie du langage et science de l'homme.* Geneva: Droz, 1993.

Golan, Romy. *Modernity and Nostalgia: Art and Politics in France Between the Wars.* New Haven, CT: Yale University Press, 1995.

González Casanova, J. A. *Federalisme i autonomia a Catalunya, 1868–1936: Documents.* Barcelona: Curail, 1974.

Goodrick-Clarke, Nicolas. *The Occult Roots of Nazism: Secret Aryan Cults and Their Influence on Nazi Ideology.* New York: New York University Press, 1985.

Grandas, M. C. *L'Exposició Internacional de Barcelona de 1929.* Barcelona: Els Llibres de la Frontera, 1988.

Greenblatt, Stephen. *Hamlet in Purgatory.* Princeton, NJ: Princeton University Press, 2001.

———. *Shakespearean Negotiations: The Circulation of Social Energy in Renaissance England.* Berkeley: University of California Press, 1988.

Griffin, Roger. *The Nature of Fascism.* London: Routledge, 1993.

Grivel, Charles. "Le retournement parodique des discours à leurres constants." In *Dire la parodie: colloque de Cerisy.* Eds. Clive Thomson and Alain Pagès. New York: P. Lang, 1989.

Großmann, G. Ulrich, and Petra Krutisch, eds. *Renaissance der Renaissance: Ein bürgerlicher Kunststil im 19. Jarhrhundert. I: Aufsätze*. München: Deutscher Kunstverlag, 1992.

Guise, René, ed. *Ponson du Terrail: Éléments pour une histoire des textes*. Nancy: Centre de Recherches sur le Roman populaire, 1986.

Gumbrecht, Hans Ulrich. *In Praise of Athletic Beauty*. Cambridge, MA: Harvard University Press, 2006.

———. "'I redentori della vittoria.' Über den Ort Fiumes in der Genealogie des Faschismus." *Der Dichter als Kommandant. D'Annunzio erobert Fiume*. Eds. Hans Ulrich Gumbrecht, Friedrich Kittler, and Bernhard Siegert. Munich: Wilhelm Fink Verlag, 1996. 83–116.

———. *Production of Presence: What Meaning Cannot Convey*. Stanford, CA: Stanford University Press, 2004.

———. "Stendhals nervöser Ernst." *Sprachen der Ironie/Sprachen des Ernstes*. Ed. Karl Heinz Bohrer. Frankfurt: Suhrkamp, 2000, 206–32.

Gunning, Tom. "An Aesthetic of Astonishment: Early Film and the (In)Credulous Spectator," in *Film Theory and Criticism: Introductory Readings*. Eds. Leo Braudy and Marshall Cohen. New York: Oxford University Press, 1999, 818–32.

Habermas, Jürgen. *The Structural Transformation of the Public Sphere*. Trans. Thomas Burger. Cambridge, MA: MIT Press, 1992.

Haeckel, Ernst. *Die Welträthsel. Gemeinverständliche Studien über Monistische Philosophie* Bonn: Verlag von Emil Strauß, 1899.

Hahn, Roger. *The Anatomy of a Scientific Institution: The Paris Academy of Sciences, 1666–1803*. Berkeley: University of California Press, 1971.

Hall, Marcia. *Color and Meaning: Practice and Theory in Renaissance Painting*. Cambridge: Cambridge University Press, 1992.

———, ed. *The Cambridge Companion to Raphael*. Cambridge: Cambridge University Press, 2005.

Halpern, Ben. "'Myth' and 'Ideology' in Modern Usage." *History and Theory* 1, no. 2 (1961): 141–49.

Hannon, Patricia. *Fabulous Identities: Women's Fairy Tales in Seventeenth-Century France*. Amsterdam: Rodopi, 1998.

Harris, Marvin. *The Rise of Anthropological Theory: A History of Theories of Culture*. New York: Crowell, 1968.

Harrison, Joseph. "An Espanya Catalana: Catalanist Plans to Transform Spain into a Modern Capitalist Economy, 1898–1923." *Journal of Iberian and Latin American Studies* 7, no. 2 (2001): 143–56.

Harrison, Robert. *Forests: The Shadow of Civilization*. Chicago: University of Chicago Press, 1992.

Hartley, Keith et al., eds. *The Romantic Spirit in German Art 1790–1990*. London: Thames & Hudson, 1994.

Hartmann, Kristiana. "Bruno Taut—the Architect, the Painter, the Colour." *Daidalus* 42.15 (1991): 24–39.

Hartmann-Virnich, Andreas. *Was ist Romanik? Geschichte, Formen und Technik des romanischen Kirchenbaus.* Darmstadt: Wissenschaftliche Buchgesellschaft, 2004.

Harty, Siobhan. "Lawyers, Codifications, and the Origins of Catalan Nationalism, 1881–1901." *Law and History Review* 20.2 (2002): 349–84.

Hathaway, Baxter. *Marvels and Commonplaces: Renaissance Literary Criticism.* New York: Random House, 1968.

Hearn, M. F., ed. *The Architectural Theory of Viollet-le-Duc: Readings and Commentary.* Cambridge, MA: MIT Press, 1995.

Heidegger, Martin. *An Introduction to Metaphysics.* Trans. Ralph Manheim. New Haven, CT: Yale University Press, 1986.

———. *Basic Questions of Philosophy.* Trans. R. Rojcewicz and A. Shuwer. Bloomington: Indiana University Press, 1994.

———. *Being and Time.* Trans. J. Stambaugh. Albany: State University of New York Press, 1996.

———. "Creative Landscape: Why do we stay in the provinces?" *The Weimar Republic Sourcebook.* Ed. Anton Kayes and Martin Jay. Berkeley: University of California Press, 1994.

———. *The Fundamental Concepts of Metaphysics: World, Finitude, Solitude.* Trans. William McNeil and Nicholas Walker. Bloomington: Indiana University Press, 1995.

———. *Nietzsche.* Pfullingen: Neske, 1961.

———. "The Origin of the Work of Art." *Basic Writings.* Ed. David F. Krell. San Francisco: Harper & Row, 1977.

Herbert, Christopher. *Culture and Anomie: Ethnographic Imagination in the Nineteenth Century.* Chicago: University of Chicago Press, 1991.

Herman, Arthur. *The Idea of Decline in Western History.* New York: Free Press, 1997.

Hernàndez-Cros, Josep Emili, Gabriel Mora, and Xavier Pouplana. *Arquitectura de Barcelona.* Barcelona: Demarcació de Barcelona del Collegi d'Arquitectes de Catalunya, 1989.

Herrmann, Wolfgang. *Gottfried Semper: In Search of Architecture.* Cambridge, MA: MIT Press, 1984.

Hill, David. *Greek Words and Hebrew Meanings: Studies in the Semantics of Soteriological Terms.* Cambridge: Cambridge University Press, 1967.

Hina, Horst. *Kastilien und Katalonien in der Kulturdiskussion, 1714–1939.* Tübingen: Niemeyer, 1978.

Hitler's Secret Conversations, 1941–44. Trans. Norman Cameron and R. H. Stevens. New York: Signet Books, 1953.

Hollinger, David. *In the American Province.* Bloomington: Indiana University Press, 1985.

Horkheimer, Max, and Theodor Adorno. *Dialektik der Aufklärung: Philosophiche Fragmente.* Frankfurt am Main: S. Fischer, 1969.

———. *Dialectic of Enlightenment: Philosophical Fragments*. Trans. Gunzelin Schmid Noerr and Edmund Jephcott. Stanford: Stanford University Press, 2002.

Hösle, Johannes. *Die katalanische Literatur von der Renaixença bis zur Gegenwart*. Tübingen: Max Niemeyer Verlag, 1982.

Hughes, H. Stuart. *Consciousness and Society: The Reorientation of European Social Thought, 1890–1930*. New York: Vintage Books, 1961.

Hugo, Victor. *Les Contemplations*. Paris: Hachette, 1922 [1856].

———. *Les Misérables*. Paris: Pléiade, 1951, 125.

Huysmans, Joris-Karl. *Oeuvres Complètes XII*. Genève: Slatkine Reprints, 1972.

Hvattum, Mari. *Gottfried Semper and the Problem of Historicism*. Cambridge: Cambridge University Press, 2004.

Ionesco, Eugène. *Le roi se meurt*. Paris: Gallimard, 1963.

Irwin, Robert. Introduction to *Là Bas: A Journey into the Self* by Joris-Karl Huysmans. Trans. Brendan King. London: Daedalus, 1986.

Israel, Jonathan. *Radical Enlightenment: Philosophy and the Making of Modernity, 1650–1750*. Oxford: Oxford University Press, 2001.

Jacobson, Stephen. "Law and Nationalism in Nineteenth-Century Europe: The Case of Catalonia in Comparative Perspective." *Law and History Review* 20.2 (2002): 307–47.

Jakobson, Roman. "The Dominant." Trans. by Herbert Eagle. *Readings in Russian Poetics*. Ed. Ladislav Matejka and Krystyna Pomorska. Cambridge, MA: MIT Press, 1971, 82–87.

James, William. *The Correspondence of William James*. Vol. IV. Ed. Ignas K. Skrupskelis and Elizabeth M. Berkeley. Charlottesville: University of Virginia Press, 1997.

———. "The Energies of Men." *The Writings of William James*. Ed. John J. McDermott. Chicago: University of Chicago Press, 1977.

———. *Essays in Psychical Research*. Cambridge, MA: Harvard University Press, 1986.

———. *Essays in Radical Empiricism*. Cambridge, MA: Harvard University Press, 1976.

———. *Manuscript Lectures*. Cambridge, MA: Harvard University Press, 1988.

———. "On Some Omissions in Introspective Psychology," *Mind* 9 (January 1884): 146.

———. *A Pluralistic Universe*. Lincoln: University of Nebraska, 1996 [1909].

———. *Pragmatism*. Cambridge: Harvard University Press, 1978.

———. *Principles of Psychology*. Vol. I. New York: Henry Holt and Company, 1910.

———. *Some Problems of Philosophy*. Cambridge, MA: Harvard University Press, 1979.

———. *The Varieties of Religious Experience*. Cambridge, MA: Harvard University Press, 1985.

———. *The Will to Believe and Other Essays in Popular Philosophy*. New York: Dover, 1956.

Jameson, Fredric. "Progress Versus Utopia: Or, Can We Imagine the Future?" *Art after Modernism: Rethinking Representation.* Ed. Brian Wallis. New York: New Museum of Contemporary Art, 1984, 239–52.

Jardí, Enric. *Puig i Cadafalch: arquitecte, politic i historiador de l'art.* Barcelona: Editorial Ariel, 1975.

Jaspers, Karl. *Nietzsche and Christianity.* Trans. E. B. Ashton. Chicago: H. Regnery Co., 1961 [1938].

Jaume, Lucien. *Le Discours jacobin et la démocratie.* Paris: Fayard, 1989.

Jennings, Michael W. *Dialectical Images: Walter Benjamin's Theory of Literary Criticism.* Ithaca, NY: Cornell University Press, 1987.

John, Peter C. "Wittgenstein's 'Wonderful Life.'" *Journal of the History of Ideas* 49, no. 3 (July–September, 1988): 495–510.

Johnson, Barbara. "Les Fleurs Du Mal Armé: Some Reflections on Intertextuality." *Lyric Poetry: Beyond New Criticism.* Eds. Chavia Parker, Patricia Hosek, and Jonathan Arac. Ithaca, NY: Cornell University Press, 1985, 264–80.

Johnston, Arthur. *Enchanted Ground: The Study of Medieval Romance in the Eighteenth Century.* London: Athlone Press, 1964.

Jonas, Hans. *The Gnostic Religion. The Message of the Alien God and the Beginnings of Christianity.* 2nd ed. Boston: Beacon Press, 1958 [1963].

Jordan, David P. *The Revolutionary Career of Maximilien Robespierre.* New York: Free Press, 1985.

Joshi, Sanjay. *Fractured Modernity: Making of a Middle Class in Colonial North India.* New York: Oxford University Press, 2001.

Joyce, James. *Ulysses.* New York: Vintage, 1990.

Juden, Brian. *Traditions orphiques et tendances mystiques dans le romantisme français (1800–1855).* Geneva: Slatkine Reprints, 1984.

Julia de Fontenelle, Jean Sébastien Eugène. *Nouveau Manuel Complet Des Sorciers, Ou La Magie Blanche, Dévoilée Par Les Découvertes De La Chimie, De La Physique Et De La Mécanique, Contenant Un Grand Nombre De Tours Dus À L'électricité, Au Calorique, À La Lumière, À L'air, Aux Nombres, Aux Cartes, À L'escamotage, Etc.* Paris: Roret, 1837.

Kaempfert, Manfred. *Säkularisation und neue Heiligkeit: Religiöse und religionsbezogene Sprache bei Friedrich Nietzsche.* Berlin: Erich Schmidt Verlag, 1971.

Kalberg, Stephen. "Max Weber's Types of Rationality." *American Journal of Sociology* 85.5 (1980): 2245–79.

Kammen, Michael. *American Culture, American Tastes: Social Change in the Twentieth Century.* New York: Alfred A. Knopf, 1999.

Kany, Roland. *Mnemosyne als Programm. Geschichte, Erinnerung und die Andacht zum Unbedeutenden im Werk von Usener, Warburg und Benjamin.* Tübingen: Max Niemeyer, 1987.

Kaplan, Alice Yaeger. *Reproductions of Banality: Fascism, Literature, and French Intellectual Life.* Minneapolis: University of Minnesota Press, 1986.

Kasper, W. et al. *Lexikon für Theologie und Kirche.* Freiburg: Herder, 1995.

Kaufmann, Vincent. *Le Livre Et Ses Adresses (Mallarmé, Ponge, Valéry, Blanchot).* Paris: Méridiens Klincksieck, 1986.

Kennedy, Emmet. *A Philosophe in the Age of Revolution: Destutt de Tracy and the Origins of "Ideology."* Philadelphia: American Philosophical Society, 1978.

Kepler, Johannes. *Harmonices mundi.* Bologna: Ferri, 1969 [1619].

Kerbs, Diethart, and Jürgen Reulecke. *Handbuch der deutschen Reformbewegungen 1880 bis 1933.* Wuppertal: Hammer, 1998.

Kern, Stephen. *The Culture of Time and Space, 1880–1918.* Cambridge, MA: Harvard University Press, 1983.

Kierkegaard, Søren. *The Sickness unto Death.* Trans. H. V. Hong and E. H. Hong. Princeton, NJ: Princeton University Press, 1980 [1849].

King, Karen L. *What is Gnosticism?* Cambridge, MA: The Belknap Press of Harvard University Press, 2003.

Kingsley-Porter, Arthur. *Lombard Architecture* (4 vols). New Haven, CT: Yale University Press, 1915–17.

Kintzler, Catherine. *Poétique de l'opéra français, de Corneille à Rousseau.* Paris: Minèrve, 1991.

Klagge, James C., ed. *Wittgenstein: Biography and Philosophy.* Cambridge: Cambridge University Press, 2001.

Klagge, James C., and Alfred Nordmann. *Ludwig Wittgenstein: Public and Private Occasions.* Lanham, MD: Roman & Littlefield Publishers, Inc., 2003.

Knight, Isabel. *The Geometric Spirit: The Abbé de Condillac and the French Enlightenment.* New Haven, CT: Yale University Press, 1968.

Koselleck, Reinhart. "Historical Criteria of the Modern Concept of Revolution." In *Futures Past: On the Semantics of the Historical Time.* Trans. Keith Tribe. New York: Columbia University Press, 2004.

Kubach, Erich. "Die Architektur zur Zeit der Karolinger und Ottonen." *Das frühmittelalterliche Imperium.* Eds. Erich Kubach and Victor H. Elberm. Baden-Baden: Holle, 1968.

Kymlicka, Will. "Liberal Egalitarianism and Civic Republicanism: Friends or Enemies?" *In Debating Democracy's Discontent.* Eds. Anita L. Allen and Milton C. Regan Jr. Oxford: Oxford University Press, 1998.

Labrousse, Elisabeth. *L'Entrée de Saturne au lion (l'éclipse de soleil du 12 août 1654).* The Hague: M. Nijhoff, 1974.

Lakoff, George. *Don't Think of an Elephant: Know Your Values and Frame the Debate—The Essentail Guide for Progressives.* White River Junction, VT: Chelsea Green Publishing Company, 2004.

———. *Moral Politics: How Liberals and Conservatives Think.* Chicago: University of Chicago Press, 2002.

Lamb, Geoffrey. *Victorian Magic.* London: Routledge, 1976.

Landy, Joshua. "Music, Letters, Truth and Lies: 'L'après-Midi D'un Faune' as an Ars Poetica." *Yearbook of Comparative and General Literature 1994* (1994): 57–69.

Laqueur, Thomas W. *Solitary Sex: A Cultural History of Masturbation.* New York: Zone, 2004.

Lash, Scott, and Jonathan Friedman, eds. *Modernity and Identity.* Oxford: Blackwell Publishing, 1992.

Lasky, Melvin J. *Utopia and Revolution.* Chicago: University of Chicago Press, 1976.

Laslett, Peter. *The World We Have Lost.* New York: Routledge, 2004 [1965].

Latour, Bruno. "How to Be Iconophilic in Art, Science, and Religion?" *Picturing Science, Producing Art.* Ed. Caroline A. Jones and Peter Galison. New York: Routledge, 1998.

———. *We Have Never Been Modern.* Trans. Catherine Porter. Cambridge, MA: Harvard University Press, 1993.

———. "Why Has Critique Run out of Steam? From Matters of Fact to Matters of Concern," *Critical Inquiry* 30 (2004): 225–48.

Lears, T. J. Jackson. *No Place of Grace: Antimodernism and the Transformation of American Culture, 1880–1920.* New York: Pantheon Books, 1981.

Leroux, Pierre. "*Encyclopédie nouvelle,* v. v. 'Culte.'" *A la source perdue du socialisme français: Peirre Leroux.* Ed. Bruno Viard. Paris: Desclée de Brouwer, 1997.

Lévi, Eliphas. *Eliphas Lévi, visionnaire romantique.* Ed. Frank Bowman. Paris: PUF, 1969.

Levine, Lawrence. *Highbrow/Lowbrow: The Emergence of Cultural Hierarchy in America.* Cambridge, MA: Harvard University Press, 1988.

Lichtheim, George. *The Concept of Ideology and Other Essays.* New York: Random House, 1967.

Liefeld, W. L. "Transfigure." In Colin Brown et al. *The New International Dictionary of New Testament Theology.* Grand Rapids, MI: Zondervan, 1978.

Lincoln, Bruce. *Theorizing Myth: Narrative, Ideology, and Scholarship.* Chicago: University of Chicago Press, 2000.

Linton, Marisa. "Robespierre's Political Principles." *Robespierre.* Eds. Colin Haydon and William Doyle. Cambridge: Cambridge University Press, 1999.

Llorenz i Vil, Jordi. *La Unió Catalanista i els orígens del catalnisme polític.* Barcelona: Barcelona Publicacions de l'Abadia de Montserrat, 1992.

Lofficier, Jean-Marc, and Randy Lofficier. *Shadowmen: Heroes and Villains of French Pulp Fiction.* Encino: Black Coat Press, 2003.

Löwith, Karl. *Nietzsche's Philosophy of the Eternal Recurrence.* Trans. J. H. Lomax. Berkeley: University of California Press, 1997 [1935].

Loy, J. Robert. *Diderot's Determined Fatalist: A Critical Appreciation of Jacques Le Fataliste.* New York: King's Crown Press, 1950.

Lukács, Georg. *The Theory of the Novel.* Trans. Anna Bostock. Cambridge, MA: MIT Press, 1971.

Lunn, Eugene. *Marxism and Modernism.* Berkeley: University of California Press, 1982.

Lyotard, Jean-Francois. *The Postmodern Condition: A Report on Knowledge.* Trans. Geoff Bennington and Brian Massumi. Minneapolis: University of Minnesota Press, 1984.

Mabille, Pierre. *The Mirror of the Marvelous: The Classic Surrealist Work on Myth.* Preface by André Breton. Trans. Jody Gladding. Rochester, VT: Inner Traditions, 1998.

MacIntyre, Alasdair. *Dependent Rational Animals*. Chicago: University of Chicago Press, 1999.

Mackay, Charles. *Memoirs of Extraordinary Popular Delusions*. London: Routledge, 1869.

Malcolm, Norman. *Ludwig Wittgenstein: A Memoir*. Oxford: Oxford University Press, 1984 [1958].

Mallarmé, Stéphane. *Correspondance*. Ed. Henri Mondor. Paris: Gallimard, 1959–1985.

———. *Oeuvres Complètes*. Paris: Gallimard, 1998 and 2003.

Mannheim, Karl. *Ideology and Utopia: An Introduction to the Sociology of Knowledge*. Trans. Louis Wirth and Edward Shils. London: Routledge, 1966 [1929].

Manuel, Frank. *The Eighteenth Century Confronts the Gods*. Cambridge, MA: Harvard University Press, 1959.

———. *The New World of Henri Saint-Simon*. Cambridge, MA: Harvard University Press, 1956.

———. *The Prophets of Paris*. New York: Harper, 1965.

Marchal, Bertrand. *Lecture de Mallarmé : Poésies, Igitur, Le coup de dés*. Paris: Corti, 1985.

Marfany, Joan-Lluís. *La cultura del catalnisme: El nacionalisme català en els seus incisis*. Barcelona: Empuréis, 1995.

———. *La llengua maltractada. El castellà i el català a Catalunya del segle XVI al segle XIX*. Barcelona: Editorial Empúries, 2001.

———. "El Modernisme." Martí de Riquer, Antoni Comas and Joaquim Molas. Eds. *Història de la literatura catalana*. 11 vols. Barcelona: Ariel, 1984–88. Vol. 8, 76–142.

Mariel, Pierre. *Dictionnaire Des Sociétés Secrètes En Occident*. Paris: Culture, Art, Loisirs, 1971.

———. *Cagliostro: Imposteur Ou Martyr?* Paris: Culture, Art, Loisirs, 1973.

Marin, Louis. *La Critique du discours: Sur la "Logique de Port-Royal" et les "Pensées" de Pascal*. Collection Le Sens commun. Paris: Minuit, 1975.

Marsh, Jan. *The Pre-Raphaelites*. London: National Portrait Gallery, 1998.

Martin, Henri-Jean, and Roger Chartier, eds. *L'Histoire de l'édition française*. Vol. III *Les temps des éditeurs: Du Romantisme à la Belle Époque*. Paris: Promodis, 1985.

Marx, Jacques. "Le Concept d'imagination au XVIIIe siècle." *Thèmes et figures du siècle des Lumières: Mélanges offerts à Roland Mortier*. Ed. Raymond Trousson. Geneva: Droz, 1980, 147–59.

Marx, Karl, and Friedrich Engels. *The Holy Family*. Moscow: Foreign Language Publishing, 1956.

May, Georges. *Les Mille et une nuits d'Antoine Galland, ou, le chef-d'oeuvre invisible*. Paris: PUF, 1986.

Mayeur, Jean-Marie and Madeleine Rebirioux. *The Third Republic from Its Origins to the Great War, 1871–1914*. Trans. J. R. Foster. Cambridge: Cambridge University Press, 1984.

McDonald, Christie. *The Proustian Fabric: Associations of Memory*. Lincoln: University of Michigan Press, 2005.

McGuckin, John Anthony. *The Transfiguration of Christ in Scripture and Tradition. Studies in the Bible and Early Christianity*, Vol. 9. Lewiston: Edwin Mellin Press, 1986.

McKeon, Michael. *The Origins of the English Novel, 1600–1740*. Baltimore: Johns Hopkins University Press, 1987.

McMahon, Darrin. *Enemies of the Enlightenment: The French Counter-Enlightenment and the Making of Modernity*. Oxford: Oxford University Press, 2001.

Mercier-Faivre, Anne-Marie. *Un Supplément à l' "Encyclopédie:" Le "Monde Primitif" d'Antoine Court de Gébelin*. Paris: Champion, 1999.

Mesecke, Andrea. *Josep Puig i Cadafalch, 1867–1956: Katalanisches Selbstverständnis und Internationalität in der Architektur*. Frankfurt: Lang, 1995.

Messac, Régis. *Le "Detective Novel" et l'influence de la pensée scientifique*. Paris: Honré Champion, 1929.

Meyer zur Capellen, Jürg. *Raphael: a Critical Catalogue of his Paintings*. Trans. Stefan Polter. Landshut: Arcos, 2005.

Michaud, Guy. *Biographe universelle ancienne et moderne*. Paris: Mme. C. Desplaces, 1885.

———. *Mallarmé*. Paris: Hatier, 1958.

Michonneau, Stéphane. "Barcelone 1900–1910: la construction d'un espace symbolique." *Rives nord–méditerranéennes, Patrimonie et politiques urbaines en Méditerranée* 16 November 2005 <http://rives.revues.org/document438.html>.

———. *Barcelona, memòria i identitat. Monuments, commemoracions i mites*. Barcelona: Eumo, 2002.

Miller, James. *The Passion of Michel Foucault*. New York: Simon & Schuster, 1993.

Milner, Max. *Le Diable dans la littérature française de Cazotte à Baudelaire, 1772–1861*. 2 vols. Paris: Corti, 1960.

Miró y Murtó, Juan. *El Palacio de Justícia y la Ciudad de Barcelona*. Barcelona: Imp. L. Tasso Serra, 1883.

Molas, Isidro. *Lliga Catalana: Un estudi d'estasiologia*. 2 vols. Barcelona: Edicions 62, 1972. I: 27.

Monk, Ray. *Ludwig Wittgenstein: The Duty of Genius*. New York: Penguin, 1990.

Moore, Henrietta L., and Todd Sanders, eds. *Magical Interpretations, Material Realities: Modernity, Witchcraft, and the Occult in Postcolonial Africa*. London: Routledge, 2001.

Moravia, Sergio. *Il pensiero degli ideologues*. Florence: Nuova Italia, 1974.

———. *Il tramonto dell'illuminismo*. Bari: Laterza, 1968.

Moretti, Franco. "Graphs, Maps, Trees: Abstract Models for Literary History—1." *New Left Review* 24 (2003): 67–93.

Morton, Margaret, and Diana Balmori. *Transitory Gardens, Uprooted Lives*. New Haven, CT: Yale University Press, 1995.

Mücke, Dorothea E. Von. *The Seduction of the Ocult and the Rise of the Fantastic Tale*. Stanford: Stanford University Press, 2003.

Muecke, D. C. *The Compass of Irony*. London: Methuen, 1967.

Munsterberg, Hugo et al. *Subconscious Phenomena.* Boston: Richard G. Badger, 1910.

Muravchik, Joshua. "Our Worst Ex-President." *Commentary,* February 2007, 17–26.

Murphy, Kevin D. *Memory and Modernity: Viollet-le-Duc at Vézelay.* University Park: Pennsylvania State University Press, 2000.

Musset, Alfred de. *La Confession d'un enfant du siècle.* Paris: GF, 1993 [1836].

Mussolini, Benito. "The Naples Speech." In *Fascism,* ed. and trans. Roger Griffin. New York: Oxford University Press, 1995, 44.

Myers, Frederic W. H. *Human Personality and Its Survival of Bodily Death.* Ed. Susy Smith. New Hyde Park, NY: University Books, 1961 [1903].

Myers, Gerald E. "Introspection and the Unconscious." In *Theories of the Unconscious and Theories of the Self.* Hillsdale, NJ: The Analytic Press, 1987, 91–108.

Nancy, Jean-Luc, and Philippe Lacoue-Labarthe. "The Nazi Myth." Trans. Brian Holmes. *Critical Inquiry* 16.2 (1990): 291–312.

Nead, Lynda. *Victorian Babylon: People, Streets and Images in Nineteenth-Century London.* New Haven, CT: Yale University Press, 2005 [2000].

Nehamas, Alexander. *Nietzsche: Life as Literature.* Cambridge, MA: Harvard University Press, 1985.

———. "The Eternal Recurrence." *Philosophical Review* 89 (1980): 331–56.

———. "How One Becomes What One Is." *Philosophical Review* 92 (1983): 385–417.

Nelson, Robert J. "Mallarmé's Mirror of Art: An Explication of *Ses Purs Ongles.*" *Modern Language Quarterly* 20 (1959): 49–56.

Nelson, Victoria. *The Secret Life of Puppets.* Cambridge, MA: Havard University Press, 2001.

Nelson, William. *Fact or Fiction: The Dilemma of the Renaissance Storyteller.* Cambridge, MA: Harvard University Press, 1973.

Nicolai, Bernd. "Arthur Kingsley-Porter." *Altmeister moderner Kunstgeschichte.* Ed. Heinrich Dilly. Berlin: Reimer, 1990.

Nietzsche, Friedrich. *Beyond Good and Evil.* Trans. Walter Kaufmann. New York: Vintage, 1966 [1886].

———. *The Birth of Tragedy.* Trans. Walter Kaufmann. New York: Vintage, 1966 [1872].

———. *Ecce Homo.* Trans. Walter Kaufmann. New York: Vintage, 1968 [1888].

———. *The Gay Science.* Trans. Walter Kaufmann. New York: Vintage, 1974 [1882, 1887].

———. *On the Genealogy of Morals.* Trans. Walter Kaufmann. New York: Vintage, 1968 [1887].

———. *Thus Spoke Zarathustra.* Trans. Walter Kaufmann. New York: Viking, 1954 [1883–5].

———. *Twilight of the Idols.* Trans. Walter Kaufmann. New York: Viking, 1954 [1888].

———. *Werke: Kritische Studienausgabe,* ed. G. Colli and M. Montinari. Berlin: W. de Gruyter, 1980 ff.

Noulet, Emilie. *Vingt Poèmes De Stéphane Mallarmé*. Geneva: Droz, 1967.

Nützel, Johannes M., et al. "Verklärung Jesu." In Kasper, W., et al. *Lexikon für Theologie und Kirche*. Freiburg: Herder, 1995, 678–80.

Oberhuber, Konrad. *Raphael: The Paintings*. Munich: Prestel, 1999 [1983].

Olds, Marshall C. "Mallarmé's 'Glorieux Mensonge.'" *West Virginia University Philological Papers* 30 (1984): 1–9.

Oppé, A. P. *Raphael*. Ed. C. Mitchell. New York: Praeger, 1970 [1909].

Ortega y Gasset, José. "The Dehumanization of Art." *The Dehumanization of Art and Other Essays on Art, Culture, and Literature*. Trans. Helene Weyl. Princeton. NJ: Princeton University Press, 1968 [1925], 1–54.

Ovid. *Metamorphoses*. *Metamorphoses*. Trans. A. D. Melville. Oxford: Oxford University Press, 1986.

———. *Metamorphoses*. Trans. Michael Simpson. Amherst: University of Massachusetts Press. 2001.

Owen, Alex. *The Place of Enchantment: British Occultism and the Culture of the Modern*. Chicago: University of Chicago Press, 2004.

Pagels, Elaine. *The Gnostic Gospels*. New York: Vintage, 1979.

Paige, Nicholas. "L'Affaire des poisons et l'imaginaire de l'enquête: De Molière à Thomas Corneille." *Littératures Classiques* 40 (2000): 195–208.

———. "Relearning to Read: Truth and Reference in Subligny's *La Fausse Clélie*." In *Forms of Instruction: Education, Pedagogy, and Literature in Seventeenth-Century France*. Ed. Anne Birberick. Amsterdam: Rodopi, 2008, 15–51.

Pauen, Michael. *Dithyrambiker des Untergangs. Gnostizismus in Ästhetik und Philosophie der Moderne*. Berlin: Akademie Verlag, 1994.

Pavel, Thomas. *Fictional Worlds*. Cambridge, MA: Harvard University Press, 1986.

Payne, Stanley G. "Nationalism, Regionalism and Micronationalism in Spain." *Journal of Contemporary History* 26, no. 3/4 (1991): 179–91.

Peace, Richard. "Dostoyevsky and 'The Golden Age.'" *Dostoyevsky Studies* 3 (1982): 61–78.

Pearson, Roger. *Unfolding Mallarmé: The Development of a Poetic Art*. Oxford: Oxford University Press, 1996.

Pedretti, Carlo. *Raphael: His Life and Work in the Splendors of the Italian Renaissance*. Florence: Giunti, 1989.

Permanyer, Lluís, and Lluís Casals. *Josep Puig i Cadafalch*. Barcelona: Ediciones Polígraphia, 2001.

Phelps, Reginald. "'Before Hitler Came': Thule Society and Germanen Order." *Journal of Modern History* 35 (1963): 245–61.

Pieper, Josef. *Hope and History*. Trans. Richard Winston and Clara Winston. New York: Herder, 1969.

Piette, Adam. *Remembering and the Sound of Words: Mallarmé, Proust, Joyce, Beckett*. Oxford: Clarendon Press, 1996.

Pillow, Kirk. *Sublime Understanding*. Cambridge, MA: MIT Press, 2001.

Pippin, Robert. "Technology as Ideology." *Idealism as Modernism: Hegelian Variations*. Cambridge: Cambridge University Press, 1997.

Pocock, J. G. A. *Barbarism and Religion, I. The Enlightenments of Edward Gibbon, 1737–1764.* Cambridge: Cambridge University Press, 1999.

———. *The Machiavellian Moment: Florentine Political Thought and the Atlantic Republican Tradition.* Princeton, NJ: Princeton Univeristy Press, 1975.

Poe, Edgar Allan. *The Murders in the Rue Morgue.* In *Selected Tales.* London: Penguin, 1994.

Poirion, Daniel. *Le Merveilleux dans la littérature française du moyen âge.* Paris: PUF, 1982.

Ponson du Terrail, Pierre Alexis. *Rocambole.* In 3 vols. *L'Héritage mystérieux* vol. I, *L'Héritage mystérieux* vol. II, and *Le Club des valets de cœur.* Brussels: Éditions Complexe, 1991.

———. *Rocambole.* In 2 vols. *Les Exploits de Rocambole* and *La Résurrection de Rocambole.* Preface by Laurent Bazin. Paris: Robert Laffont, 1992.

Popper, Karl. *The Open Society and Its Enemies.* London: Routledge & Kegan Paul, 1966 [1945].

Port, M. H. ed. *Houses of Parliament.* New Haven, CT: Yale University Press, 1976.

Prakash, Gyan. *Another Reason: Science and the Imagination of Modern India.* Princeton, NJ: Princeton University Press, 1999.

Prat de la Riba, Enric. *La nacionalitat catalana.* 4th edition. Barcelona: Edicions 62, 1998 [1906].

Prettejohn, Elizabeth. *The Art of the pre-Raphaelites.* London: Tate Publishing, 2000.

Proust, Marcel. *Le Côté De Guermantes.* Paris: Gallimard, 1988.

———. *The Guermantes Way.* Trans. C. K. Scott Moncrieff, Terence Kilmartin, and D. J. Enright. London: Chatto & Windus, 1992.

———. *Time Regained.* Trans. Terence Kilmartin and D. J. Enright Andreas Mayor. New York: Modern Library, 1993.

Puig i Cadafalch, Josep. *L'architectura romànica a Catalunya.* 3 vols. Barcelona: Institut d'Estudis Catalans, 1909–18.

———. *La géographie et les origines du premier art roman.* Trans. Jeanne Vielliard. Paris: H. Laurens, 1935.

Quendler, Christian. *From Romantic Irony to Postmodernist Metafiction.* Frankfurt: Peter Lang, 2001.

Rabinbach, Anson. *In the Shadow of Catastrophe: German Intellectuals between Apocalypse and Enlightenment.* Berkeley: University of California Press, 1997.

Ramaswamy, Sumathi. *The Lost Land of Lemuria: Fabulous Geographies, Catastrophic Histories.* Berkeley: University of California Press, 2004.

Rancière, Jacques. "The Aesthetic Revolution and Its Outcomes: Emplotments of Autonomy and Heteronomy." *New Left Review* 14 (2002): 133–51.

———. *La Parole muette: Essai sur les contradictions de la littérature.* Paris: Hachette, 1998.

———. *The Politics of Aesthetics: The Distribution of the Sensible.* Trans. Gabriel Rockhill. London: Continuum, 2004.

Rawls, John. *A Theory of Justice.* Cambridge, MA: Belknap Press of Harvard University Press, 1971.

Reed, Christopher, ed. *Not At Home: The Suppression of Domesticity in Modern Art and Architecture.* London: Thames and Hudson, 1996.

Reginster, Bernard. *The Affirmation of Life: Nietzsche on Overcoming of Nihilism.* Cambridge, MA: Harvard University Press, 2006.

Reiss, Timothy J. *The Discourse of Modernism.* Ithaca, NY: Cornell University Press, 1982.

Renan, Ernst. *L'avenir De La Science: Pensées De 1848.* Paris: Calmann-Lévy, 1890.

Repp, Kevin. *Reformers, Critics, and the Paths of German Modernity: Anti-Politics and the Search for Alternatives, 1890–1914.* Cambridge, MA: Harvard University Press, 2000.

Ricardou, Jean. *Mallarmé ou l'obscurité lumineuse.* Paris: Editions Hermann, 1999.

Richard, Jean-Pierre. *L'univers Imaginaire De Mallarmé.* Paris: Seuil, 1961.

Ricoeur, Paul. *Time and Narrative.* Vol. 1. Trans. K. McLaughlin and D. Pellauer. Chicago: University of Chicago Press, 1984.

Riegl, Alois. *Problems of Style: Foundations for a History of Ornament.* Trans. Evelyn Kain. Princeton, NJ: Princeton University Press, 1992.

Rilke, Rainer Maria. *Duino Elegies.* Trans. C. F. MacIntyre. Berkeley: University of California Press, 1961.

Ripoll, Elisabeth. "La fin de Rocambole?" In *Du Côté du populaire.* Saint-Etienne: Centre interdisciplinaire d'études et de recherches sur l'expression contemporaine, 1994.

Riskin, Jessica. *Science in the Age of Sensibility: The Sentimental Empiricists of the French Enlightenment.* Chicago: University of Chicago Press, 2002.

Robb, Graham. *Unlocking Mallarmé.* New Haven, CT: Yale University Press, 1996.

Robert, Raymonde. *Le Conte de fées littéraire en France de la fin du XVIIe à la fin du XVIIIe siècle.* Nancy: Presses Universitaires de Nancy, 1981.

Robert-Houdin, Jean-Eugène. *Confidences De Robert-Houdin: Une Vie D'artiste.* Paris: Librairie Nouvelle, 1861.

———. *Memoirs of Robert-Houdin.* Trans. Lascelles Wraxall. New York: Dover, 1964.

Roberts, Tyler. *Contesting Spirit: Nietzsche, Affirmation, Religion.* Princeton, NJ: Princeton University Press, 1998.

Robespierre, Maximilien, *Œuvres de Maximilien Robespierre.* Ed. Société des études robespierristes. Ivry: Phénix éditions, 2000.

"Rocambolesque." *Larousse du XXe siècle.* Paris: Librairie Larousse, 1930.

Rohrer, Judith et al. *Josep Puig i Cadafalch: L'arquitectura entre la casa i la ciutat.* Barcelona: Centre Cultural de la Fundació de Pensions, 1989.

Ronsard, Pierre. *Oeuvres complètes,* Vol. 2. Ed. Gustave Cohen. Paris: Gallimard, 1950.

Rosenberg, Daniel. "An Eighteenth-Century Time Machine: The *Encyclopedia of Denis Diderot.*" *Postmodernism and the Enlightenment.* Ed. Daniel Gordon. New York: Routledge, 2001.

Rosenberg, Robert Cecil. *The Myth of the Master Race: Alfred Rosenberg and Nazi Ideology.* New York: Dodd, Mead & Co., 1972.

Rosenfeld, Sophia. *A Revolution in Language: The Problem of Signs in Late Eighteenth-Century France.* Stanford: Stanford University Press, 2001.

Rostow, Walt Whitman. *The Stages of Economic Growth: A Non-Communist Manifesto.* Cambridge: Cambridge University Press, 1960.

Roth, Jack J. *The Cult of Violence: Sorel and the Sorelians.* Berkeley: University of California Press, 1980.

Rothstein, Eric. "Broaching a Cultural Logic of Modernity." *Modern Languages Quarterly* 61, no. 2 (2000): 359–94.

Rovira i Virgili, Antoni. *Els Corrents ideològics de la Renaixença catalana.* Barcelona: Barcino, 1966.

———. *La Renaixença: la represa cultural i política, 1833–1886.* Barcelona: Graó, 1991.

Ruf, Frederick J. *The Creation of Chaos: William James and the Stylistic Making of a Disorderly World.* Albany: State University of New York Press, 1991.

Russell, Charles. "The Context of the Concept." *Romanticism, Modernism, Postmodernism.* Ed. Harry R. Garvin. Lewisburg, PA: Bucknell University Press, 1980, 180–93.

Sadler, Ted. *Nietzsche: Truth and Redemption. Critique of the Postmodernist Nietzsche.* London: Athlone Press, 1995.

Saint Augustine. *The Confessions.* Trans. Henry Chadwick. Oxford: Oxford University Press, 1991.

Saint-Just, Louis de. *Œuvres complètes.* Ed. Michèle Duval. Paris: Lebovici, 1984.

Saint-Simon, Henri de. *De la réorganisation de la société européenne.* Paris: Egron, 1814.

———. *Lettres d'un habitant de Genève à ses contemporains.* N.p., 1803.

Saler, Michael. *The Avant-Garde in Interwar England: Medieval Modernism and the London Underground.* New York: Oxford University Press, 1999.

———. "'Clap If You Believe in Sherlock Holmes': Mass Culture and the Re-Enchantment of Modernity, c. 1890–c. 1940." *The Historical Journal* 46 (2003): 599–622.

———. "At Home in the Ironic Imagination: The Rational Vernacular and Spectacular Texts." In *Vernacular Modernism: Heimat, Globalization, and the Built Environment.* Ed. Maiken Umbach and Bernd Hüppauff. Stanford: Stanford University Press, 2005, 53–83.

———. "Modernity and Enchantment: A Historiographic Review." *The American Historical Review* 111.3 (June, 2006): 692–716.

———. "Whigs and Surrealists: The 'Subtle Links' of Humphrey Jennings' *Pandaemonium.*" *Singular Continuities: Tradition, Nostalgia, and Identity in Modern British Culture.* Eds. George Behlmer and Fred Leventhal. Stanford: Stanford University Press, 2000, 123–42.

Saltus, Edgar Evertson. *The Philosophy of Disenchantment.* New York: Houghton, Mifflin & Co., 1885.

Sandel, Michael. *Democracy's Discontent: America in Search of a Public Philosophy.* Cambridge, MA: Belknap Press of Harvard University Press, 1996.

Santayana, George. *Persons and Places.* London: Constable & Co., 1944.
———. "William James." In *William James Remembered.* Ed. Linda Simon. Lincoln: University of Nebraska, 1996.
Sartre, Jean-Paul. *The Words.* Trans. Bernard Frechtman. New York: Vintage, 1981.
Scaff, Lawrence A. *Fleeing the Iron Cage: Culture, Politics, and Modernity in the Thought of Max Weber.* Berkeley: University of California Press, 1989.
Schechner Genuth, Sara. *Comets, Popular Culture, and the Birth of Modern Cosmology.* Princeton, NJ: Princeton University Press, 1997.
Schechter, Ronald. "Rationalizing the Enlightenment: Postmodernism and Theories of Anti-Semitism." In *Postmodernism and the Enlightenment.* Ed. Daniel Gordon. New York: Routledge, 2000, 93–116.
Schelling, Friedrich von. *The Ages of the World.* Trans. Frederick de Wolfe Bolman, Jr. New York: Columbia University Press, 1942.
Schlegel, Friedrich. *Philosophische Fragmente. Kritische F. Schlegels Ausgabe,* Vol. 18. Ed. E. Behler. Paderborn: Schöningh, 1958.
———. *Lucinde and the Fragments.* Trans. Peter Firchow. Minneapolis: University of Minnesota Press, 1971.
Schneider, Mark A. *Culture and Enchantment.* Chicago: University of Chicago Press, 1993.
Schopenhauer, Arthur. *The World as Will and Representation.* Trans. E. F. J. Payne. New York: Dover, 1958.
Schrödinger, Erwin. *What Is Life? The Physical Aspect of the Living Cell.* New York: Macmillan, 1945.
Scott, James C. *Seeing Like a State: How Certain Schemes to Improve the Human Condition Have Failed.* New Haven, CT: Yale University Press, 1998.
Sedgwick, Mark J. *Against the Modern World: Traditionalism and the Secret Intellectual History of the Twentieth Century.* New York: Oxford University Press, 2004.
Seifert, Lewis Carl. *Fairy Tales, Sexuality, and Gender in France, 1690–1715: Nostalgic Utopias.* Cambridge: Cambridge University Press, 1996.
Sellier, Philippe. "L'Invention d'un merveilleux: Le Comte de Gabalis (1670)." *Amicitia Scriptor: Littérature, histoire des idées, philosophie. Mélanges offerts à Robert Mauzi.* Eds. Annie Becq, Charles Porset, and Alain Mothu. Paris: Champion, 1998, 53–62.
Sermain, Jean-Paul. *Métafictions: La Réflexivité dans la littérature d'imagination (1670–1730).* Paris: Champion, 2002.
———. *Le Singe de don Quichotte: Marivaux, Cervantes et le roman postcritique.* Oxford: Voltaire Foundation, 1999.
Serres, Michel. *Variations sur le corps.* 2nd edition. Paris: Pommier, 2002.
Serroy, Jean. *Roman et réalité: Les Histoires comiques au XVIIe siècle.* Paris: Minard, 1981.
Severn, Bill. *Magic and Magicians.* New York: Van Rees Press, 1958.
Sewell, William H. Jr. "Ideologies and Social Revolutions: Reflections on the French Case." *Journal of Modern History* 57.1 (1985): 57–85.

Shearman, John. *Raphael in Early Modern Sources (1483–1602)*. New Haven, CT: Yale University Press, 2003.

Shils, Edward. "Max Weber and the World Since 1920." *Max Weber and His Contemporaries*. Eds. Wolfgang Mommsen and Jurgen Osterhammel. London: Allen & Unwin, 1987.

Sidney, Sir Philip. "An Apology for Poetry." *The Critical Tradition: Classic Texts and Contemporary Trends*. Ed. David H. Richter. New York: St. Martin's Press, 1989.

Sigfried, Charlene. *Chaos and Context: A Study in William James*. Athens: Ohio University Press, 1978.

Simpson, Michael. *The Metamorphoses of Ovid*. Amherst: University of Massachusetts Press, 2001.

Sitte, Camillo. *Der Städtebau nach seinen künstlerischen Grundsätzen*. Basel: Birkhäuser, 2002 [1889].

Smith, Richard. "The Modern Relevance of Gnosticism," in *The Nag Hammadi Library: The Definitive Translation of the Gnostic Scriptures Complete in One Volume*. Ed. James M. Robinson et al. San Francisco: Harper Collins, 1990, 532–49.

Smyth, John Vignaux. *The Habit of Lying: Sacrificial Studies in Literature, Philosophy, and Fashion Theory*. Durham, NC: Duke University Press, 2002.

Sobrequés i Vidal, Santiago. *Història de la producció del dret català fins al decret Nova Planta*. Girona: Collegi Universitari de Girona, 1978.

Sokel, Walter. "Between Gnosticism and Jehovah: The Dilemma in Kafka's Religious Attitude," *South Atlantic Review* 50 no. 1 (Jan. 1985): 3–22.

Solà-Morales, Ignasi. "L'Exposició Internacional de Barcelona (1914–1929) com a instrument de política urbana." *Recerques* 6 (1976): 137–145.

———. *L'Exposició Interncional de Barcelona, 1914–1929: Arquitectura i ciutat*. Barcelona: Fira de Barcelona, 1985.

———. *Gaudí*. Barcelona: Edicions Poligrafa, 1982.

Soll, Ivan. "Reflections on Recurrence." *Nietzsche: a Collection of Critical Essays*. Ed. R. Solomon. Garden City, NY: Anchor Doubleday, 1973, 322–42.

Sorel, Georges. *La Décomposition du marxisme*. Paris: M. Rivière, 1908.

———. "Étude sur Vico." In *Le Devenir social* 2.9 (Oct. 1896): 785–817; 2.10 (Nov. 1896): 906–41; and 2.11 (Dec. 1896): 1013–46.

———. *Introduction à l'économie moderne*. Paris: Rivière, 1922 [1902].

———. *Reflections on Violence*. Ed. Jeremy Jennings. Cambridge: Cambridge University Press, 1999.

Soria y Puig, Arturo, ed. *Cerdà: The Five Bases of the General Theory of Urbanization*. Trans. Bernard Miller and Mary Fons I Fleming. Madrid: Electa, 1999.

The Spectator. Ed. Donald F. Bond. 3 vols. Oxford: Clarendon Press, 1965.

Stafford, Barbara Maria. *Artful Science: Enlightenment Entertainment and the Eclipse of Visual Education*. Cambridge, MA: Harvard University Press, 1994.

Stanley, John. *The Sociology of Virtue: The Political and Social Theories of George Sorel*. Berkeley: University of California Press, 1981.

Starobinski, Jean. "Jalons pour une histoire du concept d'imagination." *L'Oeil vivant II*. Paris: Gallimard, 1970, 173–95.

Staum, Martin. *Minerva's Message: Stabilizing the French Revolution*. Montreal: McGill-Queen's University Press, 1996.

Sternell, Zeev. *The Birth of Fascist Ideology: From Cultural Rebellion to Political Revolution*. Trans. David Maisel. Princeton, NJ: Princeton University Press, 1984.

Stewart, Susan. "Notes on Distressed Genres." *Crimes of Writing: Problems in the Containment of Representation*. New York: Oxford University Press, 1991, 66–101.

Strinati, Dominic. *An Introduction to Theories of Popular Culture*. New York: Routledge, 1995.

Strong, Tracy. *Friedrich Nietzsche and the Politics of Transfiguration*. Urbana: University of Illinois Press, 2000 [1975].

Sturm, Hermann. *Alltag und Kult: Gottfried Semper, Richard Wagner, Friedrich Theodor Vischer, Gottfried Keller*. Basel: Birkäuser, 2003.

Subligny, Adrien-Thomas Perdoux de. *La Fausse Clélie, histoire française, galante et comique*. 1670. Nijmegen: Regnier Smetius, 1680.

Sureda, Joan. *La Pintura románica en Cataluña*. Madrid: Alanza Editorial, 1981.

Surya, Michel. *Georges Bataille: An Intellectual Biography*. New York: Verso, 2002.

Taussig, Michael. *The Magic of the State*. New York: Routledge, 1997.

Taylor, John Tinnon. *Early Opposition to the English Novel: The Popular Reaction from 1760 to 1830*. New York: King's Crown Press, 1943.

Terdiman, Richard. *Present Past: Modernity and the Memory Crisis*. Ithaca, NY: Cornell University Press, 1993.

Terrall, Mary. "Natural Philosophy for Fashionable Readers." *Books and the Sciences in History*. Eds. Marina Frasca-Spada and Nick Jardine. Cambridge: Cambridge University Press, 2000, 239–54.

Terrasson, Jean. *Sethos, histoire, ou Vie tirée des monuments anecdotes de l'ancienne Egypte: traduite d'un manuscrit grec*. Paris: J. Guérin, 1731.

Thoreau, Henry David. "Maine Woods." *Henry David Thoreau: A Week on the Concord and Merrimack Rivers; Walden; or, Life in the Woods; The Maine Woods, Cape Cod*. Washington, DC: The Library of America, 1985.

———. *The Portable Thoreau*. Ed. C. Bode. New York: Penguin, 1982.

———. *Walden and Civil Disobedience*. New York: Penguin, 1983.

Thoveron, Gabriel. *Deux Siècles de Paralittératures: Lecture, Sociologie, Histoire*. Liège: Editions du CÉFAL, 1996.

Todorov, Tzvetan. *The Fantastic: A Structural Approach to a Literary Genre*. Trans. Richard Howard. Ithaca, NY: Cornell University Press, 1975.

Tracy, A.-L.-C. Destutt de. *Analyse raisonnée de l'"Origine de tous les cultes ou réligion universelle"*. Paris: Courcier an XII, 1804 [1795].

———. *Eléments d'idéologies, I. Idéologie proprement dite*. Paris: Vrin, 1970 [1801].

———. *Eléments d'idéologies, II. Grammaire*. Paris: Vve Courcier, 1804.

———. *Mémoire sur la faculté de penser, De la métaphysique de Kant, et d'autres texts*. Ed. Anne and Henry Deneys. Paris: Fayard, 1992.

———. *Quels sont les moyens de fonder la morale chez un peuple?* Paris: Agasse, an VI, 1798.

Traill, Nancy H. *Possible Worlds of the Fantastic: The Rise of the Paranormal in Fiction*. Toronto: University of Toronto Press, 1996.

Treitel, Corinna. *A Science for the Soul: Occultism and the Genesis of the German Modern*. Baltimore: Johns Hopkins University Press, 2004.

Tucker, Robert C., ed. *The Marx-Engels Reader*. New York: Norton, 1978.

——. *Philosophy and Myth in Karl Marx*. Cambridge: Cambridge University Press, 1961.

Tuñón de Lara, M. et al. *Revolución burguesa, oligarquía y constitucionalismo, 1834–1923*. Barcelona: Labor, 1981.

Umbach, Maiken. "A Tale of Second Cities: Autonomy, Culture and the Law in Hamburg and Barcelona in the Long Nineteenth Century." *American Historical Review* 110, no. 3 (June 2005): 659–92.

Umbach, Maiken, and Bernd Hüppauf, eds. *Vernacular Modernism: Heimat, Globalization, and the Built Environment*. Stanford: Stanford University Press, 2006.

Valli, Roberta Suzzi. "The Myth of *Squadrismo* in the Fascist Regime." *Journal of Contemporary History* 35.2 (2000): 131–50.

Varela, Joan R. *La Renaixença: la represa cultural i política, 1833–1886*. Barcelona: Graó, 1991.

Verlaine, Paul. Prologue. *Poèmes sautrniens*. Paris: Librarie Générale Française, 1996 [1866].

Veyne, Paul. *Did the Greeks Believe in Their Myths? An Essay on the Constitutive Imagination*. Trans. Paula Wissing. Chicago: University of Chicago Press, 1988.

Viard, Jacques. *Pierre Leroux et les socialistes européens*. Le Paradou: Actes Sud, 1982.

Viatte, Auguste. *Les Sources occultes du romantisme*. Paris: Champion, 1979.

Voltaire. *Romans et contes*. Paris: Garnier-Flammarion, 1966.

——. "Superstition." *Dictionnaire Philosophique*. Ed. Julien Benda and Raymond Naves. Paris: Garnier, 1954.

Walpole, Horace. *The Castle of Otranto: A Gothic Story*. Eds. W. S. Lewis and E. J. Clery. Oxford: Oxford University Press, 1996, 9–10.

Walter, Klaus-Peter. "La carrière de Ponson du Terrail." *Le Rocambole* 9 (Winter 1999): 13–48.

Walton, Kendall. *Mimesis as Make-Believe*. Cambridge, MA: Harvard University Press, 1990.

Warren, Robert Penn. "Pure and Impure Poetry." *New and Selected Essays*. New York: Random House, 1989, 3–28.

Waugh, Patricia. *Metafiction: The Theory and Practice of Self-Conscious Fiction*. London: Methuen, 1984.

Webb, James. *The Flight from Reason*. London: Macdonald, 1971.

Weber, Eugen. *Peasants into Frenchmen: The Modernization of Rural France, 1870–1914*. London: Chatto and Windus, 1977.

Weber, Max. "Science as a Vocation." *From Max Weber: Essays in Sociology*. Ed. and Trans. H. H. Gerth and C. Wright Mills. Oxford: Oxford University Press, 1946, 129–56.

Weil-Garris Posner, Kathleen. *Leonardo and Central Italian Art: 1515–1550.* New York: New York University Press, 1974. (N.B. Search under Kathleen Weil-Garris Brandt.)

White, Deborah Elise. *Romantic Returns: Superstition, Imagination, History.* Stanford: Stanford University Press, 2000.

Wieckowski, Danièle. *La Poétique De Mallarmé: La Fabrique Des Iridées.* Paris: SEDES, 1998.

Williams, Raymond. *Keywords: A Vocabulary of Culture and Society.* New York: Oxford University Press, 1983.

Wirth, Oswald. *Stanislas de Guaïta: souvenirs de son secrétaire,* Paris: Editions du symbolisme, 1935.

Wittgenstein, Ludwig. *The Blue and Brown Books: Preliminary Studies for the "Philosophical Investigations."* New York: Harper Colophon, 1965 [1958].

———. *Culture and Value.* Ed. G. H. von Wright, Trans. Peter Winch. Chicago: University of Chicago Press, 1980.

———. "A Lecture on Ethics." *Philosophical Review* 74 (1965 [1929]), 3–12.

———. *Philosophical Investigations.* Trans. G. E. M. Anscombe. New York: Macmillan, 1968 [1953].

———. *Remarks on Frazer's Golden Bough.* Ed. Rush Rhees, Trans. A. C. Miles. Atlantic Highlands, NJ: Humanities Press, 1979.

———. *Zettel.* Eds. G. E. M. Anscombe and G. H. Wright, Trans. G. E. M. Anscombe. Berkeley: University of California Press, 1970.

Yack, Bernard. *The Fetishism of Modernities: Epochal Self-Consciousness in Contemporary Social and Political Thought.* Notre Dame, IN: University of Notre Dame Press, 1997.

Ylla-Català, Gamma. *Puig i Cadafalch i la col.lecció de pintura romància del MNAC.* Barcelona: Museu Nacional d'Art de Catalunya, 2001.

Yollin, Patricia. "Bayview block in bloom: Two neighbors create public garden that's pride of the area." *San Francisco Chronicle* 2 September 2003: A-1.

Young, Julian. *Nietzsche's Philosophy of Religion.* Cambridge: Cambridge University Press, 2006.

Zerbst, Rainer. *Antoni Gaudí.* Taschen: Benedikt Taschen Verlag, 1985.

Ziesemer, John. *Studien zu Gottfriend Sempers dekorativen Arbeiten am Aussenbau und im Interieur: ein Beitrag zur Kunst des Historismus.* Weimar: VDG, 1999.

Ziolkowski, Theodore. *Disenchanted Images: A Literary Iconology.* Princeton, NJ: Princeton University Press, 1977.

———. *German Romanticism and Its Institutions.* Princeton, NJ: Princeton University Press, 1990.

Index